D1571115

THE CAMBRIDGE TRANSLATIONS OF
MEDIEVAL PHILOSOPHICAL TEXTS

The Cambridge Translations of Medieval Philosophical Texts

VOLUME ONE

LOGIC AND THE PHILOSOPHY OF LANGUAGE

EDITORS

NORMAN KRETZMANN
CORNELL UNIVERSITY

ELEONORE STUMP
VIRGINIA POLYTECHNIC INSTITUTE & STATE UNIVERSITY

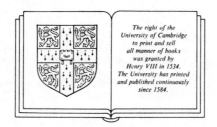

The right of the
University of Cambridge
to print and sell
all manner of books
was granted by
Henry VIII in 1534.
The University has printed
and published continuously
since 1584.

CAMBRIDGE UNIVERSITY PRESS

CAMBRIDGE

NEW YORK   NEW ROCHELLE   MELBOURNE   SYDNEY

Published by the Press Syndicate of the University of Cambridge
The Pitt Building, Trumpington Street, Cambridge CB2 1RP
32 East 57th Street, New York, NY 10022, USA
10 Stamford Road, Oakleigh, Melbourne 3166, Australia

© Cambridge University Press 1988

First published 1988

Printed in Canada

Library of Congress Cataloging-in-Publication Data
Logic and the philosophy of language / [edited by] Norman Kretzmann.
Eleonore Stump.
p.   cm. – (The Cambridge translations of medieval
philosophical texts; v. 1)
Chiefly translations from Latin.
Includes index.
ISBN 0-521-23600-2.   ISBN 0-521-28063-X (pbk.)
1. Logic – Early works to 1800.   2. Languages – Philosophy – Early
works to 1800.   I. Kretzmann, Norman.   II. Stump, Eleonore. 1947–
III. Series.
BC60.L64 1988
160–dc 19   87–30542 CIP

British Library Cataloguing in Publication Data
The Cambridge translations of Medieval
philosophical texts.
Vol. 1: Logic and the philosophy of
language
1. Philosophy, European   2. Philosophy,
Medieval
1. Kretzmann, Norman   2. Stump, Eleonore
189   B721

ISBN 0 521 23600 2 hard covers
ISBN 0 521 28063 X paperback

This volume is dedicated to the memory of Jan Pinborg,
generous scholar, gentle man, good friend.

CONTENTS

PREFACE

The idea of a series of volumes to be known as *The Cambridge Translations of Medieval Philosophical Texts* originated in the Cambridge University Press almost as soon as work on *The Cambridge History of Later Medieval Philosophy* had begun. In preparing this first volume in the series we were helped immeasurably by a grant from the Translations Program of The National Endowment for the Humanities that enabled us to devote our full time to the project for twelve months in 1983–84. Ms. Susan Mango, who was then in charge of the Translations Program, gave us good advice and encouragement, for which we are happy to thank her publicly.

Although we were able to make good progress during the period of our NEH grant, the remainder of the work had to be done in the summers, when we were free from other academic obligations. Our working arrangements during those summers were particularly convenient and pleasant because of the hospitality of the Society for the Humanities at Cornell, for which we are grateful to Professor Jonathan Culler, the director of the Society, and to his predecessor, Professor Eric Blackall.

Professors Scott MacDonald and Georgette Sinkler gave us comments on drafts of some of our translations, and we thank them for their help. We are grateful also to Professor Sten Ebbesen of the Institute for Medieval Greek and Latin Philology at the University of Copenhagen for kindly providing us with his as yet unpublished edition of Boethius of Dacia's *Sophisma I*.

The secretaries of the Department of Philosophy at Virginia Polytechnic Institute and State University, Vanessa Alexander and Christine Duncan, carried out most of the word-processing chores associated with this project, and their work was supplemented by the efforts of Debra Allen at Cornell. We certainly could not have completed this project without their help, for which we are particularly grateful.

GENERAL INTRODUCTION

Some features of medieval philosophy that distinguish it from ancient or modern philosophy are substantial and interesting, but there is also an accidental distinction that is annoying at best and often frustrating. Most of the surviving philosophical literature of the Middle Ages is still unavailable in printed editions of the Latin texts, let alone translations into modern languages. Readers of Guthrie's volumes of *The History of Greek Philosophy* have easy access to almost all the literature he discusses, in critical editions of the Greek texts for specialists, in English translations for students and general readers. Readers of *The Cambridge History of Later Medieval Philosophy*, on the other hand, lack those advantages. They will often enough be confronted with claims founded on textual evidence that still exists only in medieval manuscripts, some of which will have been consulted by no living person other than the scholar making the claim. And when such textual evidence is available in print, it will often enough be in an uncritical edition which is itself four or five hundred years old (and therefore rare), printed with typographical abbreviations that must be learned even by readers who know Latin. Only a very small percentage of the surviving medieval philosophical literature is available in modern critical editions, and a much smaller percentage is available to readers who do not read medieval Latin.

This artificial obstacle to the study and appreciation of medieval philosophy has been a concern to both of us as teachers and students of the subject, and our concern was deepened by our involvement in editing and contributing to *The Cambridge History of Later Medieval Philosophy* (CHLMP). We were particularly pleased, therefore, when, soon after we had begun work on CHLMP, editors of the Cambridge University Press proposed a companion series of volumes of new translations of medieval philosophical texts. To some extent, of course, volumes of this sort may be

thought of as giving nonspecialists access to some of the texts that
are actually discussed in CHLMP or that illustrate well some of the
historical developments or philosophical issues taken up in its
chapters. But this volume and its projected successors also have the
broader aim of alleviating a little the dearth of English translations
of medieval philosophy.

This first volume of *The Cambridge Translations of Medieval
Philosophical Texts* is devoted to logic and the philosophy of language, partly because the topically organized chapters of CHLMP
begin with discussions of developments in those fields. But the
fact that CHLMP begins in that way reflects the pattern of
medieval philosophical education, which began with the considerations of meaning and inference without which no further serious
philosophizing can be carried out. Our Volume One is designed in
keeping with that sensible program. The second volume is intended
to be devoted to metaphysics, epistemology, and natural philosophy; the third, to ethics, politics, and esthetics.

In selecting the texts in logic and philosophy of language to
translate for this volume we were guided by the philosophical and
historical considerations represented in the CHLMP chapters on
those subjects and modified by our own research. But we were also
constrained by several formal considerations. Although the material
from which we had to choose was practically boundless, we had to
keep the book to a manageable size and so had to exclude many
good things. We wanted the translated texts to be, as far as practi-
cable, complete works or at least topically complete segments of
longer works, and we wanted to present texts that were not already
available in English. Like all conscientious translators, we preferred
to base our translations on definitive editions; but in the present
state of medieval philosophical literature that was a luxury we could
not always afford (Translations 1, 11 and 13 are based on old, uncritical editions, the only ones available; Translations 14 and 15 are
based on partially completed, not yet published critical editions).

Some important categories of medieval philosophical literature
within the broad field of logic and philosophy of language are not
represented at all among our selections. We have, for instance,
included no speculative grammar texts or commentaries on
Aristotle's Organon. Both these sorts of literature are historically
important and philosophically interesting, but since we could not

find room for even every major sort of relevant literature, we tried
to omit types that are already represented in published English
translations. (For bibliographical information on these and much
else that will prove helpful, see E.J. Ashworth, *The Tradition of
Medieval Logic and Speculative Grammar from Anselm to the End of the
Seventeenth Century: A Bibliography from 1836 Onwards*; Toronto:
Pontifical Institute of Mediaeval Studies, 1978.)

Not only types of relevant literature but prominent medieval
contributors to the literature are unrepresented in this volume. It
may not seem surprising that the most illustrious theologians or
metaphysicians of the Middle Ages are not included in a volume
devoted to logic and the philosophy of language. Anselm, Aquinas,
and Duns Scotus, as illustrious as any, did make important contributions to the relevant literature – Anselm in original treatises,
Aquinas and Scotus in their commentaries. All of Anselm has been
recently translated, however, and the Aquinas commentaries exist
in published translations. As for Scotus, the editorially confused
text of his works is only now receiving its first fully critical edition.

Boethius, Abelard, Ockham, and Buridan, on the other hand, are
all well known for their contributions to medieval logic and philosophy of language in particular. Abelard and Buridan, however, are
also unrepresented in this volume. Again, their omission is
explained by limitations on space and justified by the fact that
important relevant works of theirs are already available in translation or are in the process of being translated for publication.
Among Boethius's logical treatises, those on the categorical or on
the hypothetical syllogism, for instance, might seem more directly
relevant to the history of logic than the one we have included – but
the contents of those more specifically logical treatises were pretty
fully assimilated in subsequent medieval developments. We chose
instead to translate his treatise on division, in which he provided
not only medieval logic but all of medieval philosophy with some
of its basic conceptual tools. As for Ockham, the modest length of
the selection we have translated from his *Summa logicae* is no indication of his historical and philosophical importance to the subject
matter of this volume. It is, however, a particularly important
contribution to medieval modal logic in its own right, and substantial portions of the earlier parts of Ockham's *Summa logicae* have
already appeared in translation. Of course there are other prominent

medieval logicians for whom we have not found room – Roger
Bacon, for example – but we have tried to include at least samples
of work of the sort produced by important logicians whose own
work we have not included.

We have arranged the contents of this volume in a loosely
historical order, paying more attention to the historical development of subject matter and issues than to the chronological order of
authors and their works. Boethius's analysis of division, traces of
which can be seen in the form and content of several of the later
selections, is followed by a complete elementary compendium, the
mid-twelfth-century *Abbreviatio Montana*. This introduction, which
reads like the beginners' textbook it is, has the advantage of
providing a succinct survey of the Old Logic – logic as it had
developed on the basis of Aristotle's *Categories* and *De interpretatione*, Porphyry's *Isagoge*, and Boethius's logical treatises – just
before the recovery of the rest of the Organon (the New Logic) and
the development of the distinctively medieval semantic theory (the
logica moderna). Translation 3 consists of two treatises from the
Tractatus of Peter of Spain, perhaps the oldest of the terminist
logicians, the first men whose work shows the assimilation of the
New Logic and the full development of the *logica moderna*. But the
two treatises comprising Translation 3 deal with subject matter that
belongs to the Old Logic and so provide an indication of the way
that material was being handled several generations after *Abbreviatio
Montana*.

Lambert of Auxerre is another member of the small group of
logicians most frequently mentioned as terminists. The portion of
Lambert's *Logica* that appears as Translation 4 contains his version of the logico-semantic theory that gave the terminists their
name, the theory of the properties of terms, one of two theoretical
innovations distinctive of the *logica moderna*. The second of these
innovations is the theory of syncategorematic words, or syncategoremata. It is represented in Translations 5 and 6, first in an
anonymous, primitive treatise from the late twelfth century, and
then in the full-blown analysis characteristic of the mid-thirteenth
century. We have translated the short *Syncategoremata Monacensia*
completely; from the *Syncategoremata* of Nicholas of Paris we have
translated his discussions of the syncategorematic words 'whole'

and 'besides', those which served as paradigms in CHLMP Ch. IV.11.

In Translation 7 we return to Peter of Spain's *Tractatus* for representative treatments of syllogisms, dialectical Topics, and fallacies. His treatises on syllogisms and Topics, written after Aristotle's *Prior Analytics* and *Topics* had been assimilated by medieval logicians, should be compared with the corresponding discussions in *Abbreviatio Montana*, which relied on the Old Logic only. From Peter's treatise on fallacies we have translated only his discussion of composition and division, a linguistic fallacy, and his discussion of the extra-linguistic fallacy of the consequent. Medieval logicians derived a great deal of innovative logical and semantic theory from their analysis of fallacies, as can be seen in the extensive studies of this branch of logic in the CHLMP Bibliography.

Robert Kilwardby's encyclopedic *De ortu scientiarum* provides good accounts of the understanding of the nature of logic and of its principal branches, dialectic and demonstration, at a crucial juncture in the history of this material: the mid-thirteenth century, just after the culmination of the *logica moderna* and before the wide-ranging and much more loosely structured developments of the fourteenth century. We include those accounts by Kilwardby in Translation 8.

The new departures of fourteenth-century logic and philosophy of language were outgrowths of the New Logic and the *logica moderna*, sometimes amounting to new applications of the doctrines developed during the previous century. The theory of consequences, for example, unites and extends the theory of inference that had been developing in the earlier treatments of syllogistic and dialectical reasoning (as well as in other areas of logic). Translations 9 and 10 present Burley's general account of consequences, and Ockham's specialized consideration of modal consequences. Together these two texts provide a representative sample of the theory of inference that dominated the logic of the fourteenth century.

The long medieval fascination with Aristotle's *Sophistici elenchi* may have been the ultimate source of the late medieval interest in logical and semantic paradoxes, but the concern with paradoxes took on importance because of difficulties that arose in extending logical and semantic theory itself and in applying it to problems in natural philosophy (see CHLMP Chs. IV.11, 12, V.16A, B, VII.27,

28). One family of paradoxes that received a great deal of attention in specialized treatises includes self-referential propositions of several different kinds, called 'insolubles' because of their notorious difficulty. Our sample of the *insolubilia* literature is drawn from a late-fourteenth-century logician, Albert of Saxony, one of Buridan's most eminent students. Like many other scholastic philosophical texts, Albert's discussion of insolubles exhibits many characteristics of the formal university disputation, with arguments offered for and against various theses and doubts raised about conclusions that might have seemed established.

The practice of disputation, with which every medieval academic was thoroughly familiar, was discovered to be not only an excellent method for organizing thoughts and training minds but also a source of peculiar paradoxes of its own. 'Obligational' disputations, which arose as a means of exploring certain difficulties stemming from the evaluation of disputational inferences, turned out to generate circumstances in which some of the laws of logic seemed not to apply. They thus became objects of logicians' interest in their own right, as can be seen in our extensive selections from Burley's treatise on 'obligations,' as the study of these disputational paradoxes was known.

Some of the semantic problems encountered in any use of language became sharpened for the medievals because of their marked effect on disputational reasoning. Aristotle's old distinction between composition and division came to seem applicable to a wide range of ambiguities and gave rise to the technical distinction between the compounded and divided senses of propositions. Some of the twentieth-century philosophical observations regarding the scope of various linguistic elements within a proposition are prefigured in the working out of this distinction. A mastery of it was thought to be not only theoretically important but also practically advantageous for participants in disputations, where it was often essential to be able to recognize and deal effectively with ambiguity in a proposition to which one had to respond quickly. William Heytesbury may have been the first to try to organize the scattered observations regarding the various instances of the compounded and divided senses and their special effects. Translation 13 is his complete treatise on the subject.

It seems to have been the medieval disputation again that

generated the fourteenth-century interest in epistemic logic. The respondent in a disputation is restricted almost entirely to declaring, in effect, that he knows that the proposition put to him is true, knows that it is false, or is in doubt about it because his disputational circumstances prevent his offering either of the more conclusive responses. Heytesbury's treatise on problems arising in connection with propositions whose main verbs are epistemic (or volitional) seems to have such a provenance; it is presented as our Translation 14. Not surprisingly, Heytesbury finds many opportunities to employ the distinction between the compounded and divided senses in dealing with verbs of propositional attitude.

Sophismata – propositions that in themselves or on the basis of some hypothesis give rise to at least superficial paradoxes – were part of the subject matter of medieval logic from the twelfth century onwards. In the fourteenth century they were frequently the vehicles for developing semantic theory or natural philosophy. In the thirteenth century, on the other hand, they had sometimes become the starting-points for philosophical investigations that ranged far from the topics usually associated with medieval logic. To provide a glimpse of this line of development, we conclude with the first sophisma from the *Sophismata* of Boethius of Dacia, one of the Latin Averroists with whom Thomas Aquinas contended at the University of Paris.

In order to include as much translated material as possible, and because *The Cambridge Translations of Medieval Philosophical Texts* are intended as companion volumes to CHLMP, we have kept the individual introductions short and included no explanatory notes. The relevant chapters of CHLMP listed at the end of each selection will provide not only a discussion of the material in the selection but also many explanatory and bibliographical notes, and the generous Bibliography, the Biographies, and the Indexes of CHLMP will help the reader to answer many of the questions these translations surely will raise. The present volume, too, has a detailed Index, the main entries in which are accompanied by the corresponding Latin words whenever appropriate. It will often help to check the Index for a crucial word in a difficult passage, since many difficult or unfamiliar doctrines figure in more than one of these selections.

We have adopted several typographical conventions. When we

think that our translation of a Latin word or phrase may be unusual, technical, uncertain, or otherwise noteworthy, we print the Latin in single parentheses immediately after the translated word or phrase. Bibliographical references supplied by us or taken from the references supplied by the editor of the text are printed in single parentheses at the appropriate place in the translated text. We also use single parentheses around English words, phrases, or sentences as part of our punctuation of the translated text when we think that the medieval author has written something parenthetically.

When the edition from which we translated includes section numbers, as in the Kilwardby selections, we have kept the section numbers in the translation. In every case in which we were translating from a published edition, we have indicated the page numbers of the edition within curly braces – e.g., {123} – at the appropriate places in the translation.

We indicate our own substantive additions to the text by printing the word or phrase within square brackets – e.g., [true].

Occasionally we have emended the Latin text from which we translated. All our emendations are enclosed within double parentheses, and most of them have this form: ((*verum/falsum*)), which indicates that we are replacing the word '*falsum*' in the edition with the word '*verum*,' and translating accordingly. When the word or phrase we prefer appears among the textual variants in the edition's critical apparatus, we have indicated this by including '[var.]' within the double parentheses. (A special case of this sort of emendation occurs in Translation 13, where we frequently correct our principal edition of 1494 with readings from an edition of 1501, indicated by including '[with 1501]' within the double parentheses.) The similar inclusion of '[rep.]' indicates that our emendation has been prompted by what we take to be a mistaken repetition of a word or phrase in the edition. When our translation depends on omitting a word or phrase in the edition, we indicate the omission in this way: ((om. *verum*)). The three dots near the bottom of p. 182 indicate that a passage appears to have dropped out of the Latin text.

Translation 14 is unlike the others, being based on an edition one of us is working on, and so is accompanied by a list of variants, indicated by footnote numbers in the translation.

Our translations are based on the following editions, numbered to correspond with the numbering of the translations:

1 Boethius: *On Division. De divisione*, ed. J.–P. Migne, in *Patrologia Latina* vol. 64, 875D–892A; Turnholt-Brepols, 1860.
2 Anonymous: *Abbreviatio Montana*, ed. L.M. de Rijk, in his *Logica Modernorum* vol. II. 2, pp. 77–107; Assen: Van Gorcum, 1967.
3 Peter of Spain: *Predicables; Categories. Tractatus*, ed. L.M. de Rijk; Tr. II, *De predicabilibus*, pp. 17–25; Tr. III, *De predicamentis*, pp. 26–42; Assen: Van Gorcum, 1972.
4 Lambert of Auxerre: *Properties of Terms. Logica (Summa Lamberti)*, ed. Franco Alessio; VIII: *De suppositionibus et de significationibus*, pp. 205–45; Florence: La Nuova Italia, 1971.
5 Anonymous: *Syncategoremata Monacensia. Sincategoremata Monacensia*, ed. H.A.G. Braakhuis, in his *De 13de Eeuwse Tractaten over syncategorematische Termen* vol. I, pp. 95–104; Meppel: Krips Repro, 1979.
6 Nicholas of Paris: *Syncategoremata* (selections: 'Whole,' 'Besides'). *Sincategoreumata*, ed. H.A.G. Braakhuis, in his *De 13de Eeuwse Tractaten over syncategorematische Termen* vol. II, '*Totus*,' pp. 432–6; '*Praeter*,' pp. 129–75; Meppel: Krips Repro, 1979.
7 Peter of Spain: *Syllogisms; Topics; Fallacies* (selections: Composition and Division, Fallacy of the Consequent). *Tractatus*, ed. L.M. de Rijk; Tr. IV, *De sillogismis*, pp. 43–54; Tr. V, *De locis*, pp. 55–77; Tr. VII, *De fallaciis*, '*De compositione et divisione*,' pp. 115–27; '*De fallacia secundum consequens*,' pp. 169–73; Assen: Van Gorcum, 1972.
8 Robert Kilwardby: *Nature of Logic; Dialectic and Demonstration. De ortu scientiarum*, ed. Albert G. Judy, O.P.; Cap. LIII, pp. 167–78; Cap. LVII, pp. 191–5; London: The British Academy, 1976.
9 Walter Burley: *Consequences. De puritate artis logicae Tractatus brevior*, ed. Philotheus Boehner, O.F.M.; '*Prologus*' and '*De regulis generalibus consequentiarum*,' pp. 199–219; St. Bonaventure, N.Y.: The Franciscan Institute, 1955.
10 William Ockham: *Modal Consequences. Summa logicae*, ed. Philotheus Boehner, O.F.M., Gedeon Gál, O.F.M., and Stephen Brown; III–3, Cap. 10–16, pp. 631–49; St. Bonaventure, N.Y.: The Franciscan Institute, 1974.
11 Albert of Saxony: *Insolubles. Perutilis logica*, Tr. VI, Cap. I, *De insolubilibus*, ff. 43rb–46va; Venice, 1522 (facsimile edn., Hildesheim: Olms, 1974).
12 Walter Burley: *Obligations* (selections). *Tractatus de obligationibus*, ed. Romuald Green, O.F.M., in his *An Introduction to the Logical Treatise 'De Obligationibus'* vol. II, pp. 34–7; 41–68; 84–7; 89–92; Louvain: Université Catholique, 1963.
13 William Heytesbury: *The Compounded and Divided Senses. De sensu composito et diviso*, ff. 2ra–4rb; Venice: Bonetus Locatellus, 1494

(compared with another edn. – Venice: Jacobus Pentius de Leuco, 1501).

14 William Heytesbury: *The Verbs 'Know' and 'Doubt'. Regulae solvendi sophismata*, Cap. II, *De scire et dubitare*, ff. 12va–16va; Venice: Bonetus Locatellus, 1494 (compared with several mss).

15 Boethius of Dacia: *The Sophisma 'Every Man is of Necessity an Animal.'* *Sophismata, Sophisma I: Omnis homo est de necessitate animal*, ed. Sten Ebbesen (forthcoming).

I

BOETHIUS
ON DIVISION

Introduction

Boethius (ca. 480–524/6) was born into a patrician family in Rome and, having been orphaned, was raised by the aristocrat Symmachus. He quickly gained a reputation for learning, and his public career was marked by honors. He occupied a position of trust under the Arian king Theodoric and was consul in 510. Eventually he was accused (unjustly, most scholars now hold) of treason, as well as of practicing magic and astrology. After a term of imprisonment at Pavia during which he wrote his most famous work, *The Consolation of Philosophy*, he was put to death at Theodoric's order.

It was Boethius's plan to translate all the works of Plato and Aristotle into Latin, but he succeeded only in producing translations of and commentaries on most of Aristotle's logical works. In addition, he wrote five theological treatises, two treatises on mathematics, and one on music, as well as several other works on logic, including the *De divisione* translated here. Boethius's influence on subsequent medieval philosophy and theology is hard to overestimate; he was one of the main philosophical sources for the early scholastics, second only to Augustine as an authority among Christian philosophers.

De divisione was probably written sometime between 505 and 509. It is a study of different sorts of division – e.g., the division of a genus into its species or the division of a whole into its integral parts – an important part of the logical heritage on which the scholastic period built. Boethius investigates the way in which these various divisions are distinguished from one another and the logical relations between whatever is being divided (or analyzed, or classified) and its dividing elements. For example, he points out that a genus is naturally prior to its species but a whole is naturally posterior to its integral parts; if a genus is destroyed, so are all its species, but if a whole is destroyed, some of its integral parts may remain. A large part of the treatise is devoted to the division of genus into species, in connection with which Boethius deals extensively with the predicables (genus, species, definition, differentia, proprium, and accident), their interrelationships, and the way they combine to form a Porphyrian tree. (For more on the predicables and the Porphyrian tree, see the introduction to Translation 3.)

For further reading on the role of *De divisione* in medieval philosophy and its relation to the earlier work of Porphyry and Aristotle, see CHLMP III.4, 'Ancient Scholastic Logic as the Source of Medieval Scholastic Logic'; some discussion of the philosophical content of this treatise will be found in CHLMP III.5, 'Predicables and Categories.'

On Division

[Preface]

{875D} The book on division published by Andronicus, a most painstaking ancient, teaches what great benefits the science of dividing confers on those who study it, and in what great honor this knowledge has always been held in the Peripatetic school. The same point is also confirmed by Plotinus (*Enneads,* II, 6), that most profound philosopher, {876D} and is reinforced by Porphyry in his commentaries on Plato's *Sophist* as well as by the highly valued usefulness of his *Isagoge* to Aristotle's *Categories* (1a 2–5). For he says that a practical knowledge of genus, species, differentia, proprium, and accident will be necessary not only {877A} for many other purposes but also for the incomparably great usefulness of distributing things into their parts.

Therefore, because it is of the greatest possible use and instruction in it is especially easy, I also have written this down by way of an introduction, passing on to Roman ears almost everything included in the subject with appropriate, detailed discussion, and with moderate brevity, so that my readers' minds might not be afflicted with the frustration that accompanies a truncated discourse and an unfinished line of thought. Nor should anyone who is ignorant of the subject, unsophisticated, and disdainful of everything new imagine that my hearers' minds will be subjected to pointless verbiage. And let no malice, with its hostile, vicious attacks of disparagement, vilify this digest of material both difficult by nature and unknown to our times which I have made with a great deal of effort and for the use of my readers. Let them give way to these studies – sometimes forgivingly, sometimes even approvingly – rather than {877B} reining in the beneficial arts while repudiating with shameless obstinacy whatever is novel. For who does not see what a dearth of beneficial arts there could be if men's minds were never beset with the desperation of dissatisfaction?

But enough of that for now.

[1. The Types of Division]

[1a. Introduction]

To begin with, the name of division itself has to be divided. (And the distinctive characteristics and parts of any subject matter have to be conveyed under absolutely any designation of it.)

'Division' is used in many ways, of course. There is the division of a genus into its species; there is also division when a whole is divided into its proper parts; and there is another division when an utterance that signifies many things is split into its proper significations. In addition to those three there is another division, one that is said to be carried out in connection with accidents. But it occurs in three ways: first, when we separate a subject into its accidents; second, when we divide an accident {877C} into its subjects; third, when we split an accident into accidents (which is done if both of them appear to be in the same subject).

We have to provide examples of all these [divisions], however, until the organization of division as a whole becomes clear.

[1b. Type I: The Division of a Genus into its Species]

We divide a genus into its species when we say of animals that some are rational, others irrational; or that of the rational ones some are mortal, others immortal; or when we say of colors that one is white, another black, another intermediate. Every division of a genus into its species has to be made into two or more parts, but there cannot be infinitely many or fewer than two species belonging to a genus. (The reason for this result will have to be shown later.)

[1c. Type II: The Division of a Whole into its Parts]

A whole is divided into its parts whenever we resolve anything into the things of which it is composed, as when I say that one thing that belongs to a house is the roof, {877D} another is a wall, and another is the foundation; or when I say that a man is joined together out of a soul and a body; and when we say that the parts of *man* are Cato, Virgil, Cicero, and the individuals who, because they are *particulars*, are joined together and make up the quantity of *man* as a whole. For *man* is not a genus, and individual men are not species; they are instead the parts out of which *man* as a whole is joined together.

[1d. Type III: The Division of an Utterance into its Significations]

Now a division of an utterance into its proper significations is made whenever a single utterance that signifies many things is opened up and the plurality of its significations is disclosed, as when I say of 'dog' that it is a name and designates this four-footed thing capable of barking, as well as the heavenly body that twinkles near the disease-bearing foot of Orion. (There is also the sea-dog, which grows to an enormous size and is called *Caeruleus*.)

{878A} There are, however, two varieties of this division, since either a single name or an expression already made up of names and verbs may signify many things. A name signifies many things in the way I pointed out just above, but an expression designates many things as in 'I declare that you, Aeacides, the Romans can conquer.' The division of a name through its proper significations is named a partition of equivocation, while the distribution of an expression into its proper significations is a discrimination of ambiguity, which the Greeks call *amphibolia*. So let a name that signifies many things be called equivocal but an expression that designates many things be called amphibolous and ambiguous.

[1e. Type IVa: The Division of a Subject into its Accidents]

Now of things that are divided in connection with accidents, the division of a subject into its accidents occurs when we say of all men that some are black, some white, and some of an intermediate color; for these are accidents {878B} for men, not species of men, and *man* is the subject for them, not their genus.

[1f. Type IVb: The Division of an Accident into its Subjects]

But the splitting of an accident into its subjects happens as in the case of all things that are sought after: Some are situated in the soul, others in the body. For, indeed, what is sought after is an accident, not a genus, for the soul and for the body; and the soul and the body are not the species but the subjects of a good that is situated in them.

[1g. Type IVc: The Division of an Accident into Accidents]

There is [also] a division of an accident into accidents, however, as in the case of all white things: Some are hard, such as a pearl, and others liquid, such as milk. For liquidity, whiteness, and hardness are accidents here, but white is separated into hard and liquid. Therefore, when we speak in that way we separate an accident into other accidents.

But this sort of division is always transformed in turn into one or the other of the two [preceding divisions in connection with accidents]. For we can say of things that are hard that some are {878C} black and others white and, again, of things that are liquid that some are white and others black. But we divide these again the other way around: Of those that are black, some are liquid and others hard; and of those that are white, some are liquid but others hard.

This sort of division differs from all those that were discussed above, however. For we cannot partition a signification into utterances when an utterance is distinguished into its proper significations. Nor are parts divided into a whole even though a whole is separated into its parts, and species are not split into genera although a genus is divided into species.

What was said above – that this division is made if both
[accidents] should happen to be in the same subject – is clear if it is
examined more closely. For when we say of things that are hard
that some are white and others black, such as stone and ebony, it is
obvious {878D} that both hardness and blackness are in the ebony.
(A careful reader will find this in connection with the others, too.)

[2. Differentiating the Types of Division]

[2a. Introduction]

Now in connection with things for which we seek truth's highest
work, it is essential to understand first the distinguishing characteristic of all those things taken together, and the differentiae by
which they are singly set apart from one another. For every division of an utterance, of a genus, and of a whole is called division
per se, whereas the remaining three are located in the distribution
of accident.

[2b. Differentiating Type I from Type III]

Of division *per se*, however, there is a differentia of this sort. For
the division of a genus differs from the division of an utterance in
that an utterance is of course separated into its proper significations,
whereas a genus is disjoined not into significations but into certain
things that are in some sense generations descending from it.

Also, a genus is a whole relative to its proper species, as being
more universal {879A} in nature; but an equivocation, more
universal as far as signification is concerned, is called a whole in
utterance, not a whole in nature as well.

[The division of a genus] is divided from the distribution of an
utterance in this way also: The things that are under the utterance
have nothing in common besides the name alone; the things that are
gathered together under a genus, on the other hand, take on both
the name and the definition of the genus.

Furthermore, the distribution of an utterance is not the same for
all; although many significations of the name 'dog' occur in the
Roman language, what is called 'dog' by us may be expressed

simply in a barbarian language, since the things we name by means of one name, they may signify by means of more than one name. [On the other hand,] the division and distribution of a genus remain the same for all. And so the division of an utterance pertains to the imposition [of the utterance] and to convention, whereas the division of a genus pertains to nature; for {879B} what is the same for all has to do with nature, whereas what varies from group to group has to do with convention.

These are the differentiae of the distribution of a genus and of an utterance.

[2c. Differentiating Type I from Type II]

The splitting of a genus is disjoined also from the distribution of a whole in that the division of a whole is made in respect of quantity; for the parts making up a whole substance either actually or conceptually are separated in mind ((*animo/animi*)) and thought. The distribution of a genus, on the other hand, is carried out in respect of quality; for when I have located *man* under *animal*, a division has been made in respect of quality because man is a sort of animal in that it gets a form from a quality. That is why someone answering the question 'What sort of animal is man?' will reply 'Rational,' or at least 'Mortal.'

Furthermore, every genus is naturally prior to its proper species, but a whole is [naturally] posterior to its proper parts. The parts that make up a whole {879C} precede the completion of their composite sometimes only naturally, sometimes also temporally. That is why we resolve a genus into things posterior but a whole into things prior to it. It is for this reason also that it is truly said that if a genus is destroyed its species perish immediately, [but] if a species has been destroyed, its genus is not prevented from subsisting naturally. The very opposite happens in connection with a whole; for if a part of a whole perishes, the whole of which that one part was destroyed will not exist, whereas if the whole perishes, its distributed parts remain. For example, if someone takes the roof off a complete house, he breaks up the whole that existed before, but when the whole has been destroyed [in that way], the walls and foundation will continue to exist.

Furthermore, a genus is the matter for its species. For, just as the bronze passes over into the statue when it has taken on the form, so the genus passes over into the species when it has taken on the differentia. In the case of a whole, on the other hand, the plurality of the parts is the matter, {879D} whereas the composition of those same parts is the form. For just as a species consists of a genus and a differentia, so does a whole consist of parts. That is why the difference between a whole and any one of its parts lies in the very composition of those parts, whereas the difference between a species and a genus lies in the conjunction of a differentia.

Furthermore, a species is always the same as its genus. For example, *man* is the same as *animal, virtue* the same as *habit.* A part, on the other hand, is not always the same as its whole; for a hand is not the same as the man, nor is a wall the same as the house. This is obvious in the case of things that have parts that are not alike, but it is otherwise in the case of things that have parts that are alike. For example, in the case of a rod of bronze, because its parts are continuous and of the same bronze, the parts appear to be the same as the whole is – but {880A} that is a mistake. For the parts may be the same [as the whole] as regards the sort of substance, but not also in quantity.

[2d. *Differentiating Type II from Type III*]

The differentiae between the distributions of an utterance and of a whole have not yet been given. [Those distributions] differ in that a whole consists of its parts but an utterance does not consist of the things it signifies, and a whole is divided into its parts but an utterance is divided not into its parts but into the things it signifies. That is why a whole perishes when a single part has been taken away, but an utterance designating many things remains when a single thing signified by that utterance has been taken away.

[3. The Division of a Genus]

[3a. *Genera, Species, and Differentiae*]

Now that the differentiae in division *per se* have been presented, we have to explore the distribution of genus. First we have to define what a genus is. A genus is what is predicated of more than one thing differing in species in respect of what it is. A species, on the other hand, is what we gather together under a genus; a differentia, that by means of which ((*qua/quia*)) we present one thing as standing {880B} apart from another.

Genus is indeed also what is appropriately given in reply to anyone asking what any thing is; the differentia is what is most correctly given in reply to an inquiry into what sort it is. For when anyone asks 'What is man?', the correct answer is 'Animal'; to the question 'What sort [of animal] is man?', one answers appropriately 'Rational.'

[3b. Division into Species and into Differentiae]

Now a genus is divided sometimes into the species, sometimes – if the species through which the genus is properly divided lack names – into the differentiae. For example, when I say 'Of animals some are rational, others irrational,' *rational* and *irrational* are differentiae. But since there is no single name of the species *rational animal*, we put the differentia in place of the species and connect it to the higher genus, because every differentia produces a species when it comes to its proper genus. That is why the genus is a kind of matter, the differentia a form. {880C} When species are called ((*appellantur/appellatur*)) by their own names, however, the correct division of a genus is not into the differentiae but into the species.

[3c. Division and Definition]

It is for that reason that a definition is put together out of several terms; for if all species were called by their own names, every definition would be made up of only two terms. When I say 'What is man?', for example, why would it be necessary for me to say that *mortal rational animal* completes the definition of *man* with soundest reasoning and full conclusiveness if *rational animal* had been picked out with its own name and joined with the remaining differentia *mortal*? As things are, however, division is necessary for full definitions of species. And perhaps the essential nature of division and of definition have to do with the same thing, since a single definition is made up of divisions joined together.

But some things are equivocal and others univocal, {880D} and we split those that are univocal into genera whereas for those that are equivocal there is only a division of signification. And so we first have to see what is equivocal and what is univocal so that we do not resolve an equivocal name into significant [components] as if they were species when we have been deceived [about the equivocal and the univocal]. And that is why definition is necessary for division, for by means of definition we collect together whatever is equivocal, whatever is univocal.

[3d. Differentiae Suited to Definition and the Division of Genus]

Now some differentiae are *per se* and others are *per accidens*, and some of the latter regularly follow along with [their subjects] whereas others are regularly left behind. Those that are left behind are of this sort: being asleep, being seated, standing, being awake; but those that follow along with [the subject] are, for example, curly hair (if it has not been acquired with a curling iron) and bright eyes (if they have not been affected by some extraneous {881A} disability). But these [differentiae *per accidens*] are not to be used for the division of a genus. They are not suitable for definitions either, for everything that is appropriate to the division of a genus we quite properly bring together for definitions. It is only those [differentiae] *per se* that are appropriate to the division of a genus, for they complete and give form to the substance of anything whatever, in the way rationality and mortality do [for the substance] of *man*.

But the way we can test whether [differentiae] are the sort that are regularly left behind, the sort that follow along [with the subject], or the sort that remain in the substance has to be seen along these lines (for it is not enough to know which ones we use in division unless we also know how to recognize very precisely those that are to be used and those that are to be rejected). Therefore, we have to see, first of all, whether the proposed differentia {881B} can be in every subject and at all times; if it is [ever] severed [from any subject] either actually or conceptually, it must be kept away from the division of a genus. For if [the differentiae] are often severed [from subjects] both actually and conceptually, they are the sort that are regularly left behind – *being seated*, for example, which is very often separated and actually divided from the subject itself. But those that are divided from the subject only conceptually belong to the differentiae that follow along with [the subject] – as when we conceptually sever *having bright eyes* from the subject. When I say, for example, 'There is an animal with bright eyes – e.g., any man whatever,' if this [or that] individual were not of that sort, no actual fact would prevent him from being a man.

On the other hand, there is another sort of differentia that cannot be conceptually separated [from its subject], because if it is separated, the species is destroyed. There is an example of this sort when we say that it inheres in man that he alone can use numbers or learn geometry: if {881C} that possibility is severed from man, man himself does not remain. But these are not regularly included among the differentiae that inhere in a substance; for [an animal] is a man not because it can do those things but because it is rational and mortal.

Therefore, the differentiae by means of which a species is constituted are gathered together both in the definition of a species such as *man* and in the division of the genus that contains a species such as *man*. And we have to say in general that all differentiae that are of such a sort that there can be no species without them but only in virtue of them [are the ones that] must be used either in the division of the genus or in the definition of the species.

But there are [features] that do differ which [nevertheless] must not be set against each other in division – e.g., *rational* and *two-footed* in connection with *animal* (for no one {881D} says, 'Of animals some are rational while others have two feet'). And so even though *rational* and *two-footed* differ, they are not severed from each other in respect of any opposition. [But] it is undisputed that only [features] that differ from each other in respect of some opposition can disjoin a genus, and they alone are placed under that genus as differentiae.

[3e. Excursus on Opposition]

[3e(i). The Four Oppositions]

Now there are four oppositions: either [– first –] contraries, as good to evil, or [– second –] possession and privation, as sight and blindness. (There are cases, however, in which it is hard to tell whether they have to be classified as contraries or as privation and possession - e.g., motion, rest; health, sickness; wakefulness, sleep; light, darkness. But those must be discussed another time; now we have to speak of the remaining oppositions.) The third opposition has to do with affirmation and {882A} negation – e.g., Socrates is alive, Socrates is not alive; the fourth, with relationship – e.g., father, child; master, slave.

We have to show in an altogether appropriate rational order which of these four oppositions the division of a genus is, for it is evident that there are four oppositions and that genera and species are separated by means of opposites. And so now we have to tell in which way or in accordance with which of these four oppositions it is appropriate to disjoin a species from a genus.

[3e(ii). Affirmation and Negation]

First there is the opposition of contradiction. (I call the opposition put forward in connection with affirmation and negation the opposition of contradiction.)

The negation in that opposition produces no species on its own. When I say 'man' or 'horse' or anything of that sort, they are species; but whatever a person mentions using a negation fails to express a species. *Not* {882B} *being man* is [not] a species; for every species is an ordering of being, but negation disjoins being from something that is, no matter what it presents. For example, when I say 'man,' I have spoken as if there is something; but when I say 'non-man,' with the negation I have destroyed the substance of *man*. In that respect, therefore, considered in itself, the division of a genus into species has nothing to do with negation.

All the same, it is often necessary to use negation in constructing a species when we want to use a simple name to assign a species to something that is not picked out by any word. This happens when, for example, I say 'Of odd numbers some are prime – e.g., three, five, seven, – others non-prime – e.g., nine'; and, again, 'Of figures some are rectilinear (*rectissimae*), [others non-rectilinear]'; and 'Of colors some are white, others black, others neither white nor black.' Therefore, when no single name has been applied to species, we have to designate them by means of negation; thus it is {882C} [our] need, not nature, that sometimes requires this.

So whenever we use negation to split something, it is the affirmation or the simple name that is to be said first – as in 'Of numbers some are prime, others non-prime' – because if the negation is said first there will be a delay in a person's understanding of the thing we are presenting. For when you say first that some numbers are prime (once you have taught by example or by definition which sort are prime and which sort are not prime), your listener understands at once. But if you do it the other way around, he will learn ((*coqnoscet/coqnosces*)) neither one right away, or both more slowly; and a division, which is sought after in order to reveal a genus as much as possible, must instead be reduced to the things that are more understandable.

Furthermore, affirmation is prior and negation posterior, and what is first ought also to be given first place in a division. It is always necessary, too, {882D} that finite things be prior to non-finite things – the equal to the unequal, virtue to the vices, the certain to the uncertain, the stable and fixed to the unstable and mutable. But all the things that are expressed by a part of speech that is definite or by an affirmation are more finite than a name with a negative particle or a complete negation. For that reason a division ought to be carried out with what is finite rather than with what is non-finite.

(But if anyone should be troubled by these things, or if they may be more obscure than he would like, it is not my business to promise easy learning. We put forward these [elements] of the whole art [of division] to be read and learned, not for beginners, but for the initiates, and for those who are just about to move ahead to a more advanced level. But I have carefully explained the scheme of this art – i.e., the dialectician's art – since it had to be told to me in accordance with the scheme of the Peripatetic discipline.)

[3e(iii). Possession and Privation]

The preceding remarks {883A} were made regarding the opposition constituted by affirmation and negation. But the opposition formed on the basis of possession and privation also seems to be a great deal like the preceding one, since privation is in a way the negation of possession. It differs, however, in that negation can always occur, but privation not always – only when it is possible to have possession. (The *Categories* have already taught us that, though [c. 10, 12a26–b16].) And so a privation is understood to be a kind of form, since it not only deprives but also classifies in respect of the privation each thing affected by the privation. Blindness, for instance, not only deprives the eye of light but also classifies according to the privation the one deprived of light; for he is called blind relative to the privation in such a way that it is as if he were classified and affected [in that way]. (Aristotle, too, takes this position in the *Physics* [V2, 226b15].) That is why we often use a differentia {883B} associated with a privation for the division of a genus.

But we have to proceed here just as we did in connection with contradiction; for the possession, the analogue to the affirmation, must be put first, but the privation, analogous to the negation, after it. Still, certain privations are sometimes expressed by means of a word associated with possession – e.g., 'orphaned,' 'blind,' 'widowed' – sometimes with a privative particle, as when we say 'finite,' '*in*finite'; 'equal,' '*un*equal.' But in those cases [the words like] 'equal' and 'finite' should be put first in the division, the privations second.

And let these remarks about the opposition of privation and possession suffice.

[3e(iv). Contraries]

One might be uncertain whether the opposition of contraries such as white and black seems to be a case of privation and possession, whether white is indeed the privation of black, [or] black of white; but that will have to be considered another time. For the present, {883C} we have to treat [contrariety] as if it were another genus of opposition, as it is classified by Aristotle himself in the *Categories* (c. 10, 11b17–19; 33ff.).

Much of the division of genera occurs in connection with contraries, for we bring almost all differentiae down to contraries. But since some contraries lack an intermediate and others have intermediates, division has to be carried out accordingly – as in the case of colors, for instance: some are black, others are white, others neither.

Every definition and every division would be accomplished by means of two terms, however, if it were not for the fact (discussed above) that want of a name, which often occurs, prevents it. It will be evident in the following way how both [definition and division] would be accomplished by means of two terms. When we say 'Of animals some are rational, others irrational,' *rational animal* aims at the definition of *man*. But since there is no single name for *rational animal*, {883D} let us give it the letter *A* as a name. Then: 'Of *A* (i.e., *rational animal*) some are mortal, others immortal.' Therefore, when we want to provide the definition of *man*, we will say 'Man is a mortal *A*.' For if the definition of *man* is *mortal rational animal*, but *rational animal* is signified by *A*, one reacts to 'mortal *A*' just as if 'mortal rational animal' had been said (for, as we said, *A* signifies *rational animal*). And so in that way the definition of *man* is made out of the two terms 'mortal' and '*A*.' But if names were found in connection with all things, a complete definition would always be made of two terms. So would division, if names had been imposed [on all things]. For we always split [things] into two terms, it is clear, if we impose a name on the genus and differentia {884A} when a name is lacking – as when we say 'Of figures that ((*quae/quaedam*)) are three-sided some are equilateral, others have two sides equal, and others are all unequal.' If that tripartite division were put forward, therefore, it would be made twofold: 'Of figures that are three-sided some are equal and others are unequal; of those that are unequal there are some with only two sides equal, and others with three (i.e., all) sides unequal.' And when we say 'Of all things some are good, others are bad, and others indifferent (i.e., those that are neither good nor bad),' if we were to speak in that way, a paired division would be produced: 'Of all things some are differentiated [in respect of goodness and badness] and others are indifferent; of those that are differentiated some are good and others bad.' In that way, then, every division would be split into pairs, if words for species and differentiae were not lacking.

[3e(v). Relationship]

We mentioned a fourth opposition, {884B} however, which occurs in accordance with relationship – e.g., father, child; master, slave; double, half; sense object, sense. These [opposed things], then, have no substantial differentia by which they diverge from each other.

On the contrary, they have a natural association by which they are referred to each other, and they cannot exist without each other. That is why the division of a genus must not be made into relative parts. Rather, this way of splitting things must be kept entirely separate from genus; for of *man* there is no species *slave* or *master*, nor of *number* [is there a species] *half* or *double*.

Therefore, although differentiae are to be drawn from the four oppositions of affirmation and negation, of privation and possession, of contraries, [and of relationship,] unless it is necessary, a division associated with relationship is always to be rejected. Contrariety, on the other hand, is especially to be applied in connection with differentiae. And privation as well, {884C} because one sort of contrary – such as *finite* and *infinite* – seems to be opposed to possession, for although *infinite* is a privation, it is formed on the basis of an image of the contrary since (as was said above) it is a kind of form.

[3f. More on Division into Species and Differentiae]

It is worth inquiring whether genera are correctly divided into species or into differentiae. Because the definition of division is, indeed, the distribution of a genus into its proximate species, therefore, in accordance with the nature of division and its definition, the dissection of a genus must always be made into its proper species. But sometimes this cannot be done, for the reason we gave above: there are many species for which there are no names.

(Some genera are first, others last, and others intermediate. *Substance*, for example, is a first genus; *animal*, a last genus; *body*, an intermediate genus. {884D} For *body* is the genus of *animal*; *substance*, of *body*. But just as one can find nothing above *substance* that can be assigned the role of a genus, so neither is there anything of that sort under *animal*; for *man* is a species, not a genus.)

And so the division into species will appear preferable, if there is no lack of names; but if we are not very well supplied with names for all things, it is appropriate to separate the first genera down to the last genera into differentiae. Now that is done in the following way: we dissect the first genus into its own and not into subsequent differentiae; and, again, we dissect a subsequent genus into its own and not into subsequent differentiae. For the differentiae of *body* are not the same as those of *animal*. If someone says 'Of substance one sort is corporeal, another incorporeal,' he has made the division correctly because {885A} those differentiae are indeed proper to *substance*. But if someone says 'Of substances some are animate, others inanimate,' he has not set the substantial differentiae apart correctly; for those are differentiae of *body*, not of *substance* – i.e., of a second genus, not of a first. And so it is clear that the division of prior genera must be made in accordance with their own differentiae and not in accordance with those of a subsequent genus.

But whenever a genus is resolved into differentiae or into species, definitions or examples should be supplied as soon as the division has been made. If a person is not very well supplied with definitions, however, it is enough to add examples. When, for instance, we say 'Of bodies some are animate,' we may add '– such as men or beasts; others inanimate – such as stones.'

[3g. Conversion in Division]

A division, like a term, must be neither too narrow {885B} nor too broad. One must introduce neither more nor fewer species than are under the genus, so that the division converts with itself, as a term does. For a term converts in this way: 'Virtue is the mind's best habit'; again, 'The mind's best habit is virtue.' Division also converts, in this way: 'Every genus will be one of those that are [its] species'; again, 'Each species is [its] proximate genus.'

[3h. Multiple Divisions]

The division of one and the same genus is made in many ways, like the division of all bodies and of any things having any magnitude. For we distribute a circle into semicircles and into the things the Greeks call *tōmeis* (we can call them divisions), and we sometimes separate a rectangle into triangles by means of a diagonal beginning from an angle, sometimes into parallelograms, and sometimes into rectangles. {885C} We also do the same sort of thing with a genus, as when we say 'Of numbers some are even, others odd' and, again, '[Of numbers] some are prime, others non-prime'; 'Of triangles some are equilateral, others have only two sides equal, and others are unequal on all sides' and, again, 'Of triangles some have a right angle, others have three acute angles, and others have one obtuse angle.' And so the division of a single genus is in that way multiple.

[3i. Genus, Species, and Differentia Again]

It is very useful to know that a genus is in a certain respect the likeness of many species, a likeness that brings out the substantial agreement of all of them. And it is for that reason that the genus is collective of the many species, but the species are disjunctive of the single genus. Since the species are given their form by the differentiae (as was said above), there cannot be fewer than two species under a single genus; for every {885D} differentia consists in a plurality of differences.

[4. Definition]

[4a. Transition from Division of Genus to Definition]

We have now said a great deal about the division of genus and species, and so those who follow along this path have access to a more skillful technique for defining species via the division of genus. But we must undertake not only to learn about the differentiae we use in definition, but also to comprehend with painstaking understanding the art of definition itself. I am not going to consider whether any definition can be demonstrated, or how a definition can be found by means of demonstration, or any of the issues regarding definition that Aristotle handled with precision in the *Posterior Analytics* (II 10, 93b29–94a19). I merely want to provide a thorough treatment of no more than the rule of defining.

[4b. Definition Confined to Intermediate Things]

Of things some are higher, others lower, and others intermediate. Certainly no definition {886A} encompasses the higher things, for no genera higher than they are can be found. On the other hand, however, the lower things, such as individuals, lack specifying differentiae; for that reason they too are excluded from definition.

Therefore, it is the intermediate things, those that have genera and that are predicated of the others – of genera, of species, or of individuals – that can fall under definition.

[4c. Constructing Definitions]

Therefore, when I have been given a species of the sort that both has a genus and is predicated of subsequent things, I first take up its genus, I divide the differentiae of that genus, I join a differentia to the genus, and I see whether that differentia joined to the genus can be equal to the species I have undertaken to circumscribe with a definition. If the species turns out narrower, then, again, the differentia we applied to the genus {886B} a moment ago is taken up by us as if it were a genus, and we separate it into other differentiae of its own, and, again, we conjoin those two differentiae with the higher genus. If it has succeeded in equaling the species, it will be said to be the definition of the species; but if [the species] is narrower, we again separate that second differentia into others. We conjoin all of them with the genus, and again we look to see if all the differentiae together with that genus are equal to the species that is defined. Finally, we distribute differentiae under differentiae as often as we must until all of them joined to the genus describe the species in a definition that is equal to it.

But examples will provide a clearer conception of this operation, in the following way. Suppose it is our job to define *name*. The word 'name' is predicated of many names, and in some sense [they are] species containing individuals under themselves. And so I define *name* in this way: {886C} I take up its genus, which is *utterance*, and I divide it: 'Of utterances some are significant, but others are not.' A nonsignificant utterance has nothing to do with a name because, of course, a name signifies. And so I take up the differentia *significant*, and I join it to the genus *utterance*, and I say 'significant utterance'; then I look to see whether this genus and differentia are equal to *name*.

But they are not equal yet, because an utterance can be significant without being a name; for there are certain utterances that indicate pain [naturally] and others that indicate passions of the mind naturally that are not names – e.g., interjections. I again divide *significant utterance* into other differentiae: 'Of significant utterances some are significant in accordance with men's imposition of them, others are naturally significant.' And a naturally significant utterance certainly has nothing to do with a name, but an utterance that is significant {886D} in accordance with men's imposition of it does fit a name. And so I join the two differentiae *significant* and *in accordance with imposition* to *utterance* – i.e., to the genus – and I say 'A name is an utterance significant by convention.'

But in my view this is still not equated to *name*; for of course verbs too are utterances significant in accordance with imposition, and so that is not a definition of *name* alone. I again distribute the differentia *in accordance with imposition*, and I say 'Of utterances significant in accordance with imposition some are significant with a tense, others without a tense.' And of course the differentia *with a tense* is not conjoined to *name*, because it belongs to verbs but not to names to consignify times. The result is that the differentia *without a tense* is appropriate. Therefore, I join {887A} those three differentiae to the genus, and I say 'A name is an utterance significant by convention without a tense.'

But in my view the definition is still not completely finished; for an utterance can be significant, in accordance with imposition, and without a tense, and yet be not a single name but names joined together – i.e., an expression ((*oratio/ratio*)). For example, 'Socrates together with Plato and his disciples' is an expression, even though it is of course incomplete. For that reason the last differentia, *without a tense*, must again be divided into other differentiae. And we will say 'Of utterances significant in accordance with imposition without a tense there are some having a part that signifies something independently (this pertains to an expression), others having no part that signifies anything independently.' This pertains to a name, for a part of a name signifies nothing independently. And so the definition is made in this way: {887B} A name is an utterance significant by convention, without a tense, having no part that signifies anything independently when separated.

Do you see, then, how a correct definition is constructed? For by saying 'utterance' I disjoined a name from other sounds; by adding 'significant' I separated a name from nonsignificant utterances; with 'by convention' and 'without a tense' the distinctive character of a name was disjoined from naturally significant utterances and from verbs; by proposing that its parts signify nothing independently I disjoined it from an expression, the separated parts of which do signify independently. That is why anything that is a name is included in that definition, and wherever the expression of that definition fits, you will be in no doubt whether the thing in question is a name.

[4d. Wholes and Parts in Definition and Division]

It must also be pointed out that a genus is a whole in division but a part in definition. In definition it is as if {887C} parts join together to make a kind of whole, and in division it is as if a whole is resolved into its parts; the division of a genus is like the division of a whole, definition like the composition of a whole. For in the division of the genus, *animal* is the whole belonging to *man* because it encompasses *man* within itself; in the definition, however, it is a part, since the genus joined together with the various differentiae makes up the species ((*speciem/specie*)). For example, when I say 'Of animals some are rational, others irrational' and, again, 'Of rational [animals] some are mortal, others immortal,' *animal* is the whole belonging to *rational* and, again, *rational* is the whole belonging to *mortal* ((*mortalis/mortale*)), and those three are [the whole] belonging to *man*. But if in the definition I say 'Man is a mortal rational animal,' those three join together to make the single thing that is *man*. For that reason both the genus and the differentia are ascertained to be part of *man* itself.

In division, therefore, the genus is in that way a whole and the species a part; in the same {887D} way the differentiae are also a whole, whereas the species into which they are divided are parts. In definition, on the other hand, both the genus and the differentiae are parts, whereas the species defined is the whole.

But that is enough regarding these matters.

[5. The Division of a Whole]

[5a. Introduction]

Now let us discuss the division of a whole into its parts, since that was the second division after the division of a genus. What we call a whole we signify in various ways. For a whole is what is continuous, such as a body, a line, or something of that sort. We also call what is not continuous a whole – e.g., 'the whole crowd,' 'the whole population,' 'the whole army.' We also call what is universal a whole, such as *man*, or *horse*; for they are the wholes belonging to their parts – i.e., to men, or to horses. (That is also why we call each single man a *particular*.) {888A} We also call what consists of certain powers a whole. Of the soul, for example, there is one capacity for understanding, another for sensing, and another for living; they are parts, but not species [of the soul]. Therefore, the division of a whole is to be made in as many different ways as the ways in which 'whole' is used.

[5b. Divisions of a Continuous Whole]

First, indeed, if [a whole] is continuous, [it is to be divided] into the parts it is observed to consist of; otherwise no division is made. For that is how you will divide a man's body into its parts: the head, the hands, the trunk, and the feet. (The division is also correct if it is made in accordance with proper parts in some other way.)

Of things whose composition is multiple, however, the division is also multiple. An animal, for instance, is of course separated into parts that have parts like themselves – into flesh and bone – [or,] on the other hand, into those that do not have parts like themselves – into hands and feet. The same applies to a ship and to a house. {888B} We resolve a book, too, into lines, the lines into words, the words into syllables, and the syllables into letters. It is in that way that the syllables, letters, names, and lines are seen to be some sort of parts of the whole book; taken in another way, however, they are not parts of the whole but parts of parts.

Not all things must be viewed as if they divide in fact, but [some things are to be viewed] as if [they divide] mentally and conceptually. Wine mixed with water, for example, we divide into [quantities of] wine mixed with water ((*aqua/aquae*)), and we do that in fact; [but] we also divide it into the wine and the water from which it was mixed, and we do that conceptually, because once those things are mixed, they cannot be separated in fact.

But the division of a whole is [also] made into matter and form. For in one way a statue consists of its parts, and in another of [its] matter and form – i.e., of the bronze and the image.

[5c. Divisions of Discontinuous and Universal Wholes]

Likewise, wholes that are not continuous and those {888C} that are universal must be divided in the same way. Of men, for example, some are in Europe, others in Africa, and others in Asia.

[5d. Divisions of Wholes Consisting of Powers]

The division of a whole that consists of powers is also to be made in this way: Of the soul, one part is in plants, the other in animals; and, on the other hand, of the one that is in animals one part is rational, the other sensitive; and those are dispersed in turn under other divisions. Of these, however, soul is not the genus but the whole; and yet they are parts of soul not in respect of quantity but in respect of a certain capacity and power, because it is out of those capacities that the substance of soul is joined together. And that is why this sort of division bears a certain resemblance to the division of a genus and of a whole. For the fact that each part of which *soul* is predicated is associated with soul is traced back to the division of a genus: Whenever a species of [a genus] occurs, it is directly associated with {888D} the genus itself. On the other hand, the fact that not every soul is joined together out of all the parts (but some [souls] out of these, and others out of those) must be traced back to the nature of a whole.

[6. The Division of an Utterance]

[6a. Three Ways of Dividing an Utterance]

We still have to discuss the division of an utterance into its significations. The division of an utterance is made in three ways. It is divided into more than one signification either [1] as an equivocal utterance or [2] as an ambiguous utterance; for [1] a single name, such as 'dog,' signifies more than one thing, and [2] so does a single expression, as when I say that the Greeks the Trojans have conquered. But [the division of an utterance] is made in the other way [3] in accord with manner; these utterances signify not more than one thing but [one thing] in several different manners.

When we say 'infinite,' for example, it does indeed signify a single thing – one whose limit cannot be discovered – but we call it that in respect of measure, of plurality, or of species. In respect of measure, as in {889A} 'infinite is the universe' (because we are saying that it is infinite in size); in respect of plurality, as in 'infinite is the division of bodies' (because we are signifying that the plurality of [those] divisions is infinite); and, again, in respect of species, as when we call figures infinite (because there are infinitely many species of figures). We also call something infinite in respect of time. For example, we call the world infinite [because] no limit in respect of time can be found for it, and in the same way we call God infinite [because] for his supreme life no limit in respect of time can be found. And so in itself the utterance ['infinite'] does not signify more than one thing; rather, signifying only one thing itself, it is predicated of individuals in several different manners.

[6b. Determinations of Signification]

But another way [of dividing an utterance occurs] in accord with determination; for whenever any utterance is used without a determination, it produces uncertainty in the understanding. 'Man' is of that sort, for that utterance {889B} signifies many things because when no definition confines it the hearer's understanding is carried away on many different currents and misled by errors. For what does any hearer understand when the speaker does not confine what he says by means of some determination? Unless the person who is speaking defines [the utterance 'man'] in this way: 'Every man is walking' (or at least 'Some man is walking'), and designates this by a name, if it can be done in that way, the hearer's understanding has nothing it understands with good reason.

There are other determinations, too. For example, if someone says 'Give me it,' no one understands what he is supposed to give unless the understanding and definite reason associated with a determination are added. Or if someone says 'Come to me,' we know where we are to come or when we are to come only in virtue of a determination.

Although everything ambiguous is uncertain, not everything {889C} uncertain is ambiguous; for the things we have [just] been discussing are indeed uncertain although not ambiguous. Where ambiguities are concerned, the hearer thinks, reasonably enough, that he has understood one or the other [of the significations]. For example, when someone says 'I hear that the Greeks the Trojans conquered,' one person thinks that the Greeks conquered the Trojans, another that the Trojans conquered the Greeks; and both understand those things with good reason on the basis of the words themselves ((*ipsis/ipsius*)). On the other hand, when I say 'Give me it,' no hearer understands with good reason on the basis of the words themselves what you are supposed to give; for instead of seeing clearly, with some reason, what was not said before, he will conjecture about what I did not say.

[6c. Distinguishing Among Signified Things]

Therefore, since the division of an utterance is made in all these ways – by meanings (*significantias*), by the manner of significations, or by determinations – in connection with those that are divided in accord with meaning, it is not {889D} only that the signified things are to be divided; we must also show by definition that there are various things that are signified. Aristotle painstakingly taught these things in the *Topics* (II 9, 114b16–24), e.g., that among things that are called good, some are good – those that possess the quality of goodness – [while] others are called [good] with no quality [of goodness] itself but because they bring about a good thing.

[6d. Sophistry and the Art of Division]

Now one must practice this art [of division] especially against sophistical tricks, as Aristotle himself says (*Soph. el.* 5, 166b29–36). For if there is no subject thing that the utterance signifies, it is not said to be designative; if there is one thing the utterance signifies, it is called simple; if more than one, multiple – i.e., signifying many things. And so these things must be correctly divided so that we may avoid being caught in some syllogism.

But if {890A} an expression is amphibolous – i.e., ambiguous – it sometimes turns out that things that are signified in each of the two ways are possible. What I said above is an example of this, for that the Greeks conquered the Trojans could happen, likewise that the Trojans overcame the Greeks. There are others, however, that are impossible, as when I say that the man the bread is eating. That does indeed signify that the man is eating the bread and, on the other hand, that the bread is eating the man – but that is impossible. And so when it comes to controversy, the possibilities and impossibilities have to be divided. When truth is at issue, the impossibilities are to be left to one side while only the possibilities are to be expressed.

[6e. Equivocation and Ambiguity]

Because there is more than one species of utterances that signify more than one thing, it is important to point out that some of them have their signification of multiplicity in a small part, others in the complete expression. As for those that have it in a small part, the part itself is called equivocal {890B}, whereas the complete expression [of which it is a part] is multiple in accordance with the equivocation. On the other hand, an utterance that possesses its multiplicity of signification in the complete expression is named ambiguous, as was said above.

Now the significations of equivocals or of expressions [multiple] in accordance with equivocations are sometimes divided by means of definition. For example, when I say 'The man is alive,' one understands both a real and a painted man. But it is divided in this way: 'The mortal rational animal is alive' (which is true); 'The image of a mortal rational animal is alive' (which is false). There is also division by means of any addition that determines [the utterance], whether [the addition] belongs to gender, to case, or to an article. For example, when I say 'Canna was fouled with the Romans' blood,' ['Canna'] points to both the reed and the river. But we divide it in the following ways: by an article, as when we say 'The Canna (*hic Canna*) was {890C} fouled with the Romans' blood'; by gender, as in 'Canna was full (*plenus*) of the Romans' blood'; or by case; or by number (for in connection with the one of them only the singular occurs, but with the other, the plural [as well]). And we deal in the same way with other examples.

But there are other [divisions] in accordance with accent, and still others in accordance with spelling. In accordance with accent, '*pone*' and '*ponè*'; in accordance with spelling, '*queror*' and '*quaeror*', having to do with inquiry and complaint [in reverse order]. The latter [two] are also divided again in accordance with spelling, or in accordance with action and passion, since the '*quaeror*' associated with inquiry is passive, whereas the '*queror*' associated with complaint belongs to an agent.

The division of ambiguous expressions, on the other hand, is to be made by addition ('I hear that the Trojans are conquered, that the Greeks have conquered'), by subtraction ('I hear that the Greeks have conquered'), by division ('The Greeks have conquered; the Trojans have been conquered'), or by some rearrangement (e.g., when some one says {890D} 'I hear the Trojans the Greeks have conquered', we may say 'I hear that the Greeks have conquered the Trojans'). This ambiguity is resolved in any of these ways.

[6f. A Difference between Divisions of Utterance and of Genus]

Nevertheless, not every signification of utterances is to be divided as if it were [a division] of a genus. For in a genus all the species are enumerated, but in connection with ambiguity it is enough to provide as many significations as can be useful for the discourse that one or another expression contains.

[7. Divisions *per accidens*]

[7a. Transition from Divisions per se]

We have said enough about the division of utterance, and we have also presented and explained the division of a genus and of a whole. And so we have very carefully considered all the *per se* partitionings. Now we will say something about divisions that are made *per accidens*.

[7b. General Rules of Division per accidens]

It is a general rule regarding them that anything that belongs to these [divisions] and is divided {891A} is dissected into opposites. For example, when we divide a subject in connection with accidents we do not say 'Of bodies some are white, others sweet' ([because white and sweet] are not opposed), but 'Of bodies some are white, some black, others neither.' We must also divide in the same way in other divisions *per accidens*.

And notice in particular that we must say neither too much nor too little, just as in the division of a genus. For no accident may be left out of the opposition [so] that there is something in the subject that is not expressed in the division; but neither may anything be added that cannot be in the subject.

[7c. Peripatetics on Division per se and per accidens]

The later {892A} school of Peripatetic scholarship examined the differences among division with especially careful reasoning, and it disjoined division *per se* from division *per accidens*, distributing them relative to each other. The older [Peripatetics] treated them in an undifferentiated way, however, using an accident for a genus, and using accidents for species or differentiae. And so setting forth the features common to the divisions and dissecting them by means of their own differentiae struck us as having considerable practical value.

[8. Conclusion]

And so regarding every division, indeed, we have presented with care as much as the brevity of an introduction would permit.

2

ANONYMOUS
ABBREVIATIO MONTANA

Introduction

By the middle of the twelfth century, one of the most important schools for the study of logic was the one at Mont Ste. Geneviève in Paris, from which several logic treatises or fragments remain. The treatise translated here is a twelfth-century summary (*abbreviatio*) of an introductory logic text, called '*Montana*' because of its association with Mont Ste. Geneviève.

The *abbreviatio* begins with the subjects traditional for logic texts in this period: the nature of dialectic, vocal sound, names and verbs, and expressions (i.e., phrases, clauses, or sentences). This introductory material is followed by a detailed discussion of the nature and kinds of categorical propositions and the way such propositions convert with one another. A brief analysis of hypothetical (or conditional) propositions precedes the lengthy examination of inferences that constitutes the bulk of the treatise.

The first inferences considered are Topical. Topics are warrants for the inferential move from the antecedent to the consequent in a true hypothetical proposition. The treatise analyzes Topics that bear some resemblance to the Boethian Topics traditionally discussed in this connection – *from the whole, from parts, from equals,* and *from opposites*. It then goes on to discuss combinations such as the Topic *from a double whole*, which is supposed to warrant such conditionals as 'If no tree is an animal, no oak tree is either a rational or an irrational animal.' The treatise also explains that the inferences of conversion are Topical inferences and hence that there are such Topics as *from an equal by contraposition* and *from an equal by simple conversion*.

The section devoted to categorical syllogisms, the second sort of inferences examined, begins with fairly standard descriptions of their moods and figures drawing on Boethius's treatise on the subject rather than on Aristotle's *Prior Analytics*. Scattered throughout this discussion is an analysis of composite hypothetical propositions. For example, in discussing first-figure categorical syllogisms the treatise considers the conditional propositions corresponding to such syllogisms, for example, 'If every risible thing is a man and every man is an animal, every risible thing is an animal.'

For further reading on Topical inferences and their place in formal logic, see CHLMP V.14, 'Topics: Their Development and Absorption into Consequences.' For some discussion of the relation of this early logical material to its ancient sources, see CHLMP III.4, 'Ancient Scholastic Logic as the Source of Medieval Scholastic Logic.'

Abbreviatio Montana

[1. Introduction]

{77} How many things have to be looked into as regards the starting point of the art of dialectic? Five. What are they? Its name, its purpose, its function, its subject matter, and its end.

What is the name of this art? Dialectic; but it got this name from dialectical disputation. How? '*Dia*' means two, and '*logos*' means discourse; and so 'dialectic' means discourse involving two – i.e., between an opponent and a respondent. Why [is it called by this name]? Antiquity bestowed the name on this art from dialectical disputation, since the truth belonging to the whole art is revealed through dialectical disputation.

[What is its purpose?] In order to discern the purpose of this art, you have to know that there are two practitioners of the art. Who are they? There is one who acts on the basis of the art, who disputes in accordance with the rules and precepts of the art, and he is called a dialectician – i.e., a disputant. The one who acts in a way that concerns the art is the one who teaches the art and expounds its rules and precepts, and he is named either a master or an expositor (*demonstrator*). And so we ascribe different purposes in association with the different practitioners.

What is the purpose of the one who acts on the basis of the art? To prove on the basis of readily believable arguments a question that has been proposed. What is his function? To dispute properly in keeping with the rules and precepts of the art. What is his subject matter? A thesis – i.e., a dialectical question – the proof of which is the central issue of the whole dialectical disputation. What is the end [of his activity]? To produce belief regarding the proposed question.

What is the purpose of the one who acts in a way that concerns the art? To teach the art. What is his function? To expound the rules and precepts of the art and to add new ones, if they can be properly added. What is his subject matter? Utterances signifying things, and the things signified by the utterances. What is the end [of his activity]? The discovery and judgment of reasons. What is [this] discovery? Devising the reasons by means of which we dispute. What is [this] judgment? Discriminating among those reasons.

Why must we deal with utterances before things? Because teaching about things is carried on by means of utterances. But since sound is the genus of utterance, we have to begin with sound. {78}

[2. Sound]

What is sound? A thing perceptible to hearing. How is sound divided? One sort of sound is utterance, the other is not. What sort of sound is not utterance? The impact of one stone on another, footsteps, the crashing of trees, and the like. What sort of sound is utterance? The sound that is utterance is just the same as utterance. Sound that is not utterance must be left to one side, and we must concern ourselves with sound that is utterance.

What is utterance? A percussion of the air by means of the tongue, emitted by an animal through certain parts of the throat called windpipes. How is utterance divided? One sort of utterance is significant, another not significant. What sort of utterance is not significant? Letters, for example, and syllables, which are parts of significant utterances and signify nothing themselves.

What is significant utterance? Words, for example, and expressions. How is significant utterance divided? One sort of [significant] utterance is naturally significant, another arbitrarily significant. What is naturally significant utterance? The sort that signifies the natural states of animals, such as the mooing of cows, the groaning of men, the barking of dogs. What is arbitrarily significant utterance? The sort that signifies something in accordance with what human beings have rationally established – e.g., 'man.' How is arbitrarily significant utterance divided? One sort of arbitrarily significant utterance is a name, another a verb, another an expression. And it is important to note that 'name' is taken broadly here, since it includes within its signification certain interjections and certain adverbs, such as 'well,' 'badly,' and the like. Likewise, 'verb,' too, embraces certain participles within its signification, such as 'disputing,' 'loving,' and others [that operate] in that manner.

[3. Names and Verbs]

What is a name? An arbitrarily significant utterance, without time [or tense], a part of which used by itself signifies nothing. Why is 'utterance' added? Because it is the genus of a name. For what purpose is 'significant' added? As a differentia [between names and] nonsignificant utterances. Why do you add 'arbitrarily'? So that I may thereby remove naturally significant utterances [from consideration]. Why do you say, 'without time [or tense]'? We say that as a differentia [between a name and] a verb, which signifies with time [or tense]. Why do you say, 'a part of which used by itself signifies nothing'? In order to exclude an expression, certain parts of which do signify something used by themselves.

What is a verb? An arbitrarily significant utterance, with time [or tense], a part of which used by itself signifies nothing. What are the roles of the elements [of this definition]? The same as in the definition of a name, except that 'with time [or tense]' indicates what is added on as a differentia [between a verb and] a name; for a name, as was said, signifies without time [or tense]. {79}

[4. Expressions]

What is an expression? An arbitrarily significant utterance some parts of which used by themselves do signify something. 'Some parts of which [used] by themselves do signify something' was added on as a differentia [between an expression and] a name and a verb, the parts of which, as we said, signify nothing by themselves. How is expression divided? One sort of expression is complete, another incomplete. What is an incomplete expression? One the speaking of which generates no complete sense in the hearer's mind – e.g., 'white man.' What is a complete expression? One that generates a complete sense in the hearer's mind – e.g., 'Socrates is reading.' The incomplete expression must be set aside, and we must deal with the complete sort.

How is the complete expression divided? One sort is imperative, another optative, another interrogative, another vocative, another indicative (*enuntiativa*). What is the imperative sort? The sort by means of which we command something, as in 'Get a thorough grounding in elementary [logic]!' (*Affirma introductiones*). What is the optative sort? The sort by means of which we wish for something, as in 'Would that I disputed well!' What is the vocative sort? The sort by means of which we invoke something, as in 'God be with us!' What is the interrogative sort? The sort by means of which we ask something, as in 'Lord, where are you going?' What is the indicative sort? The sort by means of which we state (*enuntiatur*) something of something, as in 'Socrates is disputing.' The [first] four must be set aside, and we must deal with the indicative sort.

[5. Indicative Expressions, or Propositions]

What is an indicative expression? The same as a proposition. What is a proposition? An expression signifying what is true or what is false. How is the proposition divided? One sort of proposition is categorical, another hypothetical. What is the hypothetical sort? One that has an antecedent and a consequent together with a condition, as in 'If Socrates is a man, Socrates is an animal.' And it is important to note that 'condition' is taken broadly here, for it includes certain locational words, such as 'where,' and certain temporal words, such as 'while,' 'when.' The hypothetical must be set aside, and we must deal with the categorical.

[6. Categorical Propositions]

What is a categorical? One that has a subject and a predicate term, such as 'Socrates is a man.' But it got this name from the more

important part – viz., from the predicate – for '*categoria*' means
predication; and so a proposition is called categorical as if to say
'predicative.' How is the categorical proposition divided? One sort
of categorical proposition is affirmative, another negative. What
sort is affirmative? The sort by means of which something is
affirmed, as in 'Socrates is reading.' What sort is negative? The sort
by means of which something is denied, as in 'Socrates is not
reading.' It is also {80} divided in another way. How? One sort of
categorical proposition is universal, another particular, another indefinite, another singular. But one should know what a universal, a
particular, an indefinite, and a singular proposition are. First, one
should consider what a universal is, and what a universal sign is,
and what a particular is.

What is a universal? That which has to apply to more than one
thing – e.g., 'man,' 'donkey.' What is a singular? That which
applies to only one thing – e.g., 'Socrates.' What is a universal sign?
'Every' or 'all,' 'no,' 'whichever.' What is a particular [sign]? 'A
certain,' 'some,' 'not every.' For these [signs] added to propositions
indicate the quantities of propositions.

What is a universal proposition? One that has a universal subject
stated with a universal sign, as in 'Every man is an animal,' 'No
man is an animal.' What is a particular proposition? One that has a
universal subject stated with a particular sign, as in 'Some man is an
animal,' 'Some man is not an animal.' What is an indefinite proposition? One that has a universal subject stated without a sign, as
in '[A] man is an animal,' '[A] man is not an animal.' What is a
singular proposition? one that has a singular subject stated with a
singular sign, as in 'Socrates is reading.'

What is the quantity of a proposition? Universality, particularity,
indefiniteness, singularity. What is the quality of a proposition?
Affirmation and negation in the proposition.

And it is important to note that some terms of propositions are
finite, others non-finite. What is a finite term? One to which no
negative particle is attached – e.g., 'man.' What is a non-finite
term? One to which the negative particle 'non-' is applied – e.g.,
'non-man.'

One should also know that some propositions share a term and
some do not. Which ones do not share a term? Those that have no
term in common, such as 'Socrates is a man,' 'Plato is a body.'

Which ones share a term? Those that do have a term in common, such as 'Socrates is a man,' 'Plato is a man.'

Propositions that share no term must be set aside, and we must deal with propositions sharing one term.

[7. Propositions Sharing One Term]

One should know that propositions sharing one term sometimes share the predicate. How? As in 'Socrates is a man,' 'Plato is a man.' Sometimes they share the subject. How? As in 'Every man is an animal,' 'No man is a stone.' There are also propositions that share one term in such a way that the predicate term in one {81} proposition is the subject in the other ((om. ⟨*predicatus*⟩)), as in 'Every man is an animal,' 'Every risible thing is a man.'

[8. Propositions Sharing Both Terms]

Some propositions that share both terms share them ordered in the same way, some with the order reversed. Which ones share both terms ordered in the same way? Those that have the same predicate and the same subject, such as 'Every risible thing is a man,' 'Some risible thing is a man.' Which ones share [both] terms with the order reversed? Those whose subject passes into the predicate and whose predicate passes into the subject, such as 'No man is an animal,' 'No animal is a man.'

[8a. Sharing Both Terms Ordered in the Same Way]

Some propositions that share both terms ordered in the same way are contraries, others subcontraries, others subalterns, others contradictories. Which ones are contraries? A universal affirmative and a universal negative, such as 'Every man is an animal,' 'No man is an animal.' Which ones are subcontraries? A particular affirmative and a particular negative, such as 'Some man is an animal,' 'Some man is not an animal.' Which ones are subalterns? A universal affirmative and a particular affirmative, and a universal negative and a particular negative, such as 'Every man is an animal,'

'Some man is an animal'; 'No man is an animal,' 'Some man is not an animal.' Which ones are contradictories? A universal affirmative and a particular negative, and a universal negative and a particular affirmative, such as 'Every man is an animal,' 'Some man is not an animal'; 'No man is an animal,' 'Some man is an animal.'

[8b. The Matter of Propositions]

In order to recognize the laws ((*leges/legem*)) of these propositions, we have to see that every proposition has to be made in [one of] three [subject] matters: natural, contingent, and remote. What sort of proposition is made in natural matter? One whose predicate naturally adheres to its subject – e.g., 'A man is an animal.' What sort is made in contingent matter? One whose predicate can be present and absent without the destruction of the subject – e.g., 'The man is white.' What sort is made in remote matter? One whose predicate can in no way be in the subject – e.g., 'A man is a stone.'

[8c. Laws of Propositions Sharing Both Terms Ordered in the Same Way]

Next, as to their laws. What is the law of contraries? If one is true, the other is false. For that reason we can argue in the following way: 'This proposition is true: "Every man is an animal"; [that] is true, [and] therefore this is false: "No man is {82} an animal."' Where does the Topic come from? *From contraries.* The rule? The law of contraries is that if one is true, the other is false. The application: But these are contraries. Therefore, if 'Every man is an animal' is true, 'No man is an animal' is false. But it does not go the other way around, that if one is false, the other is true. Why? Because in contingent matter one finds both false – as if I were to say, 'Every man is white,' 'No man is white.'

What is the law of subcontraries? If one is false, the other is true. For that reason we can argue in the following way: 'This proposition is false: "Some man is a stone"; [that] is true, [and] therefore this is true: "Some man is not a stone."' Where does the Topic come from? *From subcontraries.* The rule: The law of subcontraries is that if one is false, the other is true. The application: But these are subcontraries. Therefore, if 'Some man is a stone' is false, 'Some man is not a stone' is true. But it does not go the other way around, that if one is true, the other is false. Why? Because in contingent matter one finds both true – as if I were to say, 'Some man is white,' 'Some man is not white.'

What is the law of subalterns? If the universal is true, the particular is true. For that reason we can argue in the following way: 'This proposition is true: "Every man is an animal"; [that] is true, [and] therefore this is true: "Some man is an animal"'; ((om. *verum est*)) 'This proposition is true: "No man is an animal"; [that] is true, [and] therefore this is true: "Some man is not an animal."' Where does the Topic come from? *From subalterns.* The rule: The law of subalterns is that if the universal is true, the particular is true. [The application: But these are subalterns. Therefore, if the universal is true, the particular is true.] But it does not go the other way around, that if the particular is true, the universal is true.

There is also another law of subalterns. What is it? If the particular is false, the universal is false. For that reason we [can] prove something in the following way: 'This proposition is false: "Some man is a stone"; [that] is true, [and] therefore this is false: "Every man is a stone"'; ((om. *verum est*)) 'This proposition is false: "Some man is not an animal"; [that] is true, [and] therefore this is false: "No man is an animal."' Where does the Topic come from? *From subalterns.* The rule: The law of subalterns is that if the particular is false, the universal is false. The application: But these are subalterns. Therefore, if the particular is false, the universal is false.

What is the law of contradictories? If one is true, the other is false. For that reason we can argue in the following way: 'This proposition is true. "Every man is an animal"; [that] is true, [and therefore] this is false: "Some man is not an animal"'; and 'This proposition is false: "No man is an animal"; [that] is true [and] therefore this is true: "Some man is an animal."' Where does the Topic come from? *From things that divide.* The rule: The law of things that divide is that if one is true, the other is false; and if one is false, the other is true. The application: But these are things that divide. Therefore, if one is true, the other is false, and vice versa.

Things that divide singulars also conform to this law. For that reason we argue in the following way: 'The proposition "Socrates is a man" is true; therefore the proposition {83} "Socrates is not a man" is false.' The Topic: *From things that divide.* The rule is the same as above.

[8d. Conversions]

One should note that [propositions sharing both terms] have to be converted in three different ways: simply, *per accidens,* and by contraposition. What is it for a proposition to be converted simply? The predicate is turned into a subject, and the subject is turned into a predicate, while the signs remain the same. Universal negatives and particular affirmatives are converted with this sort of conversion. How? In this way: 'No man is an animal': 'No animal is a man'; 'Some man is an animal': 'Some animal is a man.' What is it for a proposition to be converted *per accidens*? The predicate is turned into a subject, the subject is turned into a predicate, and the universal sign is changed to a particular sign. Universal affirmatives and universal negatives are converted with this sort of conversion. How? For instance if I say, 'Every man is an animal': 'Some animal is a man'; 'No man is an animal': 'Some animal is not a man.' What is it for a proposition to be converted by contraposition? The predicate is turned into a subject, and the subject is turned into a predicate; the finite terms are made non-finite, while the signs remain the same. Universal affirmatives and particular negatives are converted with this sort of conversion. How? In this way: 'Every man is an animal': 'Every non-animal is a non-man'; 'Some man is not an animal': 'Some non-animal is [not] a non-man'; 'No man is an animal': 'No non-animal is a non-man'; 'Some man is an animal': 'Some non-animal is a non-man.'

Next, as regards the conversion of singulars. A singular proposition is a determination with respect to truth and falsity. Singular propositions are converted in two ways: simply and by contraposition. A singular affirmative proposition is converted simply by means of a particular affirmative – e.g., 'Socrates is a man': 'Some man is Socrates.' The same singular affirmative is converted by contraposition into a universal affirmative – for example, 'Socrates is a man': 'Every non-man is non-Socrates.' Moreover, a singular negative proposition is converted simply by means of a universal negative – for example, 'Socrates is not a man': 'No man is Socrates' – that is, in such a way that if one is true, the other is true; and if one is false, the other is false. The same singular negative ((*negativa/affirmativa*)) is converted by contraposition by means of a particular negative, as in this case: 'Socrates is not a man': 'Some non-man is not non-Socrates.' {84}

Let these remarks suffice as regards categorical propositions.

[9. Hypothetical Propositions]

Next, as regards hypothetical propositions. How is the hypothetical proposition divided? One sort of hypothetical proposition is conjoined, another disjoined. What is a conjoined hypothetical? One whose antecedent and consequent are linked by a conjunctive conjunction. How? 'If Socrates is reading, Socrates is doing something useful.' What is a disjoined hypothetical? One whose antecedent and consequent are conjoined with a disjunctive conjunction. How? 'Either Socrates is healthy, or he is sick.'

It is divided in another way as well. How? One sort of hypothetical proposition is simple, another composite. What is a simple hypothetical? One that consists of two categoricals. How? 'If Socrates is a man, Socrates is an animal.' What is a composite hypothetical? One that has a hypothetical in its construction. How? 'If Socrates is a man, then because he is a man he is an animal.' Composite hypotheticals must be set aside, and we must deal with the simple sort.

[9a. Simple Hypotheticals]

How is the simple hypothetical divided? One sort of simple hypothetical is natural, another temporal. What sort is natural? The sort prefixed by 'if.' How? 'If Socrates is a man, Socrates is an animal.' Why is it called natural? Because it displays the natural following between antecedent and consequent. What sort is temporal? The sort to which 'while,' 'whenever,' 'when,' or the like is prefixed. How? 'Whenever the heaven is capable of revolving, fire is hot.' Why is it called temporal? Because in it what the antecedent and the consequent signify is shown to be at the same time. Temporal hypotheticals must be set aside, and we must deal with the natural sort.

[9b. Natural Simple Hypotheticals]

What sort is natural? The sort prefixed by 'if,' as we said. What is the antecedent in a simple natural hypothetical? The one to which 'if' is prefixed. {85}

[9b(i). Inferential Power or Topical Relationship]

In a simple natural hypothetical, where is the inferential power thought to lie? Sometimes in the predicate of the antecedent, sometimes in the subject of the antecedent, sometimes in both, sometimes in the whole proposition.

When does the inferential power lie in the antecedent's subject? When the subjects of the antecedent and of the consequent are changed and the predicates remain the same. How? If, for example, I say 'If Socrates is an animal, some man is an animal.' When does the inferential power lie in the antecedent's predicate? When the predicates of the antecedent and of the consequent are changed and the subjects remain the same. How? [If I say,] 'If Socrates is a man, Socrates is an animal.'

There is also another way in which the Topical relationship is thought to lie in the antecedent's predicate. How? When the antecedent's subject and the consequent's predicate are the same, and the antecedent's predicate and the consequent's subject are different. The Topical relationship must be thought to lie in the antecedent's predicate in respect of the consequent's subject and, depending on the way the antecedent's predicate is related to the consequent's subject, the Topic must be assigned either *from the whole, from a part*, or in some other way. How? For example, 'If every man is an animal, some substance is a man.'

There is also another way in which the Topical relationship is thought to lie in the antecedent's subject. How? When the antecedent's predicate and the consequent's subject are the same, and the consequent's predicate and the antecedent's subject are different. The Topical relationship must be thought to lie in the antecedent's subject in respect of the consequent's predicate, and the assigning of the Topic depends on the way the antecedent's subject is related to the consequent's predicate. How? 'If every man is an animal, some animal is risible.'

There is also [another way] in which the Topical relationship is thought to lie in the predicate and in the subject. How? When the antecedent's predicate and the consequent's predicate, and the antecedent's subject and the consequent's subject, are different. Furthermore, depending on the way the antecedent's predicate is related to the consequent's predicate, and the antecedent's subject is related to the consequent's subject, the Topic must be assigned either from the double whole or from the double part. How? 'If every man is an animal, some risible thing is a man.'

The Topical relationship is [sometimes] thought to lie in the whole proposition. How? When the antecedent proposition converts into the consequent proposition {86} by simple conversion, by conversion by contraposition, or in any other way mentioned above. And depending on the way the antecedent proposition is related to the consequent proposition, the Topic will have to be assigned either from the simple converse or from one of the other sorts of conversion (about which enough was said above) – e.g., 'If no man is an animal, no animal is a man.'

[9b(ii). *The Topic* From a Universal Whole]

It must also be noted that when the Topical relationship is thought to lie in the antecedent's predicate in respect of the consequent's predicate, then if what is predicated in the antecedent is a whole relative to what is predicated in the consequent, the Topic is *from the whole*. How? 'If some man is an animal, some man is rational or irrational.' Where does the Topic come from? *From the whole.* The rule: If a whole is predicated of something, any of its parts is also predicated of the same thing. The application: But *animal* is a whole relative to *rational* and *irrational*. The conclusion: Therefore, if some man is an animal, some man is rational or irrational.

The Topical relationship is also thought to lie in the antecedent's predicate in respect of the consequent's predicate in negative hypotheticals. How? 'If some man is not an animal, he is neither rational nor irrational.' Where does the Topic come from? *From the whole.* The rule: Whatever a whole is removed from, its part is also removed from. The application: But in this case a whole is removed from a man. The conclusion: Therefore, if some man is not an animal, he is neither rational nor irrational. (The same thing is considered in connection with a universal [antecedent]. How? 'If no man is an animal, he is neither rational nor irrational.' Where does the Topic come from? *From the whole.* The rule and the application are the same as above.)

The Topical relationship is also thought to lie in the antecedent's predicate in a [plural] negative. How? 'If Socrates and Plato are not trees, they are neither ash nor oak.' Where does the Topic come from? *From the whole.* The rule: If a whole is removed from any parts taken together, its parts are also removed from the same things taken in the same way. The application: But *trees* are a whole relative to *ash* and *oak*. The conclusion: Therefore, if Socrates and Plato are not trees, they are neither ash nor oak.

The inferential power is sometimes thought to lie in the antecedent's subject as well. How? 'If every animal is a body, every man is a body.' Where does the Topic come from? *From the whole.* The rule: If anything is predicated of a universal whole universally, it is also predicated of each part of it. The application: But *animal* is a whole relative to *man*, and *body* is predicated of that whole universally. The conclusion: Therefore, *body* is predicated of *man* universally, and I will say, 'Every man is a body.'

The inferential power is also thought to lie in the antecedent's subject in a negative hypothetical. How? 'If no animal is wooden, no man {87} is wooden.' Where does the Topic come from? *From the whole.* The rule: If anything is removed from a universal whole universally, it is also removed from each part of it. The application: But *animal* is a whole [relative to man], and *wooden* is removed from it universally. The conclusion: Therefore, it is also removed from each part of it, and I will say, 'No man is wooden.'

The inferential power is also thought to lie in the antecedent's subject [in an affirmative hypothetical]. How? 'If some animal is white, something rational or something irrational is white.' Where does the Topic come from? *From the whole.* The rule: If anything is predicated of a universal whole particularly, it is also predicated [of] any of its parts that exhaustively divide the whole. The application: But *rational* and *irrational* exhaustively divide this whole, and *white* is predicated of it particularly. The conclusion:

Therefore, it is predicated of any of its parts, and I will say 'Something rational or irrational is white.'

The inferential power is also thought to lie in the antecedent's predicate in respect of the consequent's subject. How? 'If no stone is an animal, no man is a stone.' Where does the Topic come from? *From the whole.* The rule: That from which a universal is removed universally is removed from each part of the removed whole. The application: But the universal *animal* is removed from *stone* universally. The conclusion: Therefore, *stone* is removed universally from each part of the removed whole, and I will say 'No man is a stone.'

The inferential power is also thought to lie in the antecedent's subject in respect of the consequent's predicate. How? 'If every animal is animate, something animate is a man.' Where does the Topic come from? *From the whole.* The rule: A part of anything is predicated particularly of that which is predicated universally of its whole. The application: But *animal* is the whole belonging to man, and *animate* is predicated of it universally. The conclusion: Therefore, *man* is predicated of *animate* particularly, and I will say 'Something animate is a man.'

The inferential power is also thought to lie in the antecedent's subject in respect of the consequent's predicate in a negative [hypothetical]. How? 'If no animal is a stone, no stone is a man.' Where does the Topic come from? *From the whole.* The rule: Each part is removed universally from that which is removed universally from its whole. The application: But *animal* is the whole, and *stone* is removed from it universally. Conclusion: Therefore, each part of *animal* is removed from it [i.e., *stone*] universally, and I will say 'No stone is a man.'

We have now discussed Topics *from a universal whole.*

[9b(iii). The Topic From an Integral Whole]

We have yet to discuss Topics *from an integral whole.* 'If a house exists, a wall also exists.' Where does the Topic come from? *From the whole.* The rule: If an integral whole exists, each principal part of it exists. The application: But a house is an integral whole, and a wall is a principal part of it. The conclusion: Therefore, if the integral whole exists, each principal part of it exists, and I will say 'If the house exists, the wall also exists.' (Principal parts are those by whose {88} ordered combination the whole is produced and without which parts the whole cannot exist.)

There is also another Topic from the whole. How? 'If the whole house is white, the wall is also white.' Where does the Topic come from? *From the whole.* The rule: Whatever applies to a whole taken as a whole also applies to each of its principal parts. The application: But a house is a whole, and a wall is a principal part of it. The conclusion: Therefore, if the whole house is white, the wall is also white.

We have now discussed the Topics *from a universal whole* and *from an integral whole.*

[9b(iv). The Topic From a Part]

The inferential power is also thought to lie in the antecedent's predicate in respect of the consequent's predicate, and the Topic is *from a part of a universal whole.* How? 'If Socrates is a man, Socrates is an animal.' Where does the Topic come from? *From a part.* The rule: Whatever a part is predicated of, the whole is also predicated of. The application: But *man* is a part of *animal* and is predicated of Socrates. The conclusion: Therefore, its whole is predicated of the same thing, and I will say 'If Socrates is a man, Socrates is an animal.'

The inferential power is also thought to lie in the antecedent's predicate in respect of the consequent's predicate in a negative [hypothetical]. How? 'If Socrates is not a man, Socrates is not every animal.' Where does the Topic come from? *From a part.* The rule: Whatever a part is removed from, the whole taken universally is also removed from. The application: But *man* is a part and is removed from Socrates. The conclusion: Therefore, the whole taken universally is removed from the same thing, and I will say 'If Socrates is not a man, Socrates is not every animal.'

[An Objection and Reply]

Some people claim that there is also a Topic *from the whole* in an affirmative [hypothetical]. How? 'If Socrates is a man, he is this one or that one.' Where does the Topic come from? *From the whole.* The rule: Whatever a whole is predicated of, its parts are also predicated of disjunctively. The application: But *man* is a whole and is predicated of Socrates. The conclusion: Therefore, its parts are predicated of the same thing disjunctively.

That does not follow [however]; for names taken from things that are determinately in something are not predicated [of it] disjunctively. Boethius attests to this when he says that a crow is not white or black, because it is only black, and snow is not white or black, because it is only white. Analogously, therefore, if Socrates is a man, he is not this one or that one, because he is only this one. (It seems that that is to be granted in all cases – which is false. For we say 'A man is either white or black.' Why? Because neither is in him determinately.)

[9b(iv). Cont.]

The inferential power is also thought to lie in the antecedent's predicate in respect of the consequent's predicate in an affirmative [hypothetical]. How? 'If Socrates is a man, and Brownie is a donkey, Socrates and Brownie are animals.' Where does the Topic come from? *From the parts.* The rule: Whatever things the parts of a whole are predicated of, the whole itself is predicated of those same things. The application: But *man* and *donkey* are parts of *animal*, {89} and they are predicated of Socrates and of Brownie. The conclusion: Therefore, the whole itself is predicated of those same things, and I will say 'If Socrates is a man, and Brownie is a donkey, Socrates and Brownie are animals.'

The inferential power is also thought to lie in the antecedent's predicate in respect of the consequent's predicate. How? 'If Socrates is neither rational nor irrational, he is not an animal.' Where does the Topic come from? *From the parts.* The rule: Whatever singular the parts exhaustively dividing a whole are removed from, the whole itself is removed from that same singular. The application: But *rational* and *irrational* are parts that exhaustively divide this whole, and they are removed from Socrates. The conclusion: Therefore, the whole itself is removed from the same thing, and I will say 'If Socrates is neither rational nor irrational, he is not an animal.'

The inferential power is also thought to lie in the antecedent's subject in respect of the consequent's subject in an affirmative

[hypothetical]. How? 'If some man is white, some animal is white.'
Where does the Topic come from? *From a part*. The rule: If something is predicated of a part of some whole, the same thing is
predicated of the whole itself particularly. The application: But *man*
is a part of *animal*, and *white* is predicated of it. The conclusion:
Therefore, the same thing is predicated of that whole itself particularly, and I will say 'If some man is white, some animal is white.'

It is thought to be the same in a negative [hypothetical]. How? 'If
some man is not white, some animal is not white.' Where does the
Topic come from? *From a part*. The rule: Whatever is removed
from a part of some whole is removed from the whole itself
particularly. The application: But *man* is a part of *animal*, and *white*
is removed from it. The Conclusion: Therefore, the same thing is
removed from the whole itself particularly, and I will say 'If some
man is not white, some animal is not white.'

The inferential power is also thought to lie in the antecedent's
subject in respect of the consequent's subject. How? 'If everything
rational and irrational is colored, every animal is colored.' Where
does the Topic come from? *From the parts*. The rule: If something
is universally predicated of parts that exhaustively divide some
whole, the same thing is universally predicated of the whole itself.
The application: But *rational* and *irrational* are parts that exhaustively
divide this whole, and *colored* is universally predicated of them. The
conclusion: Therefore, the same thing is universally predicated of
the whole itself, and I will say 'If everything rational and irrational
is colored, every animal is colored.'

It is thought to be the same in a negative [hypothetical]. How? 'If
nothing rational and irrational is colored, no animal is colored.'
Where does the Topic come from? *From the parts*. The rule: If
something is universally removed from parts that exhaustively
divide some whole, the same thing is universally removed from the
whole itself. The application: But *rational* and *irrational* are parts that
exhaustively divide {90} this whole, and *colored* is universally
removed from them. The conclusion: Therefore, the same thing is
universally removed from the whole itself, and I will say 'If nothing
rational and irrational is colored, no animal is colored.'

The inferential power is also thought to lie in the antecedent's
subject in respect of the consequent's subject. How? 'If Socrates and
Plato are two, some animals are two.' Where does the Topic come

from? *From the parts.* The rule: If something is predicated of the parts of a whole, the same thing is predicated of the whole itself particularly. The application: But Socrates and Plato are parts of *animal*, and the term *two* is predicated of them. The conclusion: ((*Conclude/Concludo*)) Therefore, the same thing is predicated of the whole itself particularly, and I will say, etc.

It is thought to be the same in a negative [hypothetical]. How? 'If Socrates and Plato are not three, some animals are not three.' Where does the Topic come from? *From the parts.* The rule: Whatever is removed from some whole's parts taken together is removed from the whole itself particularly. The application: But Socrates and Plato are parts of *animal*, and the term *three* is removed from them. The conclusion: Therefore, it is removed from the whole itself particularly, and I will say, etc.

The inferential power is also thought to lie in the antecedent's predicate in respect of the consequent's subject. How? 'If everything literate is a man, some animal is literate.' Where does the Topic come from? *From a part.* The rule: The thing of which a part of some whole is predicated is itself predicated particularly of the whole to which the predicated part belongs. The application: But *man* is a part of *animal*, and it is predicated of *literate*. The conclusion: Therefore, *literate* is predicated particularly of the whole to which the predicated part belongs, and I will say 'If everything literate is a man, some animal is literate.'

It is thought to be the same in a negative [hypothetical]. How? 'If nothing literate is a man, some animal is not literate.' Where does the Topic come from? *From a part.* The rule: That from which a part of some whole is removed is removed particularly from the whole to which the removed part belongs. The application: But *man* is a part of *animal*, and it is removed from *literate*. The conclusion: Therefore, *literate* is removed from the whole to which the removed part belongs, and I will say 'If nothing literate is a man, some animal is not literate.'

The inferential power lies also in the antecedent's predicate in respect of the consequent's subject. How? 'If no stone is rational and irrational, no animal is a stone.' Where does the Topic come from? *From the parts.* The rule: That from which the parts that exhaustively divide some whole are removed is itself removed universally from the whole to which the removed parts belong.

The application: But *rational* and *irrational* are parts that exhaustively divide this whole, and they are removed from *stone*. The conclusion: Therefore, that same thing is removed universally from the whole to which the removed parts {91} belong, and I will say 'If no stone is rational and irrational, no ((*nullum/nullam*)) animal is a stone.'

The inferential power is also thought to lie in the antecedent's subject in respect of the consequent's predicate. How? 'If every man is white, something white is an animal.' Where does the Topic come from? *From a part.* The rule: If something is predicated of a part of some whole, the whole to which the part that is the subject belongs is predicated particularly of the predicate. The application: But *man* is a part of *animal*, and *white* is predicated of it. The conclusion: Therefore, the whole to which the part that is the subject belongs is predicated particularly of the predicate, and I will say 'If every man is white, something white is an animal.'

The inferential power is also thought to lie in the antecedent's subject in respect of the consequent's predicate. How? 'If nothing rational and irrational is wooden, nothing wooden is an animal.' Where does the Topic come from? *From the parts.* The rule: If something is removed from parts that exhaustively divide some whole, the whole to which those parts belong is also removed universally from what has been removed. The application: But *rational* and *irrational* are parts that exhaustively divide this whole, and *wooden* is removed from them. The conclusion: Therefore, the whole to which those parts belong is removed universally from what has been removed, and I will say 'If nothing rational, etc.'

The inferential power is also thought to lie in the antecedent's subject in respect of the consequent's predicate in an affirmative hypothetical. How? 'If Socrates and Plato are three, some three things are animals.' Where does the Topic come from? *From the parts.* The rule: If something is predicated of the parts of some whole, the whole to which those parts belong is also predicated particularly of the predicate. The application: But Socrates and Plato are parts [of this whole], and the term *three* is predicated of them. The conclusion: Therefore, the whole to which those parts belong is predicated particularly of the predicate, and I will say 'If Socrates and Plato, etc.'

The inferential power is also thought to lie in the antecedent's subject in respect of the consequent's predicate. How? 'If a house exists, a wall also exists.' Where does the Topics come from? *From an integral whole.* The rule: If an integral whole is posited, each of its principal parts is posited. The application: But a whole is posited when I say 'A house exists.' The conclusion: Therefore, each of its principal parts is posited, and I will say 'If a house exists, a wall also exists.'

The inferential power is also thought to lie in the relationship of one subject to the other. How? 'If men are not governed by God's providence, the whole world is not governed by God's providence either.' Where does the Topic come from? *From a part.* The rule: Whatever does not apply to a part does not apply to the whole taken as a whole. The application: But *men* are a part, and to be governed by God's providence does not apply to them. The conclusion: Therefore, it does not apply to the whole itself taken as a whole, and I will say 'If men are not governed by God's providence, etc.' {92}

[9b(v). The Topic From Equals]

It is important to see that equals are spoken of in four different ways: in predication, inference, concomitance, and quantity. In predication, when one equal is predicated of whatever the other is predicated of – e.g., *man* and *risible thing*. In inference, when whatever is inferred from one is also inferred from the other – e.g., 'Some man is white,' 'Some white thing is a man.' In concomitance, those that are concomitant with each other – e.g., the world and time. In quantity – e.g., containers that are of the same quantity.

The inferential power is thought to lie in the antecedent's predicate in respect of the consequent's predicate. How? 'If Socrates is a man, Socrates is risible.' Where does the Topic come from? *From an equal.* The rule: Whatever one equal is predicated of the other is predicated of also. The application: But *man* and *risible thing* are equals, and *man* is predicated of Socrates. [The conclusion:] Therefore, *risible* is predicated of the same thing, and I will say 'If Socrates is a man, Socrates is risible.'

It is thought to be the same in a negative [hypothetical]. How? 'If Socrates is not a man, Socrates is not risible.' Where does the Topic come from? *From an equal.* The rule: Whatever one equal is removed from the other is removed from also. The application: But *man* is removed from Socrates. The conclusion: Therefore, the other [equal] is removed from the same thing, and I will say 'If Socrates is not a man, Socrates is not risible.'

The inferential power is also thought to lie in the antecedent's predicate in respect of the consequent's subject. How? 'If some boy is risible, some man is a boy.' Where does the Topic come from? *From an equal.* The rule: That of which one of a pair of equals is predicated particularly is predicated of the other particularly. The application: But *risible* and *man* are equals, and *risible* is predicated of *boy* particularly. The conclusion: Therefore, that same thing is predicated of the other equal particularly, and I will say, 'If some boy, etc.'

It is thought to be the same in a negative [hypothetical]. How? 'If something white is not a man, something risible is not white.' Where does the Topic come from? *From an equal.* The rule: That from which one of a pair of equals is removed particularly is removed from the other of the pair of equals particularly. The application: But *man* and *risible* are equals and *man* is removed from *white* particularly. The conclusion: Therefore, that same thing is removed from the other of the pair of equals particularly, and I will say, 'If something white, etc.'

The inferential power is also thought to lie in the antecedent's subject in respect of the consequent's predicate. How? 'If something risible is an old person, some old person is a man.' Where does the Topic come from? *From an equal.* The rule: If something is predicated particularly of one of a pair of equals, the equal of the equal that is the subject is predicated particularly of the predicate. The application: But *risible* is one of a pair of equals, and *old person* is predicated particularly of it. The conclusion: Therefore, the equal of the equal that is the subject is predicated {93} particularly of the predicate, and I will say, 'If something risible, etc.'

It is thought to be the same in a negative [hypothetical]. How? 'If something risible is not an old person, some old person is not a man.' Where does the Topic come from? *From an equal.* The rule: If something is removed particularly from one of a pair of equals, the equal of the equal that is the subject is removed particularly from what was removed. The application: But *risible* is one of a pair of equals, and *old person* is removed particularly from it. The conclusion: Therefore, the equal of the equal that is the subject is removed particularly from what was removed, and I will say, 'If something risible is not an old person, etc.'

There is also the Topic *from a quantitative equal.* How? 'If this container holds one measure, that [equal] one also holds one measure.' Where does the Topic come from? *From a quantitative equal.* The rule: Judgment regarding quantitative equals is the same.

There is also the Topic *from a concomitant equal.* How? 'If time exists, the world also exists.' Where does the Topic come from? *From a concomitant equal.* The rule: When one concomitant equal exists, the other exists. The application: But *time* and the *world* are concomitant equals. The conclusion: Therefore, when one concomitant equal exists, the other exists.

[9b(vi). *The Topic* From Opposites]

Next, as regards opposites. Opposites are spoken of in four different ways, as Boethius says (*In Arist. Cat.* PL 64, 264C). Opposites are either relatives – e.g., father and child – or contraries – e.g., whiteness and blackness – or privation and possession – e.g., blindness and sight – or affirmation and negation – e.g., 'Socrates is a man,' 'Socrates is not a man.' Opposites in predication are also spoken of. Things that are universally removed from each other and are predicated of no singular are said to be opposites in predication.

A rule is drawn from relatives: 'If a father is, a child also is.' Where does the Topic come from? *From relatives.* The rule: If one of a pair of relatives is posited, the other is posited. The application: But *father* is one of a pair of relatives, and it is posited when I say, 'A father is.' [The conclusion:] Therefore, the other is posited, and I will say, 'If a father, etc.'

It is thought to be the same in a negative [hypothetical]. How? 'If a father is not, a child is not.' Where does the Topic come from? *From relatives.* The rule: When one of a pair of relatives is destroyed, the other is destroyed. The application: But *father* is one of a pair of relatives, and it is destroyed when I say, 'A father is not.' The conclusion: Therefore, the other is destroyed, and I will say, 'A child is not.'

Additional rules are given for relatives. Thus, suppose that we argue in this way: 'If *man* is a species of *animal, animal* is also the genus of *man.*' Where does the Topic come from? *From relatives.* The rule? If one of a pair of relatives applies to something in respect of something else, the other relative applies to it in respect of the same thing. The application: But *species* is one of a pair of relatives, and it applies to *man* in respect {94} of something else. The conclusion: Therefore, the other relative, which is *genus*, applies to it – i.e., to *animal* – in respect of the same thing – viz., of *man.*

It is thought to be the same in a negative [hypothetical]. How? 'If *man* is not a species of *stone*, neither is *stone* the genus of *man.*' Where does the Topic come from? *From relatives.* The rule: If one of a pair of relatives does not apply to something in respect of something else, neither does the other relative apply to it in respect of that other thing. The application: But *species* is one of a pair of relatives, and it does not apply to *stone* in respect of something else. The conclusion: Therefore, neither does the other relative apply to it in respect of the other thing, and I will say, 'If *man*, etc.'

We have now discussed the rules drawn from relatives; we have yet to discuss the rules drawn from contraries.

It is important to note that in this context we say that both things that are in a subject and things that are said of a subject are contraries. We also say that some contraries are mediate, others immediate. The immediate ones are those of which it is necessary that the one or the other be in that which admits of them; the mediate ones are those of which it is not necessary that the one or the other be in that which admits of them.

Rules drawn from mediate contraries come next, and they are of this sort. 'If whiteness is in Socrates, blackness is not in him.' Where does the Topic come from? *From contraries.* The rule: If one of a pair of contraries is in something, the other of those contraries is not in that same thing. The application: But *whiteness* is one of a pair of contraries, and it is presented as being in something when I say, 'Whiteness is in Socrates.' The conclusion: Therefore, the other of the contraries is not in that same thing, and I will say, 'If whiteness, etc.'

'If Socrates is white, Socrates is not black'. (Another rule drawn from contraries is given.) Where does the Topic come from? *From contraries.* The rule: If one of a pair of contraries is predicated of something, the other of those contraries is removed from that same thing. The application: But in this case one of a pair of contraries is predicated when I say 'Socrates is white.' The conclusion: Therefore, the other of those contraries is removed from that same thing, and I will say, 'If Socrates is white, etc.'

Next comes a rule drawn from immediate contraries. Thus, suppose that we argue in this way: 'If Socrates is not healthy, Socrates is sick.' Where does the Topic come from? *From immediate contraries.* The rule: If one of a pair of immediates is removed from something, the other of those immediates is predicated of that same thing. The application. But one of a pair of immediates is removed from something when I say, 'Socrates is not healthy.' The conclusion: Therefore, the other of those immediates is predicated of that same thing, and I will say, 'Socrates is sick.'

The next rule is drawn from the opposites privation and possession. Thus, we infer in this way: 'If sight is not in him, blindness is in him.' Where does the Topic come from? *From the opposites privation and possession.* The rule: If one of a pair of privative and possessive opposites ((*oppositorum/appositorum*)) is not presented as being in something, the other is presented as being in that same thing. The application: But in this case one of a pair of {95} privative and possessive opposites is not presented as being in something when I say, 'Sight is not in him.' The conclusion: Therefore, the other is presented as being in him, and I will say, 'If sight is not in him, blindness is in him.'

A rule drawn from opposites in predication is given. 'If Socrates is a man, Socrates is not a horse.' Where does the Topic come from? *From opposites in predication.* The rule: If one of a pair of opposites is predicated of something, the other is removed from that same thing. The application: But *man* is one of a pair of opposites, and it is predicated of something when I say 'Socrates is a man.' The conclusion: Therefore, the other is removed from that same thing, and I will say, 'If Socrates is a man, Socrates is not a horse.'

Another Topic *from opposites*. There is also a Topic from opposites when the Topical relationship lies in the predicate of the first categorical [in a hypothetical] in respect of the subject of the second, as in 'If every man is an animal, nothing wooden is a man.' The rule: That of which one opposite is predicated is removed universally from one of that thing's opposites. The application: But *animal* is opposed to *wooden*. [The conclusion:] Therefore, if *animal* is predicated of *man*, *man* is removed universally from *wooden*.

Another Topic *from opposites*. There is also a Topic from opposites when the relationship is considered to lie in the subject of the first categorical [and] the predicate of the second is removed, as in 'If every man is an animal (or: [If] some man is an animal), some animal is not a horse.' The rule: If something is predicated universally or particularly of one opposite, its opposite is removed from that thing particularly. The application: But *man* is an opposite of *horse*. [The conclusion:] Therefore, if *animal* is predicated of *man*, *horse* is removed from it particularly.

[9b(vii). *Topics Assigned when the Inferential Power Lies in Both Terms*]

We have now discussed the Topics that are to be assigned when a categorical implies a categorical in such a way that the inferential power lies in the predicate only or in the subject only. Now we have to discuss Topics that are to be assigned when the inferential power lies in both the predicate and the subject.

We have to see how the predicate of the first categorical is related to the predicate of the following one, and how the subject of the first is related to the subject of the following one. And on that basis a double Topic will be assigned: either *from a double whole*, or *from a double equal*, or *from a part,* or *from a whole*, or *from similars*. A double relationship is also considered, as in the following case. Rule: If a whole is predicated of some whole universally, one of the parts exhaustively dividing that whole is predicated of each individual belonging to the whole that is the subject. For example, if the whole [*animal*] is predicated universally of *biped*, one of the parts that exhaustively divide that whole is predicated of each individual contained under {96} *biped*. And it works analogously in connection with negatives: 'If no tree is an animal, no oak is either a rational or an irrational animal.' The Topic: *From a double whole*. The rule: If a whole is removed from some whole universally, any parts of the removed whole are removed from each part of the whole that is the subject.

Here is the Topic *from a double part*: 'If every man is a biped, some animal naturally has [two] feet.' The rule: If a part is predicated of some part universally, particularly, or indefinitely, the whole to which the predicated part belongs is predicated particularly of the whole to which the part that is the subject belongs. The application: But *biped* is a part relative to *having two feet*, and *man* is a part of *animal*. [The conclusion:] Therefore, if *biped* is predicated of *man naturally having [two] feet* is predicated particularly of *animal*.

Again, the Topic *from a part* and *from the parts* occurs in this way: 'If some oak is neither a rational nor an irrational animal, some tree is not an animal.' The rule: If parts that exhaustively divide a whole are removed from some part, the whole to which the removed parts belong is removed particularly from the whole to which the part that is the subject belongs. The application: But *rational animal* and *irrational animal* are parts that exhaustively divide *animal*, and *oak* is part of *tree*. [The conclusion:] Therefore, if *rational or irrational animal* is removed from *oak* in any way, *animal* is removed particularly from *tree*.

But here is the Topic *from a double equal*: 'If every man is a donkey, every thing that can laugh is a thing that can bray.' The rule: If something is predicated particularly of some equal, something equal to the predicated equal is predicated of something equal to the equal that is the subject. The application: But *man* is equal to *thing that can laugh* and *donkey* is equal to *thing that can bray*. [The conclusion:] Therefore, if *donkey* is predicated of *man, thing that can bray* is predicated of *thing that can laugh*.

It works analogously in connection with negatives: 'If no man is a donkey, no thing that can laugh is a thing that can bray.' The Topic: *From a double equal.* The rule: If an equal is removed from some equal, something equal to the removed equal is removed from something equal to the equal that is the subject.

And so wherever the Topical relationship lies in both the predicate and the subject, the simple Topics discussed above can be mixed together in many ways – as an attentive, watchful mind will be able to discover.

[9b(viii). Topics Assigned When the Inferential Power Lies in the Whole Proposition]

When the inferential power lies in the whole proposition, however, the Topical relationship is considered to lie not in the subject, in the predicate, or in both, but in the whole proposition. For that reason we have to see how the antecedent proposition is related to the following proposition. And on that basis a Topic must be assigned either *from an equal by contraposition* or *from an equal by simple conversion*, {97} and in another way. We discussed these things when we were discussing Topics from simple conversion or from conversion by contraposition.

We have discussed Topics that have to be assigned in connection with a simple hypothetical, or in connection with a categorical when one categorical implies another. Now we have to discuss composite hypotheticals.

[9c. Composite Hypotheticals]

One sort of composite hypothetical consists of a categorical and a hypothetical, another consists of a hypothetical and a categorical, another consists of two or more hypotheticals.

And first we have to discuss the sort that consists of a categorical and a hypothetical. It can consist of a categorical and a disjunctive hypothetical or of a categorical and a connected hypothetical. The connected sort can consist either of a categorical and a temporal hypothetical or of a categorical and a natural hypothetical – as in this case: 'If every man is an animal, when Socrates is a man, Socrates is an animal'; 'if' conjoins that categorical with this temporal. This one consists of a categorical and a natural hypothetical: 'If every man is an animal, then if every risible thing is a man, every risible thing is an animal.' The antecedent is 'Every man is an animal'; the consequent is the natural hypothetical 'If every risible thing is a man, every risible thing is an animal'; the first 'if' conjoins the categorical with the following hypothetical; the 'then' that is interposed indicates that the categorical that precedes it is the antecedent and the hypothetical that follows it is the consequent.

Now we will discuss the sort that consists of a hypothetical and a categorical ((*ypothetica et cathegorica/cathegorica et ypothetica*)). But since everything that will be taught has to do with categorical syllogisms and with those [composite] hypothetical propositions, and since categorical syllogisms and those hypothetical propositions are demonstrated by very nearly the same rules, we will discuss categorical syllogisms and those hypothetical propositions at the same time.

[10. Categorical Syllogisms]

'Syllogism' means a collection of sentences. '*Syn*' in Greek is '*simul*' in Latin: 'together'; '*logos*' means 'sentence'; and so we say 'syllogism' – i.e., a collection of sentences.

One sort of syllogism is categorical, the other hypothetical. A categorical syllogism is one that consists of categoricals only; a hypothetical syllogism is one that contains either one or more hypotheticals. {98} Now let us discuss categorical syllogisms.

[10a. Regular and Irregular Syllogisms]

Some categorical syllogisms are regular, others irregular. The regular ones are those contained in the rules given by the authorities – those that are contained in three terms and in three propositions – the sort that are in [Boethius's] book of categorical syllogisms. The irregular ones are those that contain four or more propositions. Let us omit them for the present and discuss the regular ones.

[10b. Regular Syllogisms]

[10b(i). General Considerations]

Regular syllogisms occur in three figures: the first, the second, and the third. [For example,] the first figure is the one in which the two propositions from which the conclusion is inferred share the same term in such a way that the term that is the subject in one [of those two propositions] is the predicate in the other – e.g., 'Every man is an animal, but every risible thing is a man; therefore every risible thing is an animal.'

As we have said, three propositions must be expressed in a syllogism. The first of them is called the syllogism's proposition, but the second is called the addition because it is added to the proposition – i.e., as joined to it – and it adds something belonging to it. The third, which is inferred from those, is called the conclusion.

There are three terms in a syllogism, and no more. One of them is the middle term, the others are the extremes. The middle term is the one that is shared by both the proposition and the addition in syllogisms. The extremes are those of which one is the major, the other the minor.

[10b(ii). *The Structure of the First Figure*]

In the first figure the middle term is the one that is the subject in one, the predicate in the other. The other two terms are the extremes. The major is the one that is predicated of the middle term; the minor is the one that is the subject relative to the middle term. For example, in this case 'Every man is an animal, but every risible thing is a man,' 'man' is the middle term because it is the subject in the one, the predicate in the other; but 'animal' is the major extreme because it is predicated of 'man', which is the middle term; 'risible thing' is the minor extreme because it is the subject relative to 'man', which is the middle term. And in the conclusion, when it is drawn directly, the major extreme is predicated of the minor.

[10b(iii). *Syllogistic Figure Generally*]

In connection with syllogism, figure is defined as follows: The figure is the property of the syllogism that is distinguished on the basis of the sharing of the middle term. [This is] because the proposition and the addition share the one middle term either in such a way that it is the subject in one and the predicate in the other (the basis on which the first figure is picked out), or they share the same term in such a way that that term is the predicate in both (the basis on which the second figure is distinguished), or they share the same term in such a way that it is the subject in both (the basis on which the third figure is distinguished). {99}

[10b(iv). *First-figure Syllogisms*]

First we have to discuss syllogisms of the first figure. The first figure includes nine moods of which the first four are perfect, the rest imperfect.

The first mood of the first figure consists of two universal affirmatives resulting in a universal affirmative conclusion. No other mood can have that.

[An Excursus on Syllogistic Mood Generally]

Mood is defined in this way in connection with syllogism. The mood is the property of the syllogism that is distinguished on the basis of the quantity and quality of the propositions that constitute the syllogism and on the basis of the order they have in its constitution. Moods are distinguished in syllogisms in that the propositions are universal, or there is a universal in the one and a particular in the other (and that is on the basis of quantity); or in that the propositions are affirmative, or the one is affirmative and the other negative (and that is on the basis of quality). The mood is also distinguished in that the affirmation precedes the negation either universally or particularly (and that is on the basis of the order they have in the syllogism's constitution).

[10b(iv). Cont.]

In the first figure, for example, the first mood is distinguished in that it consists of all universal affirmatives – e.g., 'Every man is an animal, but every risible thing is a man; therefore, every risible thing is an animal.' There is the following rule of syllogisms: If something is predicated universally of something, and [that] subject is predicated universally of something else, the first predicate is predicated universally of the second subject. The application: But in this syllogism *animal* is predicated universally of *man*, and that same subject – i.e., *man* – is predicated universally of *risible thing*.

If the terms are put ((*termini ponantur/terminus ponatur*)) in the propositions ((*propositionibus/propositione*)) in such a way that 'Every risible thing is a man' occurs as the first proposition, there will be a syllogism of the same mood and figure – e.g., 'Every risible thing is a man, but every man is an animal; therefore every risible thing is an animal.' But the rule must be stated in this way: If something is predicated universally of something, and something else is predicated universally of [that] predicate, that same thing is universally predicated of the first subject.

That rule of syllogism includes a [composite] hypothetical

composed of two categoricals joined by 'and' and one following, such as 'If every risible thing is a man and every man is an animal, every risible thing is an animal.' The antecedent is the proposition composed of two categoricals {100} joined by 'and' ((om. *et una sequente*)) – viz., 'Every risible thing is a man and every man is an animal'; the consequent is this one alone: 'Every risible thing is an animal.'

Following that same order, a composite hypothetical is made out of a categorical and a hypothetical: 'If every man is an animal, then if every risible thing is a man, every risible thing is an animal.' The antecedent is the categorical 'Every man is an animal,' the consequent is the hypothetical 'then if every risible thing is a man, every risible thing is an animal,' and 'then,' which is interposed, does not enter into the sense of the whole hypothetical but indicates that the proposition that is before it is the antecedent and the one that follows after it is the consequent. The rule must be assigned in this way: If something is predicated universally of something, then if [that] subject is universally predicated of something else, [that] predicate is universally predicated of it. The application: If *animal* is predicated universally of *man*, then if that subject – i.e., *man* – is predicated universally of *risible thing*, [that] predicate is predicated universally of that same thing.

The second mood consists of a universal negative and a universal affirmative, resulting directly in a universal negative conclusion. I say 'directly' because the sixth mood consists of the same proposition and addition but results indirectly in a universal negative conclusion, in such a way that the minor extreme is removed from the major. But in the second mood the major extreme is removed from the minor, and so it results in its conclusion directly. For example, 'No animal is a stone, but every man is an animal; therefore, no man is a stone.' The rule: If something is universally removed from ((*ab/de*)) something, and [that] subject is universally [predicated] of something else, the first predicate is universally removed from that same thing.

This rule includes a [composite] hypothetical composed of two categoricals joined by 'and' and one following – viz., 'If no animal is a stone and every man is an animal, no man is a stone.' The rule is the same. The applicaton: If *stone* is removed from *animal*, and *animal* is predicated of *man*, *stone* is removed from *man*.

In accordance with this mood, a composite hypothetical is made out of a categorical and a hypothetical – viz., 'If no animal is a stone, then if every man is an animal, no man is a stone.' The rule: If something is universally removed from something, then if [that] subject is universally predicated of something else, [that] predicate is universally removed from that same thing. [The application:] If *stone* is universally removed from *animal*, then if *animal* is universally predicated of *man*, *stone* is universally removed from that same thing.

If the terms of the propositions ((*termini propositionum/terminus propositionis*)) are put in the syllogism in this way: first 'Every {101} man is an animal,' second 'No animal is a stone,' and the same conclusion is inferred, the syllogism will be of the same mood and figure. But the rule will have to be assigned in this way: If something is universally predicated of something, and something else is universally removed from that predicate, it is universally removed from [that] subject – e.g., 'Every man is an animal, but no animal is a stone; therefore, no man is a stone.'

The third mood consists of a universal affirmative and a particular affirmative, resulting directly in a particular affirmative conclusion. I say 'directly' because of the seventh mood, which consists of the same proposition and addition but results in ((*concludit/concluditur*)) a particular affirmative conclusion indirectly. The rule of the third mood is as follows: If something is universally predicated of something, and [that] subject is predicated of something else particularly, the first predicate is predicated of that same thing particularly. For example, 'Every man is an animal, but some risible thing is a man; therefore, some risible thing is an animal.'

If the terms of the propositions are put ((*termini propositionum ponantur/terminus propositionis ponatur*)) so that 'Some risible thing is a man' is said first and 'Every man is an animal' is said second, and the same conclusion is inferred – i.e., 'Some risible thing is an animal' – then there will be a syllogism of the same mood and figure. The rule: If something is predicated of something particularly and something else is predicated of the predicate universally, that same thing is predicated of the subject particularly.

In accordance with this mood a composite hypothetical is made out of a categorical and a hypothetical – viz., 'If some risible thing is a man, then if every man is an animal, some risible thing is an animal.' The rule: If something is predicated of something particularly, then if something else is predicated universally of [that] predicate, that same thing is predicated of [that] subject particularly.

Similar composite hypotheticals can likewise be found through the individual moods composed of two categoricals joined by 'and' in the antecedent and one in the consequent, or hypotheticals composed of a categorical antecedent and a hypothetical consequent.

The fourth mood consists of a universal negative and a particular affirmative, resulting in a particular negative conclusion. For example, 'No animal is a stone, but some man is an animal; therefore, some man is not a stone.' The rule: If something is removed ((*removetur/predicatur*)) from something universally, and [that] subject [is predicated] of something else particularly, the first predicate is removed from that same thing particularly. {102}

In these four moods the major extreme is the term predicated in the conclusion. But in the five moods that remain, the minor extreme is the term predicated in the conclusion.

The fifth mood has the same proposition and addition as the first mood, but it differs in the conclusion because, whereas the first mood results in a universal affirmative conclusion, this mood results in its converse *per accidens* as a conclusion. Thus, the fifth mood consists of two universal affirmatives resulting indirectly in a particular affirmative conclusion. For example, 'Every man is an animal, but every risible thing is a man; therefore, some animal is risible.' The rule: If something is predicated universally of something, and [that] subject is universally predicated of something else, that same thing is predicated of the first predicate particularly.

The sixth mood has the same proposition and addition as the second mood, but it differs in the conclusion because the sixth mood results in a universal negative conclusion indirectly. For example, 'No animal is a stone, but every man is an animal; therefore, no stone is a man.' The rule: If something is universally removed ((*removetur/predicatur*)) from something, and [that] subject is universally predicated of something else, that same thing is universally removed from [that] predicate.

The seventh mood has the same proposition and addition as the third mood, but it differs in the conclusion because it results in a particular affirmative conclusion indirectly. For example, 'Every man is an animal, but some risible thing is a man; therefore, some animal is risible.' The rule: If something is universally predicated of something, and [that] subject is predicated of something else particularly, that same thing is predicated of the first predicate particularly.

The eighth mood consists of a universal affirmative and a universal negative, resulting in a particular negative conclusion indirectly. For example, 'Every man is an animal, but no stone is a man; therefore, some animal is not a stone.' The rule: If something is universally predicated of something, and [that] subject is universally removed from something else, that from which the subject is removed is removed from the predicate particularly.

In this mood one cannot conclude that {103} the major extreme is in any way removed from or in any way predicated of the minor. But the reason why this cannot be is given by Aristotle where he says 'something in which the middle does not inhere is something to all or to none of which the first applies' (*Prior Analytics* I 3, 26b5–6). He calls the middle term the middle, and he calls the major extreme the first; and so he means to say 'something in which the middle does not inhere' – i.e., something from which the middle term is removed – and 'to all of which the first applies' – i.e., of which the major extreme is predicated universally – and 'to none of which the first applies' – i.e., from that from which the middle term is removed the major extreme is universally removed. Thus in the syllogism that was expressed before, *man*, which is the middle term, is removed from *stone*, and *animal*, which is the major extreme, is predicated of no stone – 'to none of which the first applies.' And in this other syllogism 'Every man is an animal, but no horse is a man; therefore, some animal is not a horse,' *man*, which is the middle term, is not in *horse*, and 'to all of which the first applies,' or *animal* – which is the first, that is, the major extreme – is predicated universally of it. And so one cannot conclude that the major extreme is in any way removed from the minor.

The ninth mood is the same as the eighth except that the proposition in the ninth mood is a particular affirmative, whereas in the eighth mood it is universal. For example, 'Some man is an animal, but no stone is a man; therefore, some animal is not a stone.' The rule: If something is predicated of something particularly, and [that] subject is universally removed from ((*ab/de*)) something else, that same thing is removed from [that] predicate particularly.

These two moods, the eighth and the ninth, are demonstrated through the fourth. The eighth is demonstrated in this way: Its addition, a universal negative, is converted simply and becomes the proposition of the fourth mood; the proposition of the eighth mood, a universal affirmative, is converted *per accidens* into a particular and becomes the addition of the fourth mood; and the same conclusion results in both moods. For example, 'Every man is an animal, but no horse is a man; therefore, some animal is not a horse.' The addition of the eighth mood, 'No horse is a man,' is converted simply and becomes the proposition of the fourth mood; the proposition of the eighth mood, 'Every man is an animal,' is converted *per accidens* into 'Some animal is a man' and becomes the addition of the {104} fourth mood; and the same conclusion results. Analogously, the addition of the ninth mood is converted simply and becomes the proposition of the fourth; the proposition of the ninth is converted simply and becomes the addition of the fourth; and the conclusion is the same.

We have discussed the moods of the first figure. Now we have to discuss the second figure.

[10b(v). Second-figure Syllogisms]

The second figure occurs when the term that is predicated in the proposition is predicated in the addition. There are three terms in it: the middle term, which is predicated in the proposition and in the addition, and the two extremes – i.e., the two subject terms. The major extreme is the subject term in the proposition, but the minor extreme is the subject term in the addition and in the conclusion. The major extreme is always removed from the minor extremity, because all syllogisms of this figure are negative.

Four moods are contained in this figure. The first consists of a universal negative and a universal affirmative, resulting in a universal negative conclusion. For example, 'No stone is an animal, but every man is an animal; therefore, no man is a stone.' That this syllogism belongs to the second figure is apparent from the middle term, which is the predicate in the proposition and in the addition;

but that it is of the first mood can be seen from the quality and quantity of the propositions and from the order they have in the constitution of the syllogism because the universal negative is first and the universal affirmative is second. The rule: If something is universally removed from something, and [that] predicate is universally predicated of something, the first subject is universally removed from the second subject. The application: But in the proposition of this syllogism *animal* is universally removed from *stone*, and in the addition the predicate, *animal*, is universally predicated of *man*. Therefore, the first subject, *stone*, is universally removed from the second, *man*. The conclusion is 'Therefore, no man is a stone.'

The rule that includes the syllogism also includes this hypothetical: 'If no stone is an animal and every man is an animal, no man is a stone.' In this case two categoricals ((*cathegorice/ypothetice*)) are the antecedent and one categorical follows.

In this mood a composite hypothetical is made out of a categorical and a hypothetical in accordance with the following rule: If something is removed universally from something else, then if [that] predicate {105} is predicated universally of something else, the first subject is removed universally from that same thing. For example, 'If no stone is an animal, then if every man is an animal, no man is a stone.'

The second mood consists of a universal affirmative and a universal negative, resulting in a universal negative conclusion. For example, 'Every man is an animal, but no stone is an animal; therefore, no stone is a man.' The rule: If something is universally predicated of something, and [that] predicate is removed universally from something else, [that] subject is removed universally from that same thing.

The third mood consists of a universal negative and a particular affirmative, resulting in a particular negative conclusion. For example, 'No stone is an animal, but some man is an animal; therefore, some man is not a stone.' The rule: If something is removed universally from something, and [that] predicate is predicated particularly of something else, [that] subject is removed particularly from that same thing.

The fourth mood consists of a universal affirmative and a particular negative, resulting in a particular negative conclusion. For example, 'Every man is an animal, but some body is not an animal; therefore, some body is not a man.' The rule: If something is universally predicated of something, and [that] predicate [is removed] from ((*ab/de*)) something else particularly, the first subject is removed from that same thing particularly.

This mood cannot be demonstrated through the conversion of propositions, but it is demonstrated *per impossibile* as follows: For if the particular negative that is inferred is not true, the universal affirmative that is its contradictory is true – i.e., 'Every body is a man'; but 'Every man is an animal' has already been granted. From those two one infers in the first mood of the first figure 'Every body is an animal,' but in the addition of this syllogism 'Some body is not an animal' has been granted. And so two mutually exclusive [propositions] are true at the same time – viz., 'Every body is an animal' and 'Some body is not an animal' – which is impossible. {106}

[10b(vi). Third-figure Syllogisms]

The third figure is one in which the same term is the subject in the proposition and in the addition. This figure has six moods. In the individual moods there are three terms: the middle term and the two extremities. The middle term is the one that is the subject in the proposition and the addition. The two extremes are the two terms that are predicated. The extreme that is the major term is the one that is the predicate in the proposition; the minor extreme is the term that is predicated in the addition. And in the individual moods the major extreme is the term predicated in the conclusion. In this figure, however, there is no syllogism that is not particular – i.e., that does not have a particular conclusion.

The first mood of this third figure consists of two universal affirmatives, resulting in a particular affirmative conclusion. For example, 'Every man is an animal, but every man is a body; therefore, some body is an animal.' The rule: If something is universally predicated of something, and something else is universally predicated of [that] subject, the first predicate is predicated of the second predicate particularly. The application: But in the syllogism's proposition *animal* is universally predicated of *man*, and in the addition *body* is universally predicated of that same subject – i.e., of *man*. Therefore, *animal*, which is the first predicate, is predicated particularly of *body*, which is the second predicate.

The second mood consists of a universal negative and a universal affirmative, resulting in a particular negative conclusion. For example, 'No man is a donkey, but every man is an animal; therefore, some animal is not a donkey.' The rule: If something is universally removed ((*removetur/predicatur*)) from something, and something else is universally predicated of the same subject, the first predicate is removed from the second particularly.

This rule includes this syllogism and also a [composite] hypothetical consisting of two categoricals joined by 'and' and one consequent: 'If no man is a donkey and every man is an animal, some animal is not a donkey.' But the hypothetical consisting of a categorical and a hypothetical in accordance with this mood becomes this: 'If no man is a donkey, then if every man is an animal, some animal is not a donkey.' The rule: If something is universally removed ((*removetur/predicatur*)) from something, {107} then if something else is universally predicated of that same subject, the first predicate is removed particularly from it.

The third mood consists of a particular affirmative and a universal affirmative, resulting in a particular affirmative conclusion. For example, 'Some man is an animal, but every man is a body; therefore, some body is an animal.' The rule: If something is predicated of something particularly, and something else is universally predicated of the same subject, the first predicate is predicated of that same thing particularly.

The fourth mood consists of a universal affirmative and a particular affirmative, resulting in a particular affirmative conclusion. For example, 'Every man is an animal, but some man is white; therefore, some white thing is an animal.' The rule: If something is universally predicated of something, and something else is predicated of the same subject particularly, the first predicate is predicated of the second particularly.

The fifth mood consists of a particular negative and a universal affirmative, resulting in a particular negative conclusion. For example, 'Some animal is not a man, but every animal is a body; therefore, some body is not a man.' The rule: If something is

Anonymous

removed ((*removetur/predicatur*)) from something particularly, and something else is universally predicated of the same subject, the first predicate is removed from the second particularly.

This mood cannot be resolved through the conversion of propositions, but is proved *per impossibile*.

The sixth mood consists of a universal negative and a particular affirmative, resulting in a particular negative conclusion. For example, 'No man is a donkey, but some man is an animal; therefore, some animal is not a donkey.' The rule: If something is universally removed ((*removetur/predicatur*)) from something, and something else is predicated of the same subject particularly, the first predicate is removed from the second predicate particularly.

3

PETER OF SPAIN
PREDICABLES; CATEGORIES

Introduction

Peter of Spain seems to have been born into a noble family in Lisbon, Portugal, around 1205. He studied in Paris in the 1220s and taught medicine in Siena from 1246–1250. In 1263 he was appointed *magister scholarum* of the cathedral school of Lisbon, and in 1272 Pope Gregory X appointed him as court physician at Viterbo. He became Archbishop of Brage as well as Cardinal-Bishop of Frascati (Tusculum) in 1273. In 1276 he became Pope John XXI, though he was said to be more interested in his studies than in his duties as pope.

His most important acts as pope were his bulls of January 18 and April 28, 1277, to Stephen Tempier, Bishop of Paris. In the first, he ordered the bishop to investigate errors being taught at the University of Paris, and in the second he mandated a purification of the doctrines of the Parisian masters. He died in a way appropriate to his life and interests: In order to continue his studies even while pope, he ordered the addition of an apartment to the papal palace at Viterbo. On May 14, 1277, the roof of this apartment collapsed on him, and he died of the injuries on May 20.

Peter wrote a number of works on medicine, including the famous *Thesaurus pauperum*, composed while he was Gregory's court physician. He also wrote various psychological treatises, including a commentary on Aristotle's *De anima*, and commentaries on Dionysius the pseudo-Areopagite. His main logical works are the *Syncategoreumata* (a study of syncategorematic words) and the *Tractatus*, from which the following selections are excerpted. The *Tractatus*, written not later than the 1230s, is a basic textbook of logic that enjoyed great popularity on the continent and became one of the most famous logic books of the scholastic period.

Aristotle's *De interpretatione* and *Categories*, together with Porphyry's introduction to the *Categories*, the *Isagoge*, formed the core of what the medievals called the Old Logic. These works are the source of the lore of the predicables and categories, which informs all of medieval philosophy with its technical vocabulary, philosophical understanding of language, and metaphysical commitments.

A predicable is what is naturally suited to be said of more than one thing; that is, it is a universal in linguistic form. Peter considers five of these predicables: genus, differentia, species, proprium, and accident. There is a sixth predicable, definition, that he leaves out of account, perhaps because it can be constructed out of genus and differentia, which together constitute a definition. Peter defines and illustrates these five and then goes on to discuss the likenesses and differences among the predicables. Differentia, for example, differs from species because a differentia, unlike a species, is always predicated of more than one species. He concludes this section with some general remarks about univocal, equivocal, and denominative predication.

The section on the categories begins with further consideration of the nature of predication and with an examination of ways one thing is said to be in another. Peter analyzes and illustrates five of Aristotle's ten categories – substance, quantity, relation, action, and passion. There follows a discussion of opposition, priority, and concomitance; and the section concludes with some brief remarks on possession, the last of Aristotle's ten categories.

For some general discussion of the Old Logic, see CHLMP III.6, 'Abelard and the Culmination of the Old Logic'; a consideration of the philosophical issues posed by the Old Logic can be found in CHLMP III.5, 'Predicables and Categories.'

Predicables

[The Word 'Predicable']

{17} 1. Sometimes 'predicable' is used strictly, and in this way only what is predicated of more than one thing is called a predicable. Sometimes it is used broadly, and in this way what is predicated of one or of more than one is called a predicable. Hence, 'predicable' taken in its strict sense and 'universal' are the same, but they differ in that a predicable is defined in terms of saying and a universal in terms of being. For a predicable is what is naturally suited to be said of more than one, but a universal is what is naturally suited to be in more than one.

Predicables or universals are divided into genus, differentia, species, proprium, and accident; and our subject here is just these five.

[Genus]

2. There are three senses of 'genus.' The first sense of 'genus' is a group of many [individuals] mutually related in a certain way to each other and to one source – e.g., the group of individuals who belong to the same family and are descended from one ancestor [is a genus]. The second sense of 'genus' is the source of a race – e.g., the father, or the native country. The third sense of 'genus' is that under which a species is put, and this last sense is the one in which 'genus' is used here. ['Genus' in that sense] is defined in this way: A genus is that which is predicated of more than one thing, differing in species, in respect of what it is – e.g., *animal* is predicated of *horse*, *man* and *lion*, which differ in species.

3. To understand this part [of the definition], 'differing in species,' it is important to know that there are as many senses of 'differing' as there are of 'the same.' But 'the same' has three senses: the same in species, the same in genus, and the same in number. Things are the same in genus that are included under the same genus – e.g., *man* and *donkey* are included under *animal*. {18} Things are the same in species that are included under the same species – e.g., as Socrates and Plato are included under *man*. As for 'the same in number,' it has three senses: first, the same in name or definition; next, the same in proprium; and third, the same in accident. Things are called the same in name if there is one thing but more than one name – e.g., 'Marcus Tullius.' Things are called the same in definition if one is the definition of the other – e.g., *mortal rational animal* and *man*. They are the same in proprium if one is the proprium of the other – e.g., *man* and *risible*. They are the same in accident if one is an accident of the other – e.g., Socrates and the whiteness which is in him.

4. The senses of 'differing in genus,' 'differing in species,' and 'differing in number' are similar [to these]. Things that are under

different genera are things differing in genus – e.g., as *man* is under the genus *animal* and *tree* is under the genus *plant*. Things that belong to different species are things differing in species – e.g., Socrates and [the donkey] Brownie. Things that can be counted are things differing in number – e.g., Socrates and Plato.

5. Something that is an appropriate answer to a question asked by means of 'what' is said to be predicated in respect of what something is. For example, when one asks, 'What is man?', the appropriate answer is *'animal.'* Animal, therefore, is predicated of *man* in respect of what it is.

6. Alternatively, genus is defined in this way: A genus is that under which species are put.

7. Genus is divided into most general genus and subaltern genus. A most general genus is one over which there is no other supervening genus – e.g., substance. Or, to put it another way, a most general genus is one that, although it is a genus, cannot be a species [as well].

Most general genus is divided into ten. They are substance, quantity, relation, quality, action, passion, position, when, where, and possession. These ten are said to be most general because they have no genus {19} over them. For, although 'being' is said of these ten, it is said of them equivocally or ambiguously and so is not a genus. We will not discuss these ten now, but what we have to say about them will be presented in [the treatise] on the categories.

A subaltern genus is one that, although it is a genus, can be a species [as well]; for example, *animal* is the genus of *man* and a species of *animate body*.

[Species]

8. A species is what is predicated of more than one thing, differing in number, in respect of what it is. In this definition (as also in the others), the verb 'is predicated' indicates suitability [for predication] rather than actual [predication]; for example, *man* is predicated of Socrates and of Plato and of other individual men, who are more than one and also differ in number, as was made clear earlier. And it is predicated of them in respect of what they are. For when one asks, 'What is Socrates?' or 'What is Plato?', the appropriate answer is *'man.'*

It is also defined in this way: A species is what is put under a genus. Or in this way: A species is that of which a genus is predicated, in respect of what it is.

9. Species is divided into most specific species and subaltern species. A most specific species is one that, although it is a species, cannot be a genus [as well] - e.g., *man, horse*, and the like. Alternatively, a most specific species is that under which there is not another, lower species.

A subaltern species is one that, although it is a species, can be a genus [as well]. Thus, all those that are between the most general genus and the most specific species are both genera and species, though relative to different things. For they are genera in relation to those that are lower, and they are species in relation to those that are higher.

In order to make this point clearer, let us take an example from one category. So, for example, *substance* is a primary genus. Under it is *body*. Under *body* is *animate body*, and under that is *animal*. Under *animal* is *rational animal*, and under that is *man*. Under *man* are individuals such as Socrates, Plato, and Cicero.

10. A singular (*individuum*) is what is predicated of one only. {20}

11. All these things are made clear in the following diagram, which is called the tree of Porphyry.

[Differentia]

12. There are three senses of differentia – broad, strict, and very strict. Differentia in the broad sense is when one thing differs from another by a separable accident – e.g., as Socrates sitting differs from Socrates not sitting or from something else. Differentia in the strict sense is when one thing differs from another by an inseparable accident. {21} An inseparable accident is, for example, snub-nosed or aquiline. Differentia in the very strict sense is when one thing differs from another by a specific differentia – e.g., as *man* differs from *horse* in respect of *rational*. This last sense is the one in which 'differentia' is used here.

[Differentia in that sense] is defined in this way: A differentia is what is predicated of more than one thing, differing in species, in respect of what it is like. So, for example, *rational* is predicated of man and of the gods, who are rational, for (as Porphyry would have it [*Isagoge* 11.25–12.1]) both we and the gods are rational; but when *mortal* is added to us, it separates us from them.

Something that is an appropriate answer to a question asked by means of 'What is [it] like?' is said to be predicated in respect of what it is like. So, for example, when one asks, 'What is man like?', the appropriate answer is 'rational'; and thus *rational* is predicated of *man* in respect of what he is like.

[Differentia] is also defined in this way: A differentia is that by which a species exceeds a genus, as, for example, *man* exceeds *animal* by the differentiae *rational* and *mortal*.

13. It is important to know that the same differentia is both divisive and constitutive, but it is divisive of a genus and constitutive of a species. So, for example, *rational* together with the differentia opposed to it divides *animal*; for we say that some animals are rational and others are irrational, and these two differentiae constitute different species under *animal*. For every differentia added to a genus constitutes a species, and so it is designated constitutive, or specific. For when *mortal* is added to the genus *rational animal*, it constitutes *man*. And for this reason Boethius says (*De divisione* 886A 5ff.) that only a species is defined, for a definition must consist of genus and differentiae; but only a species has a genus and differentiae, and therefore only a species is defined. {22}

[Proprium]

14. There are four senses of 'proprium.' In one sense a proprium is what is in some [members] of a species but not in every [member of that species] – e.g., as being a doctor or being a geometer is in a man but not in every man. A proprium in the second sense is what is in every [member of a species] but not in them alone – e.g., as being two-footed is in every man but not in men alone. A proprium in the third sense is what is in every [member of a species] and in them alone but not always [in them] – e.g., as getting grey is in every man and in men alone, but not always, because only in old age. The fourth sense of proprium is proprium in its strict designation; and it is defined in this way: A proprium is what is in every [member of a species] and in them alone and always [in them]. So, for example, *risible* is in every man and in men alone and always; for a man is not said to be risible because he is always actually laughing but rather because he is naturally suited to laugh.

And it is in this fourth sense that proprium is said to be one of the five predicables. Also, Aristotle defines it in the following way (*Topics* I 5, 102a18–19): A proprium is that which is in a single species, which is predicated of a thing in such a way that [the predication] converts, and which does not indicate what the thing is – e.g., as risible is in man. 'Which does not indicate what the thing is' is put in the description of a proprium to differentiate it from a definition. For a definition is predicated of a thing in such a way that [the predication] converts, and it does indicate what the thing is. So, for example, *sensitive animate substance* is predicated convertibly with *animal* and indicates what it is, because every definition is made by means of substantial [characteristics]; for everything higher belongs to the essence of what is lower with respect to it. Aristotle defines definition in this way: A definition is an expression signifying what a thing is (*Topics* I 5, 101b38–102a1 and VII 3, 153a15–16), but a proprium does not signify what a thing is. {23}

[Accident]

15. An accident is what is present to and absent from a thing without the destruction of its subject – e.g., white, black, and

sitting, for these can be in a man and absent from him without his being destroyed.

[Accident] is defined in this way also: An accident is what is not a genus, species, differentia, or proprium and yet is in a thing. Alternatively: An accident is what can be in and not be in the same subject – e.g., as white and sitting [can be in and not be in] a man.

Regarding these two definitions, Aristotle says that

the second definition of accident is better, because in order to understand the first we must first know what a genus and differentia and the rest are, but the meaning of the second definition can be known independently. (*Topics* I 5, 102b10–15)

16. Some accidents are separable and others are inseparable – separable, as, for example, white and sitting are separable accidents of a man; inseparable, as, for example, black is an inseparable accident of the crow and the Ethiopian, and white is an inseparable accident of the swan. And although black is an inseparable accident of the Ethiopian and the crow, this is nonetheless not contrary to the definition that says that an accident can be present and absent without the destruction of its subject, because (as Porphyry claims [*Isagoge* 13.1–3, 20.10–12]) we can conceive a crow to be white and an Ethiopian to be shining with brilliant whiteness without the destruction of the subject.

Furthermore, some accidents are common – e.g., white and snub-nosed – and others are proper – e.g., Socrates's whiteness and Socrates's snubnosedness. {24}

[The Likenesses and Differences of the Predicables]

17. All five predicables are alike in being predicated of more than one. But they differ because a genus is predicated of more than the others, and in this it differs from the others. Differentia, on the other hand, differs from genus in virtue of the fact that it is predicated in respect of what a thing is like whereas a genus is predicated in respect of what a thing is. Furthermore, differentia differs from species and from proprium because differentia is predicated of more than one species, but the others are not. It also differs from accident, because accidents admit of intensification and

diminution, but differentia does not admit of more and less. Species differs from genus, however, because a genus contains all its species but is not contained by them.

18. Species differ from differentia, however, because more than one differentia can produce one [species] – e.g., the two differentiae *rational* and *mortal* are conjoined to constitute the species *man*. But one species is not conjoined to another in order to give rise to some other species. For in order to generate a mule an individual mare is united to an individual donkey – and not *mare* and *donkey* in general. Species also differs from proprium because species is by nature prior to proprium and proprium is posterior to species. Moreover, things whose terms or definitions are different are themselves also different; the definitions of proprium and species are different, and therefore they themselves are different. Species differs from accident, however, because species is predicated in respect of what [a thing is], but accident in respect of what [a thing is like] or what its condition is. And species is by nature prior to accident. But every accident is by nature posterior to its subject.

19. Proprium differs from accident, however, because a proprium is predicated of only one species, but an accident is predicated of more than one species. An accident is primarily in individuals and secondarily in genera and species. For *man* or *animal* does not run, except insofar as Socrates or {25} Plato runs. But a proprium is primarily in a species and is in an individual in virtue of being in the species. Furthermore, genus, differentia, species, and proprium are shared in equally by all the things of which they are predicated. Accident is not [shared equally] however, but admits of intensification and diminution. Furthermore, genus, differentia, species, and proprium are predicated univocally, but accident is predicated denominatively rather than univocally.

[Predication]

20. To be predicated univocally is to be predicated in accordance with one name and one analysis taken in accordance with the name. So, for example, *man* taken according to its name is predicated of Socrates and of Plato – e.g., 'Socrates is a man,' 'Plato is a man' – and it has one analysis in accordance with that name, namely, *mortal*

rational animal, in accordance with which it is predicated of the things beneath it – e.g., 'Socrates is a mortal rational animal,' 'Plato is a mortal rational animal,' and so on for the rest. And for this reason *being* cannot be a genus because it is predicated of everything in accordance with one name but not in accordance with one analysis. For the analysis of *being* in accordance with which it is said of substance is *being* [existing of itself], but the analysis in accordance with which it is said of the other nine categories is *being* [*occurring*] *in something else*. And in this way *being* is predicated in accordance with different analyses, and so it is not predicated univocally but rather equivocally or ambiguously.

To be predicated equivocally is to be predicated with one name but with different analyses taken in accordance with that name. So, for example, *dog* is predicated with one name of what can bark, of a sea creature, and of a star. The same analysis is not said of all those things in accordance with that name, however, but different analyses.

[Denominatives]

21. Those that differ from some [name] only by their ending and have their meaning in accordance with that name are called denominatives – e.g., literate [man] from literacy, and courageous [man] from courage. Hence, *literate, courageous, white,* and the like are predicated denominatively, and so an accident is said to be predicated denominatively. {26}

Categories

[Introductory Remarks]

1. {26} In order to understand the categories certain introductory remarks are necessary. First, we will distinguish with Aristotle (*Categories* 1, 1a1–15) three ways of making a predication: Some things that are said are equivocal, others are univocal, and others denominative.

Those that have a name in common but a different analysis (*ratio*) of their substance in accordance with that name are equivocal. So, for example, although 'animal' signifies a true animal and an animal in a picture, they have a common name and a different analysis of their substance in accordance with that name.

Those that have a name in common and the same analysis of their substance in accordance with that name are univocal. So, for example, the name 'animal' is common to man and to cow, and its analysis in accordance with that name is likewise the same. {27}

Those that differ from a [name] only in their ending and have their meaning in accordance with that name are called denominatives – e.g., literate [man] from literacy. They differ only in ending, that is, only the ending that is associated with the real thing, and they have their meaning in accordance with that name. And so a denominative name must agree with the univocal name in the first part [of the name] – e.g., 'literacy' and 'literate [man]', 'white [man]' and 'whiteness.'

2. Some things that are said are said without being combined – e.g., 'man' or 'runs' – and others are said combined – e.g., 'A man runs.'

But before we subdivide either part of this division, we must differentiate ways of being in, which are necessary for understanding the subsequent division and for certain things that will be said afterwards.

In the first way something is said to be in something else the way an integral part is in its whole – e.g., a finger in a hand and a wall in a house. The second way is the way an integral whole is in its parts – e.g., a house in [its] wall, roof, and foundation. The third way is the way a species is in a genus – e.g., *man* in *animal* (and, in general, anything lower [in the Porphyrian tree] in what is above it). The fourth way of being in is the way a genus is in its species – e.g., *animal* in *man* (and, [in general,] anything that defines is in its definition and every definition is in what it defines). The fifth way of being in is the way a form is in matter. And this fifth way is subdivided, because some forms are substantial, as the soul is the substantial form of man, and other {28} forms are accidental, as white is an accidental form of man. Strictly speaking, the first of these is said to be in as a form is in matter, as the soul is in the body; the other is said to be in as an accident is in a subject – e.g.,

whiteness in a wall and color in a body. The sixth way of being
in is the way something is in its primary efficient cause – e.g.,
sovereignty in the sovereign. The seventh way of being in is the
way something is in its end – e.g., virtue in happiness. The eighth
way of being in is the way anything is in a container, and, in
general, the way anything located is in its location.

These are the eight ways of being in that Aristotle distinguishes
(*Physics* IV 3, 210a14–24). Boethius, however, allots nine ways of
being in, because he divided the fifth way into two, in the way
described (*In Arist. Cat. PL* 64, 172B2–C9).

3. Some things are said of a subject but are not in any subject –
e.g., the genera and species of substance and the differentiae of
substance; and these are all called universal substances, by an
extension of the name 'substance' – e.g., *man, animal,* and *rational*.
'To be said of a subject,' as it is used here, is to be said of
something lower [in the Porphyrian tree] – e.g., *animal* is said of
man and *man* is said of Socrates, and *color* is said of *whiteness*. But 'to
be in a subject' is used [here] in the sense of an accident's being in
[its] subject.

Other things neither are said of a subject nor are in a subject –
e.g., individuals [belonging to the category] substance.

Others, however, are said of a subject and are in a subject – e.g.,
the genera and species of the other nine categories are said of the
things lower with respect to them and are in a substance as an
accident is in [its] subject. So, for example, color is said of whiteness {29} as of something lower [with respect to it] and is in a body
as in a subject.

Still others are in a subject but are not said of any subject, as this
knowledge is in the soul as an accident is in a subject, but is not said
of anything lower [with respect to it]; and this color is in a subject
but is not said of a subject, for every color is in a body.

4. When one thing is predicated of another as of a subject,
everything said of what is predicated is also said of [its] subject. So,
for example, if Socrates is a man, and a man is an animal, then
Socrates is an animal.

Different genera that are not subalternate to one another have
different species and differentiae – e.g., *animal* and *knowledge,* which
are [such] different genera. For the differentiae of *animal* are *rational*
and *irrational,* since it is divided by these differentiae. But the

differentiae of *knowledge* are *natural, moral,* and *linguistic,* for *knowledge* is divided by these differentiae – some knowledge is natural, some moral, and some linguistic.

5. Each of the things that are said without being combined signifies a substance, a quantity, a quality, being related, where, when, being positioned, possessing, doing, or undergoing. To indicate [these] by giving examples, a substance is, for example, a man and a horse; a quantity: two cubits and three cubits; a quality: whiteness and blackness; being related: double and triple; where: in a place; when: yesterday [and] tomorrow; position: sitting and lying; possessing: having shoes on and carrying weapons; doing: cutting [and] burning; undergoing: being cut [and] being burned.

On the basis of these [introductory considerations], we must discuss each of the categories; first, substance, since it is prior to the other categories. {30}

[Substance]

6. Substance is divided into primary and secondary substance. What is strictly, principally, and especially called substance is primary substance. Alternatively, primary substance is what is neither said of a subject nor is in a subject – e.g., a man or a horse.

Secondary substances are the species in which primary substances are and the genera of these species – e.g., *man* and *animal*; for a man is in *man*, which is a species, just as *man* is in *animal*, which is a genus.

Individual substances are called primary substances because they primarily underlie (*substant*) other things, and their genera and species are called secondary substances because they underlie [other things] secondarily. For a man is called a literate thing, a running thing, an animal, and a substance; and for this reason man is called literate, running, animal, and substance.

7. Furthermore, all those things that are said of a subject are predicated in name and in analysis – e.g., *man* [is predicated] of Socrates [in name and in analysis]. But with regard to those that are in a subject ((*sunt in/dicuntur de* [var.])), in many cases neither the name nor the analysis is predicated of the subject – e.g., this whiteness or this white. In other cases, however, nothing prevents

the name from being predicated of the subject while the analysis cannot be; for example, white is predicated of a subject while the analysis of white is never predicated of a subject.

Furthermore, as regards secondary substances, a species is more a substance than the genus is, because the species is nearer to the primary substance than the genus is, and also because the species underlies more things, for the species underlies whatever things the genus underlies, and it also underlies the genus itself. But the most specific species are equal to substances – e.g., *man, horse,* and the like.

[What Substances Have in Common and What is Proper to Them]

8. Having seen these things, we must discuss what substances have in common and what is proper to them. It is common to every substance not to be in a subject, because being in a subject belongs only to accidents. And this {31} is clear as regards primary substances in virtue of the definition of primary substance. It is clear of secondary substances by induction and syllogism. By induction, in this way: *Man* is not in a subject; *horse* is not in a subject; neither is *animal*; and so on for the other secondary substances; therefore, no secondary substance is in a subject. By syllogism, in this way: None of the things that are in a subject are predicated in [both] name and analysis; but every secondary substance is predicated in [both] name and analysis; therefore, no secondary substance is in a subject.

This, however, is not proper to substance but rather belongs to [its] differentiae; and this is understood regarding the differentiae of substance. And the parts of a substance that are in the whole are not a counterexample [to this]. The parts of a substance seem to be in a subject because being in as an accident is in a subject is one way of being in, and being in as a part is in a whole is another way of being in, as was made clear above.

9. Furthermore, it belongs to all secondary substances and to the differentiae of substance to be predicated univocally. For these are all predicated of primary substances in [both] name and analysis because they are predicated univocally.

10. Furthermore, every primary substance signifies a *this* (*hoc aliquid*), that is, [something] single and one in number. But a

secondary substance seems to signify a *this* insofar as it is in a primary substance and of its essence, and yet it does not signify a *this* but rather something common. For it is not the case that what is signified by a secondary substance is one in the way that what is signified by a primary substance is one.

11. Furthermore, nothing is contrary to a substance. But this is not proper to substance because it belongs to every substance, to every quantity, and to certain other things.

12. Furthermore, a substance does not admit of more and less. But I do not mean that one substance does not underlie more than another. Rather I mean that no given substance is intensified or diminished with respect to its own being. So, for example, a white [thing] is sometimes more white and sometimes less, but Socrates is not more a man at {32} one time than at another, nor is he more a man than Plato is.

13. Furthermore, it is proper to substances to admit of contraries in accordance with a change in them. So, for example, the same man is sometimes black, sometimes white, sometimes hot, sometimes cold, and both lax and diligent.

An expression does not constitute a counterexample, because although the same expression – e.g., the proposition 'Socrates is sitting' – can be sometimes true and sometimes false, this does not happen in accordance with a change in it but with a change in reality – e.g., because Socrates gets up or runs. And we should take note of the fact that [being] true and false are in things as in a subject but in an expression as in a sign. Hence when we say that [being] true and false are in things and in an expression, we are equivocating on the way of being in. And in the same way, we equivocate on 'admits of' when we say that urine admits of health and an animal admits of health, for the former admits of health because it is a sign of health but the latter because it is the subject of health. And so this [admitting of contraries] is proper only to substances and does not belong to expressions.

[Quantity]

14. Some quantities are continuous and others are discrete. A discrete quantity is, for example, a number, and an expression.

(Thus, there are two species of quantity, [the continuous and the discrete].) For there is no common limit in number to which the parts of number are united; so, for example, in ten, five and five (or three and seven) are not united to any common limit but are always discrete and separate. And number is a multitude {33} of unities gathered together. In the same way in an expression the syllables are not united to some common limit, but each one is separated from the other.

15. Some continuous quantities are lines, some are surfaces, some are bodies, some are times, and some are places. Thus, there are five species of continuous quantity. That a line is continuous is clear, because its parts are united to a common limit – i.e., to a point. The parts of a surface are united to a line, and the parts of a body are united to a surface. The parts of time are united to now, as the past and the future to the present. The parts of a place are united to the same limit as the particles of a body [in that space].{34}

[What is Common to Quantity]

16. Having seen these things, we must discuss what is common to quantity. The first thing that is common is that nothing is contrary to a quantity. So, for example, there is no contrary to two cubits, to three cubits, or to a surface. This is because contrariety is primarily in qualities (and not in all of them but only in some), but quantity is not a quality; therefore, contrariety is not in quantity.

Furthermore, quantity does not admit of more and less, for one line is no more a quantity than another line, and three is no less a number than four.

Furthermore, it is proper to quantity that something is said to be equal or unequal in accordance with it – e.g., a number is equal or unequal to another number, a body to another body, a line to another line, and so on.

[Being Related]

17. Things that are what they are in virtue of being said to be *of* other things or to be *to* other things in any other way are said to be related. So, for example, what is double is double of its half, and a

half is half of its double; and a father is the father of a child, and a child is a child of its father; and what is greater is greater than what is less; and what is similar is similar to what is similar.

18. Some things are called relatives on the basis of a comparison – e.g., relatives that are expressed by means of the same name, as similar is similar to similar, equal is equal to equal, and neighbor is neighbor to neighbor. Others are called relatives on the basis of {35} the superiority of one to another – e.g., master, double, and triple. Still others are called relatives on the basis of the subordination of one to another – e.g., a slave, a half of what is double, and a third of what is triple. For these are subordinate to the others and the others are superior to them: a master is superior to a slave, a father to a child, and what is double to its half; and a slave is subordinate to a master, a child to a father, and a half to its double.

[What is Common to Relation]

19. Next after these things comes what is common to relation. The first thing common is that there is contrariety in relation. So, for example, virtue is contrary to vice, although both of them are relatives. Not every relation has a contrary, however, for there is no contrary to double, or to triple.

Furthermore, relatives admit of more and less. So, for example, what is similar is said to be more or less similar, and likewise for what is equal. This does not apply to all relatives, however, for what is double is not said to be more or less double, what is triple is not said to be more or less triple, and a father is not said to be more or less a father.

Furthermore, all relatives are expressed in such a way that they convert. For example, if there is a father, there is a child, and conversely; if there is a master, there is a slave, and conversely; and if there is a double, there is a half, and conversely.

Furthermore, relatives seem by nature to be concomitant (*simul*), for double and half are concomitant, and so are father and child.

Furthermore, if one relative is posited, so is the other; and if one relative is removed, so is the other. So, for example, if there is not a double, there is not a half; and if there is not a father, there is not a child.

20. Furthermore, the definition of relatives is this: Those things

are related whose being consists in being in a certain condition with respect to something else. And this definition is proper to relatives. {36}

Furthermore, it is proper to relatives that if any one knows distinctly (*diffinite*) one of a pair of correlatives, he also knows the other distinctly. For example, if one distinctly knows a double, one also distinctly knows that of which it is a double, for one must use the analysis of each [correlative] in connection with the other.

[Quality]

21. A quality is that on the basis of which we are said to be qualified [in some respect or other]. For example, we are said to be white on the basis of whiteness, colored on the basis of color, and just on the basis of justice.

There are four species of quality. The first species is habit and disposition. A habit differs from a disposition, because a habit is more stable and longer-lasting – e.g., virtues and knowledge. For it is difficult to change knowledge unless perhaps there is some great alteration, either as a result of sickness or from something else of that sort, in the knower – or in one who has virtues, for justice or chastity are not easily altered. Those that are easily altered are called dispositions – e.g., heat and cold, sickness and health, and the like. Habits can nonetheless be called dispositions, but not vice versa, for people who have a habit are said to be disposed in a certain way, either better or worse, with respect to the habits they have. But dispositions are not habits. Thus, a habit can be defined in this way: A habit is a quality that is hard to change. A disposition, on the other hand, is a quality that is easy to change.

22. The second species of quality is a natural power or lack of power for doing or undergoing something easily. So, for example, something is said to be health-giving insofar as it has a natural power of preventing any suffering from certain accidents; and something is said to be sickening insofar as it has a natural lack of power for preventing any suffering. And what is hard has a natural power for not being readily cut. Runners and fighters are so-called likewise {37} not because they are exercising their [characteristic] activities, but because they have a natural power for doing so easily.

23. The third species of quality is passion and passive quality, as,

for example, those qualities that produce passions in the senses – e.g., in taste, sweetness or bitterness and the like. Qualities that arise from passions that are stable and changed only with difficulty are also included under this species. For blackness is called a quality whether it is generated by a natural passion, by sickness, or by heat.

24. The fourth species of quality is a form or a figure including something, as, for example, the disposition of a body – e.g., triangularity, rectangularity, straightness, or curvedness.

25. Those things are said to be qualified that are expressed denominatively on the basis of this (as, for example, literate from literacy, and just from justice), or that are expressed non-denominatively from some quality. This happens in two ways. Some things are expressed nondenominatively from some quality, in that the name is not imposed on the quality itself; so, for example, a runner is not so-called denominatively, in that the name is not imposed on the quality [i.e., on the natural power in virtue of which he is called a runner]. Other things are called non-denominatively qualified in that they do not share the name of the quality by which they are said [to be qualified], although the name is imposed – e.g., diligent from virtue.

And thus there are three ways of deriving what is qualified from a quality. {38}

[What is Proper to Quality]

26. There is contrariety in qualities – e.g., whiteness is contrary to blackness, and justice is contrary to injustice. But this is not proper to quality, because it does not belong to every quality; for a figure does not have a contrary, nor does any color intermediate [between black and white].

Furthermore, if one of a pair of contraries is something qualified, the other will be something qualified also. So, for example, justice is the contrary of injustice, but justice is a quality; therefore, injustice is a quality also. And what is just is something qualified; therefore, what is unjust is also something qualified.

Furthermore, quality admits of more and less, for one is said to be more or less just, or literate, or white. But this is not proper to quality, because what is rectangular does not admit of more and less, neither does a circle, nor do rectangularity and circularity.

Furthermore, it is proper to quality that something is said to be similar or dissimilar in accordance with it. For example, someone white is said to be similar to someone white, and someone just is said to be similar to someone just, and someone white is said to be dissimilar to someone black.

[Action]

27. Action is that in the subject in accordance with which we are said to act. So, for example, a person cutting is said to act in that he cuts. Thus, cutting is an action, and the person who cuts, insofar as he cuts, acts in accordance with cutting. Beating is also an action.

It is proper to action that it implies a passion.

Doing and undergoing admit of contrariety. For heating is the contrary of cooling, and being heated is the contrary of being cooled, and being gladdened is the contrary of being saddened.

Furthermore, doing and undergoing admit of more and less. For heating is said [to be] more or less, and being heated, being gladdened, and being saddened are also said to be more or less. {39}

[Passion]

28. Passion is an effect and consequence of action – e.g., being heated is the effect and the consequence of heating.

It is proper to passion that it be primarily a consequence of action.

Furthermore, passion is not in the one acting but in the one undergoing.

And as for the rest, the things that were said above are sufficient for now.

[The Four Ways of Opposition]

29. One thing is said to be opposed to another in four different ways. Some opposites are relative opposites – e.g., father and child, double and half, or master and slave. Others are privative opposites

– e.g., privation and possession, such as sight and blindness, or hearing and deafness. Others are contraries – e.g., white and black. Others are contradictory opposites – e.g., affirmation and negation, as in 'He is seated' and 'He is not seated.'

Which ones are relative opposites was said above.

Contraries are those that are located in the same genus and [yet] are as far as possible from one another, mutually exclusive of one another, and are by turns in one and the same thing that admits of them unless either one of them is in [that thing] by nature – as whiteness is in snow, or heat in fire.

Privative opposites are those that have to occur in connection with the same thing in an irreversible order – e.g., one must go from the possession to the privation and not {40} vice versa. For there cannot be a regress from a privation back to the possession. So, for example, blindness and sight have to occur in connection with the eye, and by nature a change can occur from sight to blindness but not vice versa.

[Priority]

30. There are four senses of 'prior.' First, and strictly speaking, one thing is said to be prior to another with regard to time, as, for example, one person is said to be senior to and older than another – e.g., a man who is forty years old is said to be senior to and older than a man who is twenty.

What is prior in the second sense is what is not interchangeable in an existential consequence. It is in this way that one is prior to two; for when two exist, the immediate consequent is that one exists – e.g., if two are, one is; but not vice versa.

What is prior in the third sense has to do with order. It is in this way that the principles of a discipline are prior to its conclusions – e.g., ((*ut/et*)) in grammar the letters are prior to the syllables, and in a speech the proemium is prior to the narration with regard to order.

What is prior in the fourth sense is what is better and more honorable, for most men are accustomed to calling prior the people whom they honor or cherish more.

Besides the four senses already mentioned, there is another sense of 'prior.' When things are interchangeable in a consequence having to do with essence and one of them is somehow the cause of the other's existing, it is appropriately said to be prior by nature. So, for example, things in reality are the cause of the truth of a proposition or expression about those things. For example, that a man is running is interchangeable with the expression 'A man is running' – e.g., if it is true that a man is running, 'A man is running' is also true, and vice versa. For things in reality are the cause of a true expression about them, but the true expression is not the cause of the things' existing. For it is from the fact that [this] thing exists or does not exist that the expression is said to be true or false. {41}

[Concomitance (*simul*)]

31. There are three senses of 'concomitant.' In the first sense things are said to be concomitant if they arise at the same time and neither of them is prior or posterior to the other. Such things are said to be concomitant in time.

In the second sense things are said to be concomitant if they are interchangeable and neither of them is the cause of the other's existing, as, for example, all relatives – e.g., double and half, and the like.

In the third sense things are said to be concomitant if they severally condivide a genus – e.g., [the species] *man, horse, lion,* and the like, which condivide the genus *animal,* or even the differentiae, such as *rational* and *irrational,* [which severally condivide *animal*].

In these two last senses things are said to be concomitant in nature, but in the first sense they are said to be concomitant in time.

[Change]

32. There are six species of change: generation, destruction, increase, decrease, alteration, and local motion.

Generation is coming out of nonbeing into being. Corruption is going from being into nonbeing. Increase is an addition to an already existing quantity. Decrease is a lessening of an already existing quantity. Alteration is a change from one quality into its contrary quality or some intermediate quality – e.g., when one is changed from whiteness into blackness or into intermediate colors. Local motion is a change from one place to another.

There are six species or differentiae of local motion, namely, up, down, forwards, backwards, right, and left; for there is local motion with regard to all these parts.

[Possession]

33. There are many senses of possessing. The first sense is possessing a certain quality – e.g., a discipline or virtue. {42} The second sense is possessing a quantity, which occurs with regard to things that have size – e.g., two cubits and three cubits. The third sense is possessing things that go around the body – e.g., a cloak or tunic – or that are on a part [of the body] – e.g., a ring on a finger. It is in this third sense that possession is taken as one of the ten categories, and it is defined in this way: Possession has to do with bodies and things that are in contact with them – e.g., carrying weapons and having shoes on (and similar names might be devised for other instances). In connection with such contact, the one thing is said to possess and the other to be possessed.

The fourth sense is possessing a part [of the body], such as a hand or a foot.

The fifth sense is possessing contents – e.g., as a bottle possesses wine, or a bushel possesses grains of wheat.

The sixth sense is possessing ownership – e.g., a house or a field.

The seventh sense is possessing a wife. And Aristotle says regarding this last sense that it is the most foreign to the nature of possessing [*Categories* 15, 15b28–33]. He also says that other senses may perhaps appear evident from the nature of possessing, but virtually all the familiar senses have been listed.

4

LAMBERT OF AUXERRE
PROPERTIES OF TERMS

Introduction

Not much is known about the life of Lambert of Auxerre except that he was a Dominican in the Dominican house at Auxerre around the middle of the thirteenth century, and that he wrote a logic text known as *Summa Lamberti* or just *Logica*. Lambert is usually grouped with the other, mostly older, terminist logicians of this period – Peter of Spain, William of Sherwood, and Roger Bacon. All wrote roughly similar logic texts. The section translated here is taken from the last chapter of Lambert's *Logica*.

Medieval logicians took a word's natural property to be signification, which they understood as a word's presentation of a universal nature to the mind. But a word acquires other properties by being used in various ways in propositions. These other properties include supposition, appellation, copulation, ampliation, and restriction. Supposition is by far the most important of these properties, roughly analogous to reference in twentieth-century terminology. Medieval logicians divided supposition into several subcategories; personal supposition, for example, is a property a term has when it is used to refer to individuals of which it is truly predicable, and simple supposition is the use of a term to refer to the associated universal. Appellation is a property of terms similar to supposition, except that a term appellates only those things that actually exist at the time of utterance and of which the term is truly predicated. Copulation is a property modifiers have by virtue of being linked to nouns either as predicates (e.g., 'The cat is black') or as attributive adjectives (e.g., 'the black cat'). Ampliation is the extension of a term's supposition to a broader range that can be brought about by certain verbs, such as 'can,' that cause the terms to which they are linked to stand also for things that only possibly exist. Restriction, on the other hand, is the contraction of a term's supposition to a narrower range, brought about, for example, by the tense of the verb linked to the restricted term, as the present tense of the verb in the proposition 'Men are running' restricts the supposition of 'men' to currently existing things.

In the following selection, Lambert explains his general views on signification, the difference between signification and supposition, the nature of supposition, copulation, and syncategorematic words, and the relationship between supposition and copulation. He also analyzes supposition into its various subcategories. The following diagram illustrates his division of supposition:

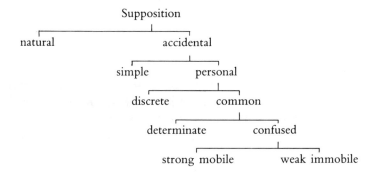

After dealing with supposition, Lambert turns to appellation, a common term's reference to the actually existing things the term is truly predicated of. An exception to this general description is given in the complicated rule of appellation Lambert presents and discusses: 'A substantial or accidental common term that is not restricted by any other means and that serves as the subject or the predicate of a present-tense verb that has no ampliating force of its own or from anything else is restricted to suppositing for present things if it has appellata; but if it does not have appellata, it reverts to nonexistents.' Because of the use of restriction in this rule, it leads naturally into a discussion of restriction. Lambert divides restriction into natural and use-governed, and each of these divisions is further subdivided. After a brief discussion of ampliation, Lambert ends this section with a detailed consideration of distribution and relatives, notions that figure in the analysis of the properties of terms.

For further reading on the properties of terms, see CHLMP IV.7,

'The Origins of the Theory of the Properties of Terms,' and IV.9, 'The Semantics of Terms.'

Properties of Terms

[1. General Introduction]

{205} Because the logician considers terms, it is appropriate for him to give an account of the term itself and its properties, for the person who is to consider something as a subject must consider its properties also. Now, there are many properties of terms: supposition, appellation, restriction, distinction, and relation. (Of these, relation was discussed ((*dictum/dicendum*)) earlier.) But because signification is, as it were, the fulfillment of a term, and the properties of terms are founded on signification, for the sake of clarity in what follows we must at the outset consider what the signification of a term is, and how it differs from supposition.

[2. Signification]

[2a. Definition of Signification]

The signification of a term is the concept of a thing, a concept on which an utterance is imposed by the will of the person instituting the term. For, as Aristotle maintains in the first book of *De interpretatione* (16a3–5), utterances are signs of states in the soul – i.e., in the understanding – but concepts are the signs of things.

[2b. Explanation of the Definition]

In order to understand this, it is essential to know that four things are required for an utterance to be significant: a thing, a concept of the thing, an utterance, and the union of the utterance with the concept of the thing. What we are calling the thing is something existing outside the soul, which is apprehended by the soul by means of an idea of it – e.g., a man, or a stone. What we call the concept of the thing is the idea or likeness of the thing, which exists in the soul; for according to Aristotle in the third book of *De anima* (III, 8, 431b30–432a1), not the stone but rather an appearance of the stone is in the soul; and it is by means of the appearance that the soul grasps the thing. The utterance is that which is put forward along with the concept of the thing; in that case a signification is united to the utterance ((*voci/vocis*)), and the utterance is made significant. And although both the concept of the thing and the utterance are natural in the same way (since they are formed by natural sources), the utterance is nevertheless said to signify by the will of the person instituting it because the union of the concept of the thing with the utterance is effected by the will, and it is in that [action] that the imposition of the utterance consists.

In this way, therefore, an utterance is primarily – in itself – and directly the sign of a concept of the thing; but in addition it is indirectly the sign of the thing. For just as we say that whatever is a cause of the cause is a cause of the thing caused, so we can {206} say that in its own way whatever is a sign of the sign is a sign of the thing signified. Thus, since an utterance is a sign of a concept, and a concept is a sign of a thing, in this way [the utterance] is a sign ((*signum/significatum*)) of the thing as well. An utterance that is a sign of a sign – i.e., of a concept – will be a sign of the thing signified – i.e., of the thing; it is, however, a sign of the concept directly but a sign of the thing indirectly.

[2c. The Difference between Signification and Supposition]

Now signification differs from supposition in that signification is prior to supposition. For the signification is the concept of the thing represented by means of the utterance, and before the union of it with the utterance there is no term; rather, a term is constituted in the union of that concept of a thing with an utterance. Supposition, on the other hand, is a certain property of a term that has been constituted in that way.

There is another difference, because signification extends only to the thing the term is imposed to signify; supposition, however, extends not only to the thing signified by means of the term but can extend to supposita contained ((*contenta/contempta*)) under that thing. For example, the signification of 'man' extends only to *man*, not to the things contained ((*contenta/contempta* [et passim])) under *man*; for 'man' signifies *man*, not Socrates and not Plato. 'Man' can, nevertheless, supposit for Socrates, and for Plato, and for *man*.

[3. Supposition]

[3a. Four Ways of Using 'Supposition']

Next, as regards supposition. It is important to know that 'supposition' is used in four ways. In one way, supposition is said to be the substantive designation or indication of a thing. In a second way, supposition is said to be the acceptance of a proposition as true and proven (it is often taken in this way in disputations). In the third way, supposition is said to be the ordering of a part of an expression in the role of something that something else is said of, as supposition is said to be in a noun with respect to a verb; for [in this sense] a noun supposits relative to a verb, and the verb is said of the noun. (Appellation corresponds to this sort of supposition, and appellation can be said to be a locational arrangement of that which is said of something else.) In the fourth way, supposition is said to be the acceptance of a term for ((*pro/per*)) itself, for its [signified] thing, for some suppositum contained under its [signified] thing, or for more than one suppositum contained under its [signified] thing.

It is in this fourth way that 'supposition' is meant here, for it is in that way, and not in the three preceding ways, that supposition is a property of a term. For 'supposition' used in the third way is the business of the grammarian, not of the logician. Supposition in the second way belongs to a proposition and not to a term, for in disputations it is not a term but a proposition that is supposited. In the first way, however, supposition is a kind of signification of a species term and not a property of a term. This is evident in the following way. A predication is true if it is put in this way: Signification is the substantive signification of a thing. Therefore, since {207} whatever is said of a definition can be said of the thing defined, if the substantive designation or signification of a thing is the definition of supposition, it could be said that supposition is signification. If it is signification, however, it is not the supposition that is a property of terms. Therefore, we are left with the conclusion that 'supposition' used in the first way is not the supposition meant here. That is true, but 'supposition' used in the first way is the signification of a substantive term, and copulation, which is the adjectival signification of a thing, corresponds to this sort of supposition.

[3b. Broad and Strict Supposition]

It is important to know, however, that the supposition meant here is talked about in two ways: broadly and strictly. Supposition broadly speaking is, as has already been said, the acceptance of a term for itself, or for its [signified] thing (as when one says '*Man* is a species,' '*White* distinguishes'), or the acceptance of a term for some suppositum or for supposita belonging to its [signified] thing (as if one were to say 'A man is running,' 'A white thing is running'). For when one says '*Man* is a species,' 'man' is interpreted for itself or for its [signified] thing, and not for any suppositum; whereas if one says 'A man is running,' it is interpreted for a suppositum. Likewise, when one says '*White* distinguishes,' 'white' is interpreted here for itself ((*se/re*)) or for its [signified] thing; for that predicate applies to *white* not by reason of a suppositum but by reason of its form. When, however, one says 'A white thing is running,' it is interpreted for a suppositum.

Supposition ((*suppositio/supposito*)) broadly speaking is divided into supposition strictly speaking and copulation. For broadly speaking both substantival and adjectival terms supposit; strictly speaking, however, supposition is attached to substantival terms and copulation to adjectival terms.

Supposition strictly speaking is the acceptance of a term representing a thing that is stable and stands on its own, an acceptance in accordance with which the term can be interpreted for its [signified] thing, not for a suppositum or any supposita contained under its [signified] thing.

[3c. Copulation]

Copulation is the acceptance of a term representing a dependent thing, an acceptance in accordance with which it can be interpreted for its [signified] thing, or for a suppositum or supposita contained under its [signified] thing. Some words, such as substantival names, supposit a term; others, such as adjectival names used adjectivally, copulate a term. Still others, however, both supposit and copulate: adjectival substantives and those that are adjectival with respect to things but substantival with respect to utterance – such as 'knight,' 'duke,' 'count,' and the like – and, likewise, those that determine a concrete suppositum – such as 'Quirinus,' 'Gradivus,' and 'Enosigeus.' For, as Priscian says in the treatise on the name in *Priscian Major* (II, 28), 'they do not need the addition of other names.' Thus they can supposit by themselves in that they determine a concrete suppositum by associating it with themselves {208} – as 'Quirinus' determines Romulus, 'Gradivus' Mars, 'Enosigeus' Neptune. For Quirinus is the same as a spear, and so to be called 'Quirinus' is the same as being said to be armed with a spear; and because Romulus was accustomed to march along at all times armed with a spear, he was called Quirinus. 'Gradivus' comes from '*gradus*,' 'step'; and because he goes to battle in step – i.e., in good order – Mars, who is called the god of war, is called Gradivus ((*Gradivus/Gravidus*)). 'Enosigeus' comes from '*enos*,' which means deep, and '*sicheus*,' which means silence – as if to say deep silence; and so Neptune, who is the god of the sea, is called Enosigeus from the depth of the sea and the silence there is in the depth of the sea.

[3d. Syncategorematic Words]

Some words, such as syncategorematic ((*sincategorematice/sincategorice*)) words, neither supposit nor copulate.

[3e. Signification and Property of a Term]

From the things already said it is clear that supposition is both the signification of a term and a property of a term, and copulation likewise. Nevertheless, 'supposition' is taken differently ((om. *supponitur vel*)) depending on whether it is the signification of a term or a property of a term, and so is copulation, as we have seen. And our concern here is with the supposition and copulation that are properties of terms, not insofar as they are the significations of terms.

[3f. Supposition and Substantives, Copulation and Adjectives]

Again, if anyone asks why supposition is appropriate to substantives and copulation to adjectives, it is clear from the things that have been said what we must say. For suppositing belongs to what stands on its own and to what represents its stable [signified] thing, but to stand on its own and to represent its stable [signified] thing is a property of substantives. Copulating, on the other hand, belongs to what adjoins ((*adiacentis/adiectivis*)) [something else] and to what represents a dependent thing, but to adjoin and to represent a dependent thing is a property of adjectives. Therefore, speaking strictly, supposition belongs to substantives, but copulation to adjectives.

[3g. Divisions of Supposition]

[3g(i). Natural and Accidental]

Supposition is divided first in this way: One sort of supposition is natural, the other accidental.

Natural supposition is what a term has on its own and by its nature. A term is said to have this sort of supposition when it is used by itself – i.e., when it is not joined to any other. But a term having that sort of supposition supposits not only for the things that share its form, but instead for all the things that share, [have shared, and will share] its form – i.e., for present, past, and future things [of that form]. And this supposition is called natural because it is not an extrinsic but an intrinsic propensity; for whatever has an internal source is natural.

Accidental supposition is what a term has from what is adjoined to it, and a term supposits in this supposition in keeping with the requirement of that to which it is adjoined. For if someone says 'A man exists,' ['man'] supposits for present things because it is adjoined to a present-tense verb; if someone says 'A man existed,' for past things; if someone says 'A man will exist,' for future things. And this supposition is called accidental because it inheres in a term extrinsically; for what inheres extrinsically in something is accidental to it.

[3g(ii). Simple and Personal]

{209} One sort of accidental supposition is simple, the other personal.

Simple supposition is the kind according to which a term is interpreted for itself or for its [signified] thing, without relation to the supposita contained under it. The supposition that is in the term by reason of its form is called simple; and it is because form is of itself simple and indivisible that the supposition that is in a term as a result of form is called simple. (That form is simple and indivisible is established in the book *Six Principles* [I.1].)

It should be noted, however, that [a term's] having no relation to the supposita can occur either in such a way that there is no sort of relation to them, neither determinately nor indeterminately, or in such a way that there is a relation to them, not determinately, but indeterminately. It is on that basis that one can say that there is a certain sort of simple supposition in which the term is in no way related to the supposita but is interpreted only for its [signified] form. The term 'man' has this sort of supposition when one says '*Man* is a species,' and this is simple supposition speaking strictly. But there is another simple supposition in which a common term is not related to the supposita determinately and yet has a relation to them indeterminately. The term 'man' has this sort of supposition when one says 'I know there is a man in England'; similarly, the term 'pepper' when one says 'Pepper is sold here and in Rome.' This, however ((*autem/enim*)), is called simple supposition less strictly than the first sort.

Personal supposition is [the sort] according to which a term is interpreted for a suppositum or for supposita. It is called personal for the following reason, however: In the case of rational substance a suppositum or individual is the same as a person. For Boethius (*Against Eutyches and Nestorius*) defines person in this way: A person is an individual substance belonging to rational nature; for an individual in the case of rational substance is a person. And because in the case of other things individuals are picked out in accordance with an analogy drawn from rational things, the supposition in which a term is interpreted for supposita or individuals is called personal – not because all individuals are persons (for only individuals that have to do with rational substance are persons, certainly not other sorts of individuals); but all individuals either are persons or are picked out by analogy with those that are persons.

[3g(iii). Discrete and Common]

One sort of personal supposition is discrete, the other common.

Discrete supposition is what a discrete term has in itself, as in 'Socrates is running' or in something equivalent, as when a common term is taken together with a determinate pronoun, as in 'This man is running.' {210} It is called discrete, however, because a term having such supposition is interpreted for something absolutely discrete.

Common supposition is the kind that is appropriate to a common term, and it is called common because it is appropriate to a common term.

[3g(iv). Determinate and Confused]

One sort of common supposition is determinate, the other confused.

Determinate supposition is what a common term has when it can be taken equally well for one or for more than one, as when one says 'A man is running.' In that proposition 'man' has determinate supposition because it is true if one man is running or if more than one are running. But it is called determinate because for the truth of a proposition in which ((*qua/una*)) a common term that has that sort of supposition is used, it is enough that that common term is interpreted necessarily for some suppositum, and it is not required that it be interpreted necessarily for more than one, although in supposition of this sort it can be interpreted for more than one. It is necessary, therefore, that a common term in this sort of supposition be interpreted for one [suppositum] determinately; if it is interpreted for more than one, that is accidental.

Confused supposition is what a common term has when it is interpreted necessarily for all its supposita or for more than one. It is called confused, however, from the plurality of supposita for which a term having this sort of supposition is interpreted; for where there is plurality there is confusion.

[3g(v). Strong Mobile and Weak Immobile]

One sort of confused supposition is strong [and] mobile, the other weak [and] immobile.

Strong mobile supposition is what a common term has when it is interpreted for all its supposita necessarily and a [logical] descent can be made under it. This happens when an affirmative universal sign is added directly to a common term, as when one says 'Every man is running,' and likewise when a negative universal sign is added indirectly or directly to a common term, as when one says 'No man is a stone.' For in this latter proposition the term to which the sign 'no' is indirectly ((*mediate/immediate*)) added – 'stone' – and likewise the one to which it is directly added have strong ((*vehementem/vehementer*)) mobile confused supposition. For the affirmative universal sign confuses and distributes the term to which it is directly added. When it is indirectly adjoined, however, it confuses but does not distribute. The negative universal sign, on the other hand, confuses and distributes a common term adjoined to it both directly and indirectly.

Similarly, a common term to which negation is directly added has this sort of supposition, as when one says 'Not a man is running,' which is to say 'No man is running.' Indirectly, too, as when one says 'I do not see a man,' which is to say 'No man do I see.'

This sort of supposition is called strong because a term that has it cannot {211} be interpreted for more than it is interpreted for. It is called mobile because in connection with a term having this sort of supposition a descent can be made for the supposita contained under it.

Weak immobile supposition is what a common term has when it is interpreted necessarily for more than one suppositum contained under it but not for all, and a descent cannot be made under it. A term to which the affirmative universal sign is indirectly added has this sort of supposition, as when one says 'Every man is an animal.' Here 'animal' has weak immobile confused supposition because 'animal' is not interpreted for all its supposita, nor can a descent be made under it. It is called weak because in connection with such supposition a common term is not interpreted for all its supposita. It is called immobile because one is not allowed to make a descent under a term having that sort of supposition.

Notice that confused supposition is strong whenever it is mobile, but not conversely – mobile whenever it is strong – for it can indeed be strong and immobile. When one says 'Only every man is running,' 'man' has strong but immobile confused supposition; for the exclusive word ((*dictio/dicto*)) ['only'] added to the distributed term impedes it so that a descent cannot be made under it. Similarly, there is confused but immobile supposition when a [distributive] sign is added to a common term in the singular or the plural and it is interpreted collectively, as when one says 'Every man is hauling a boat,' supposing that all the men are hauling a boat, and none of them by himself. Likewise, when one says 'All the apostles are twelve.'

[4. Appellation]

[4a. Introduction]

Because appellation is a kind of supposition, supposition was considered first. Now we must discuss appellation.

[4b. Four Ways of Using 'Appellation']

Now it is essential to know that 'appellation' is used in four ways. In one way, proper names, or the proper name of any person, is called appellation. In this connection it is said that someone has the appellation 'Peter' or 'William.' Taken in this way, appellation is nothing other than the establishment of an utterance for signifying some complex or noncomplex thing; and 'appellation' is often used this way in obligations, in connection with which it is said that '*A*' appellates ((*appellare/appellat*)) Socrates or appellates that a man is running. 'Appellation' used in the second way is a property of names in accordance with which names are called appellative. In this sense appellation is nothing other than the positing ((*positio/petitio*)) of a common nature containing more than one suppositum under it. (Appellation is something common when it belongs to more than one but something proper when it belongs to one.) 'Appellation' used in the third way is the acceptance of a term for a suppositum or {212} for supposita contained under its thing signified, whether or not those supposita are existing things. 'Appellation' taken in this way applies to terms having supposita under them either actually or potentially, and also to names of things signified. Used in the fourth way, 'appellation' is the acceptance of a term for a suppositum or for supposita actually existing. And it is appellation spoken of in this fourth way that is meant at present.

[4c. Appellation and Supposition]

It is important to know that appellation as understood here differs from supposition as a superior differs from its inferior or vice versa, because appellation is inferior to supposition ((*suppositionem/ suppositum*)); for wherever there is appellation there is supposition, but not vice versa. For appellation, speaking strictly, occurs in a common term only when it is interpreted for a suppositum or for supposita actually existing under it; supposition, on the other hand, can occur both in a discrete term and in a common term when it is interpreted for a suppositum or supposita either actually or potentially existing under it. Supposition can even occur in a common term when it is interpreted for ((*pro/per*)) itself, without any relation to its supposita. It is for this reason that there can be natural and accidental, discrete and common, simple and personal supposition, as was seen above. (Appellation is always personal supposition, and so just as supposition is superior to personal supposition, and personal supposition is a kind of supposition, [so appellation is a kind of supposition].)

[4d. Appellative Words and Appellata]

Again, it is important to know that some words are appellative and have appellata on their own – common substantival names are of that sort ((*cuiusmodi/cuius*)) – whereas others are appellative and have appellata not on their own but in virtue of something else. Common adjectival names are of that sort ((*cuiusmodi/cuius*)); for they are appellative, but they have appellata only through their substantives because there is individuation in accidents only in virtue of substance. There are other names that are not appellative and have no appellata – e.g., names of things signified, such as 'chimera' and 'goat-stag' – and others that are not appellative but are appellata. Proper names are of that sort ((*cuiusmodi/cuius*)), for proper names are called appellata, supposita, and singulars. They are thus named by different names, but for different reasons. They are called appellata because they are appellated or named by their [logical] superiors; for the superiors are predicated of their inferiors according to name and according to definition. For it is right to say 'Socrates is a man'; here the superior is predicated of the inferior explicitly according to its name and implicitly according to definition. Similarly, Socrates is rightly called a mortal rational animal; here the superior is predicated of the inferior explicitly according to definition and implicitly according to name, for the definition of *man* is *mortal rational animal*. Therefore the superiors give themselves to their inferiors {213} because they are predicated of them according to name and definition. They also give their names to them because they are predicated of them according to name and definition, since the superiors give their names to the inferiors. They are called appellata because they are named or appellated by them. They are called supposita because they are 'put under' (*supponuntur*) their superiors or made into subjects for them. They are called singulars, however, because they name something discrete and individual, which applies to one thing singularly.

[4e. Appellation and Existence]

It is important to know, however, that appellata are not properly so-called unless they are actual existents; for what is, and not what is not, is properly appellated. And so it is right to say that appellation is for existent supposita or for an [existent] suppositum.

[4f. Appellation and Common Terms]

Again, it is important to know that appellation applies only to a common term; for it is a property of a common term (and not of any other term) to have appellata. But sometimes [appellation] applies to it for its supposita – i.e., when by the addition of a sign [the term] is distributed for its actually existing supposita, as when one says 'Every man is running' – but sometimes it applies to it determinately for some one of its supposita – i.e., when nothing that distributes it is assigned to it but it stands determinately, [as] when one says 'A man is running.'

[4g. Substantial and Accidental Terms]

Again, for the clarification of the rules that are laid down in connection with appellations it is important to know that some names or terms are substantial, such as substantival names, others accidental, such as adjectival names. And as far as predication ((*appositio/appellatio*)) is concerned, there is no difference between accidental and substantial terms, since accidental and substantial terms are predicated in the same way, no matter what tense the verb to which they are added ((*addantur/addatur*)) may be in. Similarly, where serving as a subject (*suppositio*) is concerned, there is no difference between substantial and accidental terms with a present-tense verb, for substantial and accidental terms serve as subjects in the same way when they are added to a present-tense verb. But there is a difference between accidental and substantial terms as far as serving as a subject is concerned with a past- or future-tense verb. This will become clear in the following rules.

[4h. Rule 1]

The first rule is this:

> [Rule 1] *A substantial or accidental common term that is not restricted by any other means and that serves as the subject or the predicate of a present-tense verb that has no ampliating force of its own or from anything else is restricted to suppositing for present things if it has appellata; but if it does not have appellata, it reverts to nonexistents ((existentes/ existentiam)).*

For an explanation of this rule it is important to know [these things]. 'Common term' is used in it because of the difference between it and a discrete term, which cannot be restricted or ampliated. 'Substantial or accidental' is used in it because there is no difference between {214} a substantial and an accidental term serving as a subject with a present-tense verb. 'Not restricted by any other means' is used in it because in virtue of something added to a term serving as the subject ((*supponenti/suppositi*)) of a present-tense verb the term can indeed supposit for something other than a present thing (for instance, when one says 'A man who has been is,' 'man' serves as the subject of the verb 'is,' and yet because of the modifying clause used there it supposits for a past thing). 'Serves as the subject or the predicate' is used in it because there is no difference between a substantial and an accidental term when it serves as the subject or the predicate of a present-tense verb. 'Of a present-tense verb' is used in it because of the difference between it and a verb of any other tense, for a term when added to a present-tense verb supposits differently from the way it supposits when added to a verb of any other tense. 'That has no ampliating force' is used in it because of the difference between it and verbs that do have ampliating force (such ((*ut/et*)) as 'can,' 'is thought about,' 'is praised').

(Thus if one says 'A man can run,' 'man' is ampliated in that case to supposit for present and future things; likewise when one says 'A man is thought about,' it supposits for present and future things. But in order to recognize which verbs ampliate and which ones do not, it is important to know that an action can be related to substance in two different ways: in one way as regards that in which it is and of which it is stated – as when one says 'Socrates is running,' where the running that is in Socrates and is said of Socrates is stated relative to or is related to Socrates – in the other way as regards that of which it is stated although it is not in it – as when one says 'Caesar is praised,' where the praise is stated of Caesar and yet is not in Caesar but in the one doing the praising. Similarly, when one says 'A chimera is thought about' – i.e., is a being in thought – where the thought is stated of the chimera and yet is not in the chimera but in the one doing the thinking. Similarly, when one says 'Antichrist can exist,' where the potentiality for existing is stated of Antichrist. It must be said, therefore, that the verbs that signify an action that is related to the subject, is in the subject, and is said of the subject do not ampliate; but those that signify an action that is related to the subject of which it is said but is not in the subject do ampliate.)

'Of its own or from anything else' is used in the rule because there are certain verbs that have ampliating force on their own, as is evident, but there are others that have ampliating force from an adjunct – e.g., if one says 'A man is thinkable,' 'man' is ampliated, but not because ((*quia/hic*)) the verb 'is' has ampliating force of its own; rather, [the ampliating force comes] from the adjunct 'thinkable.' 'Is restricted to suppositing for present things' is used in it in order to show that a present-tense verb restricts a term added to it to present things ((*presentes/presens*)) and not to others. 'If [it has] appellata' is used in it because there are certain {215} common terms that have more than one appellatum at once in actuality – e.g., 'man,' 'donkey' – there are others, however, that do not have more than one appellatum at once or successively, but are unique terms ((*unici termini/unicum terminum*)) – e.g., 'sun' and 'moon.' (There is another common term that never has more than one appellated suppositum at once in actuality but always just one successively and not simultaneously, although it can indeed have more than one – i.e., 'phoenix.') Therefore, when there is a common term that has a unique appellatum or more than one appellatum, and it serves as the subject of a present-tense verb that has no ampliating force, it always supposits for the appellatum or for the appellata it actually has ((*habet/habent*)), but it never supposits for any nonexistent thing or things. On the other hand, if it does not have appellata, then it does revert to nonexistent things – i.e., if a common term ((*si terminus/situs*)) serves as the subject of a present-tense verb and does not have appellata, then it is necessary for it to revert to nonexistent things – i.e., [it is necessary] that it supposit for nonexistent things. Thus, if we suppose that no rose exists, if someone says 'Every rose exists,' the term 'rose' supposits for nonexistent things.

In brief, therefore, it can be said that the point of the rule stated above is this: When a common term serves as the subject of a present-tense verb and there is no impediment either on the part of the term or on the part of the verb, then the term always supposits for existing things if it has appellata; but if it does not have any, then it supposits for nonexistent things.

[4i. A Problem Regarding 'Every Time Exists']

In connection with the things already discussed, a question can arise regarding the truth of the proposition 'Every time exists.'

On the basis of what has been said, it seems to be true; for in it ((*hac/hoc*)) a common term, 'time,' serves as the subject of a present-tense verb, and so since 'time' has an appellatum – viz., the present time – it is restricted to suppositing for present things and thus for existing things. Therefore, its sense will be 'Every time exists' - i.e., every time that exists, exists. And since that is true, so is the first proposition.

It seems, however, that it is false. 'Every time exists; therefore, the past exists' follows, likewise 'therefore, the future exists,' but those are false; therefore, so is the first proposition.

In reply it must be said that 'Every time exists' is false, and so the argument that proves that must be granted.

For the resolution of the opposing argument it must be noted that there are some terms that signify permanent things, such as 'man' [and] 'donkey,' but there are others that signify successive things, such as 'day.' Notice also that some things [actually] exist under a term and other things exist actually. Those things are said to exist actually that exist presently ((*presentialiter/presenter*)), while those things are said actually to exist under a term ((*dicuntur esse actu sub termino/que sunt actu sub termino dicuntur*)) of which the term is presently ((*presentialiter/presenter*)) predicated in an affirmative proposition. Notice, therefore, that when a term is distributed, it is distributed not only for things that exist actually but [also] for things that are presently ((*presentialiter/presenter*)) {216} or actually contained under the term, whether the term is significant of a permanent or a successive thing. But it is important to know that in connection with terms signifying a permanent thing there is no difference between existing actually and actually existing under the term, although there is [such] a difference in connection with terms signifying a successive thing. For example, 'man' is a term signifying a permanent thing, and what actually exists under that term, a man, exists actually; for that of which 'man' is presently ((*presentialiter/presenter*)) predicated in an affirmative proposition exists actually, supposing that a man exists. 'Time,' on the other hand, is a term signifying a successive thing, and something actually exists under that term that nevertheless does not exist actually; for 'time' is predicated of past and future time in an affirmative proposition since these propositions are true: 'Past time is time' and 'Future time is time.' But the past does not exist actually, and neither does the future, although they are times.

In reply to the argument, therefore, it must be said that it is true that the term has an appellatum, and in the proposition 'Every time exists,' it serves as the subject of a present-tense verb; thus it does supposit for existing things – not only for things that exist actually, but [also] for things that actually exist under the term. Therefore the sense of that proposition is this: 'Every time exists' – i.e., every time that exists, and every time that is a time, exist. Thus, since the past ((*preteritum/presens*)) is a time, and the future [is a time] too, it follows from this that past and future time exist – which is false. And so the first proposition is false. For that reason the sense of the proposition 'Every time exists' is inadequately presented when one says that the sense is this: Every time that exists, exists. And so the argument does not come to a correct conclusion.

If someone asks why in connection with terms signifying a permanent thing there is no difference between existing actually and actually existing under the term, although there is [such] a difference in connection with terms signifying a successive thing, it must be said that a term signifying a successive thing is a kind of whole composed of parts that do not exist simultaneously but in respect of earlier and later, as is evident in the case of time. For that reason something that does not exist actually can indeed be a part of such a whole existing actually; and so something can actually exist under that whole or under that term that nevertheless does not exist actually. On the other hand, a term signifying a permanent thing is a kind of whole composed of parts that exist simultaneously; for while such a whole exists, all its parts must exist simultaneously. And so whatever actually exists under that whole or under that term exists actually in virtue of its permanence.

[4j. Three Questions Regarding Restriction]

[4j(i). Introduction]

Again, because we supposed in connection with the rule introduced above that a common term is restricted by a present-tense verb, and that it is restricted to suppositing for present things, {217} we briefly raise three questions for the sake of clarifying that rule. The first is whether a present-tense verb can restrict a common term serving as its subject; the second, whether such a verb restricts the term to suppositing for present things; the third, whether that restriction is produced by that verb in the same way in an affirmative and in a negative proposition.

[4j(ii). First Question]

In the first place, it seems that a present-tense verb cannot restrict a common term serving as its subject, because the restrictor and the restricted must be in the same place. This is evident when one says 'A white man is running'; 'man' is restricted by 'white' because 'man' and 'white' are in the same place. On the other hand, if one says 'A man is white,' in this case 'man' is not restricted by ((ab/ad)) 'white,' because they are not in the same place. But the term serving as subject and the verb are not in the same place, because one is in the subject and the other in the predicate. Therefore, the term cannot be restricted by the verb ((verbo/termino)).

Again, if the term is restricted by the verb, that happens only because of the tense of the verb. But ((om. quia)) it cannot happen because of the verb's tense. Proof: Tense is the consignification of a verb, which is accidental to the verb; but in a verb its signification is prior to its consignification. A verb does not restrict a common term by reason of its signification, however. For when one says 'A man is running,' 'man' is not restricted to those who are running. Therefore, neither will a verb restrict in virtue of its consignification (as is apparent by the Topic *from the greater*), and so it will not restrict by reason of tense.

On the other hand, it is possible that a universal proposition with contingent subject matter be true, since 'Every man is running' can be true. But it could not be true if the term were not restricted by the present-tense verb in such a proposition, because if 'man' is interpreted for past and future men, [the proposition] is impossible. Therefore, it must be either that the common term is interpreted for present things and is restricted by the verb, or that [the proposition] is impossible. But it must not be called impossible. Therefore, it remains to be said that the common term is restricted by the verb. (And the reasoning is the same in other cases.)

In reply to this it must be said that a present-tense verb restricts a common term serving as its subject only ((tantum/tamen)) as long as the verb signifies an action that is related to the subject, is stated of the subject, and is in the subject. For if there is such a verb that signifies an action that is [stated] of the subject but is not in the subject, it does not restrict but rather ampliates, as was seen above. (It is restricted in this way analogously by a past-tense and a future-tense verb, as will be said below.)

But it is important to note that this restriction is brought about in the following way. In a verb there are these two: the action and the composition. The action considered in itself is indifferent {218} with respect to any time whatever, but the action is restricted by time (which is the measure of motion) to being in that time which is its measure. Thus the action of a present-tense verb is placed in the present, the action of one in the past tense in the past, and the action of one in the future tense in the future. In this way, then, the action of a verb is restricted by the verb's time [or tense]. And because the time that is the measure of the action is the measure of the composition of the parts, the composition is restricted when the action has been restricted. And because the action is something that cannot be expressed ((*dici/esse*)) without the verb, [the action] is even said of the subject by means of the composition that unites [one] extreme with [the other] extreme in an expression. And so the subject of the action is placed in the same time in which the action and the composition are placed, and in that way the subject is restricted to the time to which the action and the composition [are restricted]. But the subject of the action is a common term serving as the subject of the verb. It is evident, therefore, that the verb restricts a common term serving as its subject, and so restriction is brought about not directly but indirectly by the time [or tense] of the verb. For first the action of the verb is restricted by the time [or tense], then the composition, and finally the common term serving as the verb's subject. And so we have to grant the argument that proves this.

To the first argument on the other side I reply that we have to say that there are two kinds of restriction. One is the kind in which the restrictor is a principle of understanding that which is restricted and [its] disposition. This kind has to be brought about by the addition ((*additionem/additum*)) of a name and by ampliation, and it is of this kind that it is true that the restrictor and the restricted must be in the same place. The other kind is a restriction in which the restrictor is not a principle of understanding the thing restricted or its disposition. This kind has to be brought about by a verb by reason of the verb's tense, and of this kind it is not true that the restrictor and the restricted have to be in the same place. And since the argument under discussion drew its conclusion concerning the second sort of restriction, it is invalid.

In reply to the other argument [on the other side] it must be said that there is no doubt that the restriction is brought about only by reason of the verb's tense. It is also true that time is the verb's consignification, and that the verb's signification is prior to its consignification. But it does not follow on that basis that a restriction cannot be brought about by reason of the consignification if it cannot be brought about by reason of the signification; for the consignification that is the verb's time [or tense] is more efficacious than is its signification for bringing about restriction. That is because the consignification that is its time [or tense] is first the measure of the verb's signification, or action, and last the measure of the suppositum, or the subject of the action. But a measure restricts the thing measured (since if [a thing] is measured with respect to quantity there is [a restriction] of the quantity of the thing measured). And so even though the restriction is not brought about by reason of the verb's signification, it can be brought about by reason of the verb's consignification. Therefore, when in arguing on the other side one says {219} that the argument appears to hold on the basis of the Topic *from the greater*, it must be said that that is false, because the signification cannot contribute more to restriction than can the consignification – on the contrary, [it contributes] less, as has been seen.

[4j(iii). Second Question]

Next we inquire into the second question: [Does a present-tense verb restrict the term to suppositing for present things?]

And it seems that a common term serving as the subject of a present-tense verb is not restricted to suppositing for existing things, because when no man is in existence 'Every man exists' is false, and so its contradictory 'Some man does not exist' will be true. But if the common term in the negative proposition supposits for existing things, the proposition will be false – which is impossible, because it is impossible that two contradictories be false at the same time. It remains, therefore, that [the term 'man'] does not supposit for existing things although it serves as the subject of a present-tense verb. That it is ((*sit/fit*)) false if the common term supposits for existing things is evident. If when no one is running someone assigns running to a runner, it will be assigned truly – if, for example, someone says 'A runner runs.' Similarly, if existence is removed from something that exists, it will be removed falsely. But when one says 'Some man does not exist,' if 'man' supposits for existing things, existence will be removed from something that exists; for the sense is this: Some man who exists does not exist. Therefore, it will be false.

Again, 'No man exists; therefore, Caesar does not exist' follows, and '[No man exists; therefore,] Antichrist does not exist' also follows. But Caesar is past and Antichrist is future. Since they are taken under the common term 'man' serving as the subject of a present-tense verb, however, it seems that that common term supposits not only for present things but [also] for past and future things.

An argument that was made in connection with the first problem can be used as an argument on the other side. For 'Every man is running' is possible, but it would be impossible if that common term were not restricted to suppositing for present things, because running cannot presently ((*presentialiter/presenter*)) apply to anything that does not exist – i.e., anything past or future. Therefore, since [the proposition] is not impossible, what remains is that a common term serving as the subject of a present-tense verb is restricted by the verb to suppositing in that proposition for present things. (And it will be the same way in other propositions.)

Some people are accustomed to say in reply to this that we have to speak in two different ways about a proposition in which a common term serves as the subject of a present-tense verb. In one way, insofar as it is considered in itself and absolutely, in its character as a statement; and they say that [when it is considered] in that way, the common term serving as the subject in it is restricted to suppositing for present things. In the other way, it can be considered insofar as it is a source for inferring something from itself, in its character as a premise; and they say that [when it is considered] in that way, the common term [serving as the subject] in it is not restricted to suppositing for present things. Instead, it can supposit for existent and nonexistent things, and it can do so by reason of the implication that is based on the relationship of the terms, {220} a relationship of terms that has nothing to do with any difference of time [or tense].

One can argue against this in the following way: One sort of restriction is brought about by an adjunct, and another is brought about by a verb by reason of the verb's time [or tense]. But a restriction brought about by an adjunct restricts a term to the same thing both in a proposition considered in itself and in the proposition insofar as it is a source for inferring something. For if one says 'Every white man is running,' 'man' is restricted to white ones whether the proposition is considered in itself or something is inferred from it. Therefore, [by the Topic] *from a similar*, a restriction ((*restrictio/restrinctio*)) brought about by reason of time [or tense] will restrict a term in a proposition to the same thing whether that proposition is considered in itself or something is inferred from it.

Again, if we suppose that every man who exists is running, 'Every man is running' is true if it is considered in its own right. If something is inferred from it, however, it will be false on our supposition, because in the original proposition [considered] insofar as something is inferred from it, the term supposits not only for existing things but also for things that do not exist. Therefore, the same proposition will be true and false; for it is true considered absolutely but false [considered] in relation to another – which is absurd. For the thing considered absolutely and the thing considered in relation [to something else] do not produce a real difference; instead, the cause of truth and falsity lies in things, according to Aristotle in the *Categories* [5, 4b5–10]: 'from the fact that the thing is,' etc. For this reason we have to say that the solution offered above seems not to work. Instead, it must be said that a common term serving as the subject of a present-tense verb is restricted to suppositing for present things (as was said), but [only] as long as the verb signifies an action that is related to the subject, is stated of the subject, and is in the subject, and the common term serving as that verb's subject has one or more appellata. And so we have to grant the argument that proves this.

In reply to the first argument on the other side we have to reply by saying that it is indeed true that if no man exists 'Every man exists' is false, because [in that case] existence is attributed to things that do not exist. But 'Some man does not exist' is true, although its sense is not this: Some man who exists does not exist, but this: Some man who does not exist does not exist. Thus existence is removed from what does not exist. For in both these propositions the common term supposits for something that does not exist, because it does not have one or more appellata and so must revert to nonexistent things. The argument is worthless, however, because it concludes in a term that has no appellata; for it must conclude in the term that has one or more appellata. {221} But such a term, and not the term that does not have one or more appellata, is restricted to suppositing for present things.

In reply to the other argument it must be said that this does not follow: 'No man exists; therefore, Caesar does not exist,' nor does 'therefore, Antichrist does not exist' follow. For when one says 'No man exists' while things are as they are now, since 'man' has at least ((*saltem/solum*)) one appellatum, it supposits for things that exist. Thus, what does not exist cannot be included under it, and so, since Caesar and Antichrist do not exist, they must not be included under 'man.' But just as there would be no [logical] relationship in 'No one who exists is a man; therefore, some man who does not exist does not exist,' so there is no [logical] relationship if one infers, 'No man exists; therefore, Caesar and Antichrist do not exist.'

But someone will say that 'No man exists; therefore, Caesar does not exist' does indeed seem to follow because 'Caesar exists; therefore, a man exists' follows. Therefore, by an inverse consequence (which holds good in connection with a contradictory) it seems that 'No man exists; therefore, Caesar does not exist' does follow correctly. But here is a proof that 'Caesar exists; therefore, a man exists' follows. For when one says 'Caesar exists,' I ask whether 'Caesar' stands for that which there now is of Caesar or for that which there was of Caesar. But it cannot be said that it stands for that which there now is of Caesar, or for the dust to which Caesar has been reduced; for if it did stand for that which there now is of Caesar, 'Caesar exists' would be true – which no one would grant. We are therefore left with the conclusion that when one says 'Caesar exists,' ['Caesar'] stands for that which there was of Caesar. Therefore, since he was a man, this follows perfectly: 'Caesar exists; therefore, a man exists.'

In reply to this we have to say that 'Caesar exists; therefore, a man exists' does not follow, just as 'No man exists; therefore, Caesar is not Caesar' does not follow. And to the proof that 'Caesar exists; therefore, a man exists' follows, we have to reply in this way. It is indeed true that when one says 'Caesar exists,' 'Caesar' stands for that which there was of Caesar; and so it stands for the man who was, and thus for something that does not exist. Nevertheless, 'Caesar exists; therefore, a man exists' does not follow. For just as there would be no [logical] relationship if one were to say 'A man who does not exist [exists]; therefore, a man who exists [exists],' so there is no [logical] relationship [when one says] 'Caesar exists; therefore, a man exists.' For when one says 'Caesar exists,' 'Caesar' stands for a man who does not exist, but when one says 'A man exists,' since 'man' has appellata, it stands for a man who exists.

And so it is important to notice that just as when a common term serves as the subject of a present-tense verb it supposits for nonexistent things if it does not have appellata, so when a discrete term serves as the subject of a present-tense verb it actually stands for a nonexistent thing if it does not have an appellatum belonging to any common term.

Again, since an inverse consequence was mentioned, {222} in order to know what is meant by that name take note that according to Aristotle in Book II of the *Topics* (II 8, 113b30), there are two sorts of consequence: The direct consequence and the inverse consequence. A consequence is direct when the opposite of the consequent follows from the opposite of the antecedent, as in 'If it is a strength, it is a virtue; therefore, if it is a weakness, it is a vice.' It is an inverse consequence when the opposite of the antecedent follows from the opposite of the consequent – e.g., 'If a man exists, an animal exists; therefore, if an animal does not exist, a man does not exist' or '[therefore,] if there is no animal, there is no man.'

[4j(iv). Third Question]

Next ((*Postea/Contra*)) we inquire into the third question ((*tertio/termino*)): [Is the restriction produced by a present-tense verb in the same way in an affirmative and in a negative proposition?]

And it seems that the restriction is produced by the verb in the same way in an affirmative and in a negative proposition. For, as we have seen, a verb restricts a term by reason of its time [or tense], but the same time [or tense] remains in the verb in both an affirmative and a negative proposition, since negation does not remove the tense. Therefore ((*quare/quia*)), the verb restricts the term in the same way in an affirmative and in a negative proposition.

Again, if the verb did not restrict the term in the same way in both an affirmative and a negative proposition, there would be no contradiction, since ((*cum/sed*)) contradiction is affirmation and negation, and of the same thing. But it is certain that there is contradiction, and so it is also certain that the verb restricts the term in the same way in both an affirmative and a negative proposition.

On the other side, an affirmative adjunct restricts a term to one thing, and a negative adjunct to another, for 'white' and 'not white' do not restrict a term to the same things. Analogously, an affirmative modifying clause restricts [a term] to something other than a negative modifying clause does; for 'man' is restricted to one sort of thing when one says 'man who is running' and to another when one says 'man who is not running.' Therefore, [by the Topic] *from a similar*, an affirmative verb restricts [a term] to something other than a negative verb does, and so the restriction will not be produced by the verb in the same way in both an affirmative and a negative proposition.

In reply to this we have to say that the verb does restrict the term in the same way in both an affirmative and a negative proposition, as is proved by the first two arguments (which must be granted).

In reply to the argument on the other side we have to say that the restriction that is produced by a verb is not the same as that produced by an adjunct and a modifying clause. For the kind that is produced by a verb is brought about by reason of consignification (because [it is produced] by reason of the verb's time [or tense]); and because negation neither removes nor alters consignification in a verb, that sort of restriction is produced in the same way when it is affirmed and when it is denied. But the sort that is produced by an adjoined negation or by a modifying clause is produced by reason of a special signification; and because negation removes special signification in an adjective {223} and in a modifying clause, restriction is not produced in the same way by an affirmed and a negated adjective or by an affirmed and a negated modifying clause.

[4k. Rule 2]

The second rule of appellations is this:

> [Rule 2] *A common term pertaining to accident that is not restricted by any other means and that serves as the subject of a past-tense verb can supposit for present and past things even though the term serving as the predicate supposits [only] for past things; but if a term pertaining to substance serves as the subject or the predicate of a past-tense verb, it always supposits for past things.*

[4l. Rule 3]

The third rule is this:

> [Rule 3] *A common term pertaining to accident that is not restricted by any other means and that serves as the subject of a future-tense verb can supposit for present and future things even though when serving as the predicate it is interpreted only for future things; but if a term pertaining to substance serves as the subject or the predicate of a future-tense verb, it is always interpreted for future things.*

[4m. Proof of Rule 2]

That ((*Quod/Quarta*)) a term pertaining to accident and serving as the subject of a past-tense verb can supposit for present and past things is evident. For 'This old man was boy' is true if someone who is at present an old man is indicated, but it cannot be true unless the subject in that proposition is interpreted for a present thing while the predicate is interpreted for a past thing. And its sense is this: He who is an old man now was a boy before. And so the term 'old man' is interpreted for present things even though it serves as the subject of a past-tense verb. Therefore, a common term pertaining to accident and serving as the subject of a past-tense verb does supposit for present things, and there is no doubt that it can supposit for past things; therefore, etc.

[4n. Proof of Rule 3]

Again, that a common term pertaining to accident and serving as the subject of a future-tense verb can supposit for present and future things is evident in the following way. Suppose that Socrates is at almost the last instant of his youth, and that he lives until ((*quousque/quotienscumque*)) he is an old man. Then it can be truly said, indicating Socrates, 'That boy will be an old man.' That proposition is true because it can have two senses – namely, this one: He who will be a boy will be an old man; or this one: He who is a boy will be an old man. And since it is not true in the sense 'He who will be a boy will be an old man' (because from now on, as was supposed, he will not be a boy), we are left with its being true in this sense: He who is a boy will be an old man. And in that way 'boy' supposits for present things even though it serves as the subject of a future-tense verb. Therefore, a term pertaining to accident and serving as the subject of a future-tense verb can supposit for present things, and there is no doubt that it can supposit for future things.

[40. Summary of Rules 2 and 3]

Thus, if one says, 'A white thing was running' ((*cucurrit/currit*)), the sense is this: What is or what was white was running ((*cucurrit/currit*)). Similarly, if one says, 'A white thing will be running,' the sense is this: That which is or will be white will be running.

[4p. Problems Regarding Terms Pertaining to Substances and Pertaining to Accidents]

{224} [Question 1] The following question arises, however. Because a term pertaining to substance and serving as the subject or as the predicate of a verb is interpreted according to the verb's requirement (for if it serves as the subject or as the predicate of a present-tense verb it is always interpreted for present things, if of a past-tense verb it is interpreted for past things, but if of a future-tense verb it is interpreted for future things), why is it not like that for a term pertaining to accident?

And it seems that it must be just the same as it is in connection with a term pertaining to substance. For a verb restricts by reason of its time [or tense], but the time [or tense] remains the same in a verb whether a term pertaining to substance or a term pertaining to accident serves as the subject. Therefore, a term pertaining to substance and a term pertaining to accident must be restricted in the same way.

[Question 2] Another question: Why is a term pertaining to accident interpreted according to the verb's requirement when it serves as the verb's predicate but not when it serves as its subject?

And it seems that a term pertaining to accident would have to supposit according to the verb's requirement when it serves as the subject just as when it serves as the predicate. For, as was said above, the verb's tense restricts ((*restringit/restringi*)) the action first, then the composition; and it restricts the subject in the second way ((*secundo modo/primus modus*)). Therefore, since the composition is related equally to the extremes (since it is the intermediary uniting the extremes), it seems that the way restriction is in the subject or suppositum – via the composition – is the way it must be in the predicate (*predicato vel apposito*). And so a term pertaining to accident will be restricted in the same way serving as a subject and as a predicate.

Again, 'A white thing will be Socrates' is indefinite and affirmative; therefore, it can undergo simple conversion into 'Socrates will be white.' But the judgment regarding things that can be converted is one and the same, and so if 'white' is interpreted for a future thing in 'Socrates will be white,' in the same way 'a white thing' ((*album/albus*)) is interpreted only for a future thing in 'A white thing ((*album/albus*)) will be Socrates.' And so 'white' will restrict in the same way when it serves as the subject and when it serves as the predicate.

[Reply to Question 1] In reply to the first of these, we have to say that it is true that a term pertaining to substance and serving as the subject of a past- or future-tense verb is interpreted according to the verb's requirement, but that is not the way it is with a term pertaining to accident. For a term pertaining to substance, but not a term pertaining to accident, is restricted by a past- or future-tense verb when it serves as its subject. The reason for this may be that a subject is not restricted by a verb by reason of time [or tense] directly but by means of the thing [signified], which is the verb's action, as was said above. Thus, a restriction is brought about in the subject just as the thing [signified] by the verb requires ((*verbi ita fit/verbi fit*)); but the thing [signified] by a verb has to do with the subject in which it is by reason of a substantial rather than an accidental form, because the thing [signified] by a verb is an accident and requires something stable and constant in which it occurs as a subject, and it is a substantial rather than an accidental form that is of that sort. Likewise, the reason a subject is subject to a verb is just the reason the subject must be stable and constant, and so the nature {225} of the subject *qua* subject is incompatible with an accidental form. And so it is not because of an accidental form but only because of a substantial form that a subject is restricted by the verb, by the verb's time [or tense], or by the thing the verb [signifies]. Therefore, since a term pertaining to substance is given its form ((*informatur/imponatur*)) by a substantial form and a term pertaining to accident [is given its form] by an accidental form, a term pertaining to substance is restricted by the verb whose subject it serves as, but a term pertaining to accident and serving as its subject [is] not [restricted by the verb].

In reply to the argument to the contrary [in Question 1], we have to say that of course it is true that the time [or tense] remains the same in the verb whether a term pertaining to substance or a term pertaining to accident serves as its subject; it is of course also true that a verb restricts a term by reason of its time [or tense], but it does not follow that it restricts a term pertaining to substance and a term pertaining to accident in the same way when they serve as its subject. For since the restriction is brought about not directly by the time [or tense] but by means of the thing [signified] by the verb, it is brought about in accordance with what the thing [signified] by the verb requires. And because the thing [signified] by the verb has to do with the term not because of an accidental form but only because of a substantial form, the restriction is brought about in a term pertaining to substance, which is given its form ((*informatur/imponitur*)) by a substantial ((*substantiali/accidentali*)) form.

[Reply to Question 2] As for the second question, it must be said that it is of course true that a term pertaining to accident and serving as a verb's predicate is interpreted according to the verb's requirement, but not when it serves as the subject. The reason for this may be that, as was said, the nature of a subject *qua* subject is incompatible with an accidental form; for a term pertaining to accident cannot be a subject because of an accidental form. But the nature of a predicate *qua* predicate is not incompatible with an accidental form; for a term can indeed be predicated because of an accidental form. And so, although a verb does not have to do with a term pertaining to accident in its character as a subject, it does indeed have to do with it in its character as a predicate. And so a term pertaining to accident is restricted by a verb when it serves as a predicate and not when it serves as a subject.

In reply to the first argument to the contrary [in Question 2], we have to say that it is true that the composition has to do equally with [both] extremes since it is the intermediary uniting them. But it does not follow from this that the restriction is brought about via the composition in a term pertaining to accident and serving as a subject even though it is so in a term pertaining to accident and serving as a predicate; for the composition does not have to do with a term pertaining to accident and serving as a subject considered as an extreme in virtue of its pertaining to accident, although it does indeed have to do with a term pertaining to accident [and] serving as a predicate considered as an extreme. For a term pertaining to accident can fit the definition of a predicate but not the definition of a subject.

In reply to the second [argument to the contrary in Question 2] we have to say that 'A white thing will be Socrates' has two interpretations; for it can be interpreted in this sense: That which will be white will be Socrates; or in this sense: What is white will be Socrates. {226} In the sense of what will be white will be Socrates it undergoes simple conversion into 'Socrates will be white,' but not in the other sense. And the judgment is the same regarding both of them, because in both 'white' is interpreted for a future thing. But in the sense of that which is white will be Socrates it converts this way: 'Socrates will be that which is white,' so that the modification occurs in the predicate just as in the subject in such a way that in virtue of the modification the term pertaining to accident is interpreted for a present thing when it serves as a predicate just as it was interpreted when serving as a subject. Therefore, the reasoning is invalid, for it presupposes that 'A white thing ((*album/albus*)) will be Socrates' undergoes conversion in both its interpretations into 'Socrates will be white' ((*albus/album*)) – which, as we have seen, is not true.

[5. Restriction]

[5a. Restriction and Ampliation]

Next to be considered are restriction and ampliation, and first, restriction, which is the opposite of ampliation; for no one can learn about one opposite completely without learning about the other. As Aristotle says near the beginning of Book Six of the *Topics* (VI 1, 139a24–30), 'those who define well show the contraries together' – i.e., those who do well at assigning the definition of one contrary introduce ((*insinuant/insinuat*)) along with it ((*hoc/hic*)) the definition of the other contrary.

[5b. Definition of Restriction]

First of all we have to see what restriction is, and that can be shown in this way: Restriction is a lessening of the scope of a common term as a consequence of which the common term is interpreted for fewer supposita than its actual supposition requires.

This is evident, [for] when one says 'white man,' 'man' is restricted by means of 'white.' For although as regards its actual supposition it can be interpreted for men of any color whatever, its supposition is lessened by means of the nature of the adjective 'white' to such an extent that it is interpreted for white ones only.

Notice, too, that it is quite right to add 'common term' in the definition of restriction because of the difference [between a common and] a discrete term, which cannot be restricted or ampliated.

[5c. Divisions of Restriction]

[5c(i). Natural and Use-governed]

Restriction is brought about in many ways. It is brought about in one way by means of something else added to the restricted term; it is brought about in another way when nothing has been added to that which is restricted. On this basis the one sort of restriction can be called natural, the other use-governed. That sort is called natural that is brought about by means of something added to the restricted term in that the term is restricted in accordance with the nature of what is adjoined to it. The use-governed sort is in the term, not [brought about] by means of any addition; and it is called use-governed because it arises from [linguistic] usage and not from the nature of anything added to the restricted term. This sort of restriction has to occur in the {227} term 'king.' When one says 'The king is coming,' the term 'king' is restricted to suppositing for the king of the country in which the sentence is spoken.

[5c(ii). Natural Restriction by Means
of a Clause and by Means of a Word]

'Natural restriction' is used in many different ways. [For instance,] it can be brought about either by means of a word or by means of a clause.

It is brought about by means of a clause when a clause that does not imply diminution or modification modifies a term, since in that case the term is restricted to suppositing for those [supposita] to which the modifying clause applies. For example, when one says 'A man who is white is running,' 'man' is restricted to white ones. There is a kind of modifying clause that does imply diminution, however ((*autem/enim*)) – e.g., 'who has died' or 'who does not exist' – and another that implies ampliation – e.g., 'who can exist.' Those clauses do not restrict, however ((*autem/enim*)); for restriction is said to occur in a term when the term is not destroyed by means of what is added to it but is instead interpreted for fewer supposita than its actual supposition requires. And it is because the sort of clause that implies diminution ((*diminutionem/divisionem*)) destroys what it modifies, whereas the sort that implies ampliation makes the term be interpreted for more [supposita] than its actual supposition requires, that clauses of those sorts do not restrict.

[5c(iii). By means of Signification and by Means of Consignification]

The kind of restriction that is brought about by means of a word can occur because of signification or because of consignification.

It can occur because of consignification by means of a name as well as by means of a verb: by means of a name because of its gender, by means of a verb because of its time [or tense]. For an adjectival name ((om. *masculini*)) restricts its substantive because of its gender, since if the adjective is of the masculine gender it restricts the substantive to males and if of the feminine gender to females. Thus, when one says 'That human being is white (*albus*),' 'human being' is restricted to men; if one says, 'That human being is white (*alba*),' it is restricted to women.

Restriction brought about by means of a verb occurs because of the past, present, and future tense, since a present-tense verb restricts [a term] to present things, a past-tense verb to past things, and a future-tense verb to future things (as was seen in connection with appellation).

It should be noted that restriction brought about because of consignification differs from the kind brought about because of signification in virtue of the fact that in the restriction brought about because of signification it is always necessary that what does the restricting and what gets restricted be put in the same place and that the one be directly adjoined to the other. On the other hand, in the restriction that is brought about because of consignification it is not necessary that what does the restricting and what gets restricted be put in the same place, nor is it necessary that the one be directly adjoined to the other. The reason for this is that in restriction brought about because of signification what does the restricting is the source of understanding that which gets restricted, whereas in restriction brought about because of consignification what does the restricting is not the source of understanding that which gets restricted.

[5c(iv). *Types of Restriction by Means of Signification*]

The restriction that is brought about by means of a word because of signification can be brought about in many different ways.

{228} One sort is brought about by something that is not in the same case as that which is restricted. For example, when one says 'Socrates's donkey,' 'donkey' is restricted here to suppositing for Socrates's donkey.

Another sort is brought about by means of something that is in the same case as that which is restricted. This can be brought about by means of a term pertaining to substance, and it occurs when an inferior is added to its superior in an appositive construction. For example, if one says 'An animal – a man – is running,' 'animal' is restricted here to suppositing for an animal that is a man. This can also ((*etiam/enim*)) be brought about by means of the specific differentia added to the genus. For example, if one says 'rational animal,' animal is restricted here [to suppositing] for the sort that is rational. It can be brought about also by means of a determinate pronoun – e.g., if one says 'That man is running,' 'man' is restricted [to suppositing] for the man determined [by the pronoun]. It can also be brought about by means of a term pertaining to accident – e.g., by means of an adjectival name or a participle ((*participium/proprium*)). For when one says 'A white man is running,' 'man' is restricted to white ones; likewise when one says 'The man running is a disputant,' 'man' is restricted to running ones.

[5d. Restriction, Diminution, and Ampliation]

Now ((*autem/enim*)) every adjective that is not diminutional and has no ampliating force restricts the term it is directly adjoined to. An adjective such as 'dead' is diminutional, and strictly speaking it ((*hoc/hic*)) does not restrict but rather destroys [the term]. If, for example, one says 'dead man,' 'man' is not ((*non/enim*)) restricted but turned aside or destroyed. Another sort of adjective causes a term to be interpreted for more things than its actual supposition requires, and it ((*hoc/hic*)) does not restrict but rather ampliates [the term]. Thus, if one says 'A man can run,' ['man'] is not restricted but ampliated.

[6. Ampliation]

[6a. Definition of Ampliation]

Next, ampliation. Ampliation ((*ampliatio/ampliato*)) is an extension of the scope of a common term as a consequence of which ((*quam/quod*)) the common term can be interpreted for more supposita than its actual supposition requires.

This is evident. When one says 'A man can be the Antichrist,' 'man' is ampliated by means of 'can'; for, although as regards its actual supposition 'man' serving as the subject of a present-tense verb is interpreted only for present things, by the nature of the verb 'can' 'man' is ampliated in such a way that it is interpreted for a future thing, and so its supposition is extended.

[6b. Ampliation by Means of Names, Verbs, Adverbs, and Participles]

Ampliation is brought about sometimes by means of names, sometimes by means of verbs, sometimes by means of adverbs, sometimes by means of participles. For there are certain names that have the power of ampliating – e.g., 'possible,' 'necessary' – and certain verbs likewise – e.g., 'can,' 'is praised' – similarly also certain adverbs – e.g., 'potentially,' 'necessarily' – and likewise certain participles – e.g., 'being able,' 'praised.'

[6c. Relative to Supposita and Relative to Times]

Ampliation can be divided in this way. One sort of ampliation is brought about because of supposita, the other because of times; for some things that ampliate {229} ampliate relative to supposita and others relative to times.

Those that cause a term to be interpreted for both actual and nonexistent supposita are said to ampliate relative to supposita. Of this sort ((*cuiusmodi/cuius*)) are the verbs whose corresponding action is related to the subject and said of the subject but is not in the subject – such as 'can,' 'is thought,' 'is praised.' Other things that have the power of those verbs ampliate in that same way, such as certain names, adverbs, and participles, if they derive from those verbs.

Those that cause a term to be extended to all the differences of time are said to ampliate relative to times – e.g., those words that include all the differences of time within themselves, as do 'necessarily,' 'necessary,' 'always.' Thus when one says 'A man is an animal necessarily,' it is the same ((*non aliud/aliud*)) as if one had said 'That is, in every time being an animal applies to a man: in the present, the past, and the future.'

[7. Distribution]

[7a. Introduction]

Many things could be said about distributions, but for the sake of brevity let us say only a few things about them now.

[7b. Distribution and Distributing]

For the present we have to consider what distribution is and what it is to distribute. Distribution is the division of one thing into divided [parts] ((*in divisa/indivisa*)); to distribute is to divide one thing into divided [parts] ((*in divisa/indivisa*)).

[7c. Signs, Wholes, and Parts]

Distribution is brought about by means of the addition ((*additionem/addictionem*)) of a universal sign to a term that has subjective or ((*vel/et*)) integral parts under it; for there are two kinds of parts, subjective and integral. Accordingly, there is a kind of universal sign that is distributive of integral parts – e.g., 'whole' – and another universal sign that is distributive of subjective parts – e.g., 'every' or 'all,' 'each' or 'any,' and the like.

A sign distributive of integral parts has to be added to an integral whole, indicating that that whole is divided into integral parts; for ((*enim/autem*)) distribution is brought about in a whole by means of a sign. The sign distributes, and so the distribution is in it actively, but the whole is distributed ((*distribuitur/distribuit*)), and so the distribution is in it passively.

On the other hand, signs distributive of subjective parts have to be added to a universal whole.

[7d. Universals]

It is important to know, however, that 'universal' is ambiguous. For there is one sort of universal that has the nature of a universal completely and perfectly, but there are other universals that fall short in some respect of the nature of a complete and perfect universal.

That is said to have the nature of a universal completely and perfectly that is actually in many things and is said of many things at once, and that is existent in the nature of things – e.g., *man*; for, while things are as they are now, *man* is in many singulars and is said of many things at once and actually, and it is something existent in the nature of things.

There are, however, other universals that fall short in some of these respects. For *sun* and *moon* are universals and are in many things, but not actually; nor are they said of many things either at once or successively, {230} because the sun is unique and there is one moon. Similarly, *phoenix* is a kind of universal, and even though it is in many things and is said of many things, it is so successively, because when one phoenix has been destroyed another is generated; and yet it is never in many things at once, nor is it said of many things at once, since there is always only one phoenix in actuality. Similarly, names of imaginary entities, such as 'chimera' [or] 'goat-stag,' have to be in many things and to be said of many things, and yet they are not anything existing in the nature of things, but only in the mind.

Notice, therefore, that universal signs distributive of subjective parts can be added correctly and completely to any of the above-mentioned universals. Thus it is correct to say 'every sun,' 'every moon,' 'every phoenix,' 'every chimera.' The reason for this might be that every universal sign distributive of subjective parts in a term to which it is added requires only that that term be informed ((*informatur/imponatur*)) by a universal form, a form in which more than one suppositum can participate, actually or potentially, in reality or in the mind. And because that condition is found in each of the above-mentioned universals, [such] a sign can be added to any of them.

[7e. Distribution in Several Categories]

It should be known that some signs distributive of subjective parts are distributive of things that are in the genus of substance e.g., 'every' or 'all,' 'no,' 'each' or 'any,' 'both,' 'neither'; others are distributive of things that are in the genus of quality – e.g., 'of any sort,' and the like; others are distributive of things that are in the genus of quantity – e.g., 'as much as you please,' 'however much,' and the like; others are distributive of things that are in the genus of discrete quantity – e.g., 'however many,' 'as many as you please,' and the like.

[7f. Universal and Particular Signs]

Notice, however, that distribution is not brought about by means of particular signs but only by means of universal signs; for universal but not particular signs have the power of distributing.

[7g. Distribution by Means of Negation]

[7g(i). Rule 1]

Again, it is important to know that not only universal signs have the power of distributing, but also negation. For this first rule is given:

> [Rule 1] *When a negation encounters mobile supposition in a term it precedes, it renders it immobile; and when it encounters immobile supposition, it renders it mobile.*

Thus if one says, 'Not every man is running,' the supposition of the term 'man,' which was mobile before the arrival of the negation, is made ((*efficitur/manet*)) immobile. But if one says 'Socrates does not see a man,' the supposition of the term 'man' is made mobile, and a [logical] descent can be made under that term, although before the arrival of the negation the supposition of the term was immobile; and so the term is distributed by the negation.

The reason for the rule may be that negation is of a destructive nature, and so it establishes the opposite of what it encounters. For that reason, when it encounters mobile supposition it renders it immobile, and when it encounters immobile supposition, it renders it mobile.

[7g(ii). Rule 2]

Again, {231} another rule is given regarding negation:

> [Rule 2] *When two universal negative signs are used in an expression, the first is equipollent to its contrary, the second to its contradictory.*

For example, if one says, 'Nothing is nothing,' it is the same as if 'Everything is something' had been said.

The reason [for the rule] may be that a rule of this sort is given in connection with equipollent [signs]: *A universal negative sign with a negation placed after ((postposita/posposita)) it is equipollent to its contrary.* But when two universal negative signs are placed in the same expression, the negation belonging to the second sign is placed after the first sign; and so, because of the negation placed after it, the first universal negative sign is equipollent to its contrary. But in connection with equipollent [signs] there is [also] this rule: *A universal sign with a negation placed before ((preposita/postposita)) it is equipollent to its contradictory.* When two universal negative signs are placed in the same expression, however, the negation belonging to the first sign is placed before the second sign; and so, because of the negation placed before it, the second universal negative sign is equipollent to its contradictory.

[7g(iii). Distributive Powers of Negative and Affirmative Signs]

Again, it must be known that a universal negative sign has more distributive power ((*virtutem/universalitatem*)) than a universal affirmative sign. For a universal affirmative sign confuses and distributes a common term adjoined ((*adiunctum/additum*)) directly to it but confuses and does not distribute a term indirectly adjoined to it, whereas a universal negative sign confuses and distributes a common term that it precedes, whether it is directly or indirectly adjoined to it. Thus, if one says, 'No man is a donkey,' a descent can be made both in the subject and in the predicate.

The reason a universal negative sign both confuses and distributes a common term that it precedes and that is indirectly adjoined to it may be this: saying 'No man is a donkey' is the same as saying 'Every man is not a donkey,' and so the negation belonging to the universal sign placed in the subject follows the term placed in the subject but precedes the term placed in the predicate; and because the term placed in the predicate had immobile supposition before the arrival of the negation, after the arrival of the negation it has mobile supposition. For, as was said, when a negation encounters immobile supposition in a term it precedes, it renders it mobile; and so it is by virtue of the negation in it that a universal negative sign distributes a term that it precedes and directly adjoins.

[7h. 'Every' Taken Divisively and Collectively]

Again, it is important to know that the universal affirmative sign 'every' or 'all,' which is distributive of a universal whole, is interpreted sometimes divisively, sometimes collectively. It is said to be interpreted collectively when it indicates that the predicate is attributed to its parts collected together and not to any one in its own right; and in that case {232} a descent in the parts of the subject is not permitted – as when one says, 'Every man is hauling a boat, and no one by himself.' On the other hand, it is said to be interpreted divisively when it indicates that the predicate is attributed to the subject for the parts of the subject, and in that case a descent in the parts of the subject is indeed permitted – as when one says 'Every man is running.' And notice that a universal affirmative sign distributive of a universal whole especially has to be interpreted collectively in the plural, as when one says, 'All the apostles are twelve,' but it does not have to be taken so strictly collectively in the singular.

We have to say the same thing about a universal sign distributive of an integral whole; for it can be interpreted divisively – as when one says, 'The whole house is white' – or collectively – as when one says, 'The whole house is worth a hundred marks.'

[7i. Rule 3]

Again, this first rule is given [regarding universal affirmative signs]:

> [Rule 3] *When a universal affirmative sign is added to a term that has two kinds of parts under it – species and individuals – the sign can distribute the term for the species or for the individuals, or for the proximate parts or for the remote parts, or for the single things belonging to the genera or for the genera of single things*

(the way it is usually applied to the proposition 'Every soul exists in you.') Notice also that saying 'species,' 'proximate parts,' and 'genera of single things' is the same; for species are called the proximate parts of genera because a genus is said of the species first and is said of the individuals via the species. Species are called genera of single things, however – i.e., of singulars – because singulars are under species just as species are under genera. Likewise, saying 'individuals,' 'remote parts,' and 'single things belonging to the genera' is the same; for individuals are more remote from the genus than the species are, and yet they participate in the genus only via the species. They are called 'single things belonging to the genera,' however, because the single things have the relationship to the species that the species have to the genus.

[7j. Adaptive Distribution]

Again, it is important to know that a universal sign sometimes produces adaptive distribution. Distribution is said to be adaptive when the common term to which the universal sign is added [is] restricted neither by means of any adjective nor by means of any modifying clause [and] is interpreted not for all its supposita but for some. For example, when one says, 'Every man is afraid at sea,' 'man' does not supposit here for all its supposita but only for those who are at sea; for the sense of it is this: every man who is at sea is afraid at sea. But this sort of distribution is called adaptive – i.e., [it has been] adapted – because strictly speaking no such distribution ought to belong to a term in such circumstances, but it has been adapted to it in order that a locution that is considered true in ordinary discourse might be true, a locution that would otherwise be false.

[7k. Distribution in Connection with Oblique Cases]

{233} Because a universal sign is added not only to a term in the nominative case but also [to a term] in an oblique case, the question arises whether a sign taken in an oblique case indicates the quantity of a proposition as it does when it is taken in the nominative. Take, for example, 'Socrates sees every man.' What is its quantity?

It seems to be singular. For a proposition in which a discrete term is the subject is a singular proposition; but a discrete or singular term is the subject in this proposition; therefore, it is singular.

And yet it seems it is universal. The syllogism 'Every man Socrates sees, Plato is a man; therefore Plato Socrates sees' is good, but no [good] syllogism is made without a universal proposition. But that is a [good] syllogism, and so there is a universal proposition in it. But there isn't any except 'Every man Socrates sees' (or vice versa). Therefore, it seems to be a universal proposition.

In reply we have to say that 'Socrates sees every man' (and any

proposition of that sort) can be taken either in the role of a statement or in the role of a proposition, as is clear from the fact that
both the principles of a statement and the principles of a proposition
are found in it. (The principles of a statement are a name in the
nominative case and a verb or some grammatical form of a verb, as
is explained in *De interpretatione* (5, 17a10).) Therefore, since there
are a name in the nominative case and a verb in 'Socrates sees every
man,' it has the principles of a statement. On the other hand, it has
the principles of a proposition insofar as a proposition is either a
beginning ((*primum/principium*)) and a middle, or a middle and an
end. For, since a syllogism is made up of propositions, the parts of
a syllogism and of a proposition are the same. But the parts of a
syllogism are the beginning ((*primum/principium*)), the middle, and
the end – i.e., the major extreme, the minor extreme, and the
middle term, as we find in *Prior Analytics* (I 4, 25b31–34). Thus,
since the major extreme and the middle term occur in the major
proposition, the principles ((*principia/principium*)) of the major proposition are the beginning and the middle; but since the minor
extreme and the middle term occur in the minor proposition, its
principles are the middle and the end. Therefore, since 'Socrates
sees every man' can be a major proposition (as was seen in the
complete syllogism), it has in itself a beginning and a middle,
which are the principles of a proposition.

That ['Socrates sees every man'] can be taken in the role of a
statement and in the role of a proposition is clear on the basis of
another argument also. According to Aristotle in *De interpretatione*
(4, 17a3), a statement is an expression signifying what is true or
what is false. Therefore, since the expression 'Socrates sees every
man' is of that sort, it can be taken in the role of a statement. {234}
But it is a proposition when it is put into an orderly arrangement to
imply some proposition or conclusion; and since it is of that sort
((*huiusmodi/huius*)) (because, as we saw, it can be the major proposition in a syllogism), it is clear that it can be taken in the role
of a proposition.

Therefore, when one asks regarding 'Socrates sees every man'
what quantity it is, it must be said that if it is taken in its role as a
statement, it is singular; because when it is taken in that way the
subject in it is a discrete term. But when it is taken in its role as a
proposition, it is universal; because when it is taken in that way it is

possible to syllogize on the basis of it. (Syllogizing cannot be done without a universal proposition, and there is no universal proposition besides it in the syllogism presented above.)

[Both] the arguments that have been presented conclude correctly, therefore; for they work in different ways. The first of them concludes that ['Socrates sees every man'] is singular considered in its role as a statement, whereas the second concludes that it is universal considered in its role as a proposition. And so both of them have to be granted.

And it should be noted that when 'Socrates sees every man' is taken in its role as a statement, the subject is a name in the nominative case; and because in a statement the subject occupies the first place, the statement must be organized in such a way that the name in the nominative case is put first: 'Socrates sees every man.' On the other hand, when it is taken in its role as a proposition, 'man' (*hominem*) is the subject; for, as we saw in the syllogism presented above, 'man' (*hominem* or *homo*) is the middle, but according to the arrangement of the first figure, the middle is what serves as the subject in the first proposition and is predicated in the second. Therefore, since 'man' (*homo*) is predicated in the second proposition, 'man' (*hominem*) must serve as the subject in the first; and in that case it is to be organized by putting 'man' (*hominem*) before [the verb]: 'Every man Socrates sees.'

It should also be noted that when the expression under discussion is a statement it derives its quantity from [a term in] the nominative case, but when it is a proposition it derives its quantity from [a term in] an oblique case. Thus, it is important to know in general that every statement derives its quantity from [a term in] the nominative case, since it derives its quantity from the subject, and in a statement the subject is always a name in the nominative case. A proposition, on the other hand, derives its quantity sometimes from [a term in] the nominative case, sometimes from [a term in] an oblique case. The reason for this is that a proposition is a positing for something else – viz., for the sake of acquiring [something else] – or a positing for the sake of concluding something else. Thus, a proposition indicates an ordered relationship to something else. And since a proposition is sometimes relative to something else by reason of [something in] the nominative case and sometimes by reason of [something in] an oblique case, it derives its quantity sometimes from [a term in] the nominative case, sometimes from [a term in] an oblique case. For when one says, 'Every man is running, Socrates is a man; therefore, Socrates is running,' the major is in an ordered relationship to the others by reason of [a term in] the nominative case. But when one says, 'Every man Socrates sees, Plato is a man; {235} therefore, Plato Socrates sees,' the major is in an ordered relationship to the others by reason of [a term in] an oblique case.

[8. Relation]

[8a. Aristotelian Relatives]

Next we have to consider relation. And the first thing to learn is that in one way 'relation' is applied to a reciprocal connection of certain things that have a mutual dependence on one another. In the *Categories* (7, 6a36) Aristotle takes relatives in accordance with 'relation' used in that way, relatives being defined as follows: Relatives are those things whose essence is that they are said of other things, and whose being is to be associated with something else. For relatives are those things that both as regards being and as regards speaking have a dependence on something else.

Some relatives of the sort just presented have to do with superiority ((*superpositionis/suppositionis*)) – e.g., 'father,' 'master,' since they imply a certain dignity because of which they are placed over others. Others, such as 'child' and 'servant,' have to do with subordination, since they imply a kind of subjection because of which they are made subject to others. Still others are of equal status – e.g., 'companion,' 'friend,' 'alike,' 'unlike' – since they are imposed as a result of some quality that is predicated equally of ((*de/ab*)) the things in which it is; and it is because of that special character that they are called relatives of equal status. We are not concerned here with relation or with relatives as spoken of in those ways.

[8b. Calling to Mind What has Gone Before]

In another way 'relation' is applied to a calling to mind of a thing that has gone before. A relative that calls to mind what has gone before is considered in accordance with 'relation' taken in that way;

for there is a relative that makes mention of that which was put before it, and it is in that way that 'relative' and 'relation' are taken by philosophers. And it is in that way that we intend to discuss relation and relatives here, because relatives of that sort often cause difficulty in sophismata, and so learning about them is useful for logic.

[8c. Relatives of Substance and of Accidents]

Some relatives of the sort just described are relatives of substance, others are relatives of accidents. Relatives of substance are those that indicate that the calling to mind has to do with a substance that has gone before; relatives of accidents are those that hark back to accidents that have gone before.

Some relatives of substance are names, such as 'who' (*quis*) or 'the one,' 'the other' (*alius*); others are pronouns, such as 'himself' (*ipse*) or 'he' (*ille*).

[8d. Relatives of Identity and of Diversity]

Again, one sort of relative of substance is the relative of identity, such as 'who' (*qui*), [and] the other is the relative of diversity, such as 'the other' (*alius*). There is a difference between the relative of identity of substance and the relative of diversity, however, because the relative of identity of substance refers to numerically the same substance as is conveyed by the antecedent and supposits for it. Thus, it refers to its antecedent and supposits for numerically the same thing as its antecedent supposits for. For when one says, 'Socrates is running, {236} who disputes,' the relative 'who' refers to Socrates and supposits for Socrates; for the sense is this: Socrates is running, who disputes – i.e., Socrates is running and ((*et/qui*)) Socrates disputes. On the other hand, the relative of diversity of substance supposits for something other than its antecedent even though it refers to its antecedent. For when one says, 'Socrates is running and the other is disputing,' 'the other' refers to Socrates but supposits for someone other than Socrates; for the sense is this: Socrates is running, and someone other than Socrates is disputing – e.g., Plato or any of the others.

[8e. A Problem Regarding Such Relatives]

Someone will say that the familiar line 'Woman, who has damned us, has saved us' is taken as true, but it can be so only if the relative 'who' supposits for something numerically distinct from its antecedent, since Eve damned us but the Virgin Mary saved us. Therefore, since 'who' is a relative of identity of substance, it seems that a relative of substance does not supposit for numerically the same thing as its antecedent supposits for – which is contrary to the things said before. One can speak in the same way in connection with these: 'Wood was the cause of death, and it was the cause of life'; similarly, 'Man sinned, and he redeemed'; similarly, 'My hands, which made you, have been pierced with nails.'

[8f. Simple and Personal Relation]

In reply to this we have to say that there are two sorts of relation: simple and personal. Now a relation is said to become simple when a relative and its antecedent do not supposit for numerically the same thing but for something the same in species, as is clear in the foregoing examples. That relation is called simple, however, in that it occurs because of the species that is shared by what the relative supposits for and what the antecedent supposits for; but a species is a form, and a form is simple and indivisible ((*indivisibilis/individualis*)), and so a relation brought about on the basis of a species is called simple.

On the other hand, it is called personal when the relative and the antecedent do supposit for [numerically] the same thing, as when one says 'Socrates is running, who disputes.' Now, that relation is called personal because it occurs on the basis of a suppositum, but a suppositum is the same as a person, or is considered in its likeness to a person (as was maintained above in the treatise on suppositions). And so a relation brought about on the basis of a suppositum is called personal.

Now, what was said to begin with in assigning the difference between the relative of identity and the relative of diversity is understood to apply when a personal relation occurs. On the other hand, the counterinstances offered apply when a simple relation occurs. For that reason there is no contradiction.

Notice, however, that, strictly speaking, a relative of identity of substance and its antecedent always supposit for numerically the same thing; if it is done otherwise, it will not be strictly correct. Thus, all those [propositions] in which a relative of identity of substance and its antecedent supposit for things numerically distinct are not strictly correct. Nor are such [propositions] to be brought together in a consequence – i.e., they are not to be accepted among people speaking in an ordinary way. {237}

[8g. Simple and Personal Demonstrativity]

Notice in this connection that just as relation is said to occur in two forms – simple and personal – so also demonstrativity. Personal demonstrativity occurs when a certain suppositum is indicated by a demonstrative and no suppositum other than the one indicated by that demonstrative is understood through it – e.g., if one says 'This one is Socrates,' Socrates having been indicated by the demonstrative. On the other hand, there is simple demonstrativity when a certain suppositum is indicated by a demonstrative but a suppositum other than the one indicated by that demonstrative is understood through it, the other one being nevertheless alike in species with the one that is indicated by the demonstrative. For example, if someone says 'This herb grows in my garden,' having indicated by the demonstrative a sage plant growing in someone else's garden, the sense is this: This herb – viz., one just like this one in species and nature – grows in my garden.

[8h. Reciprocal and Nonreciprocal Relatives]

Again, some relative pronouns are reciprocal and others nonreciprocal. A reciprocal relative is one that is always placed in the same clause as its antecedent, as when one says 'Socrates sees himself.' A nonreciprocal relative is one that is never placed in the same clause as its antecedent, as when one says 'Socrates is running; Plato sees him'; for 'him' is a nonreciprocal relative, but it is nevertheless referred to Socrates.

And it should be noted that a reciprocal relative is the same as its passive since it refers to a substance that is a patient relative to itself. For when one says 'Socrates is beating himself,' the same substance is both the agent and the patient of that beating. Thus 'himself' is a reciprocal relative.

[8i. Relative Pronouns as Relatives of Identity]

Again, it is important to note that every relative pronoun is a relative of identity and none is a relative of diversity. The reason for this is that every diversity stems from form, and no pronoun is imposed on the basis of any quality or any form; for a pronoun signifies the subject without any quality. And so no pronoun conveys any diversity, and for that reason no pronoun could be a relative of diversity.

[8j. Relative Pronouns as Relatives of Substance]

Notice also that every [relative] pronoun is a relative of substance and none is a relative of accident. And the reason for this is that every pronoun insofar as it depends on the force of the matter of the utterance signifies a substance. Thus no pronoun signifies an accident, and so no pronoun could be a relative of accident.

[8k. Relatives of Accidents]

Again, some relatives of accidents are names – e.g., 'of such a kind as' (*talis, qualis*) – and others are adverbs – e.g., 'in such a way as' (*qualiter, taliter*), 'as often as' (*quotiens, totiens*), 'when' (*quando*).

Moreover, some names that are relatives of accidents are relatives of identity – e.g., 'of such a kind as,' 'of such a sort' ((*huiusmodi, cuiusmodi/huius, cuius*)) – and others are relatives of diversity – e.g., 'other' (*alter*), 'of another sort' (*alterius modi*).

But there is the following sort of difference between a relative of identity of accident and a relative of diversity [of accident]. For a relative of identity of accident refers to an accident that is not numerically the same but the same in species or in genus. For example, when one says {238} 'Socrates is white, and so (*talis*) is Plato,' the sense is this: Whiteness is in Socrates as it is in Plato, but it is not numerically one and the same whiteness in both; rather, a whiteness that is the same in species is in both. On the other hand, a relative of diversity refers to an accident diverse either in species or in genus. For example, when one says 'Socrates is white, and Plato is other, or of another sort,' the sense is this: Whiteness is in Socrates and not in Plato; rather there is in Plato a color different in species from Socrates's whiteness.

If, however, one asks what 'so' is referred to when one says 'Socrates is white and so is Plato,' it must be said that 'so' (*talis*) is referred to 'as' (*qualis*), which is understood there. For the sense is this: As Socrates is, so is Plato. But it refers to the quality that is the same in species in Socrates and Plato; for its sense is this: As Socrates is, so is Plato – i.e., Socrates and Plato have a quality that is the same in species.

And if one asks what 'other' is referred to when ((om. *et quid refertur*)) one says 'Socrates is white, and Plato is other,' it must be said that 'other' is referred to 'white,' and it is referred to a quality other in species than the quality that is in Socrates; for the sense is this: Socrates is white, and Plato is other [- i.e.,] Socrates has such a quality – viz., whiteness – but Plato has a quality other in species than whiteness (such as blackness or any of the others differing from whiteness in species).

[8l. Relatives of Quality and of Quantity]

[8l(i). Description and Examples]

Again, some names that are relatives of identity of accidents are relatives of quality – e.g., 'of such a kind as' (*talis, qualis*) – and others are relatives of quantity – e.g., 'as much as' (*tantus, quantus*) – and still others are relatives of discrete quantity – e.g., 'as many as' (*tot, quot*).

[8m. Mutual Relatives]

It is important to notice also that some relatives are mutually relative – e.g., ['he' and] 'who,' and likewise 'so' and 'as,' and the like. They are called mutually relative because the one refers to the other and vice versa. For when one says 'He who is running disputes', 'who' refers to 'he,' and 'he' refers to 'who.' In the same way, when one says 'As Socrates is, so is Plato,' 'as' refers to 'so' and vice versa.

[8m(i). Objection 1]

But it seems that 'who' and 'he' cannot mutually refer to each other when one says 'He who is running disputes.' For a relative is taken on the basis of an antecedent, and so, if the one refers to the other and vice versa, the one will be the antecedent of the other and vice versa. Therefore, the one will be taken on the basis of the other and vice versa, and so each of the two will be that which terminates and that which is terminated – which seems impossible.

[8m(ii). Objection 2]

Again, a relative is posterior to its antecedent. Therefore, if one refers to the other and vice versa, each of the two will be both prior and posterior – which seems to be impossible.

[8m(iii). General Reply]

In reply we have to say that a mutual relation is of course possible; for it is indeed possible that the one relative produces the other's dependence and vice versa. This is clarified by an example of two {239} very long pieces of wood; for if one of them is erected by itself, it will not be able to stand erect unless it is fastened to the earth or supported by something standing. Nevertheless, if the top of the one piece of wood is supported by the top of the other piece of wood, the one will hold the other, and the one will stand erect in virtue of the other in such a way that neither can do it alone although they can do it when both are applied at once. In the same way, even though the one relative cannot be placed in the locution alone without an antecedent terminating it, when two relatives that have a mutual correspondence are placed in the locution, the one is terminated by the other by the application of the one to the other. In that way, then, a mutual relation is ((*est/et*)) possible.

[8m(iv). Reply to Objection 1]

In reply to the first objection we have to say that it is indeed true that each of the two is both terminating and terminated, but not in the same way. And, although it would be absurd for the same thing to be both terminating and terminated in the same way, it is not absurd if these things are done in different ways. It is clear that this happens in that way when one says 'He who is running disputes': 'He' terminates 'who' and is terminated by 'who,' and likewise vice versa. But 'he' terminates 'who' as regards a definite suppositum, whereas 'who,' because of the action belonging to [the verb] adjoined to it, terminates 'he' as a quality does. Accordingly, 'he' terminates as a suppositum does and is terminated as by a quality, whereas 'who' terminates ((*finiens/finies*)) as a quantity does but is terminated as by a definite suppositum.

[8m(v). Reply to Objection 2]

In reply to the other [objection] we have to say that as regards relatives that depend on antecedents and are terminated by antecedents it is of course true that the relative is posterior to its antecedent; but that is not true as regards relatives that depend on things subsequent to them and are not terminated by antecedents, since as regards those that are mutually relative both do not depend on an antecedent, nor are both terminated ((*finitur/finiuntur*)) by an antecedent. Instead, the one depends on something subsequent to it and is terminated ((*finitur/finiuntur*)) by that subsequent thing, and that one is prior; whereas the other depends on an antecedent and is terminated by an antecedent, and that one is posterior. In this way, then, where mutual relatives are concerned it is not that both are prior and posterior, but that one is prior and the other posterior. This is evident. When one says 'He is running who disputes,' 'he' signifies a substance that seeks to be made definite by what follows. It is for that reason that it is terminated by the subsequent thing to which it refers. 'Who,' on the other hand, signifies a substance that seeks to be made definite by that which is antecedent to it; it is for that reason that it is terminated by the antecedent to which it refers.

Notice also that where mutual relatives are concerned, the one that depends on a subsequent thing has the place and nature of an antecedent, whereas the one that depends on an antecedent rather has the place and nature of a relative.

[*8n. A Rule Regarding Relatives of Identity*]

[*8n(i). Rule 1*]

Again, it is important to know that this is a rule:

> [Rule 1] *A relative of identity related to a common term refers to it in the same way as to its antecedent.*

[*8n(ii). A Relevant Observation Regarding Common Terms*]

It is important to know, however, that a common term can {240} be taken in three different ways: for the utterance, for a suppositum or for an appellatum, and for the concept or for the form. And so there is this verse:

Now an appellatum, now itself, now the thing signified the word supposits. Each one is threefold then.

That is, a word or common term supposits now an appellatum – i.e., it is sometimes interpreted for an appellatum [or suppositum] – now it supposits itself – i.e., it is sometimes interpreted for itself, or for its utterance – now it supposits the thing signified – i.e., it is sometimes interpreted for the thing signified, which is to say, for the concept or for the common form it is imposed to signify; for 'man' is a name proper to a species, whereas 'animal' is a name proper to a genus. Therefore ((*ergo/enim*)), each common term can be interpreted in three different ways.

[*8n(iii). Relatives of Identity in the Light of this Observation*]

And so when a relative refers to a common term only ((*tantum/ terminum*)) insofar as it is taken for its utterance, it refers to it for the utterance, as in this case: 'Man is a monosyllable, and it is common in gender.' On the other hand, if it refers to a common term taken for a suppositum, it refers to it for the suppositum, as in 'A man is running who disputes.' But if it refers to a common term taken for the concept, it refers to it for the concept, as in 'Man is a species, and it is most specific.'

In this connection it should be noted that [when] some predicate suited to a common term is attributed to it under one interpretation, it is necessary that the relative clause attributes to it a predicate suited to it under the interpretation under which [the term] occurred as its antecedent; otherwise the locution will be false. Thus, if one attributes to a common term interpreted for the utterance some predicate that is suited to it [interpreted] for a suppositum, the locution will be false – e.g., if one says 'Man is a monosyllable, and he is running.'

[80. Rule 2]

Again, one should know that this is a rule:

> [Rule 2] *If two antecedents are placed before a relative, the locution is ambiguous in that the relative can refer to either one or the other.*

For example, when one says 'A man is not a donkey, and he is rational,' 'he' can refer to 'man' (in which case it is true) or to 'donkey' (in which case it is false). And it can be said that this ambiguity gives rise to the fallacy of equivocation; for since a relative derives its signification from its antecedent and signifies the same as its antecedent, insofar as it refers to different things it signifies different things; but ((*autem/ergo*)) equivocation is caused by diverse signification.

But notice that a relative must not for this reason be said to be equivocal in its own right; for there are many locutions in which relatives occur where there is nevertheless no equivocation. Therefore, because a relative derives that ambiguity from the nature of the different antecedents {241} to which it refers, the relative must be said to be equivocal not in its own right but by the nature of the different antecedents to which it refers. Therefore, it is not equivocal unless it refers to different things.

[8p. Replacing Relatives with Their Antecedents]

Again, it is important to know that this is a rule:

> [Rule 3] *Since a relative depends on the antecedent it refers to ((om. denotat)) and by which it is terminated, analogously a proposition in which a relative is used depends on a proposition in which the antecedent is used.*

And one cannot judge the quantity of a proposition that starts with a relative – i.e., in which a relative is the subject – except on the basis of a judgment regarding the quantity of a proposition in which the antecedent occurs in the subject position, since the relative proposition has the quantity [of the proposition] in which the antecedent occurs in the subject position. If, however, we want to take the contradictory of a proposition in which a relative occurs in the subject position, we should first take the contradictory of one in which the antecedent occurs in the subject position; and then we should take the contradictory of the proposition in which the relative occurs in the way we take the contradictory of the proposition in which the antecedent occurs. For example, if one says 'Every man is running, and he disputes,' we must take the contradictory of 'he disputes' just as we take the contradictory of 'Every man is running,' by putting a negation before the whole proposition, saying 'Not every man is running.' And the reason for this is that the antecedent may be put in place of the relative; for if one says 'Socrates is running, and he disputes,' the antecedent may be put in place of the relative: 'Socrates is running, and Socrates disputes.' On this basis, then, the antecedent may be put in place of the relative.

It seems that the same judgment must be made regarding the quantity of a proposition in which the antecedent is used and [the quantity] of a proposition in which a relative is used if both [the antecedent and the relative] occur in the subject position. The reason the subject position [is specified] has already been mentioned. For if the antecedent occurs in the subject position but the relative does not (or vice versa, so that the antecedent occurs in the predicate position and the relative in the subject position), the proposition in which the relative occurs could be of a quantity different from that of the proposition in which the antecedent occurs, as in this case: 'Socrates is running, every man sees him' and 'Socrates sees every man, he is running' (given that 'he' refers to every man).

[8q. Do Relatives Refer to Antecedents along with Their Dispositions?]

[8q(i). Introduction]

The question whether a relative refers to its antecedent along with its disposition or without it is often raised. And because one sort of relative is reciprocal and another is not, let us raise this question briefly first as regards reciprocal relatives and second as regards nonreciprocal relatives.

It seems that a reciprocal relative does refer to its antecedent along with its disposition in the following way. Take, for example, the proposition 'Every {242} man sees himself,' and then ((*ergo/erga*)) let the following argument be made. A reciprocal relative takes from its antecedent a definite signification and supposition, since a relative signifies the same as its antecedent and supposits for what its antecedent supposits for; therefore, a relative must supposit for everything for which its antecedent supposits. And so if the antecedent supposits universally, so does the relative. But when one says 'Every man sees himself,' 'man' supposits universally; therefore, since 'himself' is its relative, ['himself'] refers to ['man'] universally. And so it refers to it along with its disposition.

Again, an antecedent may be put in place of its relative; therefore 'every man' may be put in place of 'himself.' And so to say 'Every man sees himself' is the same as to say 'Every man sees every man.' But in that way the antecedent is repeated together with its disposition, and so it is also referred to along with its disposition.

On the contrary, if we suppose ((*posito/positio*)) that every man sees himself alone, 'Every man sees himself' is true (as is evident if it is proved inductively). But in that case ((*tunc/cum*)) it is not the same to say 'Every man sees himself' and 'Every man sees every man.' Therefore, it seems, 'himself' does not refer to 'man' along with its disposition.

In reply to this we have to say that a reciprocal relative sometimes refers to a discrete term. In that case it does refer to its antecedent along with its disposition, and then it is indeed all right to put the antecedent in place of the reciprocal relative. For example, if one says 'White Socrates sees himself,' that is the same as 'White Socrates sees white Socrates.' On the other hand, sometimes a reciprocal relative refers to a common term, and in that case the common term is taken either universally or not. If not, it is indeed all right to put the antecedent [in place] of the reciprocal relative, and it does refer to its antecedent along with its disposition. For example, if one says 'A white man sees himself,' that is the same as 'A white man sees a white man.' But if the common term to which it refers is taken universally, then the reciprocal relative refers to its distributed antecedent singularly or one by one for each and every one of the single things. And it does supposit for everything for which its antecedent supposits, but not in the same way; for the antecedent supposits universally under the aspect of the common, whereas the reciprocal relative refers to the antecedent for each and every [member] of the universality under the aspect of the discrete. And because the reciprocal relative does not supposit in the same way as its antecedent taken universally, in this case the reciprocal relative does not refer to the antecedent along with its disposition, nor can the antecedent be put in place of the relative.

The reason the reciprocal relative does not refer to the antecedent taken universally under the aspect of the common but refers to it under the aspect of the discrete for each and every [member] of the universality is this: Because of its reciprocal character a reciprocal relative conveys the greatest distinctness {243} and definiteness. The fact that the reciprocal relative has an unusual declension, which no other third-person pronoun has, is an indication of this; for ((*enim/autem*)) the unusual declension is caused by the determinacy and definiteness. And since separateness is incompatible with commonness as it is expressed by means of a universal sign, a reciprocal relative does not refer to a common term taken universally under the aspect of the common but rather refers to it in the way described. And so it is evident that a reciprocal relative sometimes refers to its antecedent along with its disposition and sometimes does not.

The last argument produced on that side must be granted; for it proves that a reciprocal relative does not refer to an antecedent taken universally along with its disposition, and that is true.

In reply to the first argument on the other side, we have to say that it is indeed true that a reciprocal relative gets its definite signification and supposition from its antecedent and so supposits for everything for which its antecedent supposits, and yet, as we have seen, not in the same way, since the nature of distinctness is an obstacle to that. And so it does not follow that a reciprocal relative supposits universally as its antecedent does, but rather singularly.

In reply to the other argument, we have to say that it is of course
true as regards a nonreciprocal relative, since its antecedent may be
put in place of it. It is of course likewise true as regards that
reciprocal relative when it refers to a discrete term and to a
common term that is not taken universally. But it is not true as
applied to a reciprocal relative when it refers to a common term
taken universally, since, as is clear enough, the nature of distinctness is an obstacle to that.

[8q(iii). The Question as Regards Nonreciprocal Relatives]

The next question is whether a nonreciprocal relative refers to its
antecedent along with its disposition.

And it seems that it does so. 'This man is white, and he is black'
is impossible in that it indicates that what is white is black at one
and the same time, which is impossible. But if the relative refers to
its antecedent without its disposition, the proposition could be true
now; because in that case what would be expressed by it is not
literally that what is white is black, but rather that a man is white
and that a man who is not under whiteness is black – which is of
course possible. Nevertheless, it is absurd that a proposition that is
impossible can be true, and so that from which it follows will be
absurd; but it does follow from the claim that a relative refers to its
antecedent without its disposition. And so it would always refer to
it along with its disposition.

On the contrary, there is an extrinsic disposition – e.g., 'white,'
'every,' and the like, which are expressed extrinsically by utterances
– but there is also an intrinsic disposition, such as a grammatical
case, since a case is a disposition of a substance in relation to an
action. Then one argues as follows: A relative does indeed refer to
its antecedent without its intrinsic disposition – i.e., under a case
other than ((*quam/quem*)) the antecedent had – {244} as when one
says 'Socrates is running, I see him.' Therefore, [by the Topic] *from
a similar*, it could refer to its antecedent without its extrinsic
disposition because it does not always refer to it along with its
disposition.

In reply to this some people say that there are two kinds of
dispositions, since one sort of disposition is absolute and the other
is relative. The absolute sort is ((om. *quedam dispositio absoluta et*

quedam respectiva; absoluta est [rep.])), for example, 'white,' 'black,' and the like – those that dispose the subject in itself and absolutely, not in relation to the predicate. Therefore, these people say that a relative refers to its antecedent along with its absolute disposition. A relative disposition is, for example, 'every,' 'no,' and the like – those that do dispose the subject in relation to the predicate. And it is not necessary that a relative always refer to its antecedent along with its relative disposition; instead, sometimes it does so and sometimes it does not, depending on the requirement of the locutions in which such a disposition occurs.

Nevertheless, one can reply otherwise, and better, as follows. A nonreciprocal relative of identity of substance always refers to its antecedent along with its disposition, whether it is absolute or relative, when a personal relation is in effect. For there seems to be no reason why it must refer to its antecedent with an absolute disposition more than with a relative disposition, and so if it refers to the antecedent with an absolute disposition, it would refer to it with a relative disposition as well. The reason for this is the one Priscian suggests in the first book of *Priscian minor* [XVII, 56.20–57.20], in the passage 'Now determination occurs to a pronoun, etc.' But relatives were invented to dispel ambiguity and to produce definiteness; for if one says 'Ajax came to Troy; Ajax fought bravely,' there is some doubt whether the same Ajax is meant since there were two men named Ajax, and it is possible to understand the action of one of them as belonging to the other. But when one says 'Ajax came to Troy, and the same fought bravely,' it is definite that those two actions are understood regarding the same Ajax in virtue of the relative serving as an appositive there. For a nonreciprocal relative of identity of substance in a personal relation refers to its antecedent, and such a relative and its antecedent supposit for numerically the same thing. Therefore, since a disposition does not introduce something numerically the same ((*idem in numero/in numerum*)) as that which it disposes – rather, the antecedent and its disposition are the same as a subject and its accident – a relative either refers to the antecedent attributed to it without its disposition, or with the disposition that disposes it, whether that disposition is absolute or relative. Thus, when one says, 'A white man is running, and he disputes,' the sense is this: A white man is running, and this white man disputes; similarly, when one says 'Every man is

running, [and he disputes,' the sense is this: Every man is
running,] and this one – {245} every man running – disputes. The
argument that proves this must be granted.

   In reply to the argument on the other side we have to say that
there is no similarity between the grammatical case, which is an
intrinsic disposition, and the extrinsic disposition that is 'white,'
'black,' 'every,' 'no,' and the like ((*consimilia/comsimilis*)); for a
change of case does not change numerical identity – instead, a thing
remains numerically the same ((*eadem/eodem*)) under various cases.
On the other hand, a change of extrinsic dispositions does change
numerical identity. And because it is required that a relative and its
antecedent supposit for numerically the same thing, as we have
seen, a relative can indeed refer to its antecedent under another case,
since numerical identity can indeed occur together with that change
of case. But it cannot refer to [its antecedent] under a different
extrinsic disposition, since numerical identity does not remain
together with that disposition of change or change of extrinsic
disposition. Therefore, neither can the relative refer to its antecedent without that extrinsic disposition, because that disposition
accompanies something numerically the same as the antecedent to
which the relative refers. But the relative and its antecedent must
supposit for what is numerically the same, which could not happen
if [the relative] referred to [the antecedent] without its disposition.

5

ANONYMOUS
SYNCATEGOREMATA MONACENSIA

Introduction

Syncategoremata Monacensia is an introductory treatise on syncategorematic words. It seems to have been written in England and probably dates from the last quarter of the twelfth century.

The basic, grammatical distinction between categorematic and syncategorematic words seems to have been that a word that can by itself serve as the subject or predicate of a sentence is categorematic and others are syncategorematic. Although there are some notable exceptions, in general these categorematic words are substantival and adjectival names, pronouns, and verbs (except auxiliary verbs), and syncategorematic words are all the others – e.g., conjunctions, adverbs, and prepositions.

Only some of those grammatically syncategorematic words were of interest to logicians – those whose inclusion in a proposition alters the inferential force of the proposition. But the logicians' list of syncategorematic words also included some grammatically categorematic words that have that sort of effect.

The treatise translated here discusses the logician's syncategorematic words 'alone' and 'only,' 'except,' 'unless,' 'begins' and 'ceases,' 'necessarily' and 'contingently,' 'same,' 'both,' 'whole,' and 'whether.' In this early textbook there is not much philosophical discussion of the nature of these syncategorematic words or of the reasons for the ways in which they function. Instead there is a brief presentation of rules the author associates with each of the syncategorematic words.

For further reading on syncategorematic words, see CHLMP IV.11, 'Syncategoremata, Exponibilia, Sophismata.'

Syncategoremata Monacensia

[0. Preface]

{95} People who are unaware of the power of names are often victims of fallacious reasoning, as Aristotle observes in the first book of the *Sophistici Elenchi* (165a15–16). Let us, therefore, explain the powers of certain words that afflict the minds of beginners with uncertainty.

[1. 'Alone' (*solus*) and 'Only' (*tantum*)]

First, as regards the words 'alone' and 'only,' which agree in first intension, since they both indicate an adequation to something else. They differ, however, in that 'alone' indicates exclusion concerning the subject (because it is an adjectival word; for [an adjective] is inclined to establish its [corresponding] reality concerning a subject), whereas 'only' indicates exclusion of both the subject and the predicate and can determine both: the predicate in itself and the subject by reason of a tacitly understood principle.

People often ask why 'alone' is exclusive rather than inclusive. The reason is that the predicate is conjoined with the subject as a consequence not of the power of 'alone' but of the power of the verb, whereas the fact that something is excluded is a consequence of the power of the exclusive word ['alone'].

> [Rule 1.1] *If 'alone' is used together with a species term, it excludes all the other species contained under the common proximate genus.*

For example, when one says 'A man alone is running,' there must be exclusion of this sort: i.e., not a donkey, not a cow, and so on as regards the various species of animal.

> [Rule 1.2] *An exclusive word used together with an individual term excludes all [the other] individuals contained under the same proximate species.*

For example, when one says 'Socrates alone is running,' there must be exclusion of this sort: therefore not Plato, not Cicero, and so on as regards the others. {96}

> [Rule 1.3] *If an exclusive word is used together with a common term that has an accidental and a substantial form, the locution has three*

senses; for the exclusion can be assigned in respect of [i] the substantial form only, or [ii] the accidental form only, or [iii] both.

For example, in the case of 'Only a white man is running,' the sense can be [ii] 'Only a white man is running; therefore, it is not the case that a black man is running,' if the exclusion is made in respect of the accidental form. [Or] the sense can be [i] 'Only a white man is running; therefore, it is not the case that a white donkey is running,' if it is excluded in respect of the substantial form. [Or] the sense can also be [iii] 'Only a white man is running; therefore, it is not the case that a black donkey [is running],' and in that case the exclusion is made in respect of both.

[Rule 1.4] *If 'only' is used together with a numerical term, it effects an exclusion in respect of the larger, not the smaller number.*

For example, when one says 'Only three things are in here,' an exclusion of this sort must be brought about: not four, not five. But not of this sort: not two. This is because when an integral whole has been posited, each part of it is also posited.

[Rule 1.5] *It must be noted that a locution in which 'only' is used has two senses.*

For example, when one says 'Only Socrates is running,' the exclusion can be assigned either to the subject or to the predicate; in respect of the subject, as in 'Only Socrates is running, and not a donkey'; in respect of the predicate, as in 'Only Socrates is running, and he is not doing anything else.'

[Rule 1.6] *If 'only' is used together with a partitive term, the locution has two senses; for the exclusion can be assigned in respect of a particular term or in respect of an opposite sign.*

In respect of a particular term, as when one says 'Only the one of them is running,' there must be exclusion of this sort: therefore, not the other. In respect of an opposite sign, as when one says 'Only the one of them is running,' there must be exclusion of this sort: therefore, not both.

[Rule 1.7] *If 'only' is used together with a quantitative whole, it excludes other quantitative wholes.*

For example, when one says 'Only every man is running,' an exclusion of this sort is effected: therefore, not every cow, not every donkey, and so on. {97}

[2. 'Except' (*praeter*)]

Next, as regards the word 'except,' which signifies exception. Exception, however, is nothing other than the taking of a part from a whole.

> [Rule 2.1] *It must be noted that if a locution in which 'except' is used is true, the locution is false without it.*

Thus if 'Every man except Socrates is running' is true, 'Every man is running' is false.

The second rule is:

> [Rule 2.2] *The excepted thing must be included within the supposition of the term from which the exception is made.*

This is because exception is nothing other than the taking of a part from a whole.

The third rule is:

> [Rule 2.3] *A distribution from which an exception is made is immobilized by the exceptive word.*

The reason for this is that, because that from which the exception is made is posited as a whole in respect of the excepted thing, the excepted thing is taken as a part of it.

> [Rule 2.4] *A distribution is considered sometimes in itself, sometimes with regard to its parts.*

When it is considered in itself, it is immobilized by an exceptive word, as in 'Every man except Socrates is running'. When it is considered with regard to its parts, it is not immobilized – e.g., 'Every man except his foot is white.'

> [Rule 2.5] *An exceptive word tends to encounter a mobile distribution, although it then immobilizes it.*

This is because an exception tends to be made dividedly; for that reason the distribution must be made dividedly. If the distribution is made conjointly, the exception would also occur conjointly.

[3. 'Unless' (*nisi*)]

Next, as regards the word 'unless,' which is used in a statement in three different ways: {98} [i] to mark a consequence – e.g., 'Nothing is a man unless it is an animal' (i.e., if it is not an animal, it is not a man); [ii] to mark an adjunct – e.g., 'I will not give you the horse unless you come to me'; [iii] to mark an exception – e.g., 'Every man is running unless [he is] Socrates; (i.e., every man is running except Socrates).

[4. 'If' (*si*)]

Next, as regards the word 'if,' which is called continuative because it is a sign that holds propositions together in a conclusion. And it denotes antecedence, which is the relationship of the antecedent to the consequent, and does not principally signify consequentiality, since consequentiality is the relationship of the consequent to the antecedent. If it did principally signify consequentiality, it would be applied directly to the consequent.

Again, 'if' sometimes unites a dictum with a dictum – as in 'If Socrates is running, he is moving' – sometimes an attribute with an attribute – as in 'Socrates if he is running is moving.'

'If' is also used to mark an adjunct and denotes adjunction, as in 'I will not give you the horse if you will not come to me.'

Moreover, there are two ways in which one thing is said to be a cause of another: sometimes through its essence and not through anything other than itself – e.g., fire, which is a cause of heat through its essence and not through anything other than itself – sometimes through something other than itself – e.g., my going to church, which is not through its essence (i.e., necessarily) called the cause of [my] praying, but through something other than itself (i.e., contingently), namely, that I am going to church in order to pray. It is causality of this [second] sort that the conjunction 'if' indicates when it is used to mark an adjunct. When it is used continuatively, however, it indicates causality of the first kind.

[5. 'Begins' (*incipit*) and 'Ceases' (*desinit*)]

Next, as regards the verbs 'begins' and 'ceases.' They are partially {99} alike because each of them is assertive of the present, and they are partially different because the one is eliminative of the past, the other eliminative of the future. This is clear from their inter-pretation. For example, 'Socrates begins to be white' – i.e., Socrates now is white and previously was not white; 'Socrates ceases to be white' – i.e., Socrates is white and from now on will not be white. From what has been said so far the following is evident:

> [Rule 5.1] *Argumentation from an inferior to its superior or from a superior to its inferior does not follow in connection with the verb 'begins.'*

This is because 'begins' blocks the movement from an inferior to its superior by its power of negation; it is for that reason that 'Socrates begins to see Plato; therefore, Socrates begins to see a man' is invalid. On the other hand ((*autem/enim*)), it blocks the movement from a superior to its inferior by its power of affirmation, which is indefinite; it is for that reason that this does not follow: 'Socrates begins to see a man; therefore, [he begins to see] Plato.'

[6. 'Necessarily' (*necessario*) and 'Contingently' (*contingenter*)]

Next, as regards the syncategorematic words 'necessarily' and 'contingently,' we should note that 'necessarily' and 'contingently' as well as 'necessary' and 'contingent' signify the same, but differently. For 'necessary' and 'contingent' signify their corresponding realities as capable of serving as subjects and predicates, while 'necessarily' and 'contingently' signify the same things but in another way, because they signify along with [their] determination of composition and division.

We should note that 'contingent' has many significations. In one way what is not necessary is called contingent. It is described in this way by Aristotle: Since the contingent is not necessary, nothing impossible happens as a result of it (*Prior Analytics* I 13, 32a18–20). And this sort of 'contingent' is taken in three different ways. For there is [i] the contingent that happens in most cases – e.g., going grey, which happens to most men. There is also [ii] a kind of contingent that happens in a few cases – viz., its opposite, not going grey. There is also [iii] a kind of contingent that happens indifferently; {100} but what is indifferent neither is nor will be more this way than not this way, as Aristotle says in *De interpretatione* (9, 18b8–9).

Again, in another way what is actually possible is called

contingent. In keeping with this [signification] everything necessary is contingent; but it does not go the other way around – that everything contingent is necessary – because at least one contingent is subject to change – e.g., that I am seated.

We should also note that the adverb 'necessarily' has two significations. Sometimes it indicates absolute necessity, as in 'It is necessary that God exists,' and sometimes it indicates relative necessity, as in 'It is necessary that I am seated when I am seated.' (It is [also] important to know that necessity as such is twofold – relative and absolute – and [those two kinds of necessity] differ only in things themselves.)

> [Rule 6.1] *It must be noted that relative necessity does not imply absolute necessity.*

Thus the argumentation 'Socrates necessarily is seated while he is seated; therefore, Socrates necessarily is seated' is invalid; it is an instance of the fallacy [of using a term] *in a certain respect as well as unconditionally (secundum quid et simpliciter).*

> [Rule 6.2] *Absolute necessity, on the other hand, does indeed imply relative necessity.*

For that reason it is clear that 'necessary' is not equivocal, because one [sense of an] equivocal does not imply the other.

We should also note that 'necessary' as well as 'contingent' is taken for what is possible, but [in each case] something is added over and above [what is possible]. Thus what is necessary is the same as what is able to be and what is not able not to be; analogously, what is contingent is the same as what is able to be and what is able not to be.

[7. 'Same' (*idem*)]

Next, as regards the word 'same,' which is taken in three different ways in discourse.

[i] Sometimes it is taken in place of a relative [pronoun] – among grammarians, for instance – and then it has the same {101} force as 'that thing' (*illud*). And it should be used in this way in the [grammatical] construction 'Socrates sees something, and Plato sees the same' with this sense: 'Socrates sees something, and Plato sees that thing.'

[ii] In another signification in respect of which it is only a relative it belongs to the dialecticians, and it is equivalent to the [adjectival] name 'non-different' (*indifferens*). Thus it must be expounded in that way in the locution 'Socrates is the same as himself' with this sense: 'Socrates does not differ from himself.' Taken in this way, ['same'] is a name and is imposed [on a thing] on the basis of [the thing's] form – i.e., identity.

[iii] In another signification it is divisive; and in that case it sometimes divides the subject, sometimes the predicate. [It divides] the subject, for example, when one says 'They at the same time are carrying a stone' – i.e., they are carrying a stone, and at any time at which the one is carrying, the other is also carrying [it] at the same time. [It divides] the predicate, for example, in 'Socrates sees them at the same time' – i.e., Socrates sees them, and at any time at which he sees the one, he sees the other also at the same time.

As Aristotle says in the *Topics* (I 7, 103a7–9), there is sameness in genus, sameness in species, sameness in number. Those things are the same in genus that agree in genus – e.g., *man* and *donkey* in the genus *animal*. Those things are the same in species that agree in species – e.g., Socrates and Plato, which agree in the species. Those things are the same in number in which no diversity is found in counting – e.g., Marcus and Tullius. Thus if all men were counted, Marcus would never be found under another number than Tullius. (Boethius explains this word differently. He says that sameness in number is sameness in accidents [*In Porph. Isag.* I 81.25–82.3; II 235.11ff].)

In just the same way, 'different' is said in three different ways; for we speak [of things being] different in genus, different in species, [or] different in number. Those things are different in genus that are under different genera – e.g., man and whiteness. Those things are different in species that are under different species – e.g., Socrates and Brownie. Those things are different in number in which we find a difference in counting – e.g., Socrates and Plato. {102}

[8. 'Both' (*ambo*)]

Next, as regards the word 'both,' which is interpreted sometimes collectively, sometimes distributively. It is interpreted collectively when it unifies and combines the suppositions of the term to which it is adjoined into a single supposition and attributes the predicate to it conjunctively. For example, 'They both are carrying a stone' – i.e., at the same time in combination they are carrying a stone in such a way that neither of them [is carrying a stone] separately. It is interpreted distributively when it attributes the predicate to each dividedly, as in 'They both are running,' in such a way that each [is running] by himself.

But the argumentation 'They both are carrying a stone; therefore, each of them is carrying a stone' is invalid; it is an instance of the fallacy of *composition and division* because the first proposition was taken conjunctively but the second dividedly.

[9. 'Whole' (*totus*)]

Next, as regards the word 'whole,' which is interpreted sometimes collectively, sometimes distributively. When it is interpreted collectively, it does not require the predicate to agree with each part of it dividedly, but conjunctively. The proposition 'The whole house is worth a hundred pounds' is true on this interpretation, since the sense is 'The house is worth a hundred pounds, and not each part of it is worth a hundred pounds.' When it is interpreted distributively, it does require that the predicate agree with each part of it dividedly. Thus this is false: 'The whole house is worth a hundred pounds; therefore, each part of it is worth a hundred pounds'.

And we should note that the signs 'every' or 'all' (*omnis*) and 'whole' differ, because the sign 'every' or 'all' distributes for subjective parts, whereas the word 'whole' distributes for integral parts. {103}

[10. The Word '*an*': 'Whether,' 'Or,' or an Interrogative Sign]

Next, as regards the word '*an*,' which is used sometimes interrogatively, sometimes indefinitely. It is used interrogatively when one says 'Is Socrates running?' (*an Sortes currit*); it is used indefinitely when it denotes that the preceding verb is carried over, as in 'I know whether (*an*) Socrates is running.'

[Rule 10.1] *It must be noted that when* 'an' *is used twice, it disjoins the things proposed.*

For example, 'I know whether (*an*) Socrates or (*an*) Plato is running' – i.e., I know either that Socrates is running or that Plato is running.

[Rule 10.2] *When* 'an' *is used once, if it is put before an affirmative or negative universal sign, it disjoins [contradictory] opposites.*

For example, 'I know whether (*an*) every man is running' – i.e., I know that every man is running or that it is not the case that every man is running. With a negative sign, as in 'I know whether (*an*) no man is running' – i.e., I know that no man is running or I know that it is not the case that no man is running.

[Rule 10.3] *But if it is put after an affirmative or negative universal sign, it disjoins contraries.*

For example, 'I know [regarding] every man whether he is running' – i.e., I know that every man is running or that every man is not running. With a negative, as in 'I know [regarding] no man whether he is running' – i.e., I know that no man is running or that no man is not running.

[Rule 10.4] *If it is put before an affirmative particular sign or an indefinite, it disjoins things said as contradictories.*

For example, 'I know whether some man is running' – i.e., I know that some man is running or that not some (or no) man is running.

[Rule 10.5] *If it is put after an affirmative particular sign or an indefinite, it disjoins things said as subcontraries.*

For example, 'I know [regarding] some man whether he is running' – i.e., I know that some man is running or that some man is not running. {104}

[Rule 10.6] *But whether it is put before or put after a singular proposition, it disjoins things said as contradictories.*

For example, 'I know whether Socrates is running' or 'I know [of] Socrates whether he is running' – i.e., I know that Socrates is running or not running.

[Rule 10.7] *It must be noted that the word 'an' has an appellation common to affirmation and negation, and as far as that common appellation is concerned, it can be immobilized or confused.*

Thus, the argumentation 'Each of them is considering whether Socrates is running; therefore, whether Socrates is running is being considered by each of them' is invalid. For the first proposition was true, if we suppose that one of them is considering the affirmative dictum but the other the negative dictum, although in the second proposition it would be required that each of them would be considering that Socrates is running or not running. And this is an instance of univocation, since it proceeds from immobile to mobile supposition.

[11. Universality]

It should be noted that 'every' (or 'all') and 'man' are universal, but in two different ways. 'Man' is universal because it agrees with many things in such a way that it agrees with each of them; 'every' (or 'all') is universal because it makes the subject agree with the predicate universally.

6

NICHOLAS OF PARIS
SYNCATEGOREMATA (SELECTIONS)

Introduction

Nicholas of Paris was a master of arts in Paris in the middle of the thirteenth century, but little more is known about him. In the hundred years from the last quarter of the twelfth century to the last quarter of the thirteenth, syncategorematic words were recognized as a special area of study and were discussed in treatises devoted exclusively to them. The *Syncategoremata* by Nicholas of Paris belongs to this period. (For some brief remarks on the distinction between categorematic and syncategorematic words, see the Introduction to Translation 5.)

In the selections translated here, Nicholas discusses two syncategorematic words, 'whole' and 'besides.' In his brief discussion of 'whole,' he is concerned with the supposition of expressions such as 'the whole Socrates,' with the basis for the inference 'The whole Socrates is white; therefore, each part of Socrates is white,' and with the grounds on which to distinguish this inference from the fallacious inference 'The whole house costs a hundred marks; therefore, each part of the house costs a hundred marks.' His discussion of 'besides' is much longer and quite complicated. 'Besides' is what medieval logicians called an exceptive word; that is, it takes something *A* from something *B* in respect of some third thing *C*. Nicholas's discussion of 'besides' includes a general consideration of the nature of exception and the rules associated with it. He analyzes a number of illustrative sophismata, such as 'Every man sees every man besides himself.'

For further reading on this subject, see CHLMP IV.11, 'Syncategoremata, Exponibilia, Sophismata.'

Syncategoremata (selections)

'Whole'

[1. Introduction]

{432} The next word to be discussed is 'whole.' We have to see what it signifies, what its power is, and which locutions involve some difficulty as a result of including it.

[2. The Signification of 'Whole']

[2a. A Basic Observation Regarding its Signification]

The first thing to see is whether the whole 'whole' signifies something or nothing. If it signifies nothing, it is pointless to use it in a locution; moreover, in that case it would not be a part of speech. If it signifies something, then [what it signifies is] nothing but wholeness.

[2b. A Problem Resulting from that Observation]

On that basis this seems not to follow: 'The whole Socrates is white; therefore, each part of Socrates is white.' Because Socrates is not a part of himself, the term 'the whole Socrates' does not supposit for a part of Socrates; therefore 'The whole Socrates is white' must not be expounded in this way: 'Each part {433} of Socrates is white.'

Furthermore, we can correctly and properly say, 'The whole Socrates is white besides his foot.' But when an exception is made for something, the thing excepted must be included within the supposition of the term from which the exception is made. Therefore, a part of Socrates is included within the supposition of the term 'the whole [Socrates].' But it is not included within the supposition of the term 'Socrates,' because 'Socrates' supposits only for Socrates. Therefore, it is included within the supposition of the term 'whole'; therefore 'whole' supposits for the parts of Socrates.

On the other hand, 'whole' is an adjectival word, but every

adjective has the same substance as does its substantive; therefore, the term 'Socrates' supposits for Socrates. And the word 'whole' will likewise supposit for Socrates; therefore, it will not supposit for the parts of Socrates.

Again, just as one thing is referred to another through similarity, so one thing is referred to another through wholeness and part-hood. Therefore, just as 'This is similar' is incomplete because it does not say in respect of what it is called similar, so is 'The whole Socrates is white' incomplete because ['whole'] is not said there in respect of a part.

Again, some say that the word 'whole' sometimes signifies universally as 'every' or 'all' does, and so 'every' or 'all' and 'whole' differ only in that the word 'whole' distributes into integral parts, whereas the sign 'every' or 'all' distributes among recognized (*inventa*) supposita.

When a distribution is made among integral parts by means of the term 'whole,' however, as when one says 'the whole Socrates,' those parts must be understood in any utterance found [to contain that word] but they cannot {434} be understood if they are not signified; therefore, they are signified either by the term 'whole' or by the term 'Socrates.' But they are not signified by the term 'Socrates,' because 'Socrates' signifies not Socrates' parts but Socrates himself. Therefore, they are signified by the term 'whole.' Therefore, 'whole' is the same as 'each part.' Therefore, just as one says, coherently, 'each part of Socrates' and 'not each part of Socrates,' one must say 'the whole Socrates' and 'not the whole Socrates' – which is false.

[2c. Solution to the Problem]

Solution: We say that the word 'partly' signifies a part in connection with the relationship designated by the expression 'as regards' (*secundum*) (and, similarly, the adverb 'here' signifies a place in connection with the relationship signified by the word 'in'). For that reason, 'partly' has to be analyzed as 'as regards a part' (as 'here' has to be analyzed as 'in this place'). In the same way, 'wholly' signifies a part in connection with the relationship signified by the expression 'as regards' *and* in connection with universality. [So] 'partly' and 'wholly' differ only in degree of fullness. Thus, just as 'partly' has to be analyzed as 'as regards a part,' in the same way 'wholly' has to be analyzed as 'as regards each part.' (We make the same claim regarding the word 'whole,' since 'whole' and 'wholly' differ only grammatically (*in casu*).)

[3. The Power of 'Whole']

[3a. A Problem Regarding its Power]

Again, from 'The whole Socrates is white' I can infer 'Socrates as regards each part is white.' Analogously, from 'The whole house costs a hundred marks' I *cannot* infer 'therefore, each part of the house {435} costs a hundred marks.'

[3b. Solution to the Problem]

In reply to this, we have to say that the word 'whole' is sometimes taken distributively, sometimes collectively. Thus, it sometimes signifies ((om. *quoniam*)) universally and dividedly, sometimes universally and conjointly. And for that reason a [logical] descent cannot be made in connection with [its] distribution.

In reply to the question about 'The whole Socrates is white,' we say that the word 'whole' sometimes signifies wholly and is imposed in virtue of wholeness, and sometimes signifies a part universally and is imposed in virtue of a part. When it signifies wholly, however, it needs to be determined by a word designating a part. It is taken in that way when one says, 'A genus is a whole relative to a species.' But when it signifies a part universally, it does not need to be determined by a word designating a part. I say, therefore, that 'The whole Socrates is white' is not incomplete, because in it the word 'whole' is taken as regards a part.

[3c. A problem Regarding Exception with 'Whole']

Again, it can be proved that no exception can be made from the term 'Socrates.' For the expression 'any sort' signifies quality universally, and yet no exception for a quality can be made from it; thus it cannot be done in this way: 'any sort of thing besides

whiteness.' Therefore, since 'whole' is an adjectival word, no exception for a part can be made from it; for the exception cannot be
made from 'whole' joining [itself to a suppositing term] through
the suppositing term. Therefore, 'The whole Socrates is white
besides his foot' is incoherent. {436}

[3d. Solution to the Problem]

Solution: We claim that just as an exception can be made from the
word 'wholly' as regards each part, so also from the word 'whole,'
since it has the same signification.

'Besides'

[1. Introduction]

{129} Because transition is particularly easy in connection with
things that have a shared distinguishing characteristic (*simbolum*) –
i.e., with things that have some similarity to each other – now that
we have examined exclusive words, we have to examine excep-
tives, which are similar. For both the latter and the former have
negation as part of their exposition. Moreover, to exclude is to
confine something outside another thing in respect of a third thing,
and, analogously, to except is to *take* something outside another
thing in respect of a third thing.

   Therefore, we have to know what it is to except, what exception
is, which words are exceptive, and how many of them there are;
likewise, we have to know about the rules, the sophismata, and the
difficulty that occurs in association with exceptive words.

[2. Excepting and Exception]

It should be noted, therefore, that to except is (as was said) to
extract some part from its whole in respect of something else. For
that reason it is important to know that four things are necessary if
an exceptive expression is produced: [i] a whole, which is also
considered as a whole, from which the exception is made (since
nothing which is not contained in a thing can be extracted {130}

from that thing); [ii] that in respect of which the exception is made, which applies to the other parts and not to the excepted part; [iii] the excepted part, which is what we call the term designating that which is excepted; [iv] the exceptive word, by means of which the exception is made. This is evident in 'Every man besides Socrates is running' (supposing that every man other than Socrates is running and Socrates is not running): [i] the term 'every man' is the whole considered as a whole from which the part is excepted or from which the exception is made; [ii] the predicate 'is running' is that in respect of which the exception is made, which applies to the parts other than Socrates and not to Socrates; [iv] the word 'besides' is the exceptive word, because the exception is made by means of it; [iii] the name 'Socrates' (in the accusative case) is the word designating that which is excepted.

[3. The Exceptive Words]

It is important to know, therefore, that the words we use exceptively are these: 'besides' (*praeter et praeterquam*) and 'unless' (*nisi*). Of these, we first have to discuss 'besides' (*praeter*).

[4. Questions about 'Besides']

About 'besides' we have to ask what it signifies (and whether it signifies anything) and about its various uses, about the difference between it and the other exceptive words, and about the rules and sophismata that occur in association with it. {131}

[5. Does 'Besides' Signify Anything?]

The question arises, therefore, whether 'besides' signifies anything. It seems that it does. It is a part of speech, but (as Priscian says [XI 7, p. 552.1–4]) every part of speech is a word signifying a concept in the mind, and everything that signifies a concept in the mind signifies something; therefore, 'besides' signifies something.

Moreover, it is an articulate utterance put forward with a mental sense; therefore, (as Priscian says [ibid.]) it is significant.

But, on the other hand, Priscian says in the *Minor* (XVII 10, p. 114.9–20) that some words behave like consonants and others like vowels. For just as vowels make an utterance on their own, so some words signify on their own; and just as consonants do not make an utterance on their own, so some words do not signify on their own – e.g., conjunctions, prepositions, and adverbs.

Again, nothing that takes on signification from things adjoined to it signifies anything on its own, but syncategorematic words are of that sort; therefore, etc.

Again, everything signifying something signifies that which can be said of something else or of which something else can be said, but 'besides' signifies nothing of that sort; therefore, etc. {132}

It must be said that 'besides' does signify something. But signifying something occurs in two ways: either signifying something in general (a signification in accordance with which the parts of speech are distinguished from one another and each of them does signify something), or signifying something specifically (and syncategorematic words do not signify in that way, as was pointed out elsewhere). On this basis the reply to the objections raised above is evident.

It is important to know, therefore, that 'besides' has the signifying of exception for its specific signification.

[6. How Does 'Besides' Signify?]

But then the following question arises. Since everything that signifies signifies either by way of a concept or by way of an emotion, in which of those ways does 'besides' signify exception? If by way of an emotion, it seems to be an interjection, since an interjection is a part of speech signifying an emotion in the mind. If by way of a concept, then since the noun 'exception' and the verb 'to except' signify the same thing by way of a concept, what is the difference between 'besides' and the exceptive words that signify exception?

We have to say that 'besides' does signify exception by way of a concept. But signifying exception by way of a concept occurs in two ways: either signifying as a sign of a thing, or signifying as a sign of a sign. I maintain that the words 'exception' and 'to except' signify exception as a thing and are signs of it as a thing, but {133} 'besides' signifies exception in such a way that it is significant of it through another [sign]. It is a sign that an exceptive proposition associated with 'Every man besides Socrates is running' is 'Every man is running, Socrates excepted.'

[7. What is the Function of 'Besides'?]

For that reason the following question arises. Since locutions are called exceptive from [their inclusion of] exceptive words of that sort, what do those words do there? And if the answer is that they except, the question is: What is excepting? And if the answer to that is that excepting is extracting a part from a whole – e.g., when one says 'Every man besides Socrates is running' one shows by means of the exceptive word that running applies to those other than Socrates and not to Socrates ((*Sorti/sore*)) – then it seems that every exception is impossible. For every impossible expression is one that shows that the same thing both applies to and fails to apply to one and the same thing, and that proposition is such an expression. Proof: That proposition is an instance of *dici de omni*; therefore, nothing is to be taken [under the subject of which the predicate is not said]. Therefore, since Socrates is taken under the subject, the predicate ((*predicatum/predicatus*)) applies to him and to the others; but by means of the exceptive word it is shown not to apply [to Socrates].

Again, that which is Socrates either is or is not a part of that which is every man. If it is a part, it is not possible that a part insofar as it is a part be outside the whole. If it is not a part, the exceptive word is added to it incoherently, since there is a rule that {134} says that an exceptive word is to be added to a part only. It is for that reason that 'Every man besides Brownie is running' is incoherent. But if it is a part, it will also remain within the whole if the predicate ((*predicatum/predicatus*)) applies [to it] as well as to the others. And the predicate is shown not to apply; therefore, [the proposition is] false.

Again, a whole one of whose parts has been removed is restricted to the other [parts]; therefore, since there is nothing in the proposition by means of which the term 'every man' is restricted, it is clear

that it supposits for each of its parts; therefore, for Socrates. If
someone maintains the contrary because it is restricted by the
phrase 'besides Socrates,' here is a proof that it is not. No determination can be the cause of a restriction unless it determines that
which it should restrict (which is why we have the rule that the
things that are in the predicate do not restrict those that are in the
subject); but the determination 'besides Socrates' is a determination
of the predicate, because a preposition together with its object is
equipollent to an adverb, and an adverb is a verb's adjective.

[Another argument] to the same effect: Suppose that there are
only three men, and that Socrates is the one of them who is not
running, and that the other two are running. Then let 'Every man
besides Socrates is running' be proposed. And then the question
whether that proposition is coherent or incoherent arises. Proof that
it is coherent: Anything true and anything false presuppose something coherent, but this is true. Proof: When one says 'Every man
is running,' that is false, and the only counterinstance has to do
with Socrates; therefore, when an exception has been made for him,
it will be true. Therefore, 'Every man besides Socrates is running' is
true, and so it is coherent. But if the word 'Socrates' were not
within the supposition of the term 'man,' it would be incoherent by
the rule that {135} says that a common term to which a universal
sign is added requires a sufficient number of appellata, which consists in three. Therefore, it is evident that the predicate ((*predicatum/
predicatus*)) is attributed to the part Socrates and also removed by
means of the word 'besides.' Therefore, the proposition is false.

In reply we have to say that a subject can be considered in three
different ways in expressions of this sort. [i] [It can be considered
as] that which is the subject, and this in two ways: either [iA] that
which is subject to a thing (*subjectum rei*) (in which case the excepted
term does not belong to its supposition) or [iB] the subject of the
discourse (as in this case). Or [ii] [it can be considered] insofar as it
is the subject, and this in two ways: either [iiA] insofar as it harks
back to the predicate (in which case the excepted term does belong
to its supposition) or [iiB] insofar as it takes on the predicate (in
which case it does not belong to its supposition). And just as there
is opposition in something insofar as ... that which is not in it
insofar as it is universal (and vice versa), so here. For that reason it
is said that an exceptive word always implies a counterinstance to a

universal taken universally or to a whole considered as a whole, because, as Aristotle says in *Topics* VIII (2, 157b32–33), a universal is that which is found in many things in such a way that in none can a counterinstance be given; and he says that a counterinstance is given when it can be falsified for one in particular or for any one at all. Therefore, when a universal [proposition] is false for some part belonging to it, an exceptive word adjoined to that part removes the falsity. It is for that reason {136} that an exceptive word is said either to *imply* a counterinstance, (because it is a sign of the counterinstance that the falsity of the part implied), or to *remove* a counterinstance (because it removes the falsity implied by a part that was signified as having an attribute applying to it when that attribute did not apply to it).

As for the objections, [the first] is to be resolved by saying that it is an instance of *dici de omni* insofar as the subject harks back to the predicate and not insofar as it takes on the predicate.

In reply to the second, we have to say that the excepted term is a part of the subject insofar as it is [the subject] and insofar as it is a whole, but it is not a part of that which takes on the predicate insofar as it takes it on.

The reply to the fourth is evident on that basis, because it does have a sufficient number of appellata when the excepted term is a part of it.

In reply to the third, we have to say that the term is not restricted in its role as subject, but something is restricted from it insofar as it takes on the predicate.

[8. A Problem Regarding the Determination of 'Besides']

For that reason it is possible to be uncertain about what the exceptive word together with the excepted term is a determination of. For instance, when one says 'Every man besides Socrates is running,' does the determination 'besides Socrates' determine {137} the subject 'every man' or the predicate 'is running'?

It seems to determine the subject, because a part, insofar as it is a part, always has to be referred to its whole, but the excepted term is a part of the distribution 'every man'; therefore, it has to be referred to it.

Again, everything that is taken away from anything by means of some indicator must be referred to that from which it is taken away (for otherwise it would seem that nothing was being taken away from anything else, since Aristotle says [*De anima* III 6, 430b20–23] that privation must be restored by means of the possession corresponding to it); therefore, since the subject is that from which the excepted term is taken away, it must be associated with it.

Moreover, if any two things are equipollent, whatever determines the one also determines the other; but 'besides Socrates' is equipollent to 'and not Socrates,' which is arranged in the subject's position, before the verb.

If that sort of thing is said, there are the following arguments to the contrary.

If one thing is put in place of another, it must determine the same thing as that [replaced thing] determines; but a preposition together with its object is put in place of an adverb (because, as Priscian says [XIV 4–5, p. 26.4ff.], it is equipollent to it); therefore, whatever an adverb determines, a preposition together with its object must determine; but an adverb determines a verb; therefore, [etc.].

Again, a preposition implies that the substance that is its object has a persistent disposition to an action; therefore, since the verb 'is running' signifies an action, the preposition implies a disposition of its object to that action; therefore, it determines it. {138}

Moreover, as Priscian says [VIII 89, p. 440.26–28; XIV 13, p. 31.18–20], a preposition has a relationship to a nominative only in virtue of the composition [of the proposition]; therefore, the preposition cannot be referred to the nominative.

In reply to this we have to say that the exceptive word together with the term designating that which is excepted, or the determination, must be referred primarily and in itself to the thing a part of which the excepted term signifies (whether that is the subject or the predicate), but in relation to the other [term]. For by the nature of the excepted name it has reference to the whole of which it is a part, [and] by the nature of the exceptive word it harks back to the verb, to which it directs itself by the nature of the adverb to which it is equipollent.

On this basis the reply to the objections is evident: Each of the two [sides] is false, but in different respects.

[9. Rule 1]

From the things that have been said so far, the following rule can be derived:

> [Rule 1] *By means of the exceptive word the predicate is removed from the term designating the expected thing.*

Thus, when one says 'Every man besides Socrates is white,' this follows: 'therefore, Socrates is not white.'

But this rule seems to be false, because the rule must apply equally to the affirmative and to the negative if it is general; but if we suppose that Socrates and no one other than Socrates is carrying a stone, then this is {139} true: 'No man besides Socrates is carrying a stone,' from which this follows: 'Socrates is carrying a stone.' Therefore, it is clear that the predicate is not always removed from the excepted thing by means of the exceptive word.

We have to say that the sense of the rule is that what is signified by means of the exceptive word is that the predicate does not apply to the excepted term in the way it applies to the other parts of the subject from which the term is excepted. But a predicate can apply to a subject in two ways: as affirmed (and in that case the excepted thing is removed from what is affirmed, and this follows: 'Every man besides Socrates is white; therefore, Socrates is not white'), or as denied (and in that case the excepted thing is removed from what is denied, and this follows: 'No man besides Socrates is running; therefore, Socrates is not not running,' from which 'therefore, Socrates is running' follows).

[10. Rule 2]

On the basis of the things said so far it is customary to give this rule:

> [Rule 2] *An exception can be made only from a whole taken as a whole.*

For that reason we have to say that 'A man besides Socrates is running' is incoherent.

But it seems to be coherent. For as an integral whole is related to its parts, so is a universal whole to its parts; but 'The house besides

its wall is white' (*domus preter parietem est alba*) is said coherently;
therefore, 'A man besides Socrates is running' (*homo preter Sortem
currit*) is said coherently.

Moreover, the term 'Socrates' either is or is not a part of 'man.' If
it is not, then it would be incoherent to say 'every man besides
Socrates,' {140} because what was not a part could not be made a
part by means of the word 'every,' as is evident in 'Every man
besides Brownie is running.' Suppose 'Socrates' is a part of 'man';
but a part can always be excepted ((*excipi/excipere*)) from its whole;
therefore, it would be coherent to say, 'A man besides Socrates is
running.'

An exceptive word, however, is constituted in such a way that it
removes the falsity of a counterinstance to the proposition's truth;
but when some man is running and some man is not running, 'A
man is running' is true; therefore, there is no counterinstance to it
of [anything] false. Therefore, it need not be removed. Therefore,
an exceptive word is not to be added.

Moreover, there is a part only where many are considered as
many, but when one man alone is running, 'A man is running' is
true; therefore, it is clear that it does not have many. But 'is
running' has the same sense (*ratio*) if one is running or if many are
running; therefore, an exception cannot be made from it.

Moreover, it seems not to be incoherence but rather falsity. For
prepositions indicate a disposition of substances to actions, and so
when one says 'That knife is made of wool,' although 'wool,' the
object of the preposition, does not signify a material suitable for
that material object, there is no incoherence but only falsity. Therefore, *from a similar*, even though the part 'Socrates' is not taken
acceptably in that proposition under the term 'man,' the proposition
will not be incoherent but rather false.

But, on the other hand, if we suppose that Socrates is running
and Plato is not running, then 'A man is running, and not Plato' is
true; therefore, *from an equipollent*, 'A man is running besides Plato'
is also true. {141}

In reply to this we have to say that in order for an exception to be
made there must be a whole considered as a whole. For although
the word 'man' is a whole, it is only potential; but what is only
potential does not have being absolutely. Therefore, an exception
cannot be made from 'man' because it has parts only in potentiality.

Nor is it like an integral whole, from the existence of which it follows that all its parts are arranged and joined together.

In reply to the question whether it is a part, we have to say that it is a part as regards predication and not as regards aggregation; for the fact that there is a whole is enough by itself, [although] it is not enough where aggregation is concerned. For the case of a universal or predicable whole is different from the case of an aggregate whole, because for an aggregate whole the many have to be in actuality, but for a universal whole the many have to be only in potentiality or suitability (unless it has been taken universally).

In reply to the question whether it is incoherent, we have to say that it is so as regards the understanding [of it] and also, in a way, as regards the modes of signifying. For the word 'besides,' insofar as it is an exceptive word, requires a whole considered as a whole; and so there is incoherence in that case just as in 'every Socrates.'

In reply to the objection that 'A knife is made of wool' is coherent, we have to say {142} that that proposition involves no incompatibility of modes of signifying, but only the incompatibility of the things signified.

In reply to the question whether 'A man besides Socrates is running' is false, we have to say that it is neither true nor false, because it is incoherent; for truth and falsity presuppose coherence.

In reply to the proof that 'A man is running, and not Socrates' is true, we have to say that that is true because 'Plato is running and Socrates is not running' is true. (Subcontraries can stand together in that way.) And that proposition is a hypothetical and is not equipollent to the one in accordance with which it seems to be exceptive; for this one is coherent, but that one is incoherent.

[11. Rule 3]

The following rule is drawn from the preceding considerations.

> [Rule 3] *That which is excepted must be a part and be considered as a part of that from which the exception is made.*

For nothing can be extracted from that in which it does not occur.

But, on the other hand, nothing extracted from another thing is in that from which it has been extracted, but a term designating an excepted thing is of that sort because it is extracted by means of the exceptive word from the distribution from which the exception is made; therefore, the term is not in that from which it has been extracted. But it is not a part unless it is in its whole; therefore, the thing excepted {143} is not a part of that from which the exception is made.

In reply we have to say, as we have already maintained, that the excepted term is, considered absolutely, a part of that from which the exception is made. Nevertheless, the excepted part is not contained [in that from which the exception is made] as regards the reception of the predicate; and so it is contained absolutely and not in a certain respect. But there is no absurdity in something's being a part of something else absolutely and not in a certain respect.

[12. Must the Term from Which the Exception is Made Have its Greatest Number of Supposita?]

In order to clarify the things that have already been said, we can ask whether there must be the greatest number in the term from which the exception is made in order for an exception to be made, so that one could say, 'Men besides Socrates are running.'

It seems that [the greatest number] is not required. For if Socrates is running and Plato is not running, and they are indicated by the pronoun 'them,' this is true: 'Both of them besides Plato are running.' But the greatest number is not in the term 'them'; therefore, the greatest number is not required for exception.

Moreover, if two things are indicated of which one is white and the other black, this is true: 'These besides this one are white' (indicating the black one), but the greatest number is not in the term 'these'; therefore, [etc.].

Again, exception is the taking of a part from its whole, but a plural [noun or pronoun] is a whole in relation to one; therefore, when one has been taken from a plural [noun or pronoun] there will be an exception. But there is not always the greatest number in a plural [noun or pronoun]; therefore, [etc.].

No part can be excepted from its whole unless it is a part that follows from the whole, however, since an exception is a counter-instance in respect of some part. But {144} 'Men are running; therefore, Socrates [is running]' does not follow; therefore, he cannot be excepted from 'men.' But that is only because there is not the greatest number in that term, since this does follow: 'All men are running; therefore, Socrates [is running].' Therefore, the greatest number is required for exception.

We grant it, maintaining that the greatest number can be conveyed in two ways: either by reason of a distributive sign (and in that way the distributive [sign] 'both' or 'neither' does have the greatest number), or by reason of the thing that is to be made many (and it is in this way that we require the actual supposition of all the things that are actually supposited in the term, and we require it in accordance with the actual existence of singulars under the subject – at least three, and as many more as there may be).

On this basis the solution to the objections raised before is evident. For, although in a plural [noun or pronoun] at least two things are signified as far as the mode of signifying is concerned, it is not just any two things, but those that are signified in the singular [noun or pronoun] – as, for instance, what is signified in 'men' is a man and a man, not Socrates or Plato. That is why this does not follow: 'Men are running; therefore, Socrates or Plato [is running].' Therefore, likewise, neither of them can be excepted.

[13. A Problem Regarding the Quantity of Exceptive Propositions]

It is possible to be uncertain about the quantity of exceptive propositions – whether they are universal or some other quantity. For example, when one says 'Every man besides Socrates is running,' it is possible to be in doubt about its quantity.

It seems that it is not universal, since wherever there is a universal, *dici de omni* applies; but *dici de omni* applies when nothing is to be taken [under the subject of which the predicate is not said], but [in this case] something is to be taken under the subject of which the predicate ((*predicatum/predicatus*)) is not said {145} – viz., the excepted term; therefore, it is not universal.

Again, if it were universal, a syllogism could be made of it in this
way: 'Every man besides Socrates is running, but Plato is a man
besides Socrates; therefore, Plato besides Socrates is running'; but
put in that way it is incoherent. If someone says that the syllogism
must not be concluded in that way but in this way: 'therefore, Plato
is running' – on the contrary, whatever is taken under the middle
term must be taken together with the determination of the middle
(as when one says 'Every triangle necessarily has three [sides], but
an isosceles is a triangle; therefore, it necessarily has three [sides]),
but 'besides Socrates' is the determination of the middle term;
therefore, [etc.].

If for that reason someone says that it is not a universal proposition – on the contrary, it is a proposition of some quantity or other;
therefore, either universal, particular, indefinite, or singular. But it
is neither singular, nor indefinite, nor particular (as is evident regarding each of them considered singly); therefore, it is universal.

Again, the subject in that proposition is determined by a universal sign; therefore, the proposition is universal.

We grant it, maintaining that *dici de omni* does apply to it, along
with a counterinstance to the [logical] descent; and a descent can be
made under it for anything other than the thing excepted.

Therefore, in reply to the argument in opposition, that *dici de
omni* does not apply to it, we have to say that it does apply, because
it is curtailed as in adjusted distributions – e.g., in 'The sky covers
all things,' where 'all things' does not distribute for {146} each and
every thing because it does not distribute for [the sky] itself but for
other things; and so 'therefore, it covers itself' does not follow, as
was maintained in the *Distributions* ((reference not found)).

To the objection that it is not a syllogism, we have to say that it
is. For from the proposition 'Every man besides Socrates is running,' a syllogism must be made in this way: 'but Plato is a man
other than Socrates; therefore, Plato is running', since 'every man
besides Socrates' is the same as 'every man other than Socrates.' But
the fact that [the middle term] is not taken together with the
determination 'besides Socrates' is brought about not by the signified thing but by the mode of signifying, which is designed to
except from a whole considered as a whole. And it is not like the
determination 'necessarily has three [sides],' which is related uniformly to 'triangle' and to 'isosceles.'

[14. Rule 4]

There seems to be a certain rule against this:

> [Rule 4] *An exceptive word is designed to encounter a mobile distribution and render it immobile.*

The reason for this is that only a part considered as a part should be excepted. If the distribution were immobile, there would not be a whole considered as a whole; and so neither would a part be taken under it as a part. The fact that the exceptive word renders the distribution immobile is the reason why one may not descend in this way: 'Only every man besides Socrates; therefore, only Plato besides Socrates.'

Then one argues in this way: No proposition is universal if one may not move to its parts, but since ((*haec/hanc*)) 'Every man besides Socrates is running' has been made immobile by exception, one may not descend to its parts; therefore, it is not universal. {147}

Moreover, a universal affirmative ((*affirmativa/affirmata*)) to which there is a counterinstance is true when a negation is placed before it ((*praeposita/proposita*)), but when Socrates is not running and the others are running, 'Every man is running' is a proposition of that sort; therefore, 'Not every man is running' is true. But that is interchangeable with 'Some man is not running,' which is altogether immobile. But this is not universal; therefore, [neither is] the one to which it is equipollent – viz., 'Every man besides Socrates is running.'

But, on the other hand, for every proposition with a common term, either it or its contradictory is universal. Suppose, then, that 'Every man besides Socrates is running' is false. In that case 'Not every man besides Socrates is running' will be true, but neither an affirmed nor a denied singular proposition is derived from that one; therefore, it is not universal. Therefore, its contradictory is universal.

[15. Is 'Not Every Man Besides Socrates is Running' a Coherent Exceptive Proposition?]

There is a further question: whether that proposition is a coherent exceptive.

And it seems that it is. If we suppose that every man is running besides Socrates and Plato, then 'Every man besides Socrates is running' is coherent and nevertheless false; therefore, its contradictory, 'Not every man besides Socrates is running' is true. But truth and falsity presuppose coherence; therefore, it is coherent.

But, on the other hand, no exceptive proposition is coherent unless an exception is made from a whole considered as a whole, as is evident in 'a man besides Socrates' or 'some man besides Socrates.' But 'not every man' is not a whole considered as a whole, since it is the same as 'some man not'; therefore, [etc.]. {148}

In reply we have to say that 'Not every man besides Socrates is running' has two senses; for it can be either the negative of an exceptive or the exceptive of a negative. If it is the exceptive of a negative it is incoherent, because an exception cannot be made from 'not every man,' since it is not a whole considered as a whole. (It can nevertheless be said that 'Not every man is running' has two different causes [of truth]: either because no man is running, or because someone is not running. Insofar as it has this cause – that no man is running – an exception can be made from it so that the sense of 'No man is running besides Socrates' insofar as it is the sense of 'Not every man besides Socrates is running' is this: What is said by means of 'Every man besides Socrates is running' is not true, because by means of that proposition ['No man is running besides Socrates'] it is asserted that running does inhere in Socrates. In accordance with the other cause [of its truth] it was incoherent, as the opposing argument maintained.) But in keeping with the view that what we have here is the negation of an exception, it is coherent and either true or false (as the opposing argument maintained); and its sense is this: What is said by means of 'Every man besides Socrates is running' is not true.

[16. A Problem Regarding Exception from a Predicate]

[16a. The Question Proper]

Again, it is possible to be uncertain whether an exception can be made from a predicate {149} as from a subject.

[16b. Sophisma 1]

According to what is ordinarily said in connection with the sophisma

NOTHING IS TRUE UNLESS AT THIS INSTANT,

in that sophisma an exception is made from 'at this instant.'

And it is proved in this way. Whatever is true is true at this instant, and nothing is true that is not true at this instant; therefore, the first proposition ['Nothing is true unless at this instant' is true]. On the other hand, nothing is true unless at this instant; therefore, that God exists is not true unless at this instant; therefore, that God exists is not true at [an instant] other than this one – which is false. Alternatively, nothing is true unless at this instant, but that you are a donkey is not true unless at this instant; therefore, that you are a donkey is true at this instant.

But it seems that that cannot be true. For every exception is made by reason of a plurality, but every plurality occurs by reason of matter; therefore, since a predicate occurs as a form, an exception will not be made from a predicate.

Moreover, to say 'Every man is running besides this running' is to say nothing. Therefore, since an exception is not made by reason of the thing predicated, so much the less will it be made by reason of the things consignified [by the verb].

Moreover, there are many accidents pertaining to a verb, such as mood, person, and gender. Therefore, whatever reason supports making an exception in respect of time [or tense] will support making an exception in respect of the other accidents. But to say 'Every man besides a running [man] is running' is to say nothing; therefore, *from a similar*, an exception will not be made in respect of time.

Again, just as a verb has within it the things it consignifies, so does a name. But in the case of a name no exception is made in respect of the things it consignifies; therefore, {150} an exception must not be made in respect of the things consignified by a verb. For to say 'every man besides the neuter gender' or 'every man besides the plural' is to say nothing. Nor [can an exception be made] in connection with the other accidents [of a noun] in virtue of their differences [from the accidents of gender and number].

Therefore, analogously, neither must exception be made by reason of the accidents of a verb.

Again, every exception must be made from a whole considered as a whole, but the time consignified in a predicated verb is not time considered as a whole, because it is not distributed ((*distribuitur/distribuit*)), and it suppoits for a single differentia of time. Therefore, an exception cannot be made from it. That it is not distributed is evident, both because there is a rule that a universal sign distributes a term only if it is directly joined to it, and because a universal sign does not distribute accidents (but time is an accident [of a verb]; therefore, it cannot be distributed by means of the sign 'nothing'). That it suppoits for a single differentia of time is evident since one and the same verb cannot consignify various differentiae of time at once (because in that case it would be present, past, and future at once – which is impossible); therefore, it is clear that since the verb consignifies the present, it suppoits for only a single differentia of time. Therefore, the verb is not a whole considered as a whole.

Moreover, every exception must be made from a designated term. It is for that reason that to say 'besides Socrates is running' is to say nothing as long as the term 'every man' or something of the sort has not been expressed. But in 'Nothing is true unless at this instant,' we do not have the expression of a time some part of which is designated by means of what is excepted. Therefore, the exception is incoherent.

On the other hand, however, an exception can be made from a temporal whole taken as a whole, and {151} likewise from a locational whole and a whole having to do with manner. Therefore, since a verb is a whole of that sort, an exception can be made from it. That a verb is a whole of that sort is evident, for affirmative argumentation from a part to the whole follows, and negative argumentation from the whole to a part follows. And this follows: 'Socrates is running now; therefore, he is running' (running now is a temporal part, the whole of which is running *per se*); likewise, this follows: 'Socrates is running here; therefore, he is running' (and so an argument from a locational part follows); likewise: 'Socrates is running well; therefore he is running' (from a part having to do with manner). (And let the running be taken as actual.) Negatively,

however, the other way around – as in 'He is not running; therefore, he is not running well'; 'He is not running; therefore, he is not
running here'; 'He is not running; therefore, he is not running at
this time (or now).'

It is evident, therefore, that an exception can be made from a
verb in accordance with time, which is what takes place in 'Nothing is true, etc.'

In reply to the question why an exception is made by reason of
time and not by reason of the other accidents, we have to say that
this accident is unlike the others. For some accidents are made
many both in virtue of themselves and in virtue of their subjects,
but others in virtue of their subjects alone. Therefore, an exception
cannot be made with respect to those that are made many in virtue
of their subjects [alone]; [but] an exception can be made with
respect to those that are made many in virtue of themselves. Time
is of that sort, as is evident both because it is possible that there be
more than one motion in the same time (even though time is the
measure of motion), and because Aristotle indicates in the *Physics*
[cf. V 1–2, 225b7–226b8] that motion {152} is made many in three
ways. First, motion is pluralized by reason of the things that are
moving ([but] only by reason of the movable thing itself, e.g.,
when Socrates and Plato are running); second, motion is pluralized
by reason of the diversity of actions (e.g., when Socrates is digging
and plowing, the motions are diverse); third, motion is pluralized by
reason of time (e.g., when Socrates runs, [and] afterwards rests, the
motions are diverse; [and if] he rests again [and] runs again, motion
is pluralized in accordance with the same motions). (This sophisma
will be the subject of a broader discussion in what follows.)

[17. Can an Exception be Made from a Relative Pronoun Related to a Distributed Term?]

[17a. The Question Proper]

Again, it may be asked whether an exception can be made from a
relative [pronoun] related to a distributed term. The claim that it
can be is usually made in connection with the following sophisma.

[17b. Sophisma 2]

Suppose that ten are white, and that nine know themselves to be white and know nothing about the tenth. Then this is proposed:

TEN KNOW THEMSELVES BESIDES ONE TO BE WHITE.

Proof: 'Ten know themselves to be white' is false, and the only counterinstance has to do with the one; therefore, when an exception has been made for that one it will be true.

Then the following question arises: Does the pronoun 'themselves' refer to the ten besides one or only to the ten? If to the ten besides one, the sense is this: Ten besides one know ten besides one to be white. But that is {153} false, because it is true without the exception (for 'Ten know nine to be white' is true by the rule which will follow, that a proposition that is true with an exception will be false without it). If it refers ((*referat/referam*)) to the ten, the sense is this: Ten know ten besides one to be white. That is true, and it presupposes that an exception can be made from a relative.

But it seems that it cannot. For there is a rule that a relative pronoun must have a discrete and definite supposition because it signifies a discrete and definite individual, but an exception cannot be made from a singular supposition because an exception requires a whole considered as a whole; therefore, an exception cannot be made from a relative pronoun.

Again, every exception is made in virtue of some part that comes together with others in something common to them, but there is no such commonness in any pronoun (since in that case pronouns would signify quality, which is contrary to the nature of pronouns); therefore, [etc.]. That such commonness is a quality is indicated by Aristotle in *Sophistici Elenchi* (178b37–39), when he says that 'man' and everything common signifies a *quale quid*.

If for this reason someone says that no exception can be made from any relative – on the contrary: Suppose that there are only three men, who see themselves [and] one another besides one, who neither sees himself nor is seen by the others but sees the others. In that case, 'Every man sees himself besides one' is true, because 'Every man sees every man besides one' is true (which {154} is evident on the basis of its singulars). Again, 'Every man sees every man' is false, and the only counterinstance has to do with the one;

therefore, when an exception has been made for him it will be true. Therefore, the proposition is true.

We have to say that an exception can be made from a pronoun, and it can fail to be made in accordance with the requirements of discourse. It is essential to note, however, that there are many sorts of plurality. One is the sort that has not arisen from one (the sort conveyed by terms for numbers); another is the sort that has arisen from one, but in two different ways: either with respect to accident or with respect to substance. If with respect to accident, that is the way it is in collective terms. Although they signify a plurality in things, they signify [it] with a unity in the mode of signifying – viz., in the singular. If with respect to substance, then in two ways: either in accordance with form (as in distributive signs and distributed terms) or in accordance with matter (as in plural pronouns). And so we have to say that there is such a plurality in relative pronouns related to a distributed term, and that an exception can be made from them by reason of the parts in matter. And on that basis the solution to the preceding objections is evident.

[18. A Rule with Accompanying Sophismata]

[18a. Rule 5]

Again, it is ordinarily given as a rule that

> [Rule 5] *The term designating what is excepted cannot be given confused supposition by the distribution from which the exception is made.*

The reason for this is that one and the same accident cannot operate in two different things unless {155} they are united in some one thing. But the distribution from which the exception is made and the excepted part differ in character relative to the predicate; therefore, etc.

Again, the production of confused supposition is a kind of action, but (as is maintained in *De generatione et corruptione* (I 6, 322b22–25), every action [takes place] through contact ((*contactum/ contantum*)); therefore, what the sign of distribution is not in contact with, it does not produce confused supposition in. But it is not in contact with the excepted term; therefore, it does not produce

confused supposition in it. In this way the truth of the rule is
evident.

[18b. Sophisma 3]

In this connection questions are raised regarding sophismata of this
sort:

EVERY ANIMAL BESIDES THE RATIONAL IS IRRATIONAL.

Proof: 'Every animal is irrational' is false, and the only counterinstance occurs in connection with the rational; therefore, when an
exception has been made for it, the proposition will be true. Therefore, the first proposition [is true].

On the other hand, the term 'irrational' as used there does not
have confused supposition; therefore, it is taken determinately.
Therefore, it can supposit for some particular. Therefore, this will
follow: 'Every animal besides the rational is irrational; therefore,
this animal, or that one, is rational, or irrational' – which is false.

[18c. Sophismata 4–7]

The following sophismata are similar:

EVERY ANIMAL BESIDES THE MORTAL IS IMMORTAL.
EVERY ANIMAL BESIDES THE HEALTHY IS SICK.
EVERY STATABLE THING BESIDES THE TRUE IS FALSE.

Proof [of Sophisma 6]: 'Every statable thing is false' is false, and the
only counterinstance occurs in connection with the true; therefore,
when an exception has been made for it, the proposition will be
true; therefore, the first proposition [is true].

But 'Every statable thing, etc.; therefore, every statable thing
besides {156} this true one, or that true one, is false' – which is
false, no matter which true one is indicated.

This one is similar:

EVERY PROPOSITION BESIDES THE TRUE IS FALSE.

And many sophismata can be similarly constructed in connection
with all immediate contraries involving one and the same subject,
supposing the one and excepting the other.

[18d. Sophisma 6 and Rules 6–8]

In order to consider them, let us inquire into this one: 'Every statable thing, etc.' For according to the rule it appears that the term 'the true' cannot be given confused supposition by the distribution, and so the term cannot supposit dividedly for this or for that singular.

If someone should happen to say that it is confused by the exceptive word, it seems that that is false. For in virtue of a lack of differentiation an exceptive word can be added to singular as well as to common terms, which would not be done if it conveyed the mode of distribution as does ((om. *nec*)) the word 'every' or 'all.'

Again, the same thing is evident on this basis. If we suppose that every animal other than man is running, 'Every animal besides man is running' is true. But if the word 'besides' produced confused supposition in a common term, then ((*tunc/tum*)) the term 'man' would supposit for each and every man. And for that reason every man would be excepted, and in that case the expression would be false.

But it is evident that that is not true, for an exceptive word does produce confused supposition.

Again, it seems that 'Every statable thing besides the true is false' is incoherent because there is this rule:

> [Rule 6] *When something is excepted that is not a part of that from which the exception is made, the exceptive proposition is incoherent.*

But this proposition is of that sort, because nothing that is an accident of a subject is a part of it, as {157} is maintained in the *Categories* (2, 1a24–25). For the being of an accident is being in a subject, and it is impossible that the accident be without that in which it is, and the accident is not a part of it. But true and false are accidents of a statement; therefore, they cannot be excepted from a statable thing as a part from a whole.

Again, it seems that 'Every statable thing besides the true is false' is false; for there is this rule:

> [Rule 7] *An expression that is wholly false cannot be made true by means of an exception.*

But 'Every statable thing, etc.' is wholly false. Proof: There is a rule in the *Appellations* [cf. *Summe Metenses*, ed. de Rijk, p. 459] that

a common term adjoined to a present-tense verb that does not have
the power of ampliating and is taken simply is restricted to present
things. But in this expression the term 'statable thing' is taken in
that way; therefore, it supposits for existents only. And 'being' and
'true' are interchangeable; therefore, it is the same ((*idem/item*)) as if
one had said, 'Each true statable thing is false.' But that is false for
each and every part of it; therefore, it is wholly false. Therefore, an
exception cannot be made from it.

Again, it seems that it is impossible; for there is this rule:

> [Rule 8] *Whenever as many things are excepted as are supposited, the*
> *locution is impossible.*

But this proposition is of that sort. Proof: There are as many true
statable things as there are false ones – which is evident because
every statable thing has a contradictory, and every statable thing or
its contradictory is true (in accordance with the rule that says of
contradictories that it is always the case that one is true and the
other is false). Therefore, since all true things are supposited by
means of the word 'true' {158} [and] all false things by means
of the word 'statable thing,' it is clear that as many things are
supposited as are excepted.

We have to say that the first proposition ['Every statable thing
besides the true is false'] is true, and that as many true things as
false are supposited by means of the word 'statable thing,' but that
only true things are supposited by means of the word 'true' – not,
however, in personal but in simple supposition. For that reason one
may not descend to true singulars, as is done when one makes such
an argument as 'Every statable thing, etc.; therefore, besides this
true one or that true one [etc.].' Instead, there is a fallacy of *figura*
dictionis, from simple supposition to determinate or personal supposition, as in this case: 'Man is a species; therefore, some man [is a
species].' Alternatively, it can be said to be a fallacy of the consequent, because when one says 'every statable thing besides the true,'
by means of the term 'statable thing' only a statable thing that is
simply other than true (and thus false) is distributed; but when one
says 'therefore, every statable thing besides this true one,' the term
'statable thing' supposits for each and every statable thing [other]
than this one (and thus for many true ones). And so in that case
there is an inference from a lesser distribution to a greater one, as if
one were to say 'every man; therefore, every animal.'

On this basis, then, it is evident that the word 'true' is not given confused supposition either by the distribution or by the exceptive word, as the arguments prove. And so the solution of the objections is evident.

In reply to the objection that it is incoherent we have to say that it is not. For some accidents are appropriated [to certain subjects] – e.g., even and odd to number, straight and curved to line, true and false to statement, and those accidents divide a subject as {159} parts divide a whole.

In reply to the objection that it is false, we have to say that there are two things in a subject: the thing that is the subject and its character as a subject insofar as it takes on the predicate. Therefore, by reason of the thing that is the subject, the term 'statable thing' supposits the true as well as the false, and in that way the true is excepted from it as a part from a whole.

In reply to the objection that it is impossible, we have to say that it is not, because false things are supposited in it and are not excepted, but true things are excepted (as we explained a little earlier).

[19. Rule 7]

Again, we stated above a rule that is often given in connection with this syncategorematic word – viz., [Rule 7]: A proposition that is wholly false cannot be made true by means of an exception. The reason for this is that exception eliminates the falsity of a counter-instance that is in some part in respect of the whole. Therefore, when [the proposition] is wholly false, there is no counterinstance of any part against the whole – e.g., when one says 'Every man is a donkey,' it is wholly false and cannot be made true by means of an exception.

On the other hand, falsity can be removed by means of negation, but {160} exception conveys negation; therefore, falsity can be removed by means of exception. Therefore, an exception can be made in a proposition false as a whole.

Again, 'Nothing that can laugh is an animal' is false (as is evident by running through the singulars), but 'Nothing that can laugh besides a man is an animal' is true; therefore, the rule is false.

In reply we have to say that the rule is true, and that the explanation of it is sufficient.

In reply to the objections we have to say that it is true that negation eliminates falsity in the whole to which it is applied, but the negation belonging to exception is not applied to the whole but always to some part of the whole, which it extracts from it in respect of some third thing, while the remaining things to which that third thing attaches are left alone.

As for the counterinstance, it can be resolved in two ways: either by saying that the rule is to be understood as concerned with affirmatives [only] or, alternatively, that that proposition is not wholly false, because the term 'animal' is used in it, and its parts are *man*, which does attach to 'can laugh,' and *donkey* (and other animals), which do not attach to 'can laugh'; and so it is not false for each and every part of it.

[20. A Rule with Accompanying Sophismata]

[20a. Rule 8]

Again, on the basis of things already said there is this rule: {161} [Rule 8] Every false exceptive expression in which as many things are supposited as are excepted is impossible. The reason for this is that [in the expression] it is signified that the predicate inheres in the things which are supposited, but it is signified that it does not inhere in those that are excepted. This is evident. When one says 'Every man besides Socrates is running,' this follows: 'Every man other than Socrates and not Socrates [is running].' Therefore, when as many things are supposited as are excepted, it is signified that the same thing both inheres and does not inhere in the same thing – which is impossible. And as a result the rule is established.

It seems, however, that a counterinstance could be constructed in the following way.

[20b. Sophisma 8]

Suppose that there are four men, and that two of them are running whereas two are not running. Then:

ALL MEN BESIDES TWO ARE RUNNING.

Proof: 'All men are running' is false, and the only counterinstance occurs in connection with the two; therefore, when an exception has been made for them, it will be true. Therefore the first proposition [is true].

On the other hand, as many are excepted as are supposited; therefore, the locution is impossible.

We have to say that that is false, because four are supposited as far as the subject itself is concerned (as was seen above), but two in relation to the predicate. And so it is not the case that as many are supposited as are excepted.

[20c. Sophisma 9]

Alternatively, one can construct a counterinstance in this sophisma:

TEN BESIDES FIVE ARE FIVE.

Proof: 'Ten are five' is false, but with five eliminated it will be true; therefore, the first proposition [is true].

On the other hand, as many are supposited as are excepted; therefore, etc.

Alternatively, ten besides five, etc.; therefore five are not five. {162} That this follows is evident by the rule [Rule 1] that says that by means of the exceptive word the predicate is removed from the term designating the excepted thing. That is why this follows: 'Every man besides Socrates is running; therefore, Socrates is not running.'

As for the first disproof, it can be resolved as before.

In reply to the second, we have to say that the rule must be understood as applying in cases where 'besides' is interpreted exceptively and not diminutionally (as here). (This will be discussed later.)

[20d. Sophisma 10]

Again, there is another counterinstance in this form:

EACH MAN HAVING BEEN EXCEPTED, EACH MAN SEES HIM

– supposing that each man sees a man other than himself and not himself. Proof: Socrates having been excepted, each man sees him;

Plato [having been excepted, each man sees him]; and so on; therefore, etc.

   On the other hand, as many are excepted as are supposited;
therefore, [etc.].

[20e. Sophisma 11]

Taking the same hypothesis as before, this sophisma is similar:

EVERY MAN SEES EVERY MAN BESIDES HIMSELF.

The proof proceeds through the singulars, and the disproof is based
on the rule.

[20f. Reply to Sophismata 10 and 11]

We have to say that the rule is to be interpreted as applying in cases
where the same number are supposited and excepted in the same
way, but here they are supposited dividedly and excepted conjointly; and so they are not supposited and excepted in the same way.
Thus, the rule is true and the disproof is invalid. {163}

[21. Rule 9]

Again, there is this rule:

> [Rule 9] *If the exception is removed from a true exceptive proposition, a*
> *false proposition remains.*

The reason for this is that by means of the exceptive word a part
was removed to which the predicate did not apply and, once it was
removed, it was signified that the predicate did apply to that [which
was left]. For example, when Socrates is not running and the others
are running. 'Every man besides Socrates is running' is true, but
'Every man is running' is false.

   One can, however, raise an objection against this rule. While
Socrates and Plato are not running, 'Every man besides Socrates is
running' is false; therefore, its contradictory is true – viz., 'Not
every man besides Socrates is running.' But when the exceptive

word has been removed, it will be true; for 'Not every man is running' is true. Therefore, the rule is false.

We have to say that the rule is to be understood as applying when the exception is against the proposition in question; but there is no exception against 'Not every man is running.'

[22. Rule 10]

Again, there is this rule:

> [Rule 10] *If a proposition is true* {164} *without an exception, it will be false with an exception.*

The reason for this is that the exceptive word eliminates the predicate from the excepted term. Therefore, a predicate that applies universally to the subject cannot be eliminated from any part of it whatever unless it is false. Thus, since 'Every man is an animal' is true, 'Every man besides Socrates is an animal' is false.

[23. Rule 1 Reconsidered]

On that basis we are left with this rule:

> [Rule 1] *The predicate is always removed from the term designating the excepted thing,*

as was maintained above. That is the reason this follows: 'Every man besides Socrates is running; therefore, Socrates is not running.' And it has to be understood as applying to affirmatives, since where negatives are concerned the predicate is, instead, affirmed of the excepted thing. That is the reason this follows: 'No man besides Socrates is white; therefore, Socrates is white.' Nevertheless, it can be said that in negative propositions the predicate is removed from the excepted thing in the same way in which it is applied to the other things. That is the reason this follows: 'No man besides Socrates is white; therefore, it is not the case that Socrates is not white.' But because two negations related to the same verb make an affirmation, this follows further ((*praeterea/propterea*)): 'therefore, Socrates is white.'

[24. A Rule with a Sophisma]

[24a. Rule 11]

Again, there is this rule:

> [Rule 11] *Argumentation from what is less general to what is more general together with an exceptive word is invalid.*

{165} The reason for this is that the word 'besides' conveys negation. Alternatively, argumentation from an inferior to its superior with an exceptive word is not valid, because the exceptive word has the force of negation.

[24b. Sophisma 12]

Thus suppose that the individual men are carrying individual stones, besides Socrates and Plato, who are carrying one stone in common. Then let the following be proposed:

EVERY MAN BESIDES SOCRATES AND PLATO IS CARRYING A
STONE.

Proof: 'Every man is carrying a stone' is false, and the only counterinstance occurs in connection with those two; therefore, when an exception has been made for them, it will be true. Therefore, the first proposition [is true].

But every man besides Socrates and Plato is carrying a stone; therefore, every man besides Socrates is carrying a stone. And there is an analogy here: 'Socrates and Plato are running; therefore, Socrates is running' – analogously, 'Socrates and Plato are excepted; therefore, Socrates is excepted.' But the same thing is signified by that one [viz., 'Every man besides Socrates and Plato is carrying a stone; therefore, every man besides Socrates is carrying a stone'].

In reply to this we have to say that the first proposition is true, and that the argument of the disproof is not valid but is a fallacy of the consequent, from the less general to the more general. For when one says 'every man besides Socrates and Plato,' all the men other than Socrates and Plato are supposited by means of the term 'every man'; but when one says 'every man besides Socrates,' all the men besides Socrates are supposited, and so Plato too. Thus its supposition is fuller, or higher. And so the argumentation is made from the less general to the more general with an exceptive word. {166}

But there is the opposing argument that in the exceptive proposition those two are excepted. In any case, they are excepted either conjointly or dividedly. If conjointly, it seems that it is incoherent; for every exceptive proposition is incoherent in which one does not except from a whole a part which is a part of it, but the whole 'every man' is a distributive and divisive whole. But the parts of a divisive whole are divided. Therefore, 'Socrates and Plato' is not a part of 'every man' but rather parts of it. Therefore, the exceptive is incoherent. If it is said that the exception is made dividedly, then it seems that the expression is impossible; for its sense is this: Every man besides Socrates is carrying a stone, and every man besides Plato is carrying a stone. But one of those two [conjuncts] claims that Socrates is carrying a stone and Plato is not, and the other claims that Plato is carrying one and Socrates is not, and those two are incompatible. Therefore, the proposition made out of them is impossible.

We have to say that the exception is made dividedly in relation to the subject but conjointly in relation to the predicate, so that the sense is this: Every man besides Socrates and Plato is carrying a stone.

Regarding the argument of the disproof, it is clear enough that there is a fallacy of the consequent in it, from a lesser distribution to a greater with an exceptive word.

It can be disproved in another way as follows: Every man besides Socrates and Plato is carrying a stone; therefore, Socrates and Plato are not carrying a stone.

We have to say that the sophisma sentence has two senses on the basis of composition and division; for carrying a stone can be related to the subject dividedly {167} or conjointly. If conjointly, the first proposition is true, and the conclusion does not follow, because it is concluded as if it were related dividedly; if dividedly, [the first proposition] is false, and what is false follows from what is false.

[25. A Rule with a Sophisma]

[25a. Rule 12]

Again, there is this rule:

> [Rule 12] *Argumentation from an inferior to its superior with an excep-*
> *tive word is not valid.*

The reason for this is that the negation occurring as part of the
meaning of an exceptive word blocks an inference of that sort, and
it does so whether the inference is made from the subject, from the
predicate, or from the excepted term. Thus, this does not follow:
'Every man besides Socrates is running; therefore, every animal
besides Socrates is running.' (The reason for it is evident on the
basis of the resolution [of the proposition].) Likewise, 'No man
besides Socrates is running; therefore, no man besides Socrates is
moving.' (This, too, is evident on the basis of resolution.) Likewise, this does not follow: 'No man besides Socrates is running;
therefore, no man besides a man [is running],' or 'besides an animal
[is running].'

But it seems that that is false. For this follows: 'Every man
besides Socrates is running; therefore, every man besides one is
running'; but 'one' is [logically] superior to 'Socrates.' Therefore,
[etc.].

[25b. Sophisma 13]

Moreover, in this connection a question arises regarding the following sophisma. Suppose that it is the case that Socrates sees every
man on one occasion and on another occasion sees every man
besides Plato. Then let this be proposed:

SOCRATES TWICE SEES EVERY MAN BESIDES PLATO.

Proof: '[Socrates] twice sees every man' is false, and the only
counterinstance occurs in connection with Plato; therefore, when an
exception has been made for him, it will be true; therefore, that
proposition is true.

And yet, Socrates twice sees, etc.; therefore on one occasion he
sees every {168} man besides Plato, and again on another occasion
– which is false and contrary to the hypothesis.

We have to say that although 'Every man besides Socrates is running' is true, as well as 'Every man besides one is running,' the form of the argumentation does not hold good. For it is the same as if one had said 'Every man other than Socrates is running, and Socrates is not running; therefore, every man other than one is running, and one is not running.'

In reply to 'Socrates twice sees every man besides Plato,' however, we have to say that it has two senses in accordance with the general rule. For it can be judged on the basis of the adverb of number (in which case it is false and disproved, and this sense is evident in the disproof), or it can be judged on the basis of the exceptive word (in which case it is true). And this sense is evident in the proof, and it is a counterinstance to 'Socrates twice sees every [man].'

Alternatively, we can say that this does not follow: 'Socrates twice sees every man besides Plato; therefore, on one occasion he sees every man besides Plato, and on another,' because the exception is made from the whole 'Socrates twice sees' conjointly, and one argues as if it were made dividedly; and so there is a fallacy of the consequent in it.

[26. A Rule with a Sophisma]

[26a. Rule 13]

Again, there is this rule:

> [Rule 13] *Argumentation from a word signifying the condition [of exception] to one that signifies the concept [of exception] is not valid.*

On that basis it is said that this does not follow: 'Every man besides {169} Socrates is running; therefore, every man, Socrates having been excepted, is running,' because it is said that the first can be true while the second is false. For suppose that Socrates is not running and the others are running; then every man besides Socrates is running, but 'Every man, Socrates having been excepted, is running' is false. For Priscian says (V 80, pp. 190.16–191.7; XVIII 30, pp. 221.25–222.3) that an ablative absolute [e.g., '*Sorte excepto*'] always has to be resolved by means of 'if,' 'while,' or 'because'; and so the sense is this: If Socrates is excepted, every man is running, or while he is excepted, or because he is excepted – each of which is false, because the antecedent can be true without the consequent.

[26b. Sophisma 14]

In this connection a question arises regarding the following sophisma. Suppose that there are four men, three of whom are excepted from some action, and that Socrates is one of their number and is not excepted. Then let this be proposed:

EVERY MAN BESIDES SOCRATES IS EXCEPTED.

Proof: 'Every man is excepted' is false, and the only counterinstance occurs in connection with Socrates; therefore, when an exception has been made for him, it will be true; therefore, the first proposition [will be true].

Then one asks 'Is Socrates excepted or not?' If not, then that to which the exceptive word is added is false. Therefore, just as 'Every man besides Socrates is running' is false when Socrates is running and the others are running, so 'Every man besides Socrates is excepted' will be false if he is excepted and the other three are excepted. Therefore, it is true without the exception. Therefore, it is false with it, by the rule [Rule 10] that says that an expression true without an exception will be false with one.

As for the sophisma, some resolve it on the basis of *transcasus*. *Transcasus* is {170} the change of the truth of a statement in accordance with the change of time. For example, if with my hand closed I say 'My hand is closed' and then, while extending [my hand, I say] 'therefore, my hand is not open,' it is said that this does not follow in virtue of *transcasus*. Analogously, this does not follow: 'Every man besides Socrates is excepted; therefore, Socrates is excepted.'

Alternatively, others say that there is a fallacy of *secundum quid et simpliciter* here, because to be excepted from that action is to be excepted in a certain respect, but when one says 'Socrates is excepted,' that involves being excepted unconditionally. And so the argument proceeds from what is the case in a certain respect to what is the case unconditionally.

[27. Exception in Connection with an Integral Whole]

[27a. Introduction]

Having considered exception made in connection with a universal whole, we have to consider exception ((*exceptione/excepto*)) made in connection with an integral whole, as when one says 'The whole house besides the wall is white.'

[27b. Is Such Exception Coherent?]

The question can arise, then, whether such exception is coherent.

And it seems that it is so, because exception is the taking of some part from some whole in respect of a third thing. Therefore, since 'the whole house' is a whole considered as a whole, and 'the wall' is a part considered as a part, it can be extracted by means of the exceptive word.

Again, exception is the elimination of the falsity of a counter-instance, which is the falsity of a part relative to the whole. But if a wall is not white, then it is false to say that the whole house is white, and this is only because of the part which is the wall. Therefore, when that part has been eliminated, it will be true. But it can be eliminated by means of exception. Therefore, an exception {171} can be made in connection with an integral whole.

On the other hand, 'the whole house' and 'the house' are the same, but 'The house besides the wall is white' is incoherent; there-fore, so is the other proposition. Proof: 'The whole house' is related to 'the house' just as 'every man' is related to 'man,' but 'man besides Socrates' is incoherent; therefore, so is 'the house besides the wall.'

Alternatively, one asks why an exception is made coherently from an undistributed integral whole, since one cannot be made from an undistributed universal whole.

[27c. Sophisma 15]

For a clarification of this, let us inquire into the following sophisma. Suppose that Socrates has no feet, and that the whole of him is white besides his hand. Then this is proposed:

THE WHOLE SOCRATES IS WHITE BESIDES HIS HAND.

Proof: 'The whole Socrates is white' is false, and the only counter-instance occurs in connection with his hand; therefore, when an exception has been made for it, the proposition will be true. Therefore, the first proposition will be true.

But the whole Socrates is white besides his hand; therefore, Socrates's foot is white. It is clear that this follows, because 'Every man besides Socrates is white; therefore, Plato is white' follows; for integral parts are related to an integral whole just as subjective parts are related to a universal whole. Therefore, 'The whole Socrates besides his hand; therefore, Socrates's foot' must follow just as 'Every [man] besides Socrates; therefore, Plato' follows. If it is said that it does not follow, then it is plain that 'the whole Socrates' is not a whole considered as a whole. Therefore, an exception cannot be made from it; therefore, the same as before.

In reply to this we have to say that an exception can be made from an integral whole {172} both taken universally and not taken universally, because the existence of an integral whole requires the positing of all its parts. Thus 'the whole Socrates' is the same as 'each and every part of Socrates,' and it is the same taken universally and not taken universally. Nevertheless, when it is taken ((*sumitur/sumit*)) together with a sign [of distribution], it is signified to be a whole considered as a whole. And so an integral whole is not the same as a universal whole, because a universal whole is preserved in each and every one of its parts, and more than one part is not required.

In reply to the objection that 'the house' is related to 'the whole house' just as 'man' is related to 'every man,' we have to say that that is not true. For in the term 'man' there is only a potential plurality, a potentiality that is reduced to actuality by means of the addition of a universal sign; but in the term 'house' there is a plurality of parts in actuality. It is for that reason that a universal sign added to a term signifies only the way in which the term supposits and does not make [the term universal].

In reply to the objection that 'The whole Socrates; therefore, Socrates's foot' does not follow, we have to say that in one way it does follow, in another way it does not. For if it is taken together with the word 'part,' it follows, as when one says 'The whole

Socrates is white, Socrates's foot is part of Socrates; therefore, Socrates's foot is white.' But because it is taken by itself, it does not follow in this way. (And that it can be taken simply is indicated by Aristotle in the *Categories*, in the chapter on relation [7, 8b15–21].) {173}

[28. Exception in Connection with Numbers]

[28a. Introduction]

Now that we have considered the word 'besides' insofar as it is exceptive, the next thing is to consider it insofar as it conveys diminution, because it can also be taken diminutionally. But because that can be done more often ((*frequentius/frequentibus*)) in connection with numerical wholes, we have to consider exception made in connection with numbers.

[28b. Sophisma 16]

In this context a question is raised regarding the following sophisma:

TEN BESIDES FIVE ARE FIVE.

Proof: 'Ten are five' is false, and the only counterinstance occurs in connection with five; therefore, when an exception has been made for them, the proposition will be true; therefore, the first proposition [is true].

But ten besides five are five; therefore, five are not five. That this follows is evident on the basis of the rule [Rule 1] that says that in affirmative exceptive ((*exceptivis/exceptionibus*)) propositions the predicate must be removed from the thing excepted. But this proposition ['Five are not five'] is false; therefore, the proposition from which it follows [is also false].

[28c. Sophisma 17]

In the same connection a question is raised regarding this sophisma:

TEN BESIDES ONE ARE NINE.

Proof: Ten with one removed are nine; therefore, the first proposition is true.

On the other hand, [Rule 7] a proposition that is wholly false cannot be made true by exception, but 'Ten are nine' is wholly false; therefore, [etc.].

If that is said, it is not true. For 'Nine are nine' is true, but nine are part of ten; therefore, some part of that proposition is {174} true. Therefore, the proposition is not wholly false.

Every predicate [is] indivisible, however, but a subject [is] divisible unless there is some obstacle. But what is divisible is divided only into its parts. Therefore, since the parts of ten are ten units, it is divided only into ten units. Therefore, it is required that being nine apply to each of the units – which is false for each and every one. Therefore, the whole is wholly false.

In reply to the first we have to say that the first proposition is true. And the disproof is invalid, because that rule is to be understood as applying only to propositions in which 'besides' is taken exceptively, but it is taken diminutionally here.

Alternatively, it could be said that the first proposition has two senses in virtue of the equivocation of the word 'besides'; for it can be taken diminutionally (and in that way the sophisma is proved), or exceptively (and in that way it is disproved).

But wherever there is exception there is diminution. Proof: Wherever there is an exception, some part is extracted from its whole; therefore, the whole is diminished by that part.

Moreover, since exception is the elimination of a counterinstance, so diminution (as it is taken here) eliminates a part for which there was falsity in the whole; therefore, since the causes ((*causae/causa*)) of things whose effects are different are themselves different, causes of things whose effects are the same will also be the same.

Again, the method of proof is the same for both ((*utrisque/utrinque*)), as is evident in connection with the sophisma 'Ten besides five are five'; therefore, it is clear that one ought not to draw the distinction that 'besides' can be taken diminutionally or {175} exceptively, since it makes no difference.

In reply to this we have to say that the distinction does hold. And diminution and exception agree in one way, as species and genus. In another way they differ, however, because exception is the removal of a part in those wholes in which the subject ((*subiectum/*

subiectus)) agreed with the predicate because of the parts, but diminution is, rather, [the removal of a part] in those in which the subject ((*subiectum/subiectus*)) agreed with the predicate because of the whole.

As for the objection that the whole 'Ten besides one are nine' is false and cannot be made true by means of an exception, we have to say that in numbers there are two sorts of parts, material and formal. Whatever is under [the number] and less than it is called a material part; what constitutes the number in being is a formal part. Therefore, although the predicate 'nine' agrees with none of the formal parts of the whole 'ten,' it does agree with one of the material parts – viz., to the one that is nine – because a small number is a part of a larger number.

Let these remarks suffice regarding the word 'besides.'

7

PETER OF SPAIN
SYLLOGISMS; TOPICS;
FALLACIES (SELECTIONS)

Introduction

(For information on Peter's life and writings, see the introduction to Translation 3.)

The following three selections are taken from Peter of Spain's *Tractatus*, tractates IV, V, and VII; they are representative of treatments of this material among thirteenth-century terminist logicians.

The selection on syllogisms begins with standard definitions of technical terms. After presenting the basic Aristotelian lore regarding the valid syllogisms in all three figures, Peter ends with a brief discussion of Aristotle's remarks on useless quasi-syllogistic combinations.

For further reading on the relation between Aristotelian and medieval logic, see CHLMP III.4, 'Ancient Scholastic Logic as the Source of Medieval Scholastic Logic.'

The medieval tradition of the Topics has its source in Aristotle's *Topics*. But the most important source for scholastic work on Topics is Boethius, who understands two different sorts of things as Topics: first, self-evidently true, universal generalizations; and second, the general headings under which maximal propositions may be classified.

Peter of Spain, whose work on Topics stands in the Boethian tradition, tries to combine the traditional views of Topics with Aristotelian syllogistic. A Topical argument is an enthymeme, as he sees it, and the function of the Topic is to confirm the validity of such enthymemes.

For further reading on the Topics, see CHLMP V.14, 'Topics: their Development and Absorption into Consequences.'

From Aristotle's *Sophistici Elenchi* medieval philosophers took the view that there are six fallacies whose deceptive appearance of validity is dependent on language in some way, and seven whose appearance of validity depends on something other than language.

Composition and division are two of the linguistic fallacies. Peter explains that both depend on the possibility of expanding certain expressions in different ways. He considers various objections to this general view, and provides an analysis of the conditions for producing each sort of fallacy. Then he turns to the individual fallacies, presenting for each of them a 'cause of the semblance' (that is, a reason for the fallacy's appearing valid) and the modes of the fallacy. As our sample of an extra-linguistic fallacy we have chosen Peter's discussion of the fallacy of the consequent.

For further reading on fallacies and their relation to ancient logic, see CHLMP III.4, 'Ancient Scholastic Logic as the Source of Medieval Scholastic Logic.'

Syllogisms

[The Proposition]

{43} 1. A proposition is an affirmative or negative expression concerning something with regard to something else or something apart from something else. A term is that into which a proposition is analyzed, namely, a subject and a predicate. *Dici de omni* occurs when nothing is to be subsumed under the subject of which the predicate is not said, as, for example, 'Every man is running'; here *running* is said of every man, and nothing is subsumed under *man* which *running* is not said of. *Dici de nullo* occurs when nothing is to be subsumed under the subject from which the predicate is not removed, as, for example, 'No man is running'; here *running* is removed from each and every man.

[The Syllogism]

2. A syllogism is an expression in which, when certain things have been asserted, something else must occur by means of the things which were asserted. For example, 'Every animal is a substance; every man is an animal; therefore, every man is a substance.' This whole thing is an expression in which, when certain things have been asserted (namely, the two propositions used as premises), something else (namely, the conclusion) must follow by means of them.

Every syllogism consists of three terms and two propositions. The first of the propositions is called the major proposition, and the second is called the minor. Now two propositions cannot arise from three terms unless one of them is taken twice; and this term will then be the subject in one proposition and the predicate in the other, or the predicate in both, or the subject in both. {44} Furthermore, one of these terms is called the middle, one the major extreme, and one the minor extreme. The middle is the term taken twice before the conclusion. The major extreme is the term taken together with the middle in the major proposition. The minor extreme is the term taken together with the middle in the minor proposition.

[Mood and Figure]

3. A syllogism requires mood and figure. Figure is the arrangement of the three terms with regard to being the subject and being the predicate. This arrangement is brought about in three ways, as was said; accordingly there are three figures.

The first figure occurs when what is the subject in the first proposition is the predicate in the second; for example, 'Every animal is a substance; every man is an animal.' The second figure occurs when the same thing is the predicate in both propositions; for example, 'Every man is an animal; no stone is an animal.' The third figure occurs when the same thing is the subject in both propositions; for example, 'Every man is an animal; every man is risible.'

Mood is the arrangement of the two propositions, dependent on quality and quantity.

[General Rules]

4. Hence, the following general rules are given for any figure. {45}

> No syllogism can be made of propositions that are entirely particular, indefinite, or singular.

Hence, one or the other of the premises must be universal.
Again,

No syllogism in any figure can be made of propositions that are entirely negative.

Hence, one or the other of the premises must be affirmative.
Again,

If one of the premises is particular, the conclusion must be particular; but not vice versa.

Again,

If one of the premises is negative, the conclusion is negative; and vice versa.

Again,

If one of the premises is particular, the conclusion must also be particular; but not vice versa.

Again,

The middle must never be used in the conclusion.

[The First Figure]

5. The first figure has nine moods, of which the first four reach their conclusion directly and the next five reach their conclusion indirectly. Concluding directly is predicating the major extreme of the minor in the conclusion; concluding indirectly is predicating the minor extreme of the major in the conclusion. {46}
   Again, this is a rule with regard to the four directly concluding moods of the first figure:

If the minor premise is negative, nothing follows.

Again, with regard to the same moods:

If the major premise is particular, nothing follows.

[The Moods of the First Figure]

6. The first mood of the first figure consists of two universal affirmative premises, resulting in a universal affirmative conclusion.

For example, 'Every animal is a substance; every man is an animal; therefore, every man is a substance.'

The second mood consists of a universal negative and a universal affirmative premise, resulting in a universal negative conclusion. For example, 'No animal is a stone; every man is an animal; therefore, no man is a stone.' {47}

The third mood consists of a universal affirmative and a particular affirmative premise, resulting in a particular affirmative conclusion. For example, 'Every animal is a substance; some man is an animal; therefore, some man is a substance.'

The fourth mood consists of a universal negative and a particular affirmative premise, resulting in a particular negative conclusion. For example, 'No animal is a stone; some man is an animal; therefore, some man is not a stone.'

The fifth mood consists of two universal affirmative premises, resulting indirectly in a particular affirmative conclusion. For example, 'Every animal is a substance; every man is an animal; therefore, some substance is a man.' And this is proved by means of the first mood of the first figure, resulting in a universal affirmative conclusion that converts into a particular proposition; and this particular proposition is the conclusion in the fifth mood.

The sixth mood consists of a universal negative and a universal affirmative premise, resulting indirectly in a universal negative conclusion. For example, 'No animal is a stone; every man is an animal; therefore no stone is a man.' And this is reduced to the second mood by means of the simple conversion of the conclusion.

The seventh mood consists of a universal affirmative and a particular affirmative premise, resulting indirectly in a particular affirmative conclusion. For example, 'Every animal is a substance; some man is an animal; therefore, some substance is a man.' And this is reduced to the third mood when the conclusion has been subjected to simple conversion.

The eighth mood consists of a universal affirmative and a universal negative premise, resulting indirectly in a particular negative conclusion. For example, 'Every animal is a substance; no stone is an animal; therefore, some substance is not a stone.' {48} And this is reduced to the fourth mood by the conversion *per accidens* of the major premise, the simple conversion of the minor premise, and by transposition.

The ninth mood consists of a particular affirmative and a universal negative premise, resulting indirectly in a particular negative conclusion. For example, 'Some animal is a substance; no stone is an animal; therefore, some substance is not a stone.' {48} And this is reduced to the fourth mood by the simple conversion of the major and minor premises and by transposition.

[The Second Figure]

7. The second figure is next. For it the following rules are given.

> *In the second figure if the major premise is particular, nothing follows.*

Again,

> *In the second figure nothing follows from premises that are entirely affirmative.*

Again,

> *In the second figure the conclusion is always negative.*

But this third rule can be understood through the second rule.

[The Moods of the Second Figure]

8. The second figure has four moods. The first mood consists of a universal negative and a universal affirmative premise, resulting in a universal negative conclusion. For example, 'No stone is an animal; every man is an animal; therefore, no man is a stone.' And this is reduced to the second mood of the first figure by the simple conversion of the major premise.

The second mood consists of a universal affirmative and a universal negative premise, resulting in a universal negative conclusion. For example, 'Every man is an animal; no stone is an animal; therefore, no stone is a man.' And this is reduced to the second mood of the first figure by the simple conversion of the minor premise and the conclusion and by transposition.

The third mood consists of a universal negative and a particular affirmative premise, resulting in a particular negative conclusion. For example, {49} 'No stone is an animal; some man is an animal;

therefore, some man is not a stone.' And this is reduced to the fourth mood of the first figure by the simple conversion of the major premise.

The fourth mood consists of a universal affirmative and a particular negative premise, resulting in a particular negative conclusion. For example, 'Every man is an animal; some stone is not an animal; therefore, some stone is not a man.' And this is reduced to the first mood of the first figure by a reduction *per impossibile*.

[Reduction *per impossibile*]

9. To reduce [a syllogism] *per impossibile* is to infer the opposite of one of the premises from the opposite of the conclusion together with the other premise. For suppose we take the opposite of the conclusion of this fourth mood (namely, 'Every stone is a man') together with the major premise and construct a syllogism in the first mood of the first figure in this way: 'Every man is an animal; every stone is a man; therefore, every stone is an animal.' This conclusion is the opposite of the minor premise of the fourth mood. And this is what it is to prove something [by reduction] *per impossibile*.

[The Third Figure]

10. The third figure is next. The third figure is the one in which the subject in both premises is the same. The following rules are given for it.

> *In the third figure if the minor premise is negative, nothing follows.*

Again,

> *In the third figure only a particular proposition is a conclusion.* {50}

[The Moods of the Third Figure]

11. The third figure has six moods. The first mood consists of two universal affirmative premises, resulting in a particular affirmative

ENHANCEMENT

conclusion. For example, 'Every man is a substance; every man is an animal; therefore, some animal is a substance.' And this is reduced to the third mood of the first figure by the conversion *per accidens* of the minor premise.

The second mood consists of a universal negative and a universal affirmative premise, resulting in a particular negative conclusion. For example, 'No man is a stone; every man is an animal; therefore, some animal is not a stone.' And this is reduced to the fourth mood of the first figure by the conversion *per accidens* of the minor premise.

The third mood consists of a particular affirmative and a universal affirmative premise, resulting in a particular affirmative conclusion. For example, 'Some man is a substance; every man is an animal; therefore, some animal is a substance.' And this is reduced to the third mood of the first figure by the simple conversion of the major premise and the conclusion and by transposition.

The fourth mood consists of a universal affirmative and a particular affirmative premise, resulting in a particular affirmative conclusion. For example, 'Every man is a substance; some man is an animal; therefore, some animal is a substance.' And this is reduced to the third mood of the first figure by the simple conversion of the minor premise.

The fifth mood consists of a particular negative and a universal affirmative premise, resulting in a particular negative conclusion. For example, 'Some man is not a stone; every man is an animal; therefore, some animal is not a stone.' {51} And this is reduced to the first mood of the first figure by reduction *per impossibile*. For suppose we take the opposite of the conclusion with one of the premises and infer the opposite of the other premise, as, for example, 'Every animal is a stone; every man is an animal; therefore, every man is a stone.' This conclusion, which is made in the first mood of the first figure, contradicts the major premise of the fifth mood.

The sixth mood consists of a universal negative and a particular affirmative premise, resulting in a particular negative conclusion. For example, 'No man is a stone; some man is an animal; therefore, some animal is not a stone.' And this is reduced to the fourth mood of the first figure by the simple conversion of the minor premise.

[Additional Rules]

12. The following rule is given for syllogisms that indirectly reach a particular negative conclusion:

> *No syllogism that reaches a particular negative conclusion indirectly can reach that conclusion directly, and no syllogism reaching a particular negative conclusion directly can reach it indirectly.*

Again,

> *Conclusions in the first figure include all types of propositions (namely, universal and particular, affirmative and negative). Conclusions in the second figure are universal and particular negative propositions. Conclusions in the third figure are affirmative and negative particular propositions but not universal propositions.* {52}

> 13. Barbara Celarent Darii Ferio Baralipton
> Celantes Dabitis Fapesmo Frisesomorum.
> Cesare Cambestres Festino Barocho Darapti.
> Felapto Disamis Datisi Bocardo Ferison.

In these four verses there are nineteen words that are associated with the nineteen moods of the three figures in such a way that the first word stands for the first mood of the first figure, the second word for the second mood, and so on. Hence, the first two verses are devoted to the moods of the first figure. Except for its last word, the third verse is devoted to the moods of the second figure in such a way that the first word of the third verse is devoted to the first mood of the second figure, the second word to the second mood, and so on. But the last word of the third verse, together with the other words of the fourth verse, is devoted to the moods of the third figure in order.

It is important to know that the vowels *A, E, I,* and *O* stand for the four types of propositions. The vowel *A* stands for a universal affirmative; *E* for a universal negative; *I* for a particular affirmative; and *O* for a particular negative.

Again, there are three syllables in each word (if there is any more, it is superfluous, except for *M,* as will be clear later). The first of these three syllables stands for the major proposition of the syllogism; the second stands for the minor; the third for the conclusion. For example, the first word – Barbara – has three syllables, in each of which *A* is used; the three occurrences of *A* signify that the first mood of the first figure consists of two universal affirmative premises resulting in a universal affirmative conclusion. (The vowels used in the other words should also be understood in this way.)

Again, it is important to know that the first four words of the first verse and all the other subsequent words begin with these consonants: *B*, *C*, *D*, and *F*. In this way we are given to understand that all the moods that a word beginning with *B* stands for should be reduced to the first mood of the first figure; all the moods signified by a word beginning with *C*, {53} to the second mood of the first figure; *D*, to the third mood; *F*, to the fourth.

Again, where *S* is used in these words, it signifies that the proposition that the immediately preceding vowel stands for requires simple conversion. And *P* signifies that the proposition requires conversion *per accidens*. And where *M* is used, it signifies that the premises require transposition. (Transposition is making the major premise the minor premise, and vice versa.) And where *C* is used [after a vowel] it signifies that the mood that word stands for should be proved by reduction *per impossibile*.

[Useless Combinations]

14. In the *Prior Analytics* (I 27, 43a20ff.), Aristotle shows that combinations in which the conclusion does not follow from the premises are useless; since [he does so] by finding terms in which a combination of that sort does not hold, there is some use in finding such terms.

And so wherever there is a useless combination that goes against the rules of syllogisms set down above, we should look for counterinstances by using {54} two species together with one genus (for example, *man, donkey, animal*), or two species together with a proprium of one of them (for example, *man, donkey, risible*), or one species together with its genus or a proprium of it (for example, *man, animal, risible*), for a counterinstance will be found in connection with these.

Finding counterinstances is using terms with regard to which the premises are true and the conclusion is false, while the propositions remain the same in quantity and quality. For example, this is a useless combination: 'No man is a donkey; no stone is a man; therefore, no stone is a donkey.' A counterinstance is raised against this useless combination in the following way: 'No donkey is a man; no risible thing is a donkey; therefore, no risible thing is a man.' Here the premises are true and the conclusion is false, while the propositions remain the same in quality and quantity in both false syllogisms.

Topics

[The Many Senses of *ratio*]

{55} 1. '*Ratio*' is used in many ways. In one way it is the same as a definition or a description, as in this passage, 'Univocal things are those that share a name, and the definition (*ratio*) of the substance corresponding to that name is the same.' In another way it is the same as a certain power of the soul [i.e., reason]. In another way it is the same as discourse that proves something – e.g., the reasonings (*rationes*) of the participants in a disputation. In another way *ratio* is the same as the form imposed on matter – e.g., in a knife iron is the matter, and the arrangement imposed on the iron is the form. In another way *ratio* is the same as a common essence predicable of many things – e.g., the essence of a genus, a species, or a differentia. In another way *ratio* is the same as a middle implying a conclusion; and it is in this last way that '*ratio*' is used in the following definition of an argument.

[Argument and Argumentation]

2. An argument is a reason (*ratio*) producing belief regarding a matter that is in doubt, that is, a middle proving a conclusion that needs to be confirmed by means of an argument. A conclusion is a proposition proved by an argument or arguments. But before it is proved, it is in doubt, and then it is the same as a question; for a question is defined in this way: A question is a proposition in doubt. (A middle is whatever has two extremes.)

An argumentation is the unfolding of an argument by means of discourse, or the discourse that unfolds the argument. But an argument differs from a middle and from an argumentation, because something is said to be a middle insofar as it has two {56} extremes, but an argument adds to a middle the power of proving a conclusion. Hence, in order for something to be an argument there needs to be a middle, and it needs to have the power of proving a conclusion. But the whole discourse composed of premises and conclusion is called an argumentation, and the power of the argument is made manifest in it. For in some cases the whole discourse can imply a universal affirmative, in some only a particular affirmative, in some only a universal negative, and in some only a particular negative.

[The Species of Argumentation]

3. There are four species of argumentation: syllogism, induction, enthymeme, and example. The definition of a syllogism was given above.

An induction proceeds from particulars to a universal. For example, 'Socrates is running, Plato is running, Cicero is running, (and so on); therefore, every man is running.'

An enthymeme is an incomplete syllogism, that is, discourse in which the hurried conclusion is inferred from propositions that are not all asserted in advance. For example, 'Every animal is running; therefore, every man is running.' For in that argumentation, the proposition {57} 'Every man is an animal' is tacitly understood; and it is not added to the argumentation (for if it were added, [the argumentation] would be a complete syllogism).

It is important to know that every enthymeme must be reduced to a syllogism. Consequently, in every enthymeme there are three terms, as in a syllogism. Two of these terms are used in the conclusion and are the extremes; the other is the middle and is never used in the conclusion. One of the extremes is taken twice in an enthymeme, the other once. In accordance with the requirement of the [syllogistic] mood, one must make a universal proposition out of the extreme that is taken once and the middle, and in this way a syllogism will be produced. For example, in the enthymeme:

'Every animal is running; therefore, every man is running,' 'man' and 'is running' are the extremes; 'animal' is the middle. But the extreme 'man' is taken once. Consequently, a universal proposition must be made from it and the middle in this way: 'Every man is an animal'; and then the syllogism is completed in this way: {58} 'Every animal is running; every man is an animal; therefore, every man is running.'

An example occurs when one particular is proved by means of another because of something similar found in them. For example, 'The Legionians' fighting against the Astoricians is evil; therefore, the Astoricians' fighting against the Zamorians is evil'; for both are cases of neighbors fighting against neighbors.

[Topics in General]

4. An argument is confirmed by means of a Topic; hence we should give the definition of a Topic, as the term is used here. For a Topic is the foundation of an argument, or that from which we draw an argument suitable for the question at issue. (What a question is was discussed above.)

One should know that a proposition, a question, and a conclusion are the same in substance but different in sense; for they have different senses or definitions, as was clear above. {59} For insofar as it is in doubt, it is a question; insofar as it is already proved by means of an argument, it is a conclusion; and insofar as it is asserted in order to prove something else, it is a proposition. (That is why insofar as something is used in the premises in order to prove the conclusion it is called a proposition.)

Topics are divided into Topical maxims and Topics, which are the differentiae of maxims. A Topical maxim is just the same as the maxim itself. A maxim is a proposition that has no other proposition prior to it (that is, more fully known than it). For example, 'Every whole is greater than its part'; 'Whatever a definition is predicated of, the thing defined is also predicated of'; 'Whatever a species is predicated of, [its] genus is also predicated of.'

A Topic that is the differentia of a maxim is that by which one maxim differs from another. For example, these two maxims – 'Whatever a definition is predicated of, the thing defined is also predicated of' [and] 'Whatever a species is predicated of, [its] genus is also predicated of' – differ in the terms of which they are composed. For one is composed of 'genus' and 'species,' and the other of 'definition' and 'thing defined'; hence, these simple terms are said to be the differentiae of the maxims.

But a Topical maxim as well as a Topic that is a differentia of a maxim is called a Topic because both confer stability on an argument. Hence, a Topic (*locus*), as the term is used here, is analogous to a place (*locus*) for natural things, because as a place gives stability to natural things and maintains them in being, a Topic analogously confirms an argument.

Topics that are the differentiae of maxims are divided into intrinsic, extrinsic, and intermediate Topics. An intrinsic Topic occurs when an argument is taken from things that pertain to the substance of a thing – for example, from a definition. An extrinsic Topic occurs when an argument is taken from those things that are entirely separated from the substance of a thing, for example, from opposites. For instance, if the question is whether Socrates is white, then a determination of the following sort may be made: 'Socrates is black; therefore, he is not white.' An intermediate Topic occurs when an argument is taken from things that to some extent agree with the terms used in the question and to some extent differ from them, as in the case of a univocal term and its denominative, which are called conjugates. For example, if the question is whether justice is good, then a determination of the following sort may be made: 'What is just is good; therefore, justice is good.' {60}

[Intrinsic Topics]

Intrinsic Topics are divided into Topics from substance and Topics from the concomitants of substance.

[Topics from Substance]

5. A Topic from substance occurs when an argument is taken from the substance of the terms used in the question. Such Topics are divided into Topics from definition and description and Topics from an explanation of the name.

[The Topic *From Definition*]

6. A definition is an expression signifying what a thing is. The Topic *from definition* is the relationship of a definition to the thing defined. It contains four arguments and four maxims: first, by making the definition the subject in an affirmation; second, by making the definition the predicate in an affirmation; third, by making the definition the subject in a negation; and, fourth, by making the definition the predicate in a negation. The following are examples of all of these.

[First,] 'A mortal rational animal is running; therefore, a man is running.' Where does the Topic come from? From definition. The maxim: Whatever is predicated of the definition is also predicated of the thing defined.

Second, 'Socrates is a mortal rational animal; therefore, Socrates is a man.' Where does the Topic come from? From definition. The maxim: Whatever the definition is predicated of, the thing defined is also predicated of.

Third, 'A mortal rational animal is not running; therefore, a man is not running.' Where does the Topic come from? From definition. The maxim: Whatever is removed from the definition is also removed from the thing defined.

Fourth, 'A stone is not a mortal rational animal; therefore, a stone is not a man.' Where does the Topic come from? From definition. The maxim: Whatever the definition is removed from, the thing defined is also removed from. {61}

[The Topic *From the Thing Defined*]

7. The Topic *from the thing defined* is the relationship of the thing defined to the definition; and it likewise contains four arguments and four maxims.

First, by making the thing defined the subject in an affirmation. For example, 'A man is running; therefore, a mortal rational animal is running.' Where does the Topic come from? From the thing defined. The maxim: Whatever is predicated of the thing defined is also predicated of the definition.

Second, by making the thing defined the predicate in an affirmation. For example, 'Socrates is a man; therefore, Socrates is a mortal rational animal.' Where does the Topic come from? From the thing defined. The maxim: Whatever the thing defined is predicated of, the definition is also predicated of.

Third, by making the thing defined the subject in a negation. For example, 'A man is not running; therefore, a mortal rational animal is not running.' Where does the Topic come from? From the thing defined. The maxim: Whatever is removed from the thing defined is also removed from the definition.

Fourth, by making the thing defined the predicate in a negation, in this way: 'A stone is not a man; therefore, a stone is not a mortal rational animal.' Where does the Topic come from? From the thing defined. The maxim: Whatever the thing defined is removed from, the definition is also removed from.

It is important to know that in every case a Topic gets its name from what implies and not from what is implied. Hence, when the definition is what implies, the Topic is *from definition*; but when the thing defined is what implies, the Topic is *from the thing defined.* Why? Because a Topic or differentia of a maxim must get its name from what implies and not from what is implied.

[The Topic *From Description*]

8. A description is an expression signifying the being of a thing through its accidental characteristics. For example, 'risible animal' is a description of man. Alternatively, a description is an expression consisting of a genus and a proprium, as, for example, 'risible animal.' {62}

The Topic *from description* is the relationship of a description to the thing described. Like the Topic *from definition*, it contains four arguments and four maxims. The arguments and maxims are formulated in this case as in the case of the Topic *from definition*, except that where 'definition' is used in that case, 'description' is used here; likewise for ['the thing defined' and] 'the thing described.'

[The Topic *From the Explanation of a Name*]

9. There are two sorts of explanation. One sort is an explanation that is not interchangeable [with the name]; for example, 'foot-wounder' (*ledens pedem*) is the explanation of 'stone' (*lapis*). The

other sort is an explanation that is interchangeable [with the name]; for example, 'lover of wisdom' is the explanation of 'philosopher.' And it is in that way that 'explanation' is used here. It is defined in this way: An explanation is the exposition of a name by something else.

The Topic *from the explanation of a name* is the relationship of the explanation to what is explained. It contains the same number of arguments and maxims as the Topics discussed above.

For example, 'A lover of wisdom is running; therefore a philosopher is running.' Where does the Topic come from? From the explanation of a name. The maxim: Whatever is predicated of the explanation is predicated also of what is explained.

And similarly with regard to the predicate. The maxim: Whatever the explanation is predicated of, what is explained is also predicated of.

Negatively in this way: 'A lover of wisdom is not envious; therefore, a philosopher is not envious.' Where does the Topic come from? From the explanation of a name. The maxim: Whatever is removed from the explanation is also removed from what is explained.

And similarly in connection with the predicate. The maxim: Whatever the explanation is removed from, what is explained is also removed from. {63}

[Topics *From Concomitants of Substance*]

10. The Topic *from concomitants of substance* is next. It occurs when an argument is taken from things that follow from the terms used in the question. And it is divided because one sort is from the whole, another from a part, another from a cause, another from generation, another from destruction, another from uses, another from associated accidents.

[The Topic *From the Whole*]

11. The Topic *from the whole* is divided in just the ways wholes are divided; for one sort is a universal whole, another is an integral

whole, another is a quantitative whole, another is a modal whole, another is a locational whole, another is a temporal whole. The Topic *from the whole* is divided in the same way, because one sort is from a universal whole, another from an integral whole, and so on for the others.

[The Topic *From a Universal Whole* or *From a Genus*]

12. A universal whole, as the term is used here, is what is superior and substantial. What is inferior under a universal is a subjective part.

The Topic *from a universal whole* or *from a genus* is the relationship of the whole to a part or to a species belonging to it; and it is always destructive. For example, 'A stone is not an animal; therefore, a stone is not a man.' Where does the Topic come from? From a genus. The maxim: When the genus or universal whole is removed, its species or subjective part is also removed. {64}

[The Topic *From a Species* or *From a Subjective Part*]

13. The Topic *from a species* or *from a subjective part* is the relationship of the subjective part to its genus or to its whole; and it is always constructive. It contains two arguments. First, by making the species the subject. For example, 'A man is running; therefore, an animal is running.' Where does the Topic come from? From a species or from a subjective part. The maxim: Whatever is predicated of the species is also predicated of its genus. Second, by making the species the predicate, in this way: 'Socrates is a man; therefore, Socrates is an animal.' Where does the Topic come from? From a species. The maxim: Whatever the species is predicated of, its genus is also predicated of.

[The Topic *From an Integral Whole*]

14. An integral whole is what is composed of parts that have quantity, and a part belonging to it is called integral. The Topic

from an integral whole is a relationship of an integral whole to its part; and it is always constructive. For example, 'A house exists; therefore, a wall exists.' Where does the Topic come from? From an integral whole. The maxim: When an integral whole is posited, any part of it is also posited.

The Topic *from an integral part* is the relationship of an integral part to its whole; and it is always destructive. For example, 'A wall does not exist; therefore, a house does not exist.' Where does the Topic come from? From an integral part. The maxim: When an integral part is destroyed, its whole is also destroyed.

[The Topic *From a Quantitative Whole*]

15. A quantitative whole is a universal taken universally, as, for example, 'every man,' 'no man.' The Topic *from a quantitative whole* is a relationship of a quantitative whole to its part; and it is both constructive and destructive. For example, 'Every man is running; therefore, Socrates is running.' Where does the Topic come from? From a quantitative whole. {65} The maxim: Whatever is predicated of a quantitative whole is also predicated of any of its parts. (Alternatively, if a universal proposition is true, each of its singular propositions is true.) Destructively in this way: 'No man is running; therefore, Socrates is not running.' Where does the Topic come from? From a quantitative whole. The maxim: Whatever is removed from a quantitative whole is also removed from any of its parts. (Alternatively, if a universal proposition is true, each of its singular propositions is true.)

The Topic *from a quantitative part* is the relationship of quantitative parts taken all together to their whole; and it is both constructive and destructive. For example, 'Socrates is running, Plato is running (and so on); therefore, every man is running.' Where does the Topic come from? From quantitative parts. The maxim: Whatever is predicated of all the quantitative parts taken together is predicated also of their whole. (Alternatively, if each singular proposition is true, their universal proposition is also true.) Negatively in this way: 'Socrates is not running, Plato is not running (and so on); therefore, no man is running.' Where does the Topic come from? From quantitative parts. The maxim: Whatever is removed from all the quantitative parts taken together is removed also from their whole. (Alternatively, if each singular proposition is true, their universal proposition is also true.) {66}

[The Topic *From a Modal Whole*]

16. A modal whole is a universal taken without a determination. (Examples are omitted because the arguments and maxims associated with this whole and its part are formulated in the same way as in the case of genus and species.)

[The Topic *From a Locational Whole*]

17. A locational whole is a word that adverbially comprises every place – e.g., 'everywhere.' A locational part is a word that adverbially comprises one place – e.g., 'here.' The Topic *from a locational whole* is the relationship of a locational whole to a part of it; and it is both constructive and destructive. For example, 'God is everywhere, therefore, God is here;' 'Caesar is nowhere; therefore, Caesar is not here.' Where does the Topic come from? From a locational whole. The maxim: Whatever a locational whole applies to, each of its parts applies to (or, whatever is removed from a locational whole is also removed from each of its parts).

The Topic *from a locational part* is the relationship of a locational part to its whole. For example, 'Caesar is not here; therefore, Caesar is not everywhere.' Where does the Topic come from? From a locational part. The maxim: Whatever a locational part does not apply to, its whole does not apply to.

[The Topic *From a Temporal Whole*]

18. A temporal whole is a word that adverbially comprises all {67} times – e.g., 'always' and 'never.' A temporal part is a word that adverbially signifies a particular time – e.g., 'now,' 'then,' 'yesterday,' 'today,' and 'tomorrow.' (The same sort of examples are used for this Topic as for a locational whole.)

[The Topic *From a Cause*]

19. A cause is that from whose existence something else naturally
follows. It is divided into efficient cause, material cause, formal
cause, and final cause. An efficient cause is what provides the source
of change. For example, a builder is the source moving and working to bring it about that a house exists, and a smith is the source
moving and working to bring it about that a knife exists.

The Topic *from an efficient cause* is the relationship of an efficient
cause to its effect; and it is both constructive and destructive. For
example, 'The builder is good; therefore, the house is good,' or,
'The smith is good; therefore, the knife is good.' Where does the
Topic come from? From an efficient cause. The maxim: That
whose efficient cause is good is itself also good. (Alternatively,
when an efficient cause has been posited, its effect is immediately
posited.)

The Topic *from an effect* is the converse of the Topic *from an
efficient cause*.

20. Matter is that from which (together with something else)
something comes to be. There are two sorts of matter, however;
one is permanent – e.g., the iron in a knife – and the other is
transient – e.g., the wheat and water in bread, and the straw and
fern in glass. Matter is also defined in this way: Matter is what
exists only in potentiality.

The Topic *from a material cause* is the relationship of a material
cause to its effect; and it is both constructive and destructive. It is
constructive in this way: 'Iron exists,' or, 'Wheat exists'; 'Therefore, there can be iron weapons,' or, 'Therefore, there can be
bread.' Where does the Topic come from? {68} From a material
cause. The maxim: When a material cause has been posited, it is
possible for the material effect to be posited also.

In the case of permanent matter it is destructive in this way: 'Iron
does not exist; therefore, iron weapons do not exist.' Where does
the Topic come from? From a material cause. The maxim: In the
case of permanent matter when the material cause is removed, its
effect is also removed. From its effect in this way(and it is constructive): 'Iron weapons exist; therefore, iron exists.' Where does the
Topic come from? From the effect of a material cause. The maxim:
In the case of permanent matter when the effect of a material cause
is posited, the permanent matter is also posited.

In the case of transient matter, from the effect of matter in this way: 'Glass exists,' or, 'Bread exists'; 'Therefore, fern existed,' or, 'Therefore, wheat existed.' (For transient matter does not remain; instead, its substance is transformed into a different nature.) The maxim: In the case of transient matter when the effect of the matter is posited, it is necessary that the matter itself have existed previously.

21. A form is what gives a thing its being and maintains it in being. The Topic *from a formal cause* is the relationship of a formal cause to its effect. Constructively, in this way: 'Whiteness exists; therefore, a white thing exists.' Where does the Topic come from? From a formal cause. The maxim: When a formal cause has been posited, its effect is posited. Destructively, in this way: 'Whiteness does not exist; therefore, a white thing does not exist.' Where does the Topic come from? From a formal cause. The maxim: When a formal cause has been removed, its effect is removed. {69}

The Topic *from the effect of a formal cause* will be the converse of this one.

22. An end [or final cause] is that for the sake of which something comes to be. The Topic *from a final cause* is the relationship of a final cause to its effect. For example, 'Happiness is good; therefore, virtue is good.' Where does the Topic come from? From a final cause. The maxim: That whose end is good is itself also good. Alternatively: 'Punishment is bad; therefore, sin is bad.' Where does the Topic come from? From the end. The maxim: That whose end is bad is itself also bad.

The Topic *from the effect of a final cause* will be the converse of this one.

[The Topic *From Generation*]

23. Generation is a coming into being from nonbeing. The Topic *from generation* is the relationship of generation to the thing generated. For example, 'The generation of the house is good; therefore, the house is good.' Where does the Topic come from? From generation. The maxim: That whose generation is good is itself also good (and that whose generation is bad is itself also bad).

The Topic *from the thing generated* will be the converse of this one,

and the maxims are these: If the thing generated is good, its generation is good; and if the thing generated is bad, its generation is bad.

[The Topic *From Destruction*]

24. Destruction is a going from being into nonbeing. The Topic
from destruction is the relationship of destruction to the thing
destroyed. For example, 'The destruction of the house is bad;
therefore, the house is good,' or, 'The destruction of Antichrist is
good; therefore, Antichrist is bad.' Where does the Topic come
from? From destruction. The maxim: That whose destruction is
bad is itself good, {70} and that whose destruction is good is itself
bad.
   The Topic *from the thing destroyed* will be the converse.

[The Topic *From Uses*]

25. A use, as the term is used here, is the functioning or the
exercise of a thing – e.g., the hacking of an ax and the riding of a
horse. The Topic *from uses* is the relationship of this functioning to
that of which it is the functioning or the use. For example, 'The
riding (or, the cleaving) is good; therefore, the horse (or, the ax) is
good.' Where does the Topic come from? From uses. The maxim:
That whose use is good is itself also good. Alternatively: 'To
murder is bad; therefore, a murderer is bad.' Where does the Topic
come from? From uses. The maxim: That whose use is bad is itself
also bad.

[The Topic *From Associated Accidents*]

26. 'Associated accidents' is used in two ways. For there are some
associated accidents that are sometimes associated with each other
and sometimes not – e.g., [being] elegantly dressed and [being an]
adulterer. No dialectical Topic is taken from these associated
accidents, but a sophistical Topic is. There are other associated
accidents, however, where the one always follows from the other,

as, for example, having done something wrong follows from repenting. And from these a dialectical Topic is taken. For example, 'He is repentant; therefore, he has done something wrong.' Where does the Topic come from? From associated accidents. The maxim: If the secondary associated accident inheres in something, the primary associated accident does also. Destructively, in this way: 'He has not done anything wrong; therefore, he is not repentant.' Where does the Topic come from? From associated accidents. The maxim: {71} if the primary associated accident does not inhere in something, neither does the secondary associated accident.

[Extrinsic Topics]

27. We said above what an extrinsic Topic is. Extrinsic Topics are from opposites, from a greater, from a lesser, from a similar, from a proportion, from transumption, and from authority.

[The Topic *From Opposites*]

There are four species of opposition, namely, relative opposition, contrariety, privative opposition, and contradiction. Relative opposites are those of which one cannot stand without the other – e.g., father and child. Contrariety is the opposition of contraries – e.g., the opposition of white and black. Privative opposites are those which must arise with regard to the same thing – e.g., sight and blindness with regard to the eyes. A contradiction is the opposition in which there is no intermediate with regard to the opposition itself, for between being and not being there is no intermediate.

[The Topic *From Relative Opposites*]

28. The Topic *from relative opposites* is the relationship of one correlate to the other; and it is both constructive and destructive. For example, 'A father is; therefore, a child is,' and vice versa; 'A father is not; therefore, a child is not,' and vice versa. Where does

the Topic come from? From relative opposites. The maxim: When one of a pair of correlates is posited, the other is also posited; and when one is destroyed, the other is also destroyed. {72}

[The Topic *From Contraries*]

29. Some contraries are mediate, as, for example, white and black, between which there are intermediate colors; others are immediate, as, for example, healthy and sick with regard to animal. The Topic *from contraries* is the relationship of one contrary to the other. Constructively, in this way: 'The animal is healthy; therefore, it is not sick,' or, 'This body is white; therefore, it is not black.' Where does the Topic come from? From contraries. The maxim: When one of a pair of contraries is posited, the other contrary is removed from the same thing. It holds destructively in the case of immediate contraries given the sameness of the subject, as, for example, 'This animal is not healthy; therefore, it is sick.' Where does the Topic come from? From immediate contraries. The maxim: when one of a pair of immediate contraries is removed, the other is posited if the subject remains the same.

[The Topic *From Privative Opposites*]

30. We said above what privative opposites are. The Topic *from privative opposites* is the relationship of a privation to a possession or of a possession to a privation. For example, 'He has sight; therefore, he is not blind,' or 'He is blind; therefore, he does not have sight.' Where does the Topic come from? From privative opposites. The maxim: When one of a pair of privative opposites is posited, the other is removed from the same thing. It does not hold destructively unless the sameness of the subject and a naturally determined period of time are given. For a kitten is not said to be blind or to have sight before it is nine days old; and a child is not said to have teeth or to be toothless before a determined time. {73}

[The Topic *From Contradictory Opposites*]

31. The Topic *from contradictory opposites* is the relationship of one contradictory opposite to the other. For example, 'That Socrates is seated is true; therefore, that Socrates is not seated is false.' Where does the Topic come from? From contradictory opposites. The maxim: If one of a pair of contradictory opposites is true, the other is false (and vice versa).

[The Topics *From a Greater* and *From a Lesser*]

32. A greater, as the term is used here, is what exceeds something else in power or in excellence. A lesser is what is exceeded by a greater. The Topic *from a greater* is the relationship of a greater to a lesser; and it is always destructive. For example, 'The king cannot capture the fortress; therefore, neither can a knight.' Where does the Topic come from? From a greater. The maxim: If that which seems the more to inhere does not inhere, neither does that which seems the less to inhere.

The Topic *from a lesser* is the relationship of a lesser to a greater; and it is constructive. For example, 'A knight can capture the fortress; therefore, the king can also.' Where does the Topic come from? From a lesser. The maxim: If what seems the less to inhere does inhere, what seems the more to inhere also inheres.

[The Topic *From a Similar*]

33. The Topic *from a similar* is the relationship of one similar to another. {74} For example, 'As *capable of laughing* inheres in a man, so *capable of neighing* inheres in a horse; but *capable of laughing* is a proprium of man; therefore, *capable of neighing* is a proprium of a horse.' Where does the Topic come from? From a similar. The maxim: The judgment concerning similars is the same. Destructively, in this way: 'As *capable of laughing* inheres in a man, so *capable of neighing* inheres in a horse; but *capable of laughing* does not belong to man as its genus ((om. *proprium*)); therefore, *capable of neighing* does not inhere in a horse as its genus.' Where does the

Topic come from? From a similar. The maxim is the one given above, or this one: If one of a pair of similars inheres, so does the other; or, if one does not inhere, neither does the other.

[The Topic *From Proportion*]

34. The Topic *from proportion* is the relationship of one proportional to the other. For example, 'As the governor of a ship is related to the ship, so is the governor of a school related to the school; but in the case of governing a ship the governor should be chosen by art and not by lot; therefore, in the case of governing a school the governor should be chosen by art and not by lot.' Where does the Topic come from? From proportion. The maxim: The judgment concerning proportionals is the same.

This Topic differs from the Topic *from a similar*, because in the case of the Topic *from a similar* a comparison is made on the basis of a similarity in the inherence, as, for example, 'As *capable of laughing* inheres in a man, so *capable of neighing* inheres in a horse.' But in the case of the Topic *from proportion* we observe not a similarity in the inherence but a comparison of a relationship, as, for example, 'As a sailor is related to a ship, so a teacher is related to a school.'

[The Topic *From Transumption*]

35. There are two sorts of transumption. One sort occurs when {75} a name or an expression that signifies one thing is transferred to signify something else in virtue of some similarity. For example, 'smiling' is transferred to 'blooming' when we say 'The meadow is smiling.' But an expression is transferred when we say 'The seashore is plowed' for 'Your labor is lost,' as is customarily said to someone who works in vain. And this sort of transumption is not the dialectician's business but the sophist's.

But there is another sort of transumption when a name that is more known is taken for another name that is less known – as, for example, if one must prove that a philosopher is not envious, and there is a transumption to 'A wise man is not envious.' And this sort of transumption is the business of the dialectician.

The Topic *from transumption* is the relationship of one transferred thing to another. For example, 'A wise man is not envious; therefore, a philosopher is not envious.' Where does the Topic come from? From transumption. The maxim: What applies to something under a name that is more known also applies to it under a name which is less known ((*noto/toto*)).

This Topic differs from the Topic *from the explanation of a name*, because in the case of the Topic *from the explanation of a name* we take a definition or description of a name or an exposition of it – e.g., '"Philosopher" is expounded by "lover of wisdom."' But in the case of the Topic *from transumption* we are not looking for an exposition of a name; rather we take a name that is more known (or anything else by means of which what is at issue will be easily proved) in place of another name that is less known.

[The Topic *From Authority*]

36. Authority, as the term is used here, is the judgment of a wise man in his own field of knowledge. Hence, 'from the judgment of a thing' is the usual designation for this Topic.

The Topic *from authority* is the relationship of an authority to that which is proved by the authority. For example, 'An astronomer says that the heaven is revolvable; therefore, the heaven is revolvable.' Where does the Topic come from? From authority. The maxim: {76} Any expert should be believed in his own field of knowledge.

[Intermediate Topics]

37. Intermediate Topics are next. We said above what an intermediate Topic is. Intermediate Topics are from conjugates, from cases, and from division. Conjugates and cases differ because a univocal word, whether principal or abstract (which come to the same thing), is said to be conjugate with its denominative – e.g., 'justice' and 'just.' But cases are so-called because they are declined (*cadunt*) from the principal word – e.g., 'just' and 'justly.' (Aristotle lays down this difference in the second book of the *Topics* [II 9, 114a27–34]).

[The Topic *From Conjugates*]

38. The Topic *from conjugates* is the relationship of one conjugate to the other. For example, 'Justice is good; therefore, what is just is good.' Where does the Topic come from? From conjugates. The maxim: What inheres in one conjugate also inheres in the other; if one conjugate inheres in something, so does the other.

[The Topic *From Cases*]

39. The Topic *from cases* is the relationship of one case to another case. For example, 'What is just is good; therefore, what is done justly is done well' (and vice versa). Where does the Topic come from? From cases. The maxim: What applies to one case also applies to the other. {77}

[The Topic *From Division*]

40. One sort of division occurs by means of negation, as, for example, 'Socrates either is a man or is not a man; but he is not not a man; therefore, he is a man.' Where does the Topic come from? From division. The maxim: If something is exhaustively divided by two things, when one is posited, the other is removed; or, when one is removed, the other is posited.

There is another sort of division, which does not occur by means of negation. It arises in six modes, three *per se* and three *per accidens*. First, there is the division of a genus into its species – e.g., 'Some animals are rational and others irrational.' Second, the division of a whole into its integral parts – e.g., 'One part of a house is the wall, another part is the roof, and another is the foundation.' Third, of an utterance into its significations – e.g., 'dog' into something capable of barking, a marine animal, and a celestial star. Of the three modes *per accidens*, one is of a subject into its accidents – e.g., 'Some animals are healthy and others are sick.' The second is of an accident into its subjects – e.g., 'Some healthy things are men and others are beasts.' The third is of an accident into accidents – e.g., 'Some healthy things are warm and others cold.'

The Topic *from division* is the relationship of one of the exhaustively dividing things to the other. For example, 'If Socrates is an animal, he is either rational or irrational; but he is not irrational; therefore, he is rational.' Where does the Topic come from? From division. The maxim is the one given above. And the argument is formulated similarly, both constructively and destructively, in any other case of division.

Fallacies (selections)

The Fallacy of Composition and Division

[Potential Ambiguity]

{115} 57. Composition and division (and accent) produce potential multiplicity according to the Commentator, as was said before. Potential ambiguity occurs when the same word or expression signifies different things in accordance with different completions. For example, the verb '*pendere*' has different completions when it is in the second conjugation and when it is in the third conjugation, because there are in this way two verbs differing in type, and therefore they must have different completions. Nonetheless, with regard to matter it is the same verb, since it consists of the same letters and syllables. Thus there is in this case sameness of matter but diversity of completions, and what is signified differs in accordance with the different completions.

Likewise, with regard to an expression, when the expression is compounded, it is completed in one way; and when it is divided, it is completed in another way. For example, the expression 'Two and three are five' is categorical and contains a conjoined subject when it is compounded; but when it is divided – in this way 'Two are five and three are five' – then it is a conjunctive proposition. But the categorical proposition and the conjunctive proposition obviously have different completions. {116}

And, similarly, with regard to every expression involving composition and division, we can always find some diversity based on completions and thereby diversity in what is signified. And since in these cases it is possible for a word or an expression to be transformed from one completion into another, and since we find there a diversity in what is signified because of this possibility, it is called a potential ambiguity. In the case of equivocation and amphiboly, however, because a word or expression that always has the same completion signifies different things, we say that there is actual ambiguity because there is ambiguity with regard to the same actualization or the same completion (for completion is called actualization).

[Objections and Replies]

58. [Objection 1] But there is an objection against what has been said, because the expression 'that the bread the dog eats' (*panem comedere canem*) is different depending on whether the accusative 'the bread' is the subject of the verb 'to eat' or whether it is the object of the verb. And yet it does not differ with regard to matter, because it consists of the same letters and syllables and words (and so is one and the same with regard to matter). Therefore, since the expression is simply different, it must be different with regard to type. And in accordance with this [difference] it signifies different things. Therefore, the expression 'that the bread the dog eats,' which is the same with regard to matter and different with regard to different completions, signifies different things. Therefore, there is in this case a potential ambiguity, since the previously given definition of potential ambiguity applies to it. Thus, since there is in this case only amphiboly, amphiboly produces potential ambiguity; and this goes against what was said before.

[Reply to Objection 1] It should be said that in the expression 'that the bread the dog eats' there is only actual ambiguity and no potential ambiguity, since the expression is always the same with regard to type, as will already be clear. But to the objection that it differs with regard to type although it is the same with regard to matter (because it consists of the same letters and syllables and words), it should be said that ambiguity is sameness and difference in expression, because sameness in expression is twofold, namely, sameness of completion and sameness of matter. And both these {117} samenesses are in the expression 'A man is running,' since in this case there is one and the same completion and so sameness of completion; and it consists of the same letters and syllables and words, which always have the same material arrangement, and so there is [also] sameness of matter in this case.

59. Furthermore, 'difference in expression' is used in many different ways. In one way it is used with regard to type – e.g., the expression 'Two and three are five' is different in type from 'Two are five and three are five.' In another way there is a difference of matter. This occurs in two ways, either because it is made out of different letters or syllables and words – e.g., 'Socrates is running and Plato is disputing' – or because it is made out of the same letters or syllables and words but arranged in different ways. And this also occurs in two ways; because in one way the expression consists of the same words arranged in different ways contributing to one and the same completion, but in another way there is a difference in the expression with regard to matter based on words arranged in different ways contributing to different completions. In this last way an expression differs with regard to composition and division, but in the penultimate way an expression differs with regard to amphiboly. For example, the expression 'that the dog the bread eats (*comedere*)' is always the same with regard to its completion, no matter which of its accusatives is the subject or the object, because this expression is completed by the inflection in it, even though '*comedere*' is an infinitive inflection. For, as an indicative expression is completed by its appropriate inflection and an imperative by its appropriate inflection, this infinitive expression is likewise completed in its own way by an infinitive inflection, although the expression is not completed unconditionally. Hence, that expression is the same with regard to type and different with regard to matter insofar as one of its accusatives is the subject or the object (and likewise for the other).

This can be clarified by an analogy drawn from nature. For this man, who is now a boy and afterwards will be a young man (or an old man), is always the same man, although his build is not always the same but differs. So does his weight, since he is sometimes plump and sometimes {118} thin, and yet he is always the same man. In this way his material parts are transformed but the human type is always the same in him, and so there is in him a difference of matter and a sameness of type. Similarly, in the expression 'that the bread the dog eats' there is that sort of difference of matter but a sameness of type.

60. [Objection 2 and its reply] If anyone asks whether expressions involving amphiboly share sameness of expression equally, we must say that in one way they do and in another way they do not. For sameness of expression occurs in two ways, as is clear already from what has been said above: One has to do with matter and the other with type. When we are speaking about sameness with regard to matter, an amphibolous expression is always the same, as, for example, 'Aristotle's book.' An amphibolous expression varies, however, because an expression is amphibolous in that some inflected form can be either the subject or the object of one and the same verb. But when we are speaking about sameness with regard to type, every amphibolous expression is equally the same, since there is no difference among its parts with regard to type. That is because an expression has in itself its appropriate completion, the one by means of which it is always completed. Therefore, an amphibolous expression in itself is simply the same as far as sameness with regard to type goes.

[Composition]

61. Given these things, we must now discuss composition specifically. But first we must consider when an expression is said to be compounded and when it is said to be divided. So it is important to know that an expression cannot be compounded or divided unless we can find in it different places in accordance with which the parts can be arranged in different ways. When the words in the expression are arranged in accordance with the more appropriate place, then the expression is said to be compounded. But if the words are divided from that place and put in a less appropriate place, then the expression is divided. For example, the expression 'Whatever lives always is' can be compounded or divided. For when the whole 'whatever lives' is the subject in the expression and the verb 'is' {119} is the predicate, then 'is' is the principal verb in the expression, and 'lives' is not the principal verb in the expression since it is included in the subject.

Proof: A verb is that which consignifies time and is always an indication of things that are predicated of something else. And so the verb that is actually predicated actually shares in the nature of a verb unconditionally, and the verb that is not actually predicated does not share in the nature of a verb unconditionally. So, since the verb 'is' is actually predicated, it will actually share in the nature of a verb unconditionally. And since the verb 'lives' is not actually predicated but is included in the subject – something that goes against the character of a verb insofar as it is a verb – it will not actually share in the nature of a verb unconditionally. Both 'is' and 'lives' are verbs unconditionally with regard to their dispositions, however, since they both have an intrinsic aptitude for being predicated. So both are verbs unconditionally as far as their dispositions go, but it is not the case that both are actually verbs unconditionally. And in that way one is the principal verb and the other is not, as was said. Therefore, since it is the nature of an adverb to determine a verb, the adverb will more correctly determine the verb that is more rather than less principal, and so it is put in the more appropriate place. For this reason when the word 'always' determines the verb 'is,' the expression is compounded in this way: 'Whatever lives, always is.' And if the word 'always' is divided from the verb 'is,' the expression will be divided in this way: 'Whatever lives always, is.' And all the other cases should be understood in a similar way in accordance with the nature of the words used in them.

62. Similar observations apply to the expression 'I made you a slave being a free man.' Since signs insofar as they are signs should be joined together and separated on the basis of what they signify, if the things can be arranged in different ways, so can the signs or words, because words are signs of things. So when the things are more joined together in their arrangement, the signs will be so also; and when the things are less joined together in their arrangement, the signs will be so also. Since {120} leaving slavery and becoming free is more joined to human nature than is falling into slavery from freedom, the participle 'being' is construed as joined to the name 'slave' more than to the name 'free man.' And in this way the expression is compounded; and the sense is 'You, being a slave, I made a free man,' that is, I turned you into a free man when you were a slave. Taken the other way around, the expression is divided; and the sense is 'You, being a free man, I made a slave,' that is, I turned you into a slave when you were a free man.

63. Notice that Aristotle includes this expression under paral-

ogisms of division (*Soph.el.* 4, 166a36–37). Notice also that whenever composition or division or accent occurs, it is not necessary
that the expression is always true in one way and false in another, because it can happen that it is false in both senses or true
in both senses. For example, 'I touch the one struck with the hand'
might be such that someone was struck with the hand and I touch
him with the hand; in that case the original expression is ambiguous
in virtue of the fact that the ablative 'with the hand' can determine
the verb 'I touch' or the participle 'struck,' and in either sense it is
true. But if the hypothesis remains the same, 'I touch with a stick
the one struck' is false in either sense. The case of equivocation is
similar. For the expression 'Every dog is a substance' has three
senses, and it is true in each of them. But the expression 'Every dog
is white' is false in each of them. The case of amphiboly is also
similar.

   On the basis of these observations it is clear that those who say
that an expression is a fallacy of composition when it is false in the
compounded sense and a fallacy of division when it is false in the
divided sense are speaking inaccurately, because that is not true in
all cases, as was said. But it is true that if a paralogism was made on
the basis of composition, the solution will come from division, and
if the paralogism was made on the basis of the fallacy of composition, the solution will come from composition. (The latter point
comes from Aristotle, but not the former. [*Soph.el.* 20, 177a33–35]).

[The Causes of This Fallacy]

64. The cause of the semblance or the source of the effectiveness of
the fallacy of composition is the unity of the expression with regard
to its type, which is brought about by composition. And I say that
it is brought about by composition because {121} an expression is
of one or another type and, likewise, has one or another truth in
virtue of its being compounded in this way or divided in that way.
But the source of the defect belonging to the fallacy of composition
is the possibility that what is signified by one and the same expression varies. And I say this because although an expression is compounded and is in that way included under one type in connection
with composition, it has a possibility for another type or another

completion that it can have by means of division. That is the reason why it has the possibility of signifying different things. (All this was clear before in the case of the expression 'Whatever lives always is.') Hence, the possibility of an expression's being of different types, which depends on the utterance, corresponds to the possibility of its signifying different things, which depends on the things [signified].

65. Some people say that the cause of the semblance belonging to the fallacy of composition is the composition itself, whereas the cause of the nonexistence is the division of the expression. But others say that the cause of the semblance belonging to the fallacy of composition is the truth of the compounded expression, whereas the cause of the nonexistence is the falsity of that same expression taken as divided. For they say that the truth of the compounded expression is effective for producing belief in the truth of that same expression when it is divided, since the source of the effectiveness always produces a belief opposite to that produced by the source of the defect.

66. That these people make mistaken distinctions among such principles of this sophistical Topic is clear first from the fact that all verbal fallacies differ from extra-verbal fallacies in that the source of the effectiveness of the verbal fallacies depends on the utterance or the sign, and the source of the defect belonging to them depends on the things [signified], whereas for extra-verbal fallacies both of these sources depend on the things [signified]. Therefore, their first opinion cannot stand because it maintains that both these sources depend on the utterance or the sign, for the composition or division of the expression itself is looked for in the utterance or sign.

Furthermore, everything moves only toward what is like it either absolutely or in part, and consequently it is not possible for one contrary to move toward another. {122} Therefore, composition cannot move toward division, or vice versa. The first of these reasons shows the falsity of the second opinion, which maintains that both sources of the fallacy of composition depend on the things [signified], since there is no truth in an expression except on the basis of the things [signified].

Furthermore, in the fallacy of equivocation the source of the effectiveness is taken from the unity of the expression, and the source of the defect is taken from the things that are signified; the same is true in the fallacy of amphiboly, in the fallacy of accent (as will be clear later), and in the fallacy of the figure of a word. Therefore, the case of composition must be similar, or else there will not be six verbal fallacies; and Aristotle taught the opposite of this by induction and syllogism (*Soph. el.* 4, 168b27–30). Therefore, one should maintain that the source of the effectiveness of the fallacy of composition depends on the utterance, and the source of the defect depends on the things [signified].

67. That is why we said that the source of the effectiveness of the fallacy of composition is the unity of the expression with regard to its type, which is brought about by composition; but the source of the defect is the possibility that the same expression signifies different things. For the unity of a compounded expression is effective for producing the belief that one thing is signified without the possibility of anything else's being signified. And in this way the source of the effectiveness moves one in a direction opposite to that in which one is moved by the source of the defect, as in the other sophistical Topics.

[The Modes of This Fallacy]

68. Two modes can be assigned for the fallacy of composition, as Aristotle seems to indicate in his chapter on composition (*Soph. el.* 4, 166a23–32).

[The First Mode]

The first mode results from the fact that a dictum can be the subject for a verb either as a whole or in part, as in 'That a seated man walk is possible.' And a paralogism is formed in this way:

If it is possible for someone to walk, it can be the case that he walks; but that a seated man walk is possible; therefore, it can be the case that a seated man walks. {123}

The minor premise is ambiguous, because if the dictum 'that a seated man walk' is as a whole the subject for the predicate 'is possible,' there is one sense. And in that sense the expression is false, because in that case acts that are mutually opposed to one another – namely, walking and sitting – are conjoined; and that is false, just as this is false: 'A seated man is walking.' But if the dictum is the subject for that predicate in part – namely, in the part which is the subject of the dictum – then the sense is this: 'A seated man has in himself the power to walk,' and in this sense the minor premise is true. (A similar distinction should be made with regard to 'That a man who is not writing write is possible,' and the paralogism should be formed in a similar way.) These expressions and others like them are compounded insofar as the whole dictum taken as a whole is the subject. They are divided when the dictum is only in part the subject, for although the dictum is always the subject, the predicate seems more suitably attributed to the whole dictum than to part of the dictum.

[Objections and Replies]

69. [Objection 1] So there is nothing to the objections that some people raise. Some say that if it is true in that way that the possibility for walking is sometimes attributed to the whole dictum and sometimes to part of it (namely, to 'seated man'), then the accusative 'seated man' is the subject of 'A seated man is possible to walk.' But that is absurd, because the expression would be ungrammatical; for an accusative cannot be the subject of a verb in the third person. And so the distinction drawn before comes to nothing.

[Reply to Objection 1] The solution is plain on the basis of what has been said so far, because the whole dictum is always the subject of the verb in the third person, but sometimes taken as a whole – in which case the possibility is referred to the whole dictum – and sometimes in part (namely, in the part that is the subject of the dictum) – in which case the possibility is referred to the subject of the dictum, 'seated man.'

70. [Objection 2] Other people draw a distinction among these expressions, saying that an association is implied by the participle 'seated' or 'writing,' as Priscian claims, (IX 8, p. 552.21) because a participle is devised to convey an association between itself and the [principal] verb, as in 'Seated I read.' And this association is explicated by the word 'while' or 'when' in this way: 'While I am seated, {124} I read' or 'When I am seated, I read.' Therefore, they say that

the expressions discussed before are ambiguous, because the association implied by the participle 'seated' can be signified either with
respect to the verb 'walk' (in which case the sense of 'A seated man
it is possible that he walk' is this: While I am seated, that I walk is
possible, which is false), or the association can be denoted with
respect to the predicate (in which case the sense of 'A seated man
it is possible that he walk' is this: While he is seated, he has the
capacity to walk later, which is true).

[Reply to Objection 2] But this distinction reduces to the same as
the one given before. For when the association is denoted with
respect to the verb 'walk,' the possibility applies to the whole
dictum; and taken in this way it is false. But when the association is
denoted with respect to the predicate, the possibility applies to the
subject of the dictum; and taken in this way it is true.

71. Expressions of this sort are also usually called *de re* or *de dicto*.
They are said to be *de dicto* when the dictum taken as a whole is the
subject, but when the dictum in part is the subject, they are said to
be *de re*. And they call the subject of a dictum the thing (*res*); but the
subject of a dictum is not a dictum. Hence, although a dictum is a
thing (*res*), it is not a thing in the sense in which they are taking
'thing' here.

[The Second Mode]

72. The second mode of the fallacy of composition results from the
fact that a word used in an expression can be a determination of
different things – e.g., 'That the alphabet you know is to be learned
now is possible.' For the adverb 'now' can determine the verb 'to
be learned' (in which case it is false, because it is not possible that
you now learn the alphabet that you know; if you learn something
new, you do not have knowledge of that thing, for as Aristotle
claims (*Topics* III 2, 117a12), 'whoever learns something new does
not have knowledge of it'). Alternatively, it can determine the
predicate 'is possible' (in which case it is true, because it is possible
now that he learn anew again the alphabet that he knows; he can
forget it, and in that way he has now in the present the power of
learning it anew). {125}

This is similar: 'That which can carry one only can carry more.'

A paralogism is formed in this way: 'That which can carry one only can carry more; but that which cannot carry more can carry one only; therefore, that which cannot carry more can carry more.' The major premise is ambiguous, because if the word 'only' determines the verb 'can,' it is false. And the sense of 'That which can carry one only, etc.' is this: That which can carry only one and cannot carry more, can carry more; because if it can only carry one, it cannot carry more. But if the word 'only' determines the verb 'carry,' it is true. And the sense of 'That which can carry one only can carry more' is this: That which has the power to carry one only can carry more, because whatever can carry more also has the power to carry one only. For example, a ship can carry ten men, and it can carry one only; and in this way it has the power to carry one only, and it can carry more. Hence, that which can carry one only can carry more.

73. In what was said before it was made clear in what way there is a potential multiplicity in an expression, whether it is compounded or divided, and when it should be said to be compounded and when divided. What remains now is to discuss the sources or causes and the modes of division.

[Division]

74. The source of the effectiveness or the cause of the semblance of the fallacy of division is the unity of an expression with regard to its type brought about by division, because it is of one type when it is divided and of another type when it is compounded. But the source of the defect or the cause of nonexistence in the fallacy of division is the possibility that in the substance of the divided expression different things are signified. And I say this because although an expression signifies one thing in the mode in which it is divided, its substance nonetheless has the possibility for composition and so for signifying something else. {126}

[The First Mode]

75. There are two modes of the fallacy of division. The first mode results from the fact that a word can conjoin (*coniungere*) terms or

propositions. It can do this in two ways, namely, by linking (*copu-lando*) or by disjoining, for conjoining is common to linking and disjoining, just as conjunction is common to the linking conjunction and the disjunctive conjunction and to the other sorts of conjunctions, for it is the genus of all of them. Therefore, conjoining terms or propositions is common to both linking and disjoining the same things. And the first mode results from this. For example, 'Five are two and three.' A paralogism is formed in this way: 'Whatever things are two and three are three; but five are two and three; therefore, five are three.' The minor premise is ambiguous. For it can be divided, in which case its sense is 'Five are two and five are three'; in this way it is a linked proposition. Or it can be compounded, and its sense is 'Five are two and three' in such a way that it is [a proposition] with a linked predicate; and in that case there is a linking of terms. (The major premise is likewise ambiguous.) 'Five are even and odd' is similar.

[A fallacy of division is produced] by disjoining in this way: 'Every animal is rational or irrational; but it is not the case that every animal is rational; therefore, every animal is irrational.' The major premise is ambiguous, because it can be divided. In that case its sense is 'Every animal is rational or every animal is irrational'; and in this way it has a disjoined predicate and so is a disjunction of terms. And in this way these expressions are said to be compounded, because the conjunction ['or'] is first and foremost a disjoining of parts of an expression and secondarily a disjoining of expressions.

These cases are similar: 'Every animal is healthy or sick'; 'Every line is straight or curved'; 'Every number is even or odd'; 'Every substance is corporeal or incorporeal.' {127}

[The Second Mode]

76. The second mode of the fallacy of division results from the fact that an inflected word or a determination can be paired with different things. For example, 'You see him struck with your eyes.' A paralogism is made in this way: 'With whatever you see a man struck, with that he is struck; but you see a man struck with your eye (or eyes); therefore, with your eye (or eyes) he is struck.' The minor premise is ambiguous, because the inflected form or ablative

phrase 'with your eyes' can be paired with the verb 'you see'; in which case it signifies the means of vision, and its sense is 'You with your eye see the man who is struck.' In this case it is compounded, because since the ablative determination is an act, and an act occurs more truly in a verb than in a participle, the ablative should determine the verb primarily and the participle secondarily. Alternatively, 'with your eyes' can be paired with the participle 'struck,' in which case it signifies the means of striking. In this case it is divided, and its sense is 'You see the man who is struck with your eyes.'

These are similar: 'I made you a slave being a free man,' and 'Fifty of men one hundred divine Achilles left.' Also, 'You know only three men are running,' supposing that six men are running and you know about only three: 'But whatever is known is true; therefore, that only three men are running is true.' The first premise is ambiguous, because the adverb 'only' can determine the verb 'you know' – in which case it is compounded and true – or it can determine the verb 'are running,' in which case it is divided and false.

Also, 'You are today born.' Proof. You are today; therefore, you are born or not born. But it is not the case that you are not born; therefore, you are born. Therefore, you are born today. The first premise is ambiguous in virtue of the fact that the adverb 'today' can determine the verb 'you are' – in which case it is compounded and true – or it can determine the participle 'born,' in which case it is divided and false.

The Fallacy of the Consequent

[Consequences]

{169} 150. Some consequences are simple, and others are composite. A simple consequence is, for example, 'If it is a man, it is an animal' or 'If he is an adulterer, he is elegantly dressed (or, he wanders about at night),' and so on for other cases. A composite consequence is one that has to do with oppositions, and this occurs in the case of contraries or contradictories, as in *Topics* II (8, 113b15ff).

151. The consequence that is composite or has to do with oppo-sitions has two species, because some composite consequences are straightforward and some are inverse.

152. A straightforward consequence occurs when the opposite of the consequent follows from the opposite of the antecedent. For example, 'If there is justice, there is virtue; therefore, if there is injustice, there is vice'; for here the opposite of the consequent (namely, vice) follows from the opposite of the antecedent (namely, injustice). For a straightforward consequence holds for practically all contraries.

153. An inverse consequence occurs when the opposite of the antecedent follows from the opposite of the consequent; for exam-ple, 'If it is a man, it is an animal; therefore, if it is a non-animal, it is a non-man.' For here the opposite of the antecedent (namely, non-man) follows from the opposite of the consequent (namely, non-animal). Only inverse consequences can hold for contradic-tories. {170}

154. There are two species of simple consequences. Some simple consequences hold by reason of Topical relationships. For example, 'If it is a man, it is an animal'; for here there is a relationship *from the species*. But other simple consequences hold by reason of circum-stances, and these are studied in rhetoric.

155. As 'consequence' is used generally for all these conse-quences, so 'consequent' is used generally insofar as there is one sophistical Topic that is said to be of the consequent. This Topic is said to be of the consequent and not of the antecedent because the consequent is here made the source of the inference in virtue of the fact that the consequent is put in the antecedent [position] and a sophistical (as well as a dialectical) Topic takes its name from what does the implying and not from what is implied.

[The Causes and Modes of This Fallacy]

156. The source of the effectiveness of the fallacy of the consequent is the agreement between the correct consequence and its converse. The source of the defect is the falsity of the converse. And Aristotle touches on this twofold cause briefly, saying 'insofar as they think a consequence converts' when it does not convert (*Soph. el.* 5, 167b1–2). For 'consequence' points to the direct consequence,

which is the source of the effectiveness in producing belief in its converse; but 'converts' points to the converse, and this is a false consequence, which is the source of the defect.

Aristotle indicates that there are three modes of the fallacy of the consequent (*Soph. el.* 5, 167b1–20).

[The First Mode]

157. The first mode occurs when a consequence made in accordance with Topical relationships is converted. For example, 'If it is a man, it is an animal; therefore, if it is an animal, it is a man.' And it depends on putting the consequent [in the antecedent position], so that in this case it is a fallacy of the consequent. Similarly in this case: {171} 'If it is not an animal, it is not a man; therefore, if it is not a man, it is not an animal.' It, too, depends on putting the consequent [in the antecedent position]. Similarly in this case: 'If it is honey, it is ruddy; therefore, if it is ruddy, it is honey; but gall is ruddy; therefore, gall is honey.'

Similarly in this case: 'If it has rained, the earth is drenched; therefore, if the earth is drenched, it has rained.' For in all these examples above, people think the consequence converts when it does not convert, and so they err with regard to the consequent.

[The Second Mode]

158. The second mode occurs when people think that a consequence holding because of certain circumstances inhering in a person (such as is found in rhetoric) converts. For example, 'If he is an adulterer, he is elegantly dressed (or, he wanders about at night, and so on with regard to other circumstances); therefore, if he is elegantly dressed (or, he wanders about at night), he is an adulterer.' Here there is a fallacy of the consequent; because if he is an adulterer, he has one of the circumstances belonging to an adulterer, but not vice versa, just as if he is a man, he has a color, but not vice versa. 'If someone stole something, he did not earn it or acquire it as a loan; therefore, if he did not earn it or acquire it as a loan, he stole it.' But this does not follow, for people think a consequence converts when it does not convert.

[The Third Mode]

159. The third mode of the fallacy of the consequent arises when they think that a consequence which has to do with oppositions converts. For example, {172} 'If it has come into being, it has a source; therefore, if it has not come into being, it does not have a source; but the world has not come into being – that is, been generated; therefore, the world does not have a source; therefore, the world is infinite in duration, and so the world is from eternity.' For Melissus went wrong in a fallacy of the consequent in the first inference (*Soph. el.* 6, 168b35–40). For this consequence is correct: 'If it has come into being, it has a source,' because anything generated has a source, since nothing comes to be from nothing; therefore, if something comes to be, it comes to be from something. Therefore, if it has come into being, it has a source. But this does not follow: 'If it has not come into being, it does not have a source.' For it argues from the destruction of the antecedent and uses a straightforward consequence in connection with contradictory opposites, although an inverse consequence should always be used in connection with contradictory opposites. For example, this follows correctly: 'If it has come into being, it has a source; therefore, if it does not have a source, it has not come into being.' Similarly, here there is a fallacy of the consequent from the destruction of the antecedent: 'If it is a man, it is an animal; therefore, if it is not a man, it is not an animal.' Hence, there is in this case a straightforward consequence when there ought to be an inverse consequence, for in connection with contradictories it is not acceptable to argue with a straightforward [consequence].

160. From what has been said so far it is clear that whenever there is a fallacy of the consequent there is always a double consequence. This is also clear from the fact that whenever Aristotle talks about the fallacy of the consequent, he always puts expressions having to do with the fallacy of the consequent in the form of a double consequence, such as 'If this is, that is'; and 'when that is, (they think) this is' (*Soph. el.* 5, 167b1ff.; 6, 168b27ff.). {173}

161. As for the substance of any paralogism, there is a source of effectiveness and a source of defect for verbal fallacies as well as for extra-verbal fallacies. And so, if in a fallacy of the consequent a correct consequence is the source of the effectiveness and a false

consequence is the source of the defect, there must be a double consequence whenever there is a paralogism of the consequent.

162. Furthermore, with regard to the same point, it is impossible for any consequence to be converted unless in that case there are two consequences; because if a consequence is converted, there is in that case the consequence that is converted and the consequence into which it is converted. So if the cause that Aristotle assigns is right, there must be a double consequence whenever there is a fallacy of the consequent.

163. This is clearly shown by the solution Aristotle gives for paralogisms of the consequent in *Sophistici Elenchi* II. For he says (*Soph. el.* 28, 181a23–27) that in that case there is a double consequence, one [consequence] when a universal follows from a particular (for example, 'If it is a man, it is an animal'), which we said before is a simple consequence, and another [consequence] that he says is in connection with oppositions, and this we called a composite consequence. (And that is the division of consequences that we presented at the beginning.) But in both cases he solves it by showing that one consequence converts into another. And so, if his solution is generally applicable, whenever there is a fallacy of the consequent, there must be a double consequence, namely, one consequence that converts and the consequence into which it is converted. (And we grant all these points.) So, in arguments such as these, 'An animal is running; therefore, a man is running' or 'A man is running; therefore, Socrates is running' and in all other similar cases there is a sophisma not of the consequent but of accident, as was clear before in connection with expressions having to do with the fallacy of accident.

8

ROBERT KILWARDBY
THE NATURE OF LOGIC;
DIALECTIC AND DEMONSTRATION

Introduction

Robert Kilwardby was born in England, probably around 1215, and seems to have studied in Paris in the 1230s. He entered the Dominican order and was made Prior Provincial of the English Dominicans in 1261. In 1272 he became Archbishop of Canterbury, a post he held for about five years. In 1277 he forbade the teaching at Oxford of thirty propositions in grammar, logic, and natural philosophy, apparently taking his cue from the more famous condemnation by Stephen Tempier at the University of Paris. In 1278 Kilwardby was named Cardinal Bishop of Porto; he died the following year.

The work from which the following selections are translated is Kilwardby's *De ortu scientiarum*, a classification of the sciences that relies heavily on Aristotle. The subject of logic is reasoning and its end is the investigation of truth, according to Kilwardby, and he builds his analysis of the nature of logic around the various books of Aristotle's Organon. After explaining that logic in general is the science of discourse, Kilwardby proceeds to discuss logic more specifically as the science of reasoning systematically. This science of reasoning can be divided into demonstration, reasoning based on considerations specific to a particular science, and dialectic, reasoning that proceeds from common considerations and results only in opinion. Both demonstration and dialectic rely on syllogisms, the subject of Aristotle's *Prior Analytics*, but differ in the sorts of syllogisms they use. Demonstrative syllogisms must be based on first principles that are known *per se*: universal, immediate, and so on. Dialectic, on the other hand, uses syllogisms involving only what is readily believable; in Kilwardby's view, dialectic is always preparatory to demonstration. Demonstration is the subject of Aristotle's *Posterior Analytics*, and dialectic is developed in his *Topics*, where Aristotle explains dialectic in terms of the predicables. Since a person may be deceived as regards either demonstrative or dialectical reasoning, it is also the function of logic to explain the ways in which reasoning may be deceptive. If the reasoning is deceptive with regard to demonstrative syllogisms, that is, if the deceptiveness of the reasoning involves something peculiar to demonstration, we have a paralogism of a discipline or a syllogism of ignorance. But if the reasoning is deceptive with regard to dialectical syllogisms, we have sophistical reasoning. The study of this second sort of deceptive reasoning involves the presentation and analysis of fallacies, first developed in Aristotle's *Sophistici Elenchi*.

The remaining two books of Aristotle's Organon are *De interpretatione* and *Categories*; Kilwardby brings them into his schematization of logic as well. Syllogistic reasoning is a matter of advancing from one term to another by means of a middle term and thus depends on the art of compounding terms (by affirmation) or dividing them (by negation) in propositions. Consequently, Aristotle had to deal with propositions in order to deal with reasoning thoroughly, and he does so in his *De interpretatione*. But the composition and division of terms in true propositions must be related to the being and not-being of things outside the mind. A good logician, therefore, must have enough knowledge of the nature and kinds of extra-linguistic, extra-mental things to be able to carry out the propositional dividing and compounding. For this purpose Aristotle wrote the *Categories*.

For the reception of Aristotle's logic in the scholastic period, see CHLMP II.2, 'Aristoteles Latinus'; Kilwardby's view of the nature of logic is discussed in CHLMP V.14, 'Topics: Their Development and Absorption into Consequences.'

The second selection concerns demonstration and dialectic. A clear and definite distinction between them was traditional in medieval logic, but by Kilwardby's time philosophers were beginning to wonder about the distinction. Characteristics that had been thought to be peculiar to demonstration began to be recognized in dialectic as well. Kilwardby points out, for example, that whereas demonstration is characterized as reasoning on the basis of definitions and causes, which it uses as middle terms, dialectic does so as well, arguing on the basis of the Topics *from definition* and *from a cause*. Kilwardby does, however, draw distinctions between the two modes of reasoning. To begin with, he says, dialectic considers definitions and causes in their common character as definitions and causes, whereas demonstration considers a specific cause or a specific definition of a particular thing. Furthermore, a dialectician takes a definition as a middle term only insofar as it is readily believable, but a demonstrator considers the middle term of his syllogism as necessary and essential. The demonstrator thus acquires knowledge by means of his syllogism; the dialectician, only opinion. Finally, demonstration is an aid to the sciences, because by means of it all the sciences are established and developed. Dialectic, on the other hand, contributes something to the sciences by finding readily believable arguments when demonstrative arguments are hard or impossible to find; but it does not establish knowledge in any of the sciences.

For further reading on demonstration, see CHLMP VI.24, 'Demonstrative Science'; the relation of demonstration to dialectic is discussed in CHLMP V.14, 'Topics: Their Development and Absorption into Consequences.'

The Nature of Logic

Chapter LIII. The Name of Logic, its Origin, Adequacy, Subject Matter, End, and Definition. {167}

492. Regarding logic, it is important to know that its very name is equivocal. For, as Hugh of St. Victor says in his *Didascalion* (i, II, ed. Buttimer, pp. 20–21), the name ['logic'] is taken from the Greek name *'logos,'* which among the Greeks signifies both speech and reason and so is equivocal among them. And so among us logic is in one sense a science of discourse, and in that sense it includes grammar, rhetoric, and logic properly so-called; in the other sense it is a science of reason, and in that sense it is a science belonging to the trivium, distinguished from grammar and rhetoric. It is our present intention to discuss logic in this latter sense.

493. Regarding logic in that sense, it is important to know that it is called a science of reason not because {168} it considers things

belonging to reason as they occur in reason alone, since in that case it would not properly be called a science of discourse, but because it teaches the method of reasoning that applies not only within the mind but also in discourse, and because it considers the things belonging to reason as well as the reasons why things set forth in discourse can be reasoned about by the mind. It is for this reason that a syllogism is called an expression in which a conclusion follows of necessity when certain things have been asserted. It is, therefore, a ratiocinative science, or science of reason, because it teaches one how to use the process of reasoning systematically, and a science of discourse because it teaches one how to put it into discourse systematically.

494. The origin of this science, as was mentioned before, was as follows. Since in connection with philosophical matters there were many contrary opinions and thus many errors (because contraries are not true at the same time regarding the same thing), thoughtful people saw that this stemmed from a lack of training in reasoning, and that there could be no certainty in knowledge without training in reasoning. And so they studied the process of reasoning in order to reduce it to an art, and they established this science by means of which they completed and organized both this [science] itself and all others; and it is the science of the method of reasoning on all [subject] matters.

495. For in the *Prior Analytics* there is a treatment of the form of reasoning not only in dialectical and demonstrative [syllogisms] but also in rhetorical [syllogisms], and generally in every art, and wherever belief occurs, as Aristotle declares toward the end of the *Prior Analytics*, in the chapter on induction (II 23, 68b9–13). Nevertheless, the form suited to the universal, scientific matters considered by philosophers, who deal with theses, properly belongs to the business of logic, while the form that is suited to the singular, sensible things considered by orators, who are concerned with hypotheses, belongs to the business of rhetoric.

496. Therefore, in order that we might see the adequacy of logic with equal depth in the methods of reasoning and in the parts of logic, we should note that, regarding philosophical questions that are to be settled, one can reason on the basis of specific considerations as well as on the basis of common considerations.

497. [We reason] on the basis of specific considerations, I main-

tain, when the argumentation is based on the things that belong and
are considered as belonging to the science to which the question to
be settled belongs – as, for example, when one concludes that the
three angles of a triangle are equal to two right angles in virtue of
an exterior angle that is equipollent to the two opposite interior
angles, and when one concludes that the moon when diametrically
opposed to the sun is eclipsed {169} in virtue of the interposed
shadow of the earth, and other cases of that sort. For middles of
that sort are the specific causes of such conclusions.

498. [We reason] on the basis of common considerations, I maintain, when the argumentation is drawn from things that occur
commonly in the things belonging to every science and that can be
suited to all sciences, and not only to the conclusions but to the
principles of all of them. For dialectic 'has the way to the principles of all methods,' as Aristotle teaches in *Topics* I (2, 101b3–4).
Common considerations of this sort are reasons belonging to whole
and part, to a contrary, to a similar, and to an associated accident and
things of that sort, from which dialectical Topics can be drawn. For
example, one can show that a triangle has three angles equal to two
right angles in virtue of the fact that every *per se* accident is in its *per
se* subject and that having three angles is a *per se* accident of a triangle;
and one can show that the moon when opposed to the sun is eclipsed
because it is hidden from its light source, or that the sun is eclipsed
because it is hidden from our sight, and other things of that sort.
For in the cases just discussed the middle is drawn from associated
accidents. And it can be suited to other conclusions and sciences as
well as to those just discussed.

499. Now, the reason we argue to scientific conclusions both on
the basis of specific considerations and on the basis of common considerations, and even to principles on the basis of common considerations, is that the truth is often hidden from us, and our cognition
begins from the more universal and tends to the more specific. And
so at first we reason by means of common, readily believable
middles until an opinion is formed, and then we penetrate to the
specific causes; and in that way genuine science comes about,
provided that they are comprehended as specific causes. Therefore,
because one must unquestionably have one method of finding,
judging, proposing, and disputing as regards the specific considerations belonging to any discipline, and another method as regards
the common considerations (since in the former one is to find only a

readily believable middle, in the latter a necessary middle, the first of which is carried out in many ways and the second in one way, or a few, to the same conclusion); and because in the one case it must be proposed with a question and disputed on the basis of a common consideration with the respondent's consent, in the other case [it is proposed] without a question and must be disputed unhesitatingly to the conclusion even if the respondent does not consent, as Aristotle teaches in *Topics* VIII (1, 155b3–28) and in *Sophistici Elenchi* I (2, 165a38–b11) – for that reason it is the business of logic, which is the method of the sciences and must teach the method of finding the truth in them, to transmit the art of reasoning on the basis of specific considerations and on the basis of common considerations. And the logic that teaches us how to reason on the basis of specific considerations is called demonstrative logic and is transmitted in Aristotle's *Posterior Analytics*, {170} whereas that which teaches us how to reason on the basis of common considerations is called dialectic and is transmitted in Aristotle's *Topics*.

500. Again, because those differentiae of reasonings on the basis of specific considerations and on the basis of common considerations are drawn from the [subject] matter (since they are drawn from the things and the middles about which the reasonings are carried out), although the form of reasoning is the same as regards every [subject] matter, logic had to offer a treatment of the method of reasoning in general insofar as it abstracts from all matter, specific or common, which both the demonstrator and the dialectician who want to reason would of course have in view. For syllogistic form is the same in every [sort of] matter, the necessary and the readily believable.

501. Notice, however, that that form is not abstracted in such a way that it is determined on its own, without matter of any sort; for that could not happen. Instead, just as mathematics is abstracted from physical matter only and yet has its own intelligible matter (as we showed in preceding discussions), so syllogistic and ratiocinative form of every sort is abstracted from matter both common and specific – i.e., both readily believable and necessary. Nevertheless, it carries a kind of simpler matter along with it, which is between both those mentioned – namely, the three terms: the two extremes and the one middle out of which the two propositions [or premises] are put together.

502. Syllogistic and ratiocinative form of every sort is established

in Aristotle's *Prior Analytics* (I 4, 25b32ff.), where we are always given three terms constituting two propositions [or premises], but [terms] that abstract from both readily believable and necessary matter. And we are taught in how many and which moods and in how many and which figures true reasoning can be carried out in connection with those [terms] in every [sort of] matter in such a way that both the demonstrator and the dialectician take the form of reasoning from it. Therefore, in the *Prior Analytics* Aristotle teaches a method of reasoning by way of all sorts of possible combinations of all sorts of propositions, and he does this in three figures, showing that there is no other figure or true combination [of propositions] than those he presents. [He] also [shows] what sort of middle [term] there must be and how it is to be found. Finally, toward the end of the book, he teaches other methods of reasoning that evidently have none of the reasoning power of syllogism except as a result of syllogism and on the basis of the figures and moods predetermined there; and he shows this regarding induction, example, deduction, counterinstance, and enthymeme.

503. Then in the *Posterior Analytics* he teaches a method of reasoning on the basis of specific considerations belonging to a particular scientific subject in order to construct a demonstrative syllogism and seek diligently after true science. And he does this not {171} by establishing a syllogistic form different from the earlier one or by reproducing the same one; instead he establishes certain material conditions of syllogism in virtue of which syllogism, [which has been considered] unconditionally, is restricted to demonstration. [He does it in such a way] that demonstration most strictly speaking must be based on the first principles of the thing to be concluded, principles that are true, [known] *per se*, universal, immediate causes, and the like; but by extension [a demonstration] can sometimes be made on the basis of conclusions that have been concluded in virtue of true principles, sometimes on the basis of an effect, sometimes on the basis of a particular cause, and the like. He also teaches how many and what sorts of questions there are to which the demonstrator attends, what sort of thing a demonstrative middle must be, and how it is to be found.

504. And those two books belong to a single sequence, as is clear from the general preface at the beginning of the *Prior Analytics* (I 1,

24b12–14), where the aim of the *Posterior Analytics* is stated, and from the general epilogue toward the end of the *Posterior Analytics* (II 19, 99b15–17), where there is a brief summation of both books. And for that reason they are called [books of] examination, or the *Prior* and *Posterior Analytics*. Now the reason for this sequential arrangement may be that the demonstrative is the preeminent method of syllogistic reasoning, the one that is principally and finally aimed at, and the one the possession of which brings human inquiry to rest. For dialectical and sophistical [syllogistic reasoning] are not principally aimed at in their own right, as will soon be clear, but on account of the science that is to be acquired in the end by means of demonstrative [syllogistic reasoning]. And it is for that reason that the method of demonstrating is transmitted in the same unbroken sequence with the form of syllogism considered unconditionally.

505. Another reason may be that much judgment must be brought to bear in connection with syllogism considered unconditionally as well as with demonstrative syllogism. For in connection with syllogism considered unconditionally one must judge regarding the terms and the conjoining of them, regarding figure, [and] regarding mood, which consists in the arrangement of the propositions, each one of which occurs in many ways, as is clear throughout almost the whole book of the *Prior Analytics*. It is also a requirement of demonstration that one consider whether or not the principles that are set down to begin with are causes and, if they are, whether they are mediate or immediate, universal or particular, and many other things, as is taught in *Posterior Analytics* I. And so there is a great deal to do with judgment as regards both [syllogism considered unconditionally and demonstration]. And both books are called [books of] analysis or examination because when a syllogism has been made, {172} one judges it on the basis of an examination of it. But there is a little in both as regards discovery in respect of judgment, as is clear in *Prior Analytics* I, where Aristotle teaches how to discover a syllogistic middle, and in *Posterior Analytics* II, where he teaches how to discover a demonstrative middle.

506. In the *Topics*, however, he teaches the method of reasoning from common considerations to all sciences – viz., from things readily believable to the construction of a dialectical syllogism, in which an opinion is diligently sought after by the inquiry of two

people, the one opposing and the other responding – not in order to come to a stop with it, but in order that by means of that opinion a complete and easier access to trustworthy knowledge might be gained. And in that book he teaches us how (by means of certain conditions pertaining to the [subject] matter) to restrict the syllogistic form considered unconditionally to the dialectical syllogism. And because dialectic is good for three things – for the philosophical disciplines (so that truth may be found in them), for opposing someone, and for [intellectual] exercise – he establishes it in respect of all three of its ends. First, up to Book Eight, [he establishes] its principal end, by which it is directed to the recognition of the truth in the sciences, distinguishing four kinds of problems in connection with four kinds of predicates – the essential interchangeable and noninterchangeable [predicates], and the accidental interchangeable and noninterchangeable [predicates] – teaching how to produce syllogisms on the basis of readily believable things on both sides of any problem whatever.

507. In connection with these things it should be noted that he does not teach us how to determine whether a genus, proprium, or definition inheres or does not inhere unconditionally, but whether anything inheres as a genus, as a proprium, or as a definition. And so the problem of genus occurs not when one asks about that which is the genus, but when one asks whether something inheres as a genus (and likewise, I maintain, as regards proprium and definition); for those three problems are recognizable by the fact that they ask only about the mode of inhering. The problem of accident, on the other hand, is recognized in two forms: if one asks whether something inheres unconditionally, and if one asks whether it inheres with a mode – i.e., whether it inheres as an accident. Thus, when one asks about the unconditional inherence of any predicate whatever, it is always a problem of accident; or every question of that sort reduces to a determination of accident, both because it is a proprium of accident to inhere, and because when something can inhere both unconditionally and in a certain respect, both of those modes of inhering are found in accident, while in the other [predicables] only unconditional inherence is to be found. For that reason a question of unconditional inherence is associated with accident rather than with the others.

508. In *Topics* VIII (1, 156a6ff., and 5, 159a25ff.), however,

dialectic for opposing {173} and dialectic for exercising are established. And, if I am not mistaken, these two exist not in their own right, but for the sake of dialectic as an inquiry into truth, so that we might become more adept at it. Aristotle does not expressly say this, although his words toward the beginning of the *Topics* suggest it (I 2, 101a25–b4). On the basis of these remarks it is clear that the three books we have been discussing are both necessary and sufficient for logic.

509. But since among the things opposed to the principles none must be better known [than the principles], as Aristotle says in the *Posterior Analytics* (I 2, 72a37–b3), and reasoning, both demonstrative and dialectical, is the source of recognizing and discovering truth, and a careless person can be deceived in connection with either, logic must determine the deceptions that can occur in either of them so that they can be avoided and one may thus come to the truth more expeditiously and recognize it more confidently. Deceptive reasoning is called sophistic because it appears to produce knowledge in some way when it does not do so. If it takes place in connection with a demonstrative syllogism having to do with specific considerations belonging to some subject, it is called a paralogism of a discipline (because it produces a paralogism on the basis of specific considerations belonging to some discipline or other) or a syllogism of ignorance (because it brings about a dispositional ignorance, which is a wrong state of mind opposed to knowledge, as Aristotle teaches in *Posterior Analytics* I (12, 77b19–22). Some also call it a syllogism deceptive with regard to a cause (*propter quid*), a name Aristotle uses in *Sophistici Elenchi* I (11, 171b7–12), because it does not indicate the cause it seems to indicate, and so is deceptive. And according to Aristotle in *Topics* I (1, 101a5–8) and *Posterior Analytics* I (16–17, 79a23–81a37ff.), this paralogism draws its conclusion from a false premise – one or the other or both – but it reasons on the basis of specific considerations and in specific terms and draws its conclusion necessarily. For it does not err as regards syllogistic form but as regards the definition of demonstration, which must always proceed on the basis of truths. (Aristotle discusses this in the same book in which he discusses demonstration – viz., *Posterior Analytics* I.)

510. But the deceptive reasoning that occurs in connection with dialectical syllogism having to do with things common to all sub-

jects is called the contentious syllogism in the *Topics* and *Sophistici Elenchi*, and the *Sophistici Elenchi* is about it. And it {174} occurs in many different ways indeed; for either it does what it should not do, or it does not do what it should. It does what it should not do when it introduces a false premise or conclusion to produce a wrong state of mind, something reasoning should not do. And that occurs in three different ways, according to Aristotle in *Topics* I (1, 100b23–101a18).

[A] It errs as regards form alone (when the consequence does not hold good, as in 'Every man is an animal, a donkey is not a man; therefore, it is not an animal'),

[B] It errs as regards matter alone (when the consequence is good but at least one of the premises is false and not readily believable even though it appears to be readily believable, as in 'Every statue is natural, the figure of Hercules is a statue; therefore, it is natural'; the first [premise], which is false and not readily believable, can appear acceptable in virtue of the fallacy of accident: 'Every statue is bronze, and all bronze is natural; therefore, every statue is natural').

[C] It errs as regards both matter and form (as in 'Every man is an animal, what is risible is not a man; therefore, it is not an animal'; the minor premise is false and not readily believable, but it can seem readily believable to someone in virtue of the fallacy of accident in this way: 'No property is a man, risible is a property; therefore, it is not a man'; and that reasoning erred also in form because it argued from the destruction of the antecedent).

511. These ways are discussed in the *Sophistici Elenchi*. The one that errs in form is discussed in the section that discusses verbal and extra-verbal sophistical Topics, for it is there that the specious syllogism is discussed, and that is the sort that errs as regards form. But in the chapter of *Sophistici Elenchi* I that begins 'But since we have ...' (8, 169b18ff.), I think Aristotle gives his view on the [syllogism] that errs as regards matter, which in that same place he calls sophistical, as he himself explains. As a result of these considerations we have sufficiently discussed the syllogism that errs as regards matter and as regards form.

512. On the other hand, the sophistical syllogism that does not do what it should do is the one that is based on readily believable things and concludes necessarily, and yet deceives in virtue of the fact that it promises to yield a conclusion producing knowledge on the basis of specific considerations and concludes on the basis of

common considerations that can produce only belief. Bryson's syllogism on the squaring of the circle was of this sort, it is said: In any genus in which one can find a greater and a lesser than something, one can find what is equal; but in the genus of squares one can find a greater and a lesser than a circle; therefore, one can also find a square equal to a circle. This syllogism is sophistical not because the consequence is false, and not because it produces a syllogism on the basis of apparently readily believable things – for it concludes {175} necessarily and on the basis of what is readily believable. Instead, it is called sophistical and contentious because it is based on common considerations and is dialectical when it should be based on specific considerations and be demonstrative ((*demonstrativus/demonstrativis*)). It is for that reason that Aristotle in *Sophistici Elenchi* I (11, 171b17–18) says that the circle is squared in Bryson's inference, but because it is not squared in reality, [the syllogism] is sophistical. And this syllogism is the third of the sorts of false inference Aristotle presents in *Topics* VIII (12, 162b8–10) – viz., when the inference yields what was sought but not in its proper discipline, which occurs when what is not medical is presented as medical, or what is not geometrical is presented as geometrical. It seems to me that it is this sort of contentious syllogism that is discussed in *Sophistici Elenchi* I in the chapter [beginning] 'And a contentious and sophistical syllogism is one that indeed appears...' (11, 171b7–9). Someone might also think that it is the same as the one that Aristotle calls deceptive with regard to a cause (in the chapter soon after the beginning) (11, 171b10–12), because it is deceptive in virtue of the fact that it is based on common considerations although it should present the cause of the thing and bring about knowledge based on the cause.

513. The contentious syllogism, therefore, occurs in the ways that have been mentioned, and *Sophistici Elenchi* deals with it in all those different ways. For since dialectic is based on common considerations regarding all the arts and the contentious syllogism is deceptive regarding common considerations and is based on common considerations, dealing with the contentious syllogism will be altogether the business of the dialectician, as dealing with a paralogism of a discipline is the business of the demonstrator, since one and the same discipline deals with opposites. And so the book of the *Topics* and the *Sophistici Elenchi* is one continuous treatise regarding

common considerations having to do with all the arts and sciences, pertaining altogether to dialectic, which is traditionally called by almost everyone the art of discovery because in it one must find a great deal and judge very little. For in connection with arguing on the affirmative or negative side of a dialectical problem one can think up a middle in innumerable different ways, in none of which is there any need to judge further than that a readily believable middle has been found {176} and that it concludes correctly. For in *Topics* VIII (12, 162b24–30) Aristotle teaches that as regards a dialectical judgment the first thing to consider is whether the inference yields a conclusion; second, whether it is true or false, third, what sort of things it is based on. For one that concludes on the basis of false though readily believable things is better than one that concludes on the basis of true things that are not readily believable; but the worst is the one that is based on things that are false and not readily believable. In connection with the contentious syllogism, on the other hand, the discovery is carried out in as many ways as [the syllogism] is made. As far as the opponent is concerned, however, the only judgment is whether [his argument] has the semblance [of good reasoning] in its matter, its form, or both. As far as the respondent is concerned, [judgment is made] in as many ways as there are causes of the semblance, as is clear in *Sophistici Elenchi* II.

514. On this basis it is clear, then, why the *Topics* and *Sophistici Elenchi* are traditionally said to be the art of discovery, the *Prior* and *Posterior Analytics* the art of judgment. For the designation comes from the greater part [of the treatises], even though in the details there is something about discovery and something about judgment [in all of them], but more or less as necessity and the suitability of the matter require.

515. It is also clear that the whole treatise on the dialectical and contentious syllogism pertains to dialectic, both because each of them is based on common considerations and because one and the same discipline deals with opposites. And Aristotle shows this clearly in *Sophistici Elenchi* I, in the chapter [beginning] 'But in accordance with the things they argue about, those who use refutations...' (9, 170a20ff.). And the continuity of the whole treatise testifies to this, because a general preamble is put at the beginning of the *Topics* (I 1, 100a18–25) and a general epilogue follows at the end of the *Sophistici Elenchi* (34, 183a27–b15). On this basis it is also clear

that those who say that the *Sophistici Elenchi* is about the sophistical syllogism in all its generality are mistaken. The sophistical [syllogism] that produces a paralogism on the basis of specific considerations belonging to some discipline concerns not the dialectician but the demonstrator, as Aristotle shows in the cited chapter of *Sophistici Elenchi* I, 'But in accordance with the things they argue about ...' (9, 170a36–39), and so it is dealt with in the *Posterior Analytics*. {177}

516. On the basis of things said so far we can assess, in a way, the general adequacy of the ways of reasoning Aristotle establishes in four books of his logic: *Prior* and *Posterior Analytics*, *Topics*, and *Sophistici Elenchi*.

517. But because reasoning is an inquiry of reason advancing from one term to another through a middle – the sort of thing that cannot happen unless it first puts the terms together with the middle, or puts the one together with it and divides the other from it, so that in this way it follows ((*consequatur/consequantur*)) the composition of terms with one another or the division of them from one another – one must be in possession of the art of compounding and dividing terms before one is taught the art of reasoning. And because composition and division are species of proposition or of statement, Aristotle had to deal with statement and its species and their nature. And for that purpose he produced the book *Perihermenias* [or *De interpretatione*].

518. Again, because the composition and division that thought brings about must have reference to the being and not-being of things outside thought (since in statements one must consider the true and the false on the basis of which the reasoning founded on those statements seeks the true and the false that are unknown, and statements are true or false only in virtue of a relationship to the being or not-being of things outside thought), the logician has to have some knowledge of things and learn their nature to the extent to which it is appropriate to their capacity for being compounded and divided by thought. And for that purpose Aristotle produced the *Categories*.

519. On the basis of these considerations the entire general adequacy of the books and parts of Aristotle's logic can now be seen. For, since reasoning is the task of the reason compounding and dividing in itself in accordance with what is outside it in real things, in order that this may be carried out systematically, one needs first

of all an understanding of things that have the capacity to be compounded and divided, which is transmitted in the *Categories*: second, the systematic composition and division of them, which is transmitted in the other books.

520. But because reasoning is not just any composition and division belonging to reason, but the sort that is of extremes via a single middle, for the science of reasoning one must, first of all, know how any sort of composition and division of two terms is systematically brought about by means of reason and, second, how the composition or division of extremes is brought about via a middle. For the first lies before the second, and reason runs through the first into the second; for from the premises reason advances to the conclusion. The first is transmitted in the *Perihermenias*, the second in the other books.

521. But because the composition and division of extremes via a middle can occur via a middle unconditionally, abstracting from every restriction having to do with matter – and I mean by matter in connection with this sort [of middle] what is readily believable or necessary ((om. ⟨*medium*⟩)) {178} whether common to all sciences or specific to any one of them – or via a middle that is restricted to some matter, one must first teach the art of reasoning unconditionally, common to every matter, both common and specific, both readily believable and necessary, in connection with terms and propositions not significant of but applicable to every matter and capable of standing for everything, such as '*A*', '*B*', '*C*'; and that is done in the *Prior Analytics*. Second, [one must teach] the art of reasoning specifically in connection with both kinds of matter, and that is done in the other books.

522. And because reasoning that is based on things necessary and specific to any science produces cognition that is knowledge, and reasoning that is based on things readily believable and common to every science produces cognition that is opinion (of which the first is more powerful and the one that is ultimately aimed at by those who reason), the first is taught in the first place in the *Posterior Analytics* and is called demonstration, and the second is taught in the second place in the *Topics* and is called dialectical syllogism. And because ambiguity and deception occur in connection with both of these reasonings, [ambiguity and deception] which must be known so as to be avoided, the paralogism of a discipline, which is

deceptive in connection with demonstration, is dealt with in the *Posterior Analytics*, and the contentious syllogism, which is deceptive in connection with dialectic, is discussed in the *Sophistici Elenchi*. And so the art of reasoning has been adequately dealt with.

523. On the basis of these considerations one can easily consider the subject of logic as well as its end and definition. For its subject is reasoning, since it is to reasoning that all the things treated in logic are traced back as subjective or integral parts, or in some such way. Those who claim that its subject is syllogism return to that same thing; for all modes of reasoning, as Aristotle teaches in the *Prior Analytics* (II 23, 68b8–37), draw their force from syllogism and are traced back to it. Thus, those who claim that its subject is reasoning propose that which is commonly predicated of every mode of reasoning, and those who claim that it is syllogism propose the most powerful reasoning, to which all modes of reasoning are traced back. Now, the end of logic is the investigation of unknown truth, especially in connection with theses that pertain to philosophical consideration. From these observations one can infer a definition of the following sort: Logic is the science of reasoning, teaching the way of investigating unknown truth in connection with a thesis or in connection with a philosophical question. From the things already said one can in one way or another infer briefly a reasoned explanation for the name of logic, its origin, adequacy, subject matter, end, and definition.

Dialectic and Demonstration

Chapter LVII. A Comparison of Dialectic and Demonstration: Their Difference and Their Agreement. {191}

555. We are still faced with a difficult question regarding dialectic and demonstration, which are parts of logic: How do they differ? For demonstration teaches us how to reveal the characteristic proper to the species to which it belongs, and that is the same as

revealing the proprium. Again, it often teaches us how to reveal a definition, since what is material is revealed by way of the formal in that form is the cause of matter; for example, the inflammation of the blood around the heart is demonstrated by a desire for misfortune for one's opponent – which are the two definitions of anger. But dialectic also teaches us how to reveal both the proprium and the definition. Again, demonstration uses cause and definition as a middle [term] – but so does dialectic. For dialectic argues on the basis of the Topic *from a cause* and on the basis of the Topic *from definition*. Again, demonstration occasionally reveals a cause by means of an effect, as when it reveals that the stars are near because they do not twinkle; but dialectic also argues *from an effect*. Therefore, since they use the same middle [terms] and [argue] to the same conclusions, we ask how they differ.

556. At the same time we also ask in what different ways they serve as auxiliaries, for each of them can be considered both in itself and as an auxiliary. (For on that basis even the whole science of reasoning can be considered in two different ways.)

557. In reply to the first question we have to say that demonstration and dialectic differ in their revealing both a proprium and a definition, [and] first in respect of the middle [term]. For dialectic reasons on the basis of many intrinsic, extrinsic, and intermediate Topics to a solution that is to be given to every sort of problem, and it does so on either side [of any problem] and on the basis of readily believable things and common considerations only. For the Topics *from a cause, from definition, from the whole*, or [any others] of that sort, as considered by the dialectician, provide a middle [term], sometimes for a problem involving accident, sometimes for a problem involving genus, and similarly as regards the other [predicables]. Also, they sometimes give us an argument in ethics, sometimes in physics, sometimes in logic.

558. Demonstration, on the other hand, does not use such a large number of middle [terms]; but, if it is demonstration of the preeminent sort, it is demonstration on the basis of the proximate and immediate cause, and it is so exclusively. But, by an extension [from] things drawn from the proximate and immediate cause, [it demonstrates] also on the basis of a remote and mediate cause, and sometimes even from the effect. {192} But the fact that it reveals things via definition is a result of the fact that a definition indicates a

cause when it is based on prior things, a result of the fact that it indicates an effect if it happens to be a definition expressed on the basis of posterior things. Demonstration is made up of these ways [of revealing and indicating]. Nor does it adduce proof for both sides of a contradiction, but for the true side only; and it does so by means of considerations that are true, necessary, and specific. For it does not consider cause, effect, or definition in its common character, but in its specific and essential character, in virtue of which one thing is the specific cause (or effect, or definition) of another, and essentially indicative of that very thing. And so, as far as the demonstrator is concerned, a Topic common to many is not under consideration; rather, his Topic is specific for a particular conclusion, as well as for things that derive from a primary and specific conclusion by means of a particular demonstration.

559. They differ, in the second place, in respect of the conclusion. For dialectic uses the art of reasoning for determining many kinds of propria, of which some are assigned as complex and others as noncomplex, as is clear from *Topics* V (1, 128b14–129a16); for as far as the dialectician is concerned, every accidental and interchangeable predicate is called a proprium. Demonstration, on the other hand, tries to demonstrate a specific characteristic that is said of the subject *per se* in the second way; and that is a noncomplex proprium. And it applies to every [thing in the subject], and only [to every such thing], and always, and also in respect of what it is, if the demonstration is based on immediate [causes].

560. Similarly, dialectic also argues in order to determine every kind of definition, whether it is made up of integral or of essential parts. Definition, similarly, is also assigned in virtue of all sorts of causes; for [Aristotle] calls definition 'every essential interchangeable predicate' [cf. *Topics* I 4, 101b20–21, VII 3, 153a15–23]. Demonstration, on the other hand, does not reveal a definition unless there is some other cause of it; so that the definition that is the middle [term] is the specific and essential cause of the revealed definition. Therefore, although both [dialectic and demonstration] reveal a proprium and a definition, the difference [between them] is clearly great.

561. Again, although both argue by means of definition and cause and effect, they are very dissimilar. For the dialectician considers his middle [term] as readily believable and possibly otherwise

than it is, and so by its means he acquires only opinion, which is cognition that can change. The demonstrator, however, considers his middle [term] as necessary and essential, and as not possibly otherwise than it is; and so he acquires knowledge, which is certain cognition that cannot change.

562. Thus, it should be noted that the same person can have first opinion and then knowledge by means of numerically the same middle [term] {193} and regarding numerically the same thing, or that at the same time one person can have opinion regarding something and another have knowledge regarding the same thing by means of the same middle [term], as Aristotle teaches near the end of *Posterior Analytics* I (33, 89a11–b6). For there he teaches that, just as there can be true and false opinion regarding the same thing in reality, differentiated in reason alone, so likewise, regarding something that is the same in reality but differentiated in reason and [considered] by means of a middle [term] that is the same in reality and differentiated in reason alone, there can be both knowledge and opinion. And he teaches that the differentiation in reason comes to this: That anyone who knows a conclusion by its essence and in accordance with pure truth, and perceives that it could not be otherwise, and judges that the middle [term] by means of which he knows it could likewise not be otherwise, does not have opinion but truly knows. On the other hand, anyone who considers the conclusion and the middle [term] associated with it as possibly being otherwise has opinion and does not truly know. For example, anyone who knows that the moon when opposite to the sun is eclipsed in virtue of falling into the earth's shadow and thinks that this could be otherwise (because, perhaps, he imagines that it can be eclipsed otherwise than by the earth's shadow – e.g., by the shadow of a cloud or some other body, or by the rotation of the moon's globe, according to those who imagine that part of it is bright and part of it dark, and that by the rotation of various parts it appears to us to be waxing and waning) – [such a person] has opinion and not knowledge. On the other hand, anyone who has seen clearly that the earth's shadow is the true essential cause of the eclipse of the moon, and that it could not be otherwise, has knowledge. In this way, then, the dialectician and the demonstrator use the same middle [terms], but in different ways, as was said.

563. And the demonstrator uses no middle [terms] other than

definition and cause, since one cannot properly know otherwise than by means of the cause, and the definition indicates the cause – except that sometimes he uses an effect, and in that case the effect must be interchangeable with and better known than the cause, as [Aristotle] teaches in *Posterior Analytics* I (13, 78a26). The dialectician, on the other hand, uses many other middle [terms] and uses those already mentioned in more ways than the demonstrator does, since a person can acquire an opinion in very many different ways.

564. In reply to the second question, we have to say that the demonstration taught in the *Posterior Analytics* is auxiliary to other sciences in virtue of setting them up and expanding those that have been set up; for a science is acquired in the first place by demonstration and {194} expanded by that means once it has been acquired. The dialectic taught in the *Topics*, however, is auxiliary to other sciences only in moving reason forward to a variable degree of cognition short of knowledge (which is invariable), a cognition by means of which the way is opened to true knowledge (which is the possession of the conclusions), up to understanding (which is called the possession of the principles). And that is why Aristotle says in *Topics* I (14, 105b19–26, 30–31) that although there are three kinds of propositions and problems – viz., ethical (e.g., whether one should obey one's parents or the laws if they disagree), physical (e.g., whether the world is eternal), and logical (e.g., whether opposites belong to the same discipline) – all of them are the business of philosophical consideration, which is called demonstration as far as truth is concerned but dialectic as regards opinion.

565. But dialectic might be called auxiliary rather than (and in a way more correctly than) demonstration, because (in the first place) to be an auxiliary is to give part of the support and not to provide all of it, and dialectic contributes something toward knowledge but does not establish it, whereas demonstration effects and completes it; and because (in the second place) in all the parts of philosophy – ethics, physics, and logic – readily believable arguments are easily found, although in all likelihood demonstrations are not. For in ethics, demonstration is either not easy or altogether impossible, and similarly in some natural [sciences] (as was said above, where we explained how the practical sciences are parts of philosophy).

566. All the same, the demonstrative science taught in logic is

called an auxiliary to other sciences, because all of them are established, expanded, and completed by means of it, and [because] it begins by offering one or only a few conclusions, [and] then many on the basis of those. And I say 'all' only to the extent to which entities have the possibility of being the subjects of sciences; for we cannot find equal necessity (or perhaps necessity at all) in connection with all things [whatsoever].

567. And we should take note of the fact that when the parts of philosophy are said to be physics, ethics, and logic, by 'physics' we understand the entire speculative science {195} that has to do with divine matters; for it speculates regarding the natures of all entities, and it includes physics properly so-called as well as mathematics and metaphysics. And by 'logic' we understand the entire science belonging to the trivium, so-called from '*logos*,' which is speech. But mechanics falls outside this division because philosophers traditionally do not trouble themselves much about it. Or perhaps it can be traced back to ethics as its handmaiden, or to physics, since mechanics is subordinated in a way to physics, commonly so-called because of the physical things with which it deals or because of its mode of operation (as was said above where the comparison of the speculative and practical sciences was sorted out).

568. On the basis of these considerations, then, the difference between dialectic and demonstration is clear, both in themselves and in their role as auxiliaries. But there is no need to inquire now into the way in which syllogistic and reasoning in general serve as auxiliaries to all the sciences, since it is clear that in its species, dialectic and demonstration, it does provide auxiliaries, as long as they serve as auxiliaries to the sciences. Nor can it be otherwise, as is clear *per se*. For [reasoning] does not stoop to contributing to any science except when there is reasoning either by means of common considerations and readily believable things – in which case it is dialectic – or by means of specific considerations and necessary things – in which case it is demonstration.

9

WALTER BURLEY
CONSEQUENCES

Introduction

Walter Burley was born around 1275, probably in Yorkshire, England. He was a master of arts by 1301/2, and a fellow of Merton College, Oxford, by 1305. By 1310 he was in Paris studying theology, and in 1327 Edward III appointed him an envoy to the papal court. The remainder of his career was devoted to diplomatic service as well as philosophical writing. He died soon after 1344.

Burley was a prolific writer. He wrote commentaries on most of Aristotle's works on natural philosophy, sometimes more than one commentary on the same work, and he also composed some influential treatises on philosophical considerations growing out of the intensification and diminution of qualities (the intension and remission of forms) and out of the assignment of first or last instants to a thing's or an event's duration. His work on the lives of the philosophers, written in the early 1340s, was very popular. Around the same time he finished his commentary on Aristotle's *Politics*. His commentary on the *Ethics* had been completed earlier, in 1333–4. He also commented on all of Aristotle's logical works and wrote several logic treatises of his own. His best-known work of this sort, *The Purity of the Art of Logic* (*De puritate artis logicae*), was published in two versions. The earlier, shorter version was written before the appearance of Ockham's *Summa logicae* in 1324. The second version, dating from 1325–8, is in many ways a response to Ockham's logic. The discussion of consequences translated here is the first of the two sections comprising the shorter version of his *De puritate*.

Under the concept of a consequence, medieval logicians understood three different relationships among propositions: implication, entailment, and argument. Burley may have been the earliest logician to develop consequences as the basis for all logic. In his *De puritate* he subsumes the treatment of the syllogism under general rules of consequences. In this discussion of consequences Burley draws some fundamental distinctions among kinds of consequences and then offers ten general rules of consequences, each of which he discusses in detail.

For further reading on the medieval theory of consequences, see CHLMP V.15, 'Consequences.'

Consequences

The Elements of the Art of Logic

[Preface]

{199} God willing, I propose compiling a treatise on the elements of the art of logic, so that young men who are disputants in connection with any problem whatever can become practiced and quick at meeting arguments. And this little book will contain four parts. The first part lays down certain general rules that must be applied in the following parts. The second part deals with the art of sophistical reasoning, the third with the art of contentious reasoning. The fourth part briefly and succinctly presents some things regarding the art of demonstration. The first part will contain three sections. The first [section] lays down general rules of consequences; the second deals with the nature of syncategorematic words; the third briefly presents some things regarding the suppositions of terms.

[Part One: General Rules]

[Section I: General Rules of consequences]

[o. Absolute and As-of-now Consequences]

First of all, then, I present a preliminary distinction: One sort of consequence is absolute, another sort is as-of-now. An absolute consequence is one that holds good for every time – e.g., 'A man is running; therefore, an animal is running.' An as-of-now consequence holds good for a determinate time and not always – e.g., 'Every man is running; therefore, Socrates is running,' since that consequence does not hold good always, but only while Socrates is a man.

[1. First Principal Rule]

The first rule of consequences is the following:

> [Rule 1] *In any good absolute consequence the antecedent cannot be true without the consequent.* {200}

(And so if an antecedent could be true without the consequent on the basis of positing any possible hypothesis, the consequence was not good [if it was an absolute consequence].)

> [Rule 1'] *In an as-of-now consequence, however, the antecedent cannot be true without the consequent as of now*

– viz., for the time for which the consequence holds good.
   Two other rules follow from that rule. The first is this:

> [Rule 1a] *In an absolute consequence what is impossible does not follow from what is contingent.*

The second is this:

> [Rule 1b] *What is contingent does not follow from what is necessary.*

And the reason for both [of these subsidiary rules] is that what is contingent can be without what is impossible, and what is necessary can be without what is contingent.

[2. Second Principal Rule]

The second principal rule is this:

> [Rule 2] *Whatever follows from the consequent follows from the antecedent.*

There is also another rule, almost the same:

[Rule 2'] *Whatever is antecedent to the antecedent is antecedent to the consequent.*

For those two rules always produce a good argument.

There are also two other *false* rules, which always produce a fallacy of the consequent, and they are these: [FR2a] Whatever follows from the antecedent follows from the consequent; [FR2b] Whatever is antecedent to the consequent is antecedent to the antecedent.

[2a. Consequences from the First to the Last]

It is on the basis of [Rule 2], whatever follows from the consequent follows from the antecedent, that a consequence from the first to the last holds good when one argues on the basis of many intermediate consequences. And it must be taken into account that a consequence from the first to the last holds good only when that which is the consequent in the preceding conditional is the antecedent in the succeeding conditional. For if the antecedent in the succeeding conditional were different from the consequent in the preceding conditional, the consequence from the first to the last would not hold good; instead, there would be a fallacy of accident based on the variation of the middle [proposition]. For the consequent in the preceding conditional is the middle joining the later conditional with the earlier one, and it is for that reason that the consequent in the preceding conditional must be the same as the antecedent in the succeeding conditional.

For example, 'If it is a man, it is an animal; if it is an animal, it is a body; if it is a body, it is a substance; therefore, from the first to the last, {201} if it is a man, it is a substance.' And the consequence from the first to the last 'If it is a man, it is a substance' holds good because ((*quia/si*)) all those consequences were joined to one another in that whatever was the consequent in an earlier consequence was the antecedent in the later consequence.

On this basis it is evident that if one argues in this way – 'If there is no time, it is not day; and if it is not day and there is some time, it is night; and if it is night, there is some time; therefore, from the first to the last, if there is no time, there is some time' – the consequence from the first to the last does not hold good because the consequent in a preceding conditional is not the same as the antecedent in the succeeding conditional. For the first consequence was 'If there is not time, it is not day,' so that in that consequence the consequent was only 'It is not day,' and in the second consequence there was only this antecedent: 'It is not day, and there is some time.' And so the [consequence] from the first to the last is not valid because the antecedent in the later consequence and the consequent in the earlier were not the same.

[2b. Sophismata]

On the basis of [Rule 2], the solution to sophismata of the following sort is evident.

It is proved that

> THE BIGGER (*quanto maius*) SOMETHING IS, THE SMALLER
> (*tanto minus*) IT APPEARS.

The proof goes this way: 'The bigger something is, the greater the distance at which it appears; and the greater the distance at which something appears, the smaller it appears; therefore, from the first to the last, the bigger something is, the smaller it appears.'

And it is similarly proved that

> THE UGLIER (*quanto magis turpis*) SOMEONE IS, THE MORE
> ATTRACTIVE (*tanto magis pulcher*) HE IS,

as follows: 'The uglier you are, the more you embellish yourself; but the more you embellish yourself, the more attractive you are; therefore, from the first to the last, the uglier you are, the more attractive you are.'

In just the same way it is proved that

> THE MORE THIRSTY (*quanto magis sitis*) YOU ARE, THE LESS
> THIRSTY (*tanto minus sitis*) YOU ARE,

for 'The more thirsty you are, the more you drink; the more you drink, the less thirsty you are; therefore, from the first to the last, the more thirsty you are, the less thirsty you are.'

The solution is evident, since the [consequence] from the first to the last does not follow because the consequent in a preceding conditional is not the same {202} as the antecedent in the succeeding conditional; for the consequent in the preceding conditional is taken with '*tanto*' and the antecedent in the succeeding conditional is taken with '*quanto*', and so it is not the same proposition.

[2c. Two Corollaries to Rule 2]

From [Rule 2], whatever follows from the consequent follows from the antecedent, other rules follow. One is that just as in a universal proposition one can [logically] descend under the subject to any suppositum of the subject in respect of the predicate, so

> [Rule 2a] *In any good consequence one can descend under the antecedent to anything that is antecedent to it in respect of the same consequent.*

For example, the consequence 'If a man is running, an animal is running; therefore, if Socrates is running, an animal is running' is good, and so is the consequence 'If every man is running, Socrates is running; therefore, if every animal is running, Socrates is running.' And one argues for both on the basis of [Rule 2], whatever follows from the consequent follows from the antecedent. For example, because 'A man is running' follows from 'Socrates is running,' whatever follows from 'A man is running' follows from 'Socrates is running,' so if 'A man is running; therefore, an animal is running' follows, this follows: 'If Socrates is running, an animal is running.'

There is also this other rule:

> [Rule 2b] *In a conditional whose antecedent is a universal proposition, the subject of the antecedent has immobile supposition in respect of the consequent in such a way that one cannot descend under the subject of the antecedent in respect of the consequent; but in a conditional whose antecedent is an indefinite or particular proposition, the subject has confused, distributive, mobile ((mobiliter/immobiliter)) supposition in respect of the consequent.*

For example, one cannot descend under the subject of the antecedent of a conditional whose antecedent is a universal proposition, as in 'If every man is running, Socrates is running'; for this does not follow: 'If every man is running, Socrates is running; therefore, if Socrates is running, Plato is running.' Instead, it is a fallacy of the consequent, because it is argued on the basis of the false rule [FR2a], whatever follows from the antecedent follows from the consequent. On the other hand, 'If a man is running, an animal is running; {203} therefore, if Socrates is running, an animal is running' follows correctly. And so in a conditional one can descend in respect of the consequent under the antecedent's subject accepted without distribution, but one cannot descend under a subject accepted with distribution.

[2d. Two More Corollaries to Rule 2]

And, further, from [Rule 2], whatever follows from the consequent follows from the antecedent, two other rules follow, one of which is

[Rule 2c] *Whatever follows from the consequent and from the antecedent follows from the antecedent by itself.*

The second rule is

[Rule 2d] *Whatever follows from the consequent with some addition, follows from the antecedent with the same addition.*

The reason for [Rule 2c] is that each proposition implies itself together with its consequent. For example, this follows: 'Socrates is running; therefore, Socrates is running, and a man is running.' Therefore, since the antecedent implies the antecedent and the consequent, and [Rule 2] whatever follows from the consequent follows from the antecedent, it follows that whatever follows from the antecedent and the consequent follows from the antecedent by itself [Rule 2c].

The reason for the second rule [Rule 2d] is this. The antecedent with some addition implies the consequent with the same addition. For this follows: 'Socrates is running, and you are seated; therefore, a man is running, and you are seated.' Therefore, since whatever follows from the consequent follows from the antecedent [Rule 2], it must be that whatever follows from the consequent with some addition follows from the antecedent with the same addition [Rule 2d].

[2e. Counterinstances to Rule 2]

But one argues against [Rule 2], Whatever follows from the consequent follows from the antecedent, by means of counterinstances.

[2e(i). First Counterinstance]

This is a good consequence: 'I say that you are a donkey; therefore, I say that you are an animal,' and yet something follows from the consequent that does not follow from the antecedent. For 'I say that you are an animal; therefore, I say what is true' follows, but this does not follow: 'I say that you are a donkey; therefore, I say what is true.'

Alternatively, one could prove by means of this rule that you are a donkey, because this follows: 'I say that you are a donkey; therefore, I say what is true; therefore that you are a donkey is true, and, consequently, you are a donkey.' Proof of the consequence 'If I say that you are a donkey, I say what is true': this follows: 'If I say that you are an animal, I say what is true,' but if I say that you are a donkey, I say that you are an animal; therefore, in saying that you are a donkey I say that you are an animal; therefore, if I say that you are not {204} an animal, I do not say what is true; therefore, the consequent is true. This consequence is evident because it is argued on the basis of [Rule 2], Whatever follows from the consequent follows from the antecedent.

[2e(ii). Second Counterinstance]

Again, one argues further against the above-mentioned rule [in this way]: The disjunctive 'Socrates is running or he is not running' is a consequent of 'Socrates is not running,' and yet something follows from that disjunctive that does not follow from 'Socrates is not running.' For from the fact that Socrates is running or he is not running it follows that a man is running, but from the fact that Socrates is not running it does not follow that a man is running; for 'Socrates is not running; therefore, a man is running' does not follow.

[2e(iii). Third Counterinstance]

Again, 'Socrates is running' is a consequent of 'Only Socrates is running,' and yet something follows from the fact that Socrates is running that does not follow from the fact that only Socrates is running. For from the fact that Socrates is running it follows that a man is running, and yet 'From the fact that only Socrates is running it follows that a man is running' is false.

[2e(iv). Fourth Counterinstance]

Again, the proposition 'Some proposition is true' is a consequent of 'Every proposition is true,' and yet something follows from the consequent that does not follow from the antecedent. For from the fact that some proposition is true it follows that it is true that you are a donkey, and yet this is not true; 'From the fact that every proposition is true it follows that it is true that you are a donkey,' since this follows: From the fact that every proposition is true it follows that it is true that you are a donkey; therefore, from the fact that it is true that God exists it follows that it is true that you are a donkey.

Alternatively, one could prove by means of this argument that you are a donkey, since this follows: From the fact that every proposition is true it follows that it is true that you are a donkey, because from 'Some proposition is true' it follows that it is true that you are a donkey. This amounts to arguing in this fashion: 'God exists; therefore, you are a donkey'; the antecedent is true; therefore, the consequent is also true. Proof of the consequence: This is true: 'From the fact that God exists is true it follows that it is true that you are a donkey.' Proof: This follows: From the fact that every proposition is true it follows that it is true that you are a donkey; therefore, from the fact that it is true that God exists it follows that it is true that you are a donkey. The antecedent is true; therefore, the consequent is also true. {205}

[2f. Replies to the Counterinstances]

[2f(i). Reply to the First Counterinstance]

In reply to the first of these we have to say that in virtue of equivocation, a distinction must be drawn regarding 'I say that you are an animal' because the dictum 'that you are an animal' can supposit either for the utterance or for the thing [signified]. What is signified in the first sense is that I say the utterance 'You are an animal'; what is signified in the second sense is that I say the thing signified by means of that utterance. And in the same way a distinction must be drawn regarding each expression in which it is not denoted that an action pertaining to a mode passes into the dictum; expressions of that sort have to have such distinctions drawn because the action can pass into the dictum either by reason of the dictum or by reason of the thing [signified]. For example, when one says 'He knows that you are a man' there can be two interpretations: one, that he knows the utterance 'You are a man,' which cannot be the case unless he knows the language; the other sense is that he knows the thing signified by means of the utterance 'You are a man,' and a layman who knows no Latin knows that.

On this basis I say in reply to the case before us that if in the proposition 'I say that you are a donkey,' the action of saying passes into the dictum by reason of the utterance, then the consequence 'I say that you are a donkey; therefore, I say that you are an animal' does not hold good. If, on the other hand, it passes into the dictum by reason of the thing [signified], then the consequence 'I say that you are a donkey; therefore, I say what is true' is not valid, since the antecedent can be true without the consequent. For if I say that you are a donkey, I say that you are an animal insofar as the action of saying passes into the dictum by reason of the thing [signified], and yet in saying that you are a donkey I am not saying what is true.

[2f(ii). Reply to the Second Counterinstance]

In reply to the second argument we have to say that the proposition 'A man is running' does not follow from the disjunctive 'Socrates is running or he is not running.' And when it says that 'From the fact that Socrates is running or he is not running it follows that a man is running' is true, I say that that [proposition] is ambiguous in respect of composition and division. In the compounded sense it is false, for what is denoted is that the proposition 'A man is running' follows from the proposition 'Socrates is running or he is not running,' and that is false. In the divided sense it is true, for what is denoted is that from the fact that Socrates is running it follows that a man {206} is running or from the fact that Socrates is not running it follows that a man is running, and that disjunctive is true, because one or the other part is true – viz., this one: 'From the fact that Socrates is running it follows that a man is running.'

[2f(iii). Reply to the Third Counterinstance]

In reply to the third [argument] we have to say that whatever follows from 'Socrates is running' follows from 'Only Socrates is running.' And when it says that 'From the fact that Socrates is running it follows that a man is running' is true, and that 'From the fact that only Socrates is running it follows that a man is running' is false, I say that 'From the fact that only Socrates is running, etc.' is ambiguous in respect of composition and division. In the compounded sense it is true, in the divided sense it is false.

[2f(iv). Reply to the Fourth Counterinstance]

In reply to the fourth argument we have to say that whatever follows from 'Some proposition is true' follows from 'Every proposition is true.' And when it says that from the fact that some proposition is true it follows that it is true that you are a donkey, I say that that is ambiguous in respect of composition and division. In the compounded sense it is false, in the divided it is true. And in the same way a distinction must be drawn regarding this: 'From the fact that every proposition is true it follows that it is true that you are a donkey'; in the divided sense it is false, and considered in that way it is universal; in the compounded sense it is true, and in that way it is singular. And in this sense this does not follow: 'From the fact that every proposition is true it follows that it is true that you are a donkey; therefore, from the fact that it is true that God exists it follows that it is true that you are a donkey.' Instead, there is a fallacy of the consequent here, since one is arguing on the basis of the false rule [FR2a], whatever follows from the antecedent follows from the consequent.

For that reason it is important to know that when a dictum serves as the subject and a mode is predicated, the whole proposition is singular. And in that case a descent need not be made under the subject, even though the subject of the dictum is distributed by means of a universal sign. And that is why this does not follow:

'That every mule is sterile is known by me; therefore, that this mule is sterile is known by me.'

It is also important to know that even though an antecedent implies a consequent, it need not be the case that that antecedent with any addition whatever implies the consequent with that addition. This is evident, since although the consequence 'I am stuck in the mud with 100 silver coins; therefore, I am stuck in the mud' is good, this does not follow: 'I would like to be stuck in the mud {207} with 100 silver coins; therefore, I would like to be stuck in the mud,' since a person who wants the antecedent need not want the consequent.

[3. Third Principal Rule]

The third principal rule is this:

> [Rule 3] *In every good nonsyllogistic consequence the [contradictory] opposite of the antecedent follows from the contradictory opposite of the consequent.*

For example, because 'A man is running; therefore, an animal is running' follows, the [contradictory] opposite of the antecedent follows from the contradictory opposite of the consequent; for this follows: 'No animal is running; therefore, no man is running.' And the opposite of [this] antecedent follows from the opposite of [this] consequent, since this follows: 'Some man is running' (the opposite of the consequent); 'therefore, some animal is running' (the opposite of the antecedent). [Moreover,] if the [contradictory] opposite of the antecedent follows from the contradictory opposite of the consequent, the original consequence was good.

The reason for this rule is that if the [contradictory] opposite of the antecedent does not follow from the contradictory opposite of the consequent, the antecedent would stand together with the opposite of the consequent; for if the one opposite does not follow, the other one stands. But whatever stands with the antecedent stands with the consequent. Therefore, if the opposite of the consequent stood with the antecedent, it would follow that the opposite of the consequent stood with the consequent; and in that case contradictories would stand together – which is impossible.

Notice that in order that the consequence be good it is required that the contradictory opposite of the antecedent follow from the contradictory opposite of the consequent, and it is not enough that a contrary opposite of the antecedent follow from a contrary opposite of the consequent. For if that were enough, it would follow that this consequence would be good: 'Every man is an animal; therefore, every animal is a man,' since a [contrary] opposite of the antecedent follows from a contrary opposite of the consequent; for this follows: 'No animal is a man; therefore, no man is an animal.'

Notice, furthermore, that the opposite of the antecedent follows from the opposite of the consequent not in every good consequence, but only in a nonsyllogistic consequence. For in a syllogistic consequence the antecedent has no opposite, since a syllogistic antecedent {208} is more than one proposition ((*propositiones/ propositio*)) not conjoined together. Such an antecedent altogether lacks an opposite because it is neither one proposition absolutely nor one proposition conjunctively. In a syllogistic consequence, however, the opposite of one of the premises follows from the opposite of the conclusion with the other premise; and if the opposite of either premise follows from the opposite of the conclusion with the other premise, then the original syllogism was good. For it is in that way that the Philosopher proves his syllogisms – viz., by arguing from the opposite of the conclusion with one of the premises – as is apparent in *Prior Analytics* I (7, 29b1ff.).

[4. Fourth Principal Rule]

But people do not understand the nature of the contradictory of propositions in general, and so I lay down a fourth principal rule:

> [Rule 4] *The formal element that is affirmed in the one contradictory must be denied in the other.*

Thus, what is both formal and principal [in a proposition] cannot be affirmed in both contradictories but must be affirmed in the one and denied in the other. For it is because the verb linking the predicate with the subject is the formal element in assertoric propositions that the same principal verb does not remain affirmed in both contradictories; instead, in order to give the contradictory

of an assertoric affirmative proposition one must add negation to
the principal verb.

In the same way, the mode is the principal and formal element of
modal propositions, and so in modal propositions the contradictory
is given by adding negation to the mode, as the Philosopher claims
in *De interpretatione* II (12, 21a36ff.).

It is done in the same way in other kinds of propositions – in
conjunctive propositions, for instance, and so on. For the principal
element in a conjunctive proposition is the mark of conjunction,
and so the mark of conjunction will not remain affirmed in both
contradictories but must be affirmed in the one and denied in the
other. It is the same for the other kinds; for in disjunctive propositions the disjunction is the principal element, in conditional
propositions, the condition; in reduplicative propositions, the reduplication; and in all of them the contradiction must be given by
adding negation to the [principal and] formal element.

On this basis it is evident that the contradictory of 'Socrates is
running and Plato is running' is not 'Socrates is not running and
Plato is not running,' because the conjunction is affirmed in both of
those [conjunctive propositions], and, furthermore, they can be
false together. Instead, the contradictory of 'Socrates is running and
Plato is running' is 'It is not the case that Socrates is running and
Plato is {209} running,' since [in this case] a single negation negates
the mark of conjunction. And in this case the sense is this: The
conjunctive proposition 'Socrates is running and Plato is running' is
not true. (And it works the same way as regards disjunctives,
conditionals, and all the others.)

[4a. Corollaries to Rule 4]

But someone might be uncertain about what the opposite of a
conjunctive proposition is equipollent to, and what the opposite of
a disjunctive proposition is equipollent to, and so on.

We have to lay it down as a rule that

> [Rule 4a] *The contradictory of a copulative proposition is equivalent to a
> disjunctive proposition that has parts that contradict the parts of the
> conjunctive proposition.*

For example, the contradictory of the copulative proposition 'Socrates is running and Plato is running' is equivalent to 'Either Socrates is not running or Plato is not running.'

There is another rule:

> [Rule 4b] *The contradictory of a disjunctive proposition is equipollent to a conjunctive proposition made up of the contradictories of the parts of the disjunctive proposition.*

For example, the contradictory of 'Either Socrates is running or Plato is running' is equivalent to 'Socrates is not running and Plato is not running.'

There is another rule:

> [Rule 4c] *The contradictory of a conditional ((conditionalis/conditionis)) proposition is equivalent to a proposition that signifies that the opposite of its consequent stands together with its antecedent.*

For the contradictory of 'If Socrates is running, a man is running' is 'It is not the case that if Socrates is running, a man is running,' which is equivalent to 'These stand together: "Socrates is running" and "No man is running."'

There is another rule:

> [Rule 4d] *There are two causes of a reduplicative proposition; for the contradictory of a reduplicative proposition can be true either because the consequent does not follow from the antecedent or because the antecedent is not the cause of the consequent.*

For example, the contradictory of 'Insofar as you are a donkey, you are an animal' is 'It is not the case that insofar as you are a donkey, you are an animal,' and that has two causes of its truth: either because 'You are a donkey; therefore, you are an animal' does not follow, or because the proposition 'You are a donkey' is not the cause of the proposition 'You are an animal.'

Moreover, it is important to know this rule:

> [Rule 4e] *Although one or the other of a pair of contradictories is affirmed truly of anything whatever considered absolutely, it need not be the case that one or the other of a pair of contradictories is said truly of anything whatever considered under some mode or other.*

Thus both of these are false: 'Insofar as you are a man, you are a donkey' and 'Insofar as you are not a man, you are not a donkey.'

Nor do they contradict each other, since the reduplication is affirmed in both of them.

[5. Fifth Principal Rule]

The fifth principal rule is this:

> [Rule 5] *The negation of any and every [logical] inferior follows from the negation of its [logical] superior.*

And this rule is to be understood as applying when the negated superior has personal supposition; for this {210} follows: 'Socrates is not an animal; therefore, Socrates is not a man, not a donkey, and so on.'

On this basis one can see the truth of something said in other connections – viz., that a negation negates more than an affirmation affirms. For the negation of the superior is the negation of any and every inferior, but the affirmation of the superior is not the affirmation of any and every inferior. For it is not necessary that running is affirmed of any and every man if it is affirmed of a man. Still, it must be known that primarily a negation negates the same as and no more than an affirmation affirms (as the Philosopher claims [*De interpretatione* 7, 17b38]); it is [only] consequently and secondarily that a negation negates more than an affirmation affirms.

[6. Sixth Principal Rule]

The sixth principal rule is this:

> [Rule 6] *Negation governs what follows it and not what precedes it.*

[6a. Corollaries to Rule 6]

Two other rules follow from that rule. The first is this:

> [Rule 6a] *A consequence from an inferior to its superior with negation put before does not hold good*

– as is clear, since this does not follow: 'Socrates is not a donkey; therefore, he is not an animal.'

The second:

[Rule 6b] *A consequence from an inferior to its superior using particular or indefinite propositions with negation put after is good.*

For 'A man is not running; therefore, an animal is not running' does indeed follow, as is clear because the opposite of the antecedent is inferred from the opposite of the consequent.

Furthermore, from [Rule 6a], a consequence from an inferior to its superior with negation put before does not hold good, another rule follows:

[Rule 6c] *A consequence from an inferior to its superior with a word implying negation preceding ((praecedente/praecedentem)) and affecting both the superior and the inferior does not hold good.*

And so the difference or otherness of a superior does not follow from the difference or otherness of its inferior; for this does not follow: 'Socrates differs from a donkey; therefore, Socrates differs from an animal,' nor is this valid: 'Socrates is other than a donkey; therefore, he is other than an animal.' Conversely, however, the difference or otherness of an inferior does follow from the difference or otherness of its superior; for this follows: 'Socrates is other than an animal; therefore, he is other than a donkey.'

And, since a superior taken together with distribution is inferior to itself without distribution and to any inferior of it, from the difference of a superior taken together with distribution the difference of that same superior without distribution or of any inferior does not follow. For this does not follow: 'Socrates differs from any man; therefore, he differs from a man,' nor does this follow: 'Socrates differs from any {211} man; therefore, Socrates differs from Socrates,' since the antecedent is true and the consequent is false. For 'Socrates differs from any man' is true because it is equivalent to 'Socrates is not the same as any man,' which is equivalent to 'Socrates relative to some man is not the same.' But 'Socrates relative to some man is not the same' is true, and so 'Socrates differs from any man' is true.

On that basis it is evident that these are not the same: 'You differ from any man' and 'You from any man differ,' since the first is true and the second is false. For 'You differ from any man' is true because it is equivalent to 'You relative to some man are not the same'; and 'You from any man differ' is false because it is equivalent ((valet/valit)) to 'You relative to no man are the same.'

It is also evident that 'You differ from anything; therefore, you differ from yourself' does not follow but is a fallacy of the consequent, as is 'You relative to something are not the same; therefore, you relative to yourself are not the same.'

[7. Seventh Principal Rule]

The seventh principle rule is this:

> [Rule 7] *A consequence from a distributed superior to its inferior taken with distribution and without distribution holds good, but a consequence from an inferior to its superior with distribution does not hold good.*

For this follows: 'Every animal is running; therefore, every man is running (and, [therefore,] a man is running),' but not vice versa.

[7a. A Corollary to Rule 7]

From that rule another rule derives – viz.,

> [Rule 7a] *When a consequence containing terms taken without distribution is good, it is good the other way around with those terms taken with distribution.*

This rule is also expressed in other words, as follows:

> [Rule 7a'] *Whenever a consequent follows from an antecedent, the distribution of the antecedent follows from the distribution of the consequent.*

'Every animal is running; therefore, every man is running' follows because 'A man is running; therefore, an animal is running' follows.

[7b. Counterinstances to Rule 7]

There are counterinstances to this rule, however.

For this follows: 'Socrates is running; therefore, a man is running,' and yet 'Every man is running; therefore, every Socrates is running' does not follow, because the consequent is unintelligible. {212}

Again, this follows: 'A man is a donkey; therefore, a man is an animal' and yet 'Every man is an animal; therefore, every man is a donkey' does not follow.

Likewise, this follows: 'An animal is a man; therefore, a man is an animal,' and yet 'Every man is an animal; therefore, every animal is a man' does not follow.

[7c. Replies to the Counterinstances]

We have to say that the rule is true when three conditions have been presupposed. The first is that the original consequence holds good by reason of [its] noncomplex elements and not by reason of the whole complex. The second, that the terms by reason of which the original consequence held good are distributable. The third condition, that the distribution is added to those terms by reason of which the original consequence was good.

Because of a failure of the first condition, it need not be the case that if 'An animal is a man; therefore, a man is an animal' follows, then this follows: 'Every man is an animal; therefore, every animal is a man'; for the consequence 'An animal is a man; therefore, a man is an animal' holds good by reason of the whole complex and not by reason of [its] noncomplex elements.

Because of a failure of the second condition, 'Every man is running; therefore, every Socrates is running' does not follow, even though it follows the other way around without distribution.

Because of a failure of the third condition, 'Every man is an animal; therefore, every man is a donkey' does not follow, even though it does follow the other way around without distribution: 'A man is a donkey; therefore, a man is an animal.' That is because the distribution is not added to those terms by reason of which the consequence held good; for the consequence 'A man is a donkey; therefore, a man is an animal' holds good by reason of the predicates, and so if distribution were added to those predicates the consequence would hold the other way around. For this does follow: 'A man is every animal; therefore, a man is every donkey.'

[8. Eighth Principal Rule]

The eighth principal rule is this:

> [Rule 8] *A consequence from a proposition that has more than one cause of its truth to one of those [causes] does not hold good but is a fallacy of the consequent.*

For example, if you argue in this way: 'Socrates is not weak; therefore, Socrates is healthy,' there is a fallacy of the consequent, since 'Socrates is not weak' has two causes of its truth – viz., these: 'Socrates does not exist' and so is not weak, and 'Socrates is healthy' – and you are arguing to [just] one of those, and so there is a fallacy of the consequent. {213}

[8a. An Alleged Corollary to Rule 8]

On the basis of this rule some people accept a [false] rule of the following sort: [FR8] From a purely negative proposition an affirmative proposition never follows. [They do so] because a negative proposition has two causes of its truth, of which one is [just] an affirmative proposition with the opposed predicate, while the other includes the persistence of the subject. [They do so] also because a negative asserts nothing and an affirmation asserts something, and when more is asserted by means of the consequent than by means of the antecedent, the consequence does not hold good. For some say that although an affirmative proposition does not follow from a purely negative proposition, an affirmative proposition does follow from a negative proposition that includes the persistence of the subject; since although 'Socrates is not weak; therefore, Socrates is healthy' does not follow, this does follow: 'Socrates is not weak, and Socrates exists; therefore, Socrates is healthy.'

[8b. Assessment of the Alleged Corollary]

Nevertheless, that claim – that from a purely negative proposition an affirmative proposition never follows – does not hold good; for the proposition 'Some proposition is true' is affirmative, and yet it follows from every negative proposition, however negative it may be, since this follows: 'Socrates is not running; therefore, that Socrates is not running is true,' since any and every proposition asserts that it is itself true; and this follows: 'That Socrates is not running is true; therefore, some proposition is true.' Therefore, from the first to the last, 'Socrates is not running; therefore, some proposition is true.' And it works the same way with any other negative proposition – that is, any and every negative proposition implies 'Some proposition is true.'

Again, any and every negative proposition implies a disjunctive proposition one part of which is that negative proposition; for this follows: 'Socrates is not running; therefore, Socrates is running or he is not running,' and this [disjunctive proposition] is affirmative; and so any and every negative proposition implies an affirmative proposition.

All the same, a purely negative proposition does not imply an affirmative proposition with a contrary or privative predicate in respect of the same subject unless the persistence of the subject is assumed. For this does not follow: 'Socrates is not healthy; therefore, he is sick'; it is, instead, a fallacy of the consequent because the antecedent has another cause of its truth. Neither does this follow: 'Socrates is not just; therefore, he is unjust.'

[8c. Two Doubts]

There is some doubt, however, over whether from a purely negative proposition an affirmative proposition with a contradictory predicate follows. {214}

[8c(i). First Doubt]

The first doubt is whether this follows: 'Socrates is not white; therefore, he is non-white,' and similarly in other cases – which amounts to asking whether an affirmative proposition with a non-finite predicate follows from a negative proposition with a finite predicate, and, likewise, whether an affirmative proposition with a finite predicate follows from a negative proposition with a non-finite predicate – whether, for example, this follows: 'Socrates is not white; therefore, Socrates is non-white,' and also 'Socrates is not non-white; therefore, Socrates is white.'

For it seems that from a negative proposition an affirmative proposition with a contradictory predicate always follows, since according to the Philosopher in *Metaphysics* IV (7, 1011b23) and V (and in many other places) regarding anything whatever, one or the other of a pair of contradictories is said [of it], but a finite and a non-finite term are contradictories; therefore, the non-finite term is attributed to anything from which the finite term is removed.

There is an argument to the contrary, since 'Socrates is not white wood; therefore, Socrates is non-white wood' does not follow, because the antecedent is true and the consequent false. (The falsity of the consequent is obvious.) Similarly, 'Better than God is not a man; therefore, better than God is a non-man' does not follow because the antecedent is true and the consequent false. The falsity of the consequent is obvious; for this does not follow: 'Better than God is a non-man; therefore, a donkey is better than God.' The consequent is false; therefore, so is the antecedent.

[8c(ii). Second Doubt]

The other doubt is whether any and every affirmative proposition implies a negative proposition with a contradictory predicate – i.e., whether in general a negative proposition with a non-finite predicate follows from an affirmative proposition with a finite predicate, and whether a negative proposition with a finite predicate follows from an affirmative proposition with a non-finite predicate.

For it seems that it does not, since 'Socrates was white; therefore, Socrates was not non-white' does not follow, nor does 'Socrates is not white; therefore, Socrates is non-white,' nor does 'Socrates sees a non-man; therefore, Socrates does not see a man.'

The Philosopher seems to claim the contrary in *De interpretatione* II (10, 20a20ff.).

[8c(iii). Consideration of the First Doubt]

As for the first of these doubts, we have to say that as long as each of the two extremes is simple, both the subject and the predicate, then in general an affirmative proposition with a non-finite predicate does follow from a negative proposition with a finite predicate, and an affirmative proposition with a finite predicate does follow from a negative proposition {215} with a non-finite predicate. The reason for this is that regarding any simple negative proposition whatever one or the other of a pair of contradictories is affirmed [of it], and so one [contradictory] is attributed to any [negative proposition] of which the other is denied; but a finite and a non-finite term are contradictories.

And so I maintain that in general where simple [terms] are concerned, a negative proposition with a finite predicate implies an affirmative proposition with a non-finite predicate, and a negative proposition with a non-finite predicate implies an affirmative proposition with a finite predicate. For this follows: 'The man is not just; therefore, the man is non-just,' and so does this: 'The man is non-just; therefore, the man is not just.'

On the other hand, if one or the other extreme, either the subject or the predicate, is composite, it does not follow; for in that case the negative proposition need not imply the affirmative. Here is an example in which the compositeness occurs in the predicate: 'Socrates is not white wood; therefore, Socrates is non-white wood' – which does not follow, since the antecedent is true and the consequent false. Here is an example in which the compositeness occurs in the subject: 'Better than God is not a man; therefore, better than God is a non-man' – which does not follow, since the antecedent is true and the consequent false. The falsity of the consequent is obvious, since this does follow: 'Better than God is a non-man; therefore, a non-man is better than God.' The consequent is false; therefore, so is the antecedent.

[8c(iv). Objections to the Consideration]

But one argues in the following way against the things that were just said. And first one proves that as regards all terms, both simple and composite, an affirmative proposition with a non-finite predicate follows from a negative proposition with a finite predicate: for, regarding anything whatever, one or the other of a pair of contradictories is said [of it]; therefore, the non-finite term must be attributed to anything from which the finite term is removed, since the finite and the non-finite term are contradictories.

Secondly, one proves that where simple terms are concerned an affirmative proposition with a non-finite predicate does not follow from a negative proposition with a finite predicate; for this does not follow: 'Caesar is not a man; therefore, Caesar is a non-man,' since when Caesar has been destroyed the antecedent is true and the consequent false, because when Caesar has died he is not a man or a non-man.

[8c(v). Replies to the Objections]

We have to reply to the first of these by replacing the rule that one of a pair of contradictory opposites is attributed to anything from which the other is removed; for when the predicate is composite, the argument is not based on the rule that one of a pair of [contradictory] opposites is attributed to anything from which the other is removed, because 'white {216} wood' and 'non-white wood' are not contradictories, since they are made false with regard to the same thing; for each of these is false: 'Socrates is white wood' and 'Socrates is non-white wood.' And the reason for this is that when one says 'non-white wood' the non-finite negation covers only 'white,' and so 'wood' remains affirmed, but if a non-finite negation could render the whole 'white wood' non-finite, the consequence would be good.

I also claim that an affirmative proposition does not follow from a negative proposition as long as the subject is composite and the predicate is simple. Nor does one argue on the basis of the rule that regarding anything whatever one or the other of a pair of contradictories is said [of it]. For that reason I grant that 'non-man' is attributed to anything from which 'man' is removed, and yet the consequence 'Better than God is not a man; therefore, better than God is a non-man' is not valid because 'Better than God' is something false. Thus if something were better than God, the consequence would be good.

In reply to the other argument I maintain that while Caesar does not exist 'Caesar is a non-man' is true, because a non-finite term is said both of a being and of a non-being. (Transcendental terms, such as 'something' and 'being' and terms of that sort, are also said both of a being and of a non-being.)

[8c(vi). Consideration of the Second Doubt]

As for the second doubt, I say that as long as the predicate is taken with personal supposition both in the affirmative and in the negative proposition, then the affirmative proposition always implies the negative proposition. An affirmative proposition with a finite predicate implies a negative proposition with a non-finite predicate, and an affirmative proposition with a non-finite predicate implies a negative proposition with a finite predicate – with composite as well as with simple terms, with past- and future-tense propositions as well as with present-tense propositions, with substantival as well as with adjectival verbs – nor is there a counterinstance in connection with any terms. But if the predicate has material or simple supposition, the consequence need not be valid. For if the antecedent is taken in such a way that the predicate has simple supposition, this does not follow: 'Some universal is non-universal; therefore, some universal is not a universal,' because the antecedent is true and the consequent false. If the predicate of the antecedent has personal supposition, however, the consequence will be good and the antecedent false.

As for the counterinstances on the other side, I say in reply to the first that the consequence 'Socrates was non-white; therefore, Socrates was not white' does not hold good. And [the antecedent] need not imply a negative proposition [in that way], but rather in this way: 'Socrates was non-white; therefore, Socrates at that time was not white.' This follows in the same way: 'Socrates will be non-white.' {217}

In reply to the second counterinstance I say that this does not follow: 'Socrates sees a non-man; therefore, Socrates does not see a man.' And the predicate of the antecedent ((*antecedentis/antecedens*)) is not non-finite, since in 'Socrates sees a non-man' the predicate is the whole 'sees a non-man'; and so [that proposition] need not imply a negative proposition with a finite predicate.

[9. Ninth Principal Rule]

The ninth rule is this:

> [Rule 9] *Whenever a term is used for one thing in the antecedent and for another in the consequent, the antecedent does not imply the consequent; but when the terms are used for the same things in the antecedent and the consequent, the consequence is good.*

And it is for that reason that this does not follow: 'Socrates is a good blacksmith; therefore, Socrates is good'; for in the antecedent, 'good' ((*bonus/bonitas*)) is used for goodness in the blacksmith's art, and in the consequent it is used for goodness absolutely – i.e., for moral goodness. Similarly, this does not follow: 'This housekeeper is a wife, this housekeeper belongs to you; therefore, a wife belongs to you,' nor does this: 'You have a housekeeper, and she is a wife; therefore, you have a wife,' since 'belongs' and 'have' are used for one thing in the conclusion and for another in the premises.

[9a. Divided and Conjoined Predicates]

On the basis of this rule it is evident when a conjoined predicate
follows from divided predicates and when it does not, and also
when divided predicates follow from a conjoined predicate and
when they do not. And let us first see when a conjoined one
follows from divided ones, next, when divided ones follow from
conjoined ones.

[9a(i). A Conjoined Predicate Following from Divided Ones]

For the first [investigation] we have to know whether or not the
divided predicates are of such a sort that one naturally determines
the other. If neither naturally determines the other, it is certain that
a conjoined predicate never follows from divided predicates of that
sort. And so 'Socrates is a man, and Socrates is risible; therefore,
Socrates is a risible man' does not follow, nor does this: 'Socrates
is a man, and he is two-legged; therefore, he is a two-legged man.'
    On the other hand, if the one does naturally determine the
other, we have to see whether the divided predicates are used for
the same things when they are used dividedly and conjointly. If
they are used for the same things dividedly and conjointly, then, I
maintain, a conjoined predicate always follows from the divided
predicates. And it is for this reason that 'Socrates is a man, and
Socrates is white; therefore, he is a white man' does follow. But
if [either of them] is used for different things when they are used
dividedly and when {218} they are used in the conjoined [term],
the consequence is not valid. And that is why 'Socrates is good,
and he is a blacksmith; therefore, he is a good blacksmith' does
not follow.

[9a(ii). Divided Predicates Following from a Conjoined One]

For the second [investigation], I maintain that divided predicates
always follow from conjoined predicates when the term is used
dividedly for the same thing for which it is used in the conjoined
[term], but that a term used dividedly does not follow from the
conjoined [term] when it is not used for the same thing in the

conjoined [term]. And it is for this reason that 'Socrates is a white man; therefore, Socrates is a man' does indeed follow, since the term 'man' is used for the same thing – viz., for a true man – in both places. But the consequence 'Socrates is a good blacksmith; therefore, he is good' is not valid, because 'good' is used for one thing in the consequent and for another in the antecedent. Nevertheless, this consequence is good: 'Socrates is a good blacksmith; therefore, he is a blacksmith,' since 'blacksmith' is used for the same thing in the antecedent and the consequent. Furthermore, the consequence 'Socrates is a dead man; therefore, he is a man' is not valid because 'man' is used for one thing in the antecedent and for another in the consequent; for in the consequent it is used for a true man, and in the antecedent it is used for a corpse. And yet this consequence is good: 'Socrates is a dead man; therefore, he is dead,' since 'dead' is used for the same thing in the antecedent and the consequent.

It is important to know, furthermore, that in *De interpretatione* II (11, 20b12ff.) the Philosopher lays down two conditions as required in order for divided predicates to follow from a conjoined predicate. The one condition is that there be no opposition in the modifiers in the conjoined predicate; the other condition is that the predication not be accidental. By an accidental predication I mean one in which a determination added to the predicate or to something determinable in the predicate position implies neither the determinable nor the opposite of the determinable. Thus there are three kinds of determination: one that implies something, one that revokes it, and one that is indifferent. An example of the first kind: 'Socrates is a white man; therefore, he is a man' – because 'white' is a determination that implies its determinable. An example of the second kind: 'Socrates is a dead man; therefore, he is a man' – this does not follow, but its opposite 'therefore, he is not a man' does follow because 'dead' is a determination that revokes, one that implies the opposite of its determinable. An example of the third kind: 'Socrates is white as regards his teeth' – from which it does not follow 'therefore, he is white,' nor, furthermore, does this follow: 'Socrates is not white'; for the determination 'as regards his teeth' is indifferent as between white and non-white and so implies neither its determinable nor the opposite. {219}

[10. Tenth Principal Rule]

The tenth rule is this:

> [Rule 10] *From every action performed there follows the action signified, and vice versa.*

For this follows: 'A man is an animal; therefore "animal" is predicated of "man,"' since the verb 'is' performs predication, and the verb 'is predicated' signifies predication. And syncategorematic words perform actions, and adjectival verbs signify actions of that sort. For example, the sign 'every' or 'all' performs distribution, and the verb 'distribute' signifies distribution; the word 'if' performs consequence, and the verb 'follows' signifies consequence.

It is important to know, however, that an action performed does not always imply the action signified in the same terms (and vice versa). For although 'A most general genus is predicated truly of a species' is true, this is false: 'A species is a most general genus.' Nevertheless, the action performed is true for the same things for which the signified action is true (and vice versa). For this is true: 'A most general genus is predicated of a species' because 'substance' is predicated of 'man,' and so 'A man is a substance' is true.

[11. Syllogistic Consequences]

Now that the general rules for every consequence have been discussed, we have to say some things about syllogistic consequence specifically.

I maintain, therefore, that there are two general rules for every syllogism in whatever figure or mood it is made – viz., that it have [i] one or the other premise universal and [ii] one or the other premise affirmative; for nothing follows syllogistically from negative or from particular propositions.

In addition to those rules that are common to every figure there are certain special rules for each figure. In connection with the first figure there are two rules – viz., that in the moods that yield their conclusions directly [I.i] the major premise must be universal, and [I.ii] the minor premise must be affirmative. There are other rules in connection with the second figure ((om. *Una*)) – viz., [II.i] the major premise must be universal, and [II.ii] one or the other premise must be negative. In connection with the third [figure], however, there are other rules – viz., [III.i] the minor premise must always be affirmative, and [III.ii] the conclusion must be particular. If a syllogism is made in any other way, it is not valid.

Let these things that have been said suffice as regards consequences.

WILLIAM OCKHAM
MODAL CONSEQUENCES

Introduction

William of Ockham was born around 1285, probably in the village of Ockham near London. He entered the Franciscan order and studied at Oxford. There he completed the requirements for a master of theology degree but never became a regent master, at least in part because the Chancellor of the University, John Lutterell, opposed his appointment. In 1323 he was accused of heresy by Lutterell and went to Avignon the following year to answer charges. He spent four years in Avignon and ended by becoming involved in the Franciscan quarrel over poverty. With other Franciscans he left Avignon in 1328 and was subsequently excommunicated. Louis of Bavaria protected the fugitive Franciscans, and Ockham came to reside with Louis at Munich, where he wrote political treatises against the pope. He died in Munich in 1347 during an outbreak of the black plague. Besides his numerous political treatises, he also wrote commentaries on Aristotle and on the Sentences of Peter Lombard, as well as various works on logic. The following selection is taken from his major logic book, *Summa logicae*, which was probably written before 1324, while he was still in England.

Well into the thirteenth century modal logic was heavily dependent on Aristotle's understanding of modality. Aristotle's modal notions can be thought of as ways of classifying what happens in the actual world at different moments of time, and his modal logic is characterized by the principle of plenitude: No genuine possibility can remain forever unactualized. This principle and other features of his modal logic suggest that it is best understood as an attempt to characterize relations between necessary and accidental properties of things in the actual world.

In the late thirteenth and early fourteenth centuries, however, a new theory of modality emerged that took the notion of possibility as involving a consideration of alternative states of affairs with respect to the same time. According to this theory, what is possible is just that whose formulation does not contain a contradiction, and it need not be that every possibility is actualized at some time or other. With this change, modal theory is no longer concerned with describing the actual world at different times but rather with conceptual consistency and compossible states of affairs. Ockham's treatment of modality belongs to the new fourteenth-century approach to modal logic.

Most of Ockham's discussion in this section has to do with rules of inference for modal propositions. He begins with a consideration of inferences in which the premise and the conclusion (or the antecedent and the consequent of the consequence) have the same modality. In order to distinguish valid from invalid modal consequences, Ockham relies heavily on the medieval distinction between the compounded and divided senses of a proposition. He says, for example, that this inference is not valid: 'A white thing can be black; therefore, this is possible: a white thing is black,' because we are inferring from a proposition in the divided sense to a corresponding proposition in the compounded sense when the subject term stands for what can be. He similarly discusses inferences in which either the premise is a modal proposition and the conclusion is not or vice versa, and inferences with mixed modalities, as, for example, when a conclusion including 'possible' is inferred from one including 'necessary.' Finally, Ockham examines the relationships that hold among the modalities. 'Necessary,' for instance, is the logical superior of 'possible' because what is necessary is always possible but not vice versa. The section concludes with a lengthy discussion of equipollence relations among modal propositions in which he explains, for example, that a certain sort of negation of a necessary proposition implies a possible proposition, and vice versa.

For further reading on medieval modal theory, see CHLMP V.17, 'Modal Logic,' and V.18, 'Future Contingents.'

Modal Consequences

Chapter 10: Consequences in Which Both the Antecedent and the Consequent Have the Same Modality

[Introduction]

{631} Now that we have considered rules for consequences involving assertoric propositions, we have to consider certain rules for consequences involving modal propositions: first, consequences in which both the antecedent and the consequent have the same modality [Chapter 10]; second, those in which the one proposition is modal and the other is assertoric [Chapter 11]; third, those in which the one has one modality and the other has another modality [Chapter 12].

[Consequences Made Up of Propositions Including 'Necessary']

Regarding the first, we should begin by discussing consequences involving propositions that include 'necessary' [in some form or other]. One of the rules regarding them is of this sort: [If one infers] affirmatively, either in the subject or in the predicate, from a logical inferior to a logical superior without distribution, the consequence is good. For example, these follow: 'Socrates is of necessity an animal; therefore, Socrates is of necessity a substance'; 'A man is of necessity a substance; therefore, an animal is of necessity a substance.'

It is important to know that almost all the rules mentioned before and laid down earlier are to be understood as having to do with propositions including 'necessary' when they are taken in the divided sense. They are also true as regards propositions including 'necessary' that are taken in the compounded sense if the consequences are simple consequences involving assertoric propositions, but if the consequences are *ut nunc*, they need not hold. And so, although 'Every being is in actuality; therefore, every man is in actuality' follows, this does not follow: 'That every being is in actuality is necessary; therefore, that every man is in actuality is necessary.' The result is that a consequence involving assertoric propositions is good *ut nunc*, but a consequence involving the corresponding necessary propositions is neither simple nor *ut nunc*.

It is also important to know that although a consequence from a superior, without distribution, to its inferiors in a disjunction is good if we are arguing in the subject, such a consequence does not hold if we are arguing in the predicate. Thus this follows correctly: 'A body is of necessity colored; therefore, this body is of necessity colored, or that body, or that one (and so on).' On the other hand, this does not follow formally: 'A body is of necessity colored; {632} therefore, a body is of necessity white, or a body is of necessity black (and so on).' In the same way, in Aristotle's view [*De generatione et corruptione* I 5, 320b16–17], this does not follow: 'Matter is of necessity under a form; therefore, matter is of necessity under this form, or matter is of necessity under that form (and so on).' Nevertheless, such a consequence is always or often good as regards the truth [of its consequent] unless the predicate signifies the equivalent of two contradictories. And on this basis it is clear that the predicate in that sort of particular proposition including 'necessary' has merely confused supposition, because we cannot descend to the inferiors either in a disjunction or in a conjunction.

Regarding consequences involving one proposition that includes 'necessary' and is taken in the compounded sense (or its equivalent), and another proposition that includes 'necessary' and is taken in the divided sense (or its equivalent), it is important to know that a consequence from the proposition including 'necessary' and taken in the compounded sense (or its equivalent) to the other proposition including 'necessary' and taken in the divided sense (or its equivalent), or vice versa, is always a good consequence if both the antecedent and the consequent are singular propositions, with a subject that is a proper name or with a subject that is just a demonstrative pronoun. For example, this follows correctly: 'Socrates is of necessity a man; therefore, this is necessary: Socrates is a man' (and vice versa). Likewise, this follows correctly: 'This is of necessity an animal (indicating anything at all); therefore, this is necessary: This is an animal' (and vice versa).

On the other hand, if the antecedent is a universal or a particular proposition, or if it has a subject made up of a demonstrative pronoun and a common term, the consequence is not acceptable. For example, this does not follow: 'Every man is of necessity God; therefore, this is necessary: Every man is God.' nor does this follow: 'This is necessary: Everything true is true; therefore, everything true is of necessity true.' In the same way, if the antecedent is particular, the consequence does not follow. For example, this does not follow: 'The one creating is of necessity God; therefore, this is necessary: The one creating is God.' In this last case, however, it does follow correctly the other way around. For this follows correctly: 'This is necessary: The one creating is God; therefore, the one creating is of necessity God.' {633} And this is always true when we are arguing from affirmative propositions; for if we were to argue from negative propositions, the consequence would not be acceptable. For this does not follow: 'This is necessary: This white thing is not black; therefore, this white thing is of necessity not black.'

[Consequences Made Up of Propositions Including 'Possible']

Regarding propositions that include 'possible' [in some form or other], it is important to know that a singular proposition with a subject that is a proper name or just a demonstrative pronoun, and taken in the divided sense, implies a proposition that includes 'possible' and is taken in the compounded sense (and vice versa). For example, this follows correctly: 'This is possible: Socrates is white; therefore, Socrates can be white' (and vice versa). Likewise, this follows: 'This can be black; therefore, this is possible: This is black' (and vice versa).

But if the subject of those propositions were a common term or a demonstrative pronoun together with a common term, then the subject in the proposition that includes 'possible' and is taken in the divided sense (or its equivalent) stands either for that which is or for that which can be.

If it stands for that which is, then the predicate is either a common term, a demonstrative pronoun alone, a proper name, or a demonstrative pronoun together with a common term. If the predicate is a common term, a demonstrative pronoun together with a common term, or a proper name, the consequence from the one proposition to the other is not acceptable. For example, this does not follow: 'This white thing can be black; therefore, this is possible: This white thing is black.' Nor does this follow: 'This is possible: This white thing is Socrates; therefore, this white thing can be Socrates,' because of the false implication in the consequent. If the predicate were a common term or [a pronoun] taken together with a common term, the consequent would be all the more unacceptable.

On the other hand, if the subject stands for that which can be, a consequence from the proposition in the divided sense to the other in the compounded sense is not acceptable. For example, this does not follow: 'A white thing can be black; therefore, this is possible: A white thing is black.' But the other way around [as regards the compounded and divided senses] an indefinite proposition follows from an indefinite and a singular proposition from a singular, but a universal proposition does not follow from a universal. For this follows correctly: 'This is possible: A white thing is sweet; therefore, something that can be white can be sweet.' The consequence is evident, for this follows: 'This is possible: A white thing is sweet; therefore, two propositions are possible in which "white" and "sweet" are predicated of a pronoun indicating the same thing.' {634} And, furthermore, 'therefore, two propositions including "possible," having the same subject – viz., the same pronoun indicating the same thing as the subject taken in the divided sense – are true' – viz., these two: 'This can be sweet' and 'This can be white.' For, as was said, a proposition including 'possible', having as its subject just a demonstrative pronoun, and taken in the compounded sense, implies a proposition that includes 'possible' and is taken in the divided sense. Therefore, the two propositions 'This is possible: This is sweet' and 'This is possible: This is white' imply these two: 'This can be sweet' and 'This can be white.' But now this follows: 'This can be sweet, this can be white; therefore, a white thing can be sweet,' if the subject is taken as standing for that which can be. Therefore, from the first proposition to the last, this follows: 'This is possible: A white thing is sweet; therefore, a white thing can be sweet.' But a universal proposition does not imply a universal proposition, since this does not follow: 'This is possible: Every white thing is a man; therefore, everything that can be white can be a man.' Nor can such a consequence be proved as the preceding one can be, because although an indefinite, a particular, or a singular proposition is implied by an expository syllogism, a universal proposition is not.

[Consequences Made Up of Propositions Including 'Contingent']

Regarding propositions that include 'contingent' [in some form or other], it is important to know that a proposition that includes 'contingent' and is taken in the compounded sense is interchangeable with such a proposition taken in the divided sense if the subject is a demonstrative pronoun or a proper name. For example, these two are interchangeable: 'It is contingent that this is white' and 'This is contingent: This is white.' But if the subject is a common term or includes a common term or a participle, that need not be the case. For this does not follow: 'This is contingent: The one creating is God; therefore, that the one creating is God is contingent.' Nor does it follow the other way around: 'It is contingent that this white thing be black; therefore, this is contingent: This white thing is black.'

On that basis it is evident that there is a difference between propositions including 'contingent' and propositions including 'possible' as regards consequences involving pairs of such propositions. For a proposition that includes 'possible' and has a common term as its subject, or has a subject that includes a common term or a participle, and is taken in the compounded sense, implies a proposition that includes 'possible' and is taken in the divided sense. But it cannot work that way as regards propositions including 'contingent.' For this does not follow: 'This is contingent: God is the one creating; therefore, [regarding] that which is contingently God, it is contingent that it is the one creating.' Nor does this follow: 'Therefore, [regarding] that which is God, it is contingent that it is the one creating.' {635}

[Consequences Made Up of Propositions Including 'Impossible']

Regarding propositions that include 'impossible' [in some form or other], it is important to know that when the subject is a demonstrative pronoun or a proper name, such a proposition in the divided sense is equipollent to one in the compounded sense. For example, these are equipollent: 'This is impossible: This is white' and 'This cannot be white.' But if the subject is a common term or includes a common term or a participle, they are not equipollent. Thus this does not follow: 'This is impossible: A white thing is black; therefore, a white thing cannot be black.' Nor does this follow: 'A white thing cannot be a man; therefore, this is impossible: A white thing is a man.'

Nevertheless, it is important to know that when we take a proposition including 'impossible' in which [the impossibility is expressed by the fact that] a modal word for possibility is negated – e.g., 'A white thing cannot be black' – if it is taken in the divided sense and if its subject is not a demonstrative pronoun only or a proper name, then we must draw a distinction regarding the proposition, for the subject can be taken for that which is or for that which can be.

If it is taken in the first way, then a universal proposition does not imply a universal proposition, nor does a particular proposition imply a particular, or a singular proposition a singular.

If it is taken in the second way, a particular proposition does not imply a particular, but a universal proposition does imply a universal. That is why this does not follow: 'Something that can be white cannot be a man; therefore, this is impossible: A white thing is a man.' On the other hand, this follows correctly: 'Everything that can be white cannot be a man; therefore, this is impossible: Everything white is a man.'

[Consequences Made Up of Other Modal Propositions]

Regarding the other modal propositions, it is important to know that when the subject is a demonstrative pronoun or a proper name, a proposition in the compounded sense is interchangeable with one in the divided sense. For example, these are interchangeable: 'This is *per se* an animal' and 'This is *per se*: This is an animal.' So are these: 'This is known to be white' and 'This is known: This is white'; and these as well: 'This is believed to be a donkey' and 'This is believed: This is a donkey.'

But if the subject is a common term or includes a common term or a participle as a part, they are not interchangeable. Thus these are not interchangeable: 'A white thing is known to be a man' and

'This is known: A white thing is a man.' Neither are these: 'A white thing is *per se* a builder' and 'This is *per se*: A white thing is a builder'; or these: 'A white thing is believed to be a man or Socrates' and 'This is believed: A white thing is a man or Socrates.' {636} Likewise, these are not interchangeable: 'The one creating is known to be God' and 'This is known: The one creating is God,' for one of them is always true and the other false.

And the explanation of all these was given before [*Summa logicae* II, ch. 20]: A modal proposition taken in the divided sense (or a proposition equivalent to it) does not denote that the mode is truly applied to its prejacent, but rather that it is truly applied to another proposition, one in which the predicate is the same, the subject is a demonstrative pronoun or a proper name, and the verb 'is' is the third ingredient. For example, the proposition 'The one creating is of necessity God,' taken in the divided sense, does not denote that its prejacent – viz., 'The one creating is God' – is necessary. Instead, it denotes that this is necessary: 'This is God,' ['this'] denoting that for which 'the one creating' supposits in the proposition 'The one creating is of necessity God.' Likewise, the proposition 'A white thing is *per se* a builder' does not denote that the corresponding assertoric proposition – viz., 'A white thing is a builder' – is *per se*, but rather that some such proposition as 'This is a builder' is *per se*, ['this'] denoting something for which 'a white thing' supposits in the proposition 'A white thing is *per se* a builder.'

From these and the foregoing considerations it is clear that such propositions as these are to be granted (in accord with Aristotle's principles): 'A man is of necessity God,' 'A white thing is *per se* a builder,' 'The one creating is known to be God,' and the like, if these propositions are true: 'The Son of God is of necessity God,' 'A builder is *per se* a builder,' 'God is known to be God.' And the reason is that the subjects of the former and of the latter propositions supposit for the same things; and so long as they supposit for the same things, if the latter propositions are true, the former will be true (and vice versa). And the reason is that such a modality is truly applied to the whole proposition in which the predicate of the one and of the other is predicated of a pronoun indicating that for which the subject supposits, because that [sort of] proposition is the same [as the original] (although others are different).

[Objection]

But some people say that 'A man is of necessity God' is false because such a proposition including 'necessity' implies that something is necessarily a man; and because that is false, the proposition is false. Likewise, the proposition 'A white thing is known to be a man' implies that something is known to be white.

[Reply to Objection]

But that is mistaken, because such modal words, since {637} they come after the subjects, do not imply that the subjects are said of something with such a modality – I mean the modal word 'contingently,' the modal word *'per accidens,'* and so on. And so 'God contingently creates' does not imply that something is contingently God and that it [contingently] creates; nor does 'God *per accidens* creates' imply that something is *per accidens* God and that he *per accidens* creates. Instead, all that is claimed is that something is God and that he contingently or *per accidens* creates. In the same way, 'A man is of necessity God' denotes only that someone is a man and that he is of necessity God; and that is true. Likewise, 'A white thing is known to be a man' denotes only that something is white and that that thing is known to be a man, which could be true even if that thing is not known to be white. And it is in this sense that it was granted earlier that such propositions as 'The three Persons are known to be God' are true, because something – i.e., God – is three Persons, and that thing is known to be God even if that thing is not known to be three Persons. 'The Father is known to be immortal' is dealt with in the same way, because this is the Father (indicating God), and this is known to be immortal.

Chapter 11: Consequences Involving One Assertoric Proposition and One Modal Proposition

[Consequences with One Modal Proposition Including 'Necessary']

Regarding consequences that involve one assertoric proposition and the other a modal proposition, it is important to know, first, that a proposition that includes 'necessary' and is taken in the compounded or the divided sense always implies the corresponding assertoric proposition, but not the other way around (unless perhaps occasionally because of the subject matter).

[Consequences with One Modal Proposition Including 'Possible']

Regarding propositions that include 'possible,' it is important to know ((om. *primo*)) that a proposition that includes 'possible' and is taken in the divided or the compounded sense does not imply the corresponding assertoric proposition. For this does not follow: 'This is possible: A man is white; therefore, a man is white'; nor does this follow: 'A man can be white; therefore, a man is white.' But the assertoric proposition always implies its corresponding proposition including 'possible,' because {638} this follows: 'Socrates is white; therefore, this is possible: Socrates is white'; likewise, 'therefore, Socrates can be white.' And that is true whether the subject of the consequent is taken for that which is or for that which can be.

[Consequences with One Modal Proposition Including 'Contingent']

Regarding propositions that include 'contingent,' it is important to know that if a proposition including 'contingent' is taken in the compounded sense (or a proposition equivalent to that sense), it does not imply the corresponding assertoric proposition (or vice versa). For this does not follow: 'This is contingent: Socrates is white; therefore, Socrates is white'; nor does this follow: 'God is immortal; therefore, this is contingent: God is immortal.' Likewise, if it is taken in the divided sense, it does not imply the corresponding assertoric proposition (or vice versa). For this does not follow: 'It is contingent that Socrates is white; therefore, Socrates is white'; nor does this follow: 'God is immortal; therefore, it is contingent that God is immortal.'

[Consequences with One Modal Proposition Including 'Impossible']

Regarding propositions that include 'impossible,' it is important to know that a proposition that includes 'impossible' and is taken in the compounded sense does not imply the corresponding assertoric proposition. For example, this does not follow: 'That every man is a donkey is impossible; therefore, every man is a donkey.' But this does follow: 'therefore, some man is not a donkey,' although that assertoric proposition does not imply the proposition including 'impossible.' Likewise, if a proposition including 'impossible' is taken in the divided sense and [the impossibility is expressed by the fact that] a modal word for possibility is negated, the proposition implies the corresponding assertoric proposition (but not vice versa). For example, this follows: 'A man cannot be a donkey; therefore, a man is not a donkey'; but it does not follow the other way around. But if the word 'impossible' or its adverb is used in the modal proposition, the proposition including 'impossible' does not imply the corresponding assertoric proposition but, rather, its contradictory. For example, this does not follow: 'That Socrates is a donkey is impossible; therefore, Socrates is a donkey'; nor does this follow: 'Socrates is impossibly a donkey; therefore, Socrates is a donkey.' Instead, this follows: 'therefore, Socrates is not a donkey'; but, as is perfectly obvious, it does not follow the other way around.

[Consequences with One Modal Proposition of Another Sort]

Regarding the other modal propositions, it is important to know that the corresponding assertoric propositions seldom or never imply the modal propositions. For example, this does not follow: 'A man is white; therefore, a man is *per se* white'; 'A man is white; therefore, a man is known to be white'; 'A man is an animal; therefore, a man is *per accidens* an animal.'

On the other hand, the modal propositions often imply the corresponding assertoric propositions. For example, this follows: 'A man is *per se* an animal; {639} therefore, a man is an animal'; 'A white thing is known to be a man; therefore, a white thing is a man'; and so on as regards many others. Still, some of them do not imply their corresponding assertoric propositions. For example, this does not follow: 'Socrates is believed to be white; therefore, Socrates is white'; nor does this follow: 'Socrates thinks a man is white; therefore, a man is white.'

Now the following rule should be used to decide when such a

consequence is good and when it is bad: If the modality is of a sort
that can be correctly applied only to a true proposition, the consequence from the modal proposition to the corresponding assertoric
proposition is good; but if the modality is such that it can be
correctly applied to a false proposition, the consequence from the
modal proposition is not acceptable. Modal words of the latter sort
are, e.g., 'believed,' 'thought,' 'granted,' 'doubted', and the like.

Chapter 12: Consequences Involving Propositions of Different Modalities

['Necessary' and 'Possible']

Next we have to consider consequences involving propositions of
different modalities. In that connection it is important to know,
first, that a proposition including 'necessary' always implies a proposition including 'possible' as long as both are taken in the compounded sense or both in the divided sense (or their equivalents).
Thus this follows correctly: 'That every man is an animal is necessary; therefore, that every man is an animal is possible.' Likewise,
this follows correctly: 'Every man is of necessity an animal; therefore, every man can be an animal.' But it does not follow the other
way around. For example, this does not follow: 'Every man can be
white; therefore, every man is of necessity white.'

['Necessary' and 'Contingent']

In the second place, it is important to know that a proposition
including 'necessary' does not imply a proposition including 'contingent' as long as the modal word expressing contingency remains
affirmed, nor does it follow the other way around. Instead, the
proposition including 'necessary' implies the contradictory of the
proposition including 'contingent.' For example, this follows correctly: 'Every man is of necessity an animal; therefore, it is not
contingent that every man is an animal.' Likewise, this follows
correctly: 'That every man is an animal is necessary; therefore, that
every man is an animal is not contingent.' {640} But it does not
follow the other way around, for this does not follow: 'That every

man is a donkey is not contingent; therefore, that every man is a donkey is necessary'; nor does this follow: 'It is not contingent that God is whiteness; therefore, God is of necessity whiteness.'

[*'Necessary' and 'Impossible'*]

Third, it is important to know that a proposition that includes 'necessary' implies the contradictory of a proposition including 'impossible.' For example, this follows: 'Every man is of necessity an animal; therefore, every man is not impossibly an animal.' Likewise, this follows correctly: 'That every man is an animal is necessary; therefore, it is not impossible that every man is an animal.' But it does not follow the other way around.

[*'Necessary' and the Other Modal Words*]

Fourth, it is important to know that many propositions that include words expressing the other modalities imply propositions that include 'necessary' (and not vice versa). For example, this follows: 'That every man is risible is demonstrable; therefore, that every man is risible is necessary.' But some of them are implied by propositions that include 'necessary' (and not vice versa). For example, this follows: 'That every man is an animal is necessary; therefore, that every man is an animal is knowable', taking 'knowable' in a broad sense. But some of them neither imply nor are implied by propositions that include 'necessary.' For example, this does not follow: 'That every man is an animal is necessary; therefore, that every man is an animal is manifestly known to you.' Obviously it does not follow the other way around, either.

[*'Possible' and 'Contingent'*]

Regarding propositions that include 'possible,' it is important to note that a proposition including 'possible' does not imply a proposition including 'contingent,' although the implication does go the other way around. For this follows correctly: 'It is contingent that Socrates is white; therefore, Socrates can be white.' But not the other way around, since this does not follow: 'It is possible that God exists; therefore, it is contingent that God exists.' And a proposition that includes 'contingent' implies not just one proposition including 'possible,' but two: affirmative and negative. But it does not follow the other way around, since this does not follow: 'A man can be God; therefore, it is contingent that a man is God.'

['Possible' and 'Impossible']

In the second place, it is important to note that a proposition that includes 'possible' implies the opposite of a proposition including 'impossible.' For example, this follows: 'That a man is running is possible; therefore, that a man is running is not impossible.' And it also follows the other way around: {641} 'That a man is running is not impossible; therefore, that a man is running is possible.'

['Possible' and the Other Modal Words]

Third, it is important to note that every proposition that includes a modality that can be correctly applied only to a true proposition implies a proposition including 'possible.' For example, this follows: 'That every man is an animal is known; therefore, that every man is an animal is possible.' But it does not follow the other way around (except occasionally because of the subject matter). But if such a modality can be correctly applied to a false proposition, [a proposition including it] does not imply a proposition that includes 'possible', although the implication does occasionally hold the other way around. Thus this does not follow: 'That the intellect is not the intellective soul is thinkable; therefore, that the intellect is not the intellective soul is possible.' But it follows correctly the other way around, since everything possible is thinkable.

[The Predicability of Modalities of One Another]

But in order to see when such consequences are good and when they aren't, we have to see how such modalities are related to one another as regards predication – i.e., whether such propositions as these are true, or false: 'Everything necessary is possible'; 'Every known proposition is a possible proposition'; 'Every demonstrated proposition is a possible proposition'; 'Every believed proposition is a possible proposition'; 'No impossible proposition is a possible proposition'; 'No proposition known *per se* is a demonstrable proposition'; 'No *per se* proposition is a *per accidens* proposition'; and so on as regards cases just like these. Thus it is a rule that there is always a good consequence from one sort of modal proposition to another sort of modal proposition when the modality of the consequent is predicated of the modality of the antecedent taken universally. Likewise, such a consequence is never acceptable when the modality of the consequent is not predicated universally of the modality of the antecedent. Likewise, there is always a good consequence from one sort of modal proposition to another sort of modal proposition with the modality negated when the modality of the consequent is universally denied of the modality of the antecedent. Thus this consequence is good: 'That every man is running is necessary; therefore, that every man is running is not contingent'; for the proposition 'No necessary proposition is a contingent proposition' is true. {642}

[General Observations]

In this connection it is important to observe that both propositions derived from such modal propositions must always be taken in the compounded sense (or their equivalents), or both must be taken in the divided sense (or their equivalents).

On the basis of these observations what is to be said regarding consequences involving such modal propositions can be discerned.

It is important to note that all the rules laid down above regarding modal propositions must be understood as applying when all the terms have significant, personal supposition. For if they were taken as having material or simple supposition, those rules would not hold.

Now something must be said about the propositions equipollent to modal propositions, if we are to have a complete treatment of them.

Chapter 13: The Relationship of the Modalities to One Another

[Introduction]

Since there are various problems having to do with the propositions equipollent to and incompatible with modal propositions, we have to discuss them briefly in order to bring this task to a conclusion.

Now it is important to know regarding the modalities that some are incompatible, some are related as logically superior and inferior, and some are independent.

[Incompatible Modalities]

Those that are incompatible are, for example, 'necessary' and 'impossible,' 'possible' and 'impossible,' 'necessary' and 'contingent as regards either of two outcomes' 'contingent as regards either of two outcomes' and 'impossible,' 'necessary' and 'unthinkable,' 'demonstrable' and 'indemonstrable,' and many others of that sort.

[Logically Superior and Inferior Modalities]

Those that are related as logically superior and inferior are, for example, 'necessary' and 'possible' (for everything necessary is possible, and not vice versa); likewise, 'contingent' and 'possible' (for everything contingent is possible, and {643} not vice versa). 'Necessary' and 'knowable,' 'necessary' and 'demonstrable,' are related in the same way.

[Independent Modalities]

Those that are independent are 'possible' and 'dubitable,' and the like.

[Jointly Exhaustive and Other Sorts of Incompatible Modalities]

The second thing to be noted is that some incompatible modalities are jointly exhaustive, so that one or the other of them is truly applied to each and every proposition. 'Possible' and 'impossible' are related in this way, since every proposition is either possible or impossible. Others are not jointly exhaustive – e.g., 'necessary' and 'impossible'; for it is impossible that any proposition – at least any that is not ambiguous – be at one and the same time both necessary and impossible, and yet some propositions are neither necessary nor impossible.

[Dual Incompatibility]

In the third place, it is important to know that sometimes one modality is incompatible with more than one other modality. For example, 'contingent' is incompatible with both 'necessary' and 'impossible,' since a proposition that is contingent as regards either of two outcomes is neither necessary nor impossible. Likewise, 'necessary' is incompatible with both 'contingent' and 'impossible.'

[Affirmative, Negative, and Other Modalities]

Fourth, it is important to know that some modalities are simply affirmative – e.g., 'necessary,' 'possible,' 'knowable,' 'demonstrable,' and the like. Others are simply negative – e.g., 'impossible' (for 'impossible' is the same as 'not possible'); likewise, 'unthinkable,' 'indemonstrable,' and the like. Still others are neither simply affirmative nor simply negative but are, as it were, equally affirmative and negative in that they simply negate one affirmative modality and simply imply another. 'Contingent' is of that sort, since 'contingent' is incompatible with 'necessary' and absolutely implies 'possible.' Thus 'contingent [proposition]' is equivalent to 'nonnecessary possible proposition.'

[Primary and Other Modal Propositions]

The fifth thing it is important to know is that some modal propositions are unconditionally primary – [i.e.,] those for which no equipollent propositions need be sought. These are all the propositions in which the modalities are either simply affirmative or nonsimply affirmative, but not negative; and their prejacents are such that no equipollent proposition need be sought in their case. Propositions of this sort are, for example, 'It is possible that every man is

running,' 'It is possible that no man is running,' 'It is possible that
some man is running,' 'It is possible that some {644} man is not
running'; 'It is necessary that every being exists in actuality,'
'It is necessary that no being exists in actuality,' 'It is necessary
that some being exists in actuality,' 'It is necessary that some
being does not exist in actuality'; 'It is contingent ((om. *non*))
that every man is running,' 'It is contingent that no man is
running,' 'It is contingent that some,' 'It is contingent that some
not,' and so on.

For other modal propositions, however, we do have to look for
propositions equipollent to them. Thus, for every proposition in
which the modal word 'impossible' is included, we must look for
what is equipollent to it.

[Affirmed and Negated Modalities]

In the sixth place, it is important to know that the modality is
sometimes affirmed and sometimes negated in a proposition for
which an equipollent proposition is sought, as is clear in these
propositions: 'It is necessary that no man is not running,' 'It is not
necessary that no man is running.'

Chapter 14: Propositions Equipollent to Propositions That Include 'Necessary' or 'Possible'

[Introduction]

Now that we have set down those things by way of introduction,
we have to consider the propositions equipollent to these propositions. For the sake of brevity we will have to discuss only the
best-known modalities, since on the basis of [a discussion of] them
a thoughtful person can work out what is to be said about the
others.

[Propositions Including 'Necessary' without Negation]

First we have to consider the proposition in which the modal word
'necessary' is included. Regarding it we have to say that either a

negation does not negate the modality or a negation does negate the modality. If no negation negates the modality, such a proposition is always equivalent to a primary proposition that includes 'necessary.' For in such a case, as long as the same modality is retained, the same thing has to be said regarding the proposition equipollent to it and the proposition equipollent to the corresponding assertoric proposition. Thus, just as 'Not every animal is a man' is equipollent to 'Some animal is not a man,' so 'It is necessary that not every animal is a man' is equivalent to 'It is necessary that some animal is not {645} a man.' And that is the way it is generally regarding all such propositions.

[Propositions Including 'Necessary' with Negation]

But if the modality of necessity is negated along with the sign [of distribution] (if it has a sign), then the negated modality is transformed into the modality it implies – i.e., into [the modality of] possibility occurring affirmatively – and the rest into its contradictory. For example, 'It is not necessary that every animal is a man' is equipollent to 'It is possible that some animal is not a man.' But if the modality is negated and not the sign, only the modality will be transformed into [the modality of] possibility occurring affirmatively. Thus, 'No man is of necessity an animal' is equipollent to 'Every man can be not an animal.' And so we need not ask what 'Every man is of necessity not an animal' is equipollent to, but rather what 'No man is of necessity an animal' is equipollent to; and what must be said is what has just been said. And that is because 'Every man is of necessity not an animal' and 'It is necessary that no man be an animal' are equipollent, but 'Not every man is of necessity an animal' is equivalent to 'Some man can be not an animal'; and so on as regards the others.

[Propositions Including 'Possible' without Negation]

The sort of thing that was said about propositions that include 'necessary' in relation to propositions that include 'possible' is what must be said (with appropriate changes) about propositions that include 'possible' in relation to propositions that include 'necessary.' For when the modality of possibility remains affirmed, the modality is not to be transformed; and as for the rest, the equipollence is to be taken along the lines of the corresponding assertoric propositions (with appropriate changes). Thus 'It is possible that not every man is an animal' is equipollent to 'It is possible that some man is not an animal.'

[Propositions Including 'Possible' with Negation]

But when both the sign and the modality are negated, then the modality of possibility has to be transformed into the modality of necessity and the rest into its contradictory, as in the case of the corresponding assertoric proposition. Thus, 'It is not possible that every animal is a man' is equivalent to 'It is necessary that some animal is not a man.'

But when not the sign but only the modality of possibility is negated, then just the modality of possibility must be transformed into the modality of necessity, and not the universal sign into the particular sign (or vice versa). For example, 'No man can be an animal' is equipollent to 'Every man is of necessity not an animal.' And in that case, even though the universal mode is not transformed into the particular mode (or vice versa), the universal {646} negative must be transformed into the universal affirmative, not negated but affirmed, as is clear in the example provided.

[Propositions Equipollent to and Incompatible with Propositions Including 'Necessary' or 'Possible']

On the basis of these considerations it is easy to show the propositions equipollent to propositions in which the modal words 'necessary' and 'possible' are included; it is also easy to show on that basis which propositions [of those sorts] are incompatible, once one knows which primary propositions are incompatible and which aren't. Thus it is important to know that the propositions 'Every man is of necessity an animal' and 'Every man is of necessity not an animal' are incompatible as contraries, as are 'It is necessary that every man is an animal' and 'It is necessary that no man is an animal.' These propositions are also incompatible: 'Every man is of necessity an animal' and 'Some man is of necessity not an animal,' but not as contraries, strictly speaking, because not both of them are universal. Nor are they contradictories, because they can be false together. And so they are more akin to contraries, because they can be false together but they cannot be true together. We have to say the same sort of thing about 'Every man is of necessity not an animal' and 'Some man is of necessity an animal.'

But the propositions 'Every man is of necessity an animal' and 'Some man can be not an animal' are contradictories; likewise, 'Every man is of necessity not an animal' and 'Some man can be an animal.' But the propositions 'Every man can be an animal' and 'Every man can be not an animal' are not incompatible; nor are 'Every man can be not an animal' and 'Some man can be an animal'; nor are 'Every man can be an animal' and 'Some man can be not an animal.' But 'Every man can be an animal' and 'Some man is of necessity not an animal' contradict each other, and so do 'Every man can be not an animal' and 'Some man is of necessity an animal.' {647}

Chapter 15: Propositions Equipollent to Propositions That Include 'Contingent'

[Primary Propositions Including 'Contingent']

Regarding propositions that include 'contingent,' the first thing it is important to know is that we do not have to look for propositions equipollent to the following propositions, because they are primary: 'It is contingent that every man is an animal,' 'It is contingent that every man is not an animal,' 'It is contingent that some man is an animal,' 'It is contingent that some man is not an animal.'

[Exposition of Primary Propositions]

Such propositions can undergo exposition, however, since each of them is equivalent to one conjunctive proposition made up of two propositions that include 'possible.' For example, 'It is contingent that every man is an animal' is equivalent to 'It is possible that every man is an animal, and it is possible that no man is an animal' (and so on as regards the others). And so negative and affirmative propositions involving 'contingent' are always interchangeable as long as the modality of contingency remains affirmed – these two, for example: 'It is contingent that every man is an animal' and 'It is contingent that no man is an animal' (and so on as regards the others).

[Propositions Equipollent to Propositions Including 'Contingent']

On the basis of these considerations the propositions equipollent to propositions that include 'contingent' can easily be known. For as such a proposition is itself equivalent to a conjunctive proposition, a proposition incompatible with it is equivalent to a disjunctive proposition made up of the incompatible parts of that conjunction. And so when we are looking for the proposition equipollent to a proposition that includes 'contingent,' that proposition must be resolved into a conjunction made up of two propositions that include 'possible.' Once that has been done, we have to see what each of those parts is equipollent to, and then from those propositions we have to form a disjunctive proposition to which the proposition including 'contingent' will be equipollent. But that is to be done only when the modality of contingency has been negated. For example, if we take the proposition 'It is not contingent that every animal is a man,' then the affirmative 'It is contingent that every animal is a man' must be resolved into the conjunctive proposition to which it is equivalent – viz., 'Every animal can be a man, and every animal can be not a man' – and a negation must be prefixed to each of those [component] propositions in a disjunction, in this way: 'Either it is not the case that every animal can be a man, or it is not the case that every animal can be not a man.' And we should take what is equipollent to that disjunctive proposition (on the basis of the rule given in the preceding chapter) – viz., 'Either it is necessary that some animal is not a man, or it is necessary that some animal is a man.' And this last disjunctive proposition will be equipollent to 'It is not contingent that every animal is a man.' {648}

In the same way and by the same rules the proposition 'No man contingently is an animal' will be equipollent to this proposition with a disjoined predicate: 'Every man either is of necessity an animal or is of necessity not an animal.' For in this case it cannot be equipollent to a disjunctive proposition, as is clear regarding 'No divine Person is contingently the Father.' Instead, it will be equipollent to a universal proposition with a disjoined predicate, but [formed] in such a way that the modality of necessity is added to each part of the disjoined predicate. But when the dictum of a proposition that includes 'contingent' (or something equivalent to it) is transformed into its contradictory, a particular proposition will be equivalent to a disjunctive, because a particular proposition, an indefinite disjunctive proposition, and one with a disjoined predicate are interchangeable.

But it is important to know that when the modality of contingency is affirmed, the equipollent proposition should be taken [in such a way that] the same modality is preserved in what remains and in the same way, with appropriate changes, as was said regarding the preceding cases. Thus, 'It is contingent that not every man is running' is equipollent to 'It is contingent that some man is running' (and so on as regards the other cases).

Chapter 16: Propositions Equipollent to Propositions That Include 'Impossible'

['Impossible' and 'Not possible']

Regarding propositions that include 'impossible,' it is important to know, first, that none of them is primary, because each of them is equipollent to the opposite of some proposition that includes 'possible.' For that reason, we have to look for what each of them is equipollent to. And since we have said that 'impossible' is equivalent to 'not possible,' by putting 'not possible' in place of the modal word 'impossible' one can readily know on the basis of the foregoing considerations what a proposition including 'impossible' is equipollent to.

['Impossible' Affirmed and Negated]

It is important to know, therefore, that this modality is sometimes affirmed – i.e., [used] in such a way that no negation negates it – as in 'It is impossible that every animal is a man.' But sometimes it is negated by another negation, as in 'It is not impossible that every animal is a man,' 'It is not impossible that every man is running.'

In the first case – i.e., when no negation negates the modality of impossibility – a proposition involving 'impossible' is equipollent to one that involves 'necessary,' {649} just as a proposition involving 'possible' in which the modality is negated is equipollent to a proposition involving 'necessary.' Thus, 'It is impossible that every animal is a man' is equipollent to 'It is necessary that some animal is not a man,' and 'It is impossible that no animal is a man' is equipollent to 'It is necessary that some animal is a man,' and 'It is impossible that some animal is a man' is equipollent to 'It is necessary that no animal is a man,' and 'It is impossible that some animal is not a man' is equipollent to 'It is necessary that every animal is a man.'

If the modality of impossibility is negated, however, then the modality of impossibility is transformed into the modality of possibility. For example, 'It is not impossible that every animal is a man' is equipollent to 'It is possible that some animal is a man.' For because the modality of possibility when it is negated must be transformed into the modality of necessity, and the modality of necessity when it is negated must be transformed into the modality of possibility affirmed, it is necessary that 'impossible' when negated be transformed into the modality of possibility.

[Concluding Observations]

On the basis of the things that have been said and on the basis of the rule regarding the equipollences of assertoric propositions – viz., A negation before the sign of distribution produces the contradictory; after, the contrary; before and after, the subalternate (*prae cotradic, post contra, prae-postque subalter*) – it is easy to know which propositions are equipollent to modal propositions.

And so let these observations regarding their equipollence suffice.

II

ALBERT OF SAXONY
INSOLUBLES

Introduction

Albert of Saxony studied at the University of Paris, where he became a master of arts in 1351. Two years later he was made rector of the University; and when a university was established at Vienna in 1365, Albert was its first rector. Beginning in the next year, however, and continuing until his death in 1390, Albert was Bishop of Halberstadt and involved chiefly in political and church affairs. Apart from his mathematical and logical treatises, Albert's work consists almost entirely of question-commentaries on Aristotle's works. The selection below is taken from his textbook of logic, *Perutilis logica*.

Insolubles are certain sorts of self-referential sentences that give rise to paradoxes, called insoluble because of their prodigious difficulty. The best-known example of an insoluble is the so-called liar's paradox: 'What I am saying now is false.' The middle of the fourteenth century was the most productive period of medieval work on insolubles. One treatment of insolubles in favor at that time was to maintain that they are false just because they signify or imply both that they are true and that they are false. Albert's approach to insolubles belongs to this tradition.

The treatise begins with some general definitions and rules about modality, the nature of true propositions, and the signification of propositions. Included among these rules is the stipulation ('the sixth thesis') that every proposition signifying that it is true and that it is false is false. Albert's examples begin with fairly simple insolubles such as a person's saying 'I say something false' and nothing else. He argues that, by the sixth thesis, such insolubles are false. He employs the same strategy for many of the succeeding insolubles, but the examples themselves quickly become much more complicated, and in discussing them Albert raises several related

philosophical issues. For example, in connection with Insoluble V
(If there are only three propositions – 'A man is a donkey,' 'God
does not exist,' and 'Every proposition is false' – is the third of
these propositions true or false?), Albert argues for apparently para-
doxical rules of inference, such as 'Some consequence is good even
though if its antecedent is true, its consequent is false.' Insolubles
XV–XIX involve someone's being mistaken or in doubt, being
deceived or pretending; and the issues they raise often fall within
the area of epistemic logic. For example, in connection with Insoluble XVII, Albert argues that although Plato can know that Socrates
is mistaken, Socrates cannot know that he himself is mistaken; and
in the discussion of the next insoluble, Albert considers the sorts of
issues involving knowing and doubting that are raised in William
Heytesbury's *Regulae* in the chapter on 'Know' and 'Doubt'
(appearing in this volume as Translation 14).

For further reading on insolubles, see CHLMP IV.12,
'Insolubilia.'

Insolubles

[Organization of the Chapter]

{43rb} It now remains for us to solve insolubles – [which are called
insoluble] not because they are in no way soluble, but because
solving them is difficult. And to that end I want to present [first],
some descriptions; second, some suppositions; third, some theses.
Fourth, I will present some insolubles as examples along with their
solutions. From those insolubles it will be readily apparent to
anyone considering them how any others that may be formulated
can be solved.

[1. Descriptions]

As for the first, here is the first description:

> A true ((versa/negativa)) proposition is one such that things are however
> it signifies they are.

Second description:

> *A possible proposition is one such that things can be however it signifies they are.*

Third description:

> *A necessary proposition is one such that it is necessary that things be however it signifies they are.*

[2. Suppositions]

As for the second, here is the first supposition:

> *Every proposition is affirmative or negative.*

Second supposition:

> *For any affirmative proposition to be true is for its subject and predicate to supposit for the same thing (and vice versa); and for it to be false is for its subject and predicate to supposit for what is not the same (and vice versa).*

Third supposition:

> *For any negative proposition to be true is for its subject and predicate to supposit for what is not the same (and vice versa); and for it to be false is for its subject and predicate to supposit for the same thing [(and vice versa)].*

Fourth supposition:

> *Every affirmative proposition signifies that what its subject and predicate supposit for is the same, and the affirmed copula in it shows this clearly.*

Fifth supposition:

> *Every negative proposition signifies that what its subject and predicate supposit for is not the same, and the negated copula in it shows this clearly.*

Sixth supposition:

> *It is impossible that the same proposition be true and false at the same time.*

[3. Theses]

As for the third, here is the first thesis:

Every affirmative proposition signifies that it is true.

This is proved, because (by the fourth supposition) every affirmative proposition signifies that what its subject and predicate supposit for is the same, and (by the second supposition) for any affirmative proposition to be true is for its subject and predicate to supposit for the same thing (and vice versa); therefore, every affirmative proposition ((*propositio/propositionis*)) signifies that it is true.

Second thesis:

Every negative proposition signifies that it is true.

This is proved, because (by the fifth supposition) every negative proposition signifies that what its subject and predicate supposit for is not the same, but (by the third supposition) for a negative proposition to be true is for its subject and predicate to supposit for what is not the same (and vice versa); therefore, every negative proposition signifies that it is true.

Third thesis:

Every proposition in the world signifies that it is true.

This is proved, [because] (by the first supposition) every proposition in the world is affirmative or negative, but (by the first thesis) every affirmative proposition signifies that it is true, and (by the second thesis) every negative proposition signifies that it is true; therefore, every proposition in the world signifies that it is true – which was to be proved.

Fourth thesis:

Every affirmative proposition signifying that it is true and that it {43va} is false, is false.

I prove this; for this follows correctly: '[This] affirmative proposition signifies that it is true and signifies that it is false; therefore, it signifies that what its subject and predicate supposit for is the same, and that what its subject and predicate supposit for is not the same.' This consequence holds good by the second supposition. And, furthermore, '[This affirmative proposition] signifies that what its subject and predicate supposit for is the same and signifies that what its subject and predicate supposit for is not the same; therefore, it is not the case that things are however it signifies they are.' This consequence holds good because it cannot be the case at one and the same time that what its subject and predicate supposit for is the same and that what its subject and predicate supposit for is not the same. Therefore, it is not the case that things are however it signifies they are. Therefore, it is false. The consequence holds by the first description. Finally, therefore, if any proposition is affirmative, signifying that it is true and that it is false, it is false.

Fifth thesis:

> *Every negative proposition signifying that it is true and that it is false, is false.*

This is evident; for if a negative proposition signifies that it is true and that it is false, then it signifies that its subject and predicate supposit for what is not the same, and that its subject and predicate supposit for the same thing (by the third supposition). And since it cannot be the case at one and the same time that what its subject and predicate supposit for is the same and that what its subject and predicate supposit for is not the same, etc., it follows that it is not the case that things are however it signifies they are. Consequently (by the first ((*primam/secundam*)) description), it will be false – which was to be proved.

Sixth thesis:

> *Every proposition signifying that it is true and that it is false, is false.*

This is proved [as follows]. If it is affirmative and signifies that it is true and that it is false, it is false (by the fourth thesis); and if it is negative and signifies that it is false and [that it is] true, it is false (by the fifth thesis); therefore, every proposition signifying that it is true and that it is false, is false – which was to be proved. And in just the same way it is impossible that the same proposition be true and false [at the same time] (by the sixth supposition); therefore, if any proposition signifies that it is true and [that it is] false, then it is not the case that things are however it signifies they are. Consequently (by the first description) it is false.

Seventh thesis:

Every conjunctive proposition is contradicted by a disjunctive composed of parts contradicting the parts of the conjunctive.

For example, the contradictory of 'Socrates is running, and Socrates is not disputing' is 'Socrates is not ((*Socrates non/non Socrates*)) running, or Socrates is disputing.' This is proved, because the law and nature of contradictory propositions applies to them – viz., if the one is true, the other is false (and vice versa). And they cannot be true or false at the same time, and the categorical propositions belonging to them have subjects and predicates that are alike, and the cause of the falsity of the one is a sufficient cause of the truth of the other (and vice versa). That is evident, because the cause of that conjunctive proposition's truth is that both parts be true, but both parts of the conjunctive proposition's being true is both parts of that disjunctive proposition's being false. Thus, the parts of the conjunctive proposition contradict the parts of the disjunctive proposition; therefore, the cause of the conjunctive proposition's truth is the cause of the disjunctive proposition's falsity. Analogously, the cause of the conjunctive proposition's falsity is the cause of the disjunctive proposition's truth. For the cause of the conjunctive proposition's falsity is that both parts be false or that one of its parts be false (because for the falsity of a conjunctive proposition it is enough that one of its parts be false). But from both parts of the conjunctive proposition's being false or from one of its parts' being false, it follows that both parts of the disjunctive proposition are true or that one of its parts is true (because the conjunctive proposition's parts contradict the disjunctive proposition's parts and because for the truth of a disjunctive proposition it is enough that one of its parts be true). Therefore, from the falsity of a conjunctive proposition there follows the truth of a disjunctive proposition made up of parts contradicting the parts of the conjunctive proposition. (Analogously, one can deduce that it works this way in the other direction.)

[4. Insolubles]

[4a. Insoluble I]

As for the fourth, I propose the following insoluble first:

I SAY SOMETHING FALSE.

Suppose that I am saying nothing other than the proposition 'I say something false.'

The question is whether the proposition spoken by me is true, or false.

If it is said [by you] to be true – on the contrary: Then things are however it signifies they are; and since it signifies that I am saying something false, that I am saying something false is the way things are; and since I am saying nothing other than the proposition 'I say something false,' it follows that the proposition 'I say something false' is false. Consequently, it is not true – the opposite of what you say. (The consequences produced [here] are evident on the basis of the suppositions.)

But if you say that it is false – then: Therefore, the way things are is the way it signifies, since it signifies that it itself {43vb} is false. And if the way things are is the way it signifies, it follows that it is true and consequently not false – the opposite of what you say.

But if you say that it is true and false at the same time, that is contrary to the sixth supposition.

The reply: The proposition introduced above is false. And by the third thesis regarding the general signification of propositions, it signifies that it is true. But its being false follows from its being true. Consequently, it follows (by the sixth thesis) that it is false.

But that its being false follows from its being true is proved in the following way. This follows: It is true, and since it is an affirmative its subject and predicate supposit for the same thing (by the second supposition). And, furthermore, its subject and predicate do supposit for the same thing. Therefore, 'I' and 'saying something false' supposit for the same thing; therefore, I and one saying something false are the same thing. Consequently, I am one saying something false. And since I say nothing other than the proposition introduced above, it follows that that proposition is false. But it is true. Therefore, its being false follows from its being true – which was to be proved. Consequently it is false.

And when it was said that if it is false, then, since it signifies that it is false, things are the way it signifies, I grant that; and when it is said further that therefore it is true, I deny the consequence. Thus although things are the way it signifies, nevertheless, it is not that things are however it signifies they are. But, as is evident on the basis of the description of a true proposition [i.e., the first description], that would have to be the case for it to be true. Thus, in order that the proposition be true it is not enough that things are the way it signifies; instead, it is required that things are however it signifies they are. For that reason the proposition 'A man is a donkey' is false, and yet things are the way it signifies because it signifies that a man is, and things are that way. But because along with that it signifies otherwise than things are, it is false. The case we are considering is of that sort, however ((*autem/enim*)). For although things are the way the proposition 'I say something false' signifies (because it signifies that it is false, and things are that way), ((om. *quia*)) nevertheless, it is not that things are however it signifies they are; for it [also] signifies that it is true, and that is not the way things are.

For that reason you should conceive of the truth of a proposition just as you conceive of the highest degree of a quality; for as soon as the quality diminishes, it ceases to be at its highest degree and begins to have been diminished. So in the case we are considering if we suppose that some proposition is true, as soon as it signifies in any way other than things are, even though along with that it signifies the way things are, it ceases to be true and begins to be false, even if it were still to have much more truth than falsity.

Similarly, one can think of truth and falsity ((*veritate et falsitate/ falsitate et veritate*)) in the way one thinks of purity and impurity. Just as what is pure becomes impure through the introduction of any contrary whatever, so a true proposition becomes false as soon as it signifies in any way other than things are.

A doubt: Someone might say, however, 'You say that this is false: "I say something false." What is its contradictory? If you say that it is "I [do not] say something false" – on the contrary: Let "I say something false" be called *A* and "I do not say something false" *B*. Then *A* signifies that *A* is false, and *B* signifies that *B* is not false; therefore, *A* and *B* do not contradict each other. The consequence holds good because a contradiction must be the affirmation and the negation of the same thing as regards the same subject, but that is not the way it is in the case we are considering. Therefore, etc. But if you say that the contradictory of "I say something false" is "I have not said something false" (as some people say), that is not acceptable. For the first one was false, and the second one does not signify that it was not false; therefore, the second is false. Consequently, the second does not contradict the first; otherwise two contradictories would be false at the same time. In the second place, these two do contradict each other: "I have said something false" and "I have not said something false"; therefore, "I say something false" does not contradict "I have not said something false."'

Reply to the doubt: Briefly, leaving aside other ways [of replying], I say that because it signifies that it is true and that it is false, its ((*eius/est*)) contradictory – viz., the proposition 'It is not the case that I say something false' – can be false insofar as that negation is not extended to cover the whole proposition 'I say something false.' And since 'It is not the case that I say something false' signifies that things are not as 'I say something false' signifies, therefore, since 'I say something false' signifies that I say something true and say something false, 'It is not the case that I say something false' thus signifies that I do not say something true or that I do not say something false. This is because (by the last conclusion) the contradictory of a conjunctive proposition is a disjunctive proposition made up of parts contradicting the parts of the conjunctive proposition. {44ra}

[4b. Insoluble II]

THE PROPOSITION I UTTER IS LIKE THE PROPOSITION PLATO UTTERS.

Suppose that Plato utters one false proposition and no other – e.g., 'A man is a donkey' – and let that be *B*; and that the proposition I utter is this [and] no other: '[The proposition] I utter is like the proposition Plato utters,' and let that be *A*.

Then the question is whether *A* is true or false.

If you say that *A* is true – on the contrary ((*contra/cum*)): *A* is like *B*, but *B* is false; therefore, *A* is false. And if that is the case, it is not true – the opposite of what you say.

If you say that *A* is false, then, since *B* is false, *A* is like *B*. But that is what *A* states. Therefore, the way things are is the way *A* states they are; therefore, *A* is true and consequently not false – the opposite of what you say.

If you say that *A* is true and false, that is contrary to the sixth supposition.

The reply: *A* is false because it signifies that it is true and its being false follows from its being true. Therefore, since it signifies that it is true and consequently false, it follows (by the sixth thesis) that it is false. For since *A* is an affirmative proposition, it signifies (by the fourth supposition) that what its subject and predicate supposit for is the same; but its being false follows from the fact that its subject and predicate supposit for the same thing (as long as the hypothesis remains the same). Therefore, etc.

And when it is said that if *A* is false, then it is like *B*, I grant that; and when it was said further that therefore the way things are is the way *A* states that they are, I grant that. [But when it was said that] therefore it is true, I deny the consequence. Although this follows: 'Things are however *A* signifies they are; therefore, *A* is true,' now the antecedent is not true because *A* signifies that it is true and that it is false. But it is not wholly the case that *A* is true, etc. And so because the proposition presented above is equivalent to a conjunctive proposition, its contradictory was a disjunctive proposition made up of parts contradicting the parts of that conjunctive proposition.

[4c. Insoluble III]

THIS PROPOSITION IS FALSE.

Suppose that by 'this' is indicated that very proposition itself; and let it be called *B*.

The question is whether this proposition, *B*, is true, or false.

If true, then things are however it signifies; but it signifies that it is false; therefore, that is the way things are. And, consequently, it is false and not true – the opposite of what you say.

But if you say that it is false, then, since it signifies that it is false, the way things are is the way it signifies. And, consequently, it is true and not false – the opposite of what you say.

The reply: It is false because, as is evident, it signifies that it is false. And since (by the third thesis) every proposition signifies that it is true, it follows that this proposition signifies that it is true and that it is false. Consequently (by the sixth thesis), it is false.

And when it was said that if it is false, then, since it signifies that it is false, the way things are is the way it signifies, I grant that. [I do] not [grant that] it is therefore true, because it is not the case that things are however it signifies.

First doubt: But you might say, 'You say that proposition B is false. On the contrary: Let A be a proposition like B. Then as follows ((*sic/sit*)): If B is false, then A is true because A states that B is false. And, further, if A is true, it follows that B is true, because A and B are propositions altogether alike. For they are just alike as regards subject, copula, and predicate; and ((om. *cum*) the subject and predicate of the one supposit for the same thing for which the subject and predicate of the other supposit (since both supposit for proposition B).'

Reply to the first doubt: B is false and A is true. And I claim that it is not impossible that there be two propositions altogether alike, such that the terms of the one supposit for the same thing for which the terms of the other supposit, and yet one of them is false and the other true in virtue of the fact that one falsifies itself and the other does not.

Second doubt: Still, you might say, 'You say that B is false. Therefore, its contradictory will be true – viz., "This proposition is not false," indicating by "this" proposition B. And let that be C. Then as follows: C is true, but C signifies that B is not false; therefore, B is not false – the opposite of what you say.'

Reply to the second doubt: {44rb} C is not the contradictory of B, because both are false. From this I infer that it is possible that there be two singular propositions, one affirmative and the other negative, with subjects, predicates, and copulas just alike, whose extremes supposit for the same thing, and which nevertheless do not contradict each other. That is evident as regards these: 'This proposition is false,' 'This proposition is not false,' indicating by the 'this' in the first that first proposition, and by the 'this' in the second that same first proposition.

But you might say, 'What is the contradictory of the proposition presented above?'

I say that it is this: 'This proposition is not true, or this proposition is not false,' indicating by both occurrences of 'this' proposition B. And that is because proposition B is equivalent to a conjunctive proposition – viz., 'This proposition is true, and this proposition is false.' And (by the last thesis) the contradictory of a conjunctive proposition is a disjunctive proposition made up of parts contradicting the parts of the conjunctive proposition.

Third doubt: But you might say, 'If B is a false proposition, then its subject and predicate supposit for the same thing in virtue of the fact that "false" is its predicate. And, further, if its subject and predicate supposit for the same thing, then, since it is affirmative, it follows (by the first thesis) that it is true in virtue of the fact that every affirmative proposition such that its subject and predicate supposit for the same thing is true.'

Reply to the third doubt: I reply by granting it except when such an affirmative proposition has incompatible significations, as in the case we are considering. For 'This proposition is false' [is false] as regards formal signification since it is an affirmative signifying ((*significans/significat*)) that its subject and predicate supposit for the same thing; as regards material signification, however – i.e., by reason of the term 'false' suppositing for that very proposition itself – it signifies that it is false. And consequently its subject and predicate do not supposit for the same thing, and ((om. *cum*)) that is what it is for an affirmative proposition to be false. And so, because its formal signification is discordant and incompatible with its material signification, it is false despite the fact that its subject and predicate supposit for the same thing.

Still, you might say, 'Isn't it possible?'

No, because things cannot be however it signifies. For it signifies that it is true and that it is false, and it is impossible that that be the case; for when that is the case, it is not, and when it is not, that is not the case. For when it is not, it is neither true nor false.

Fourth doubt: Still, you might say, 'It seems that the proposition "This proposition is false" is true because things are altogether as it signifies. This is proved, because as regards formal signification it signifies that its subject and predicate supposit for the same thing, [and] as regards material signification – viz., by reason of the term 'false' – it signifies that it is false, and so it is.'

Reply to the fourth doubt: If each of the two significations were considered apart from each other by setting aside the influence of the one over the other, things would indeed be as they are signified in each of the two significations. But these significations are related differently in the proposition under discussion, because the material signification does have an influence over the formal signification: as regards the formal signification it signifies that its subject and predicate supposit for the same thing, but as regards the material signification it signifies that it is false. Now those [conditions] are not compatible – that its subject and predicate, etc., and that it is false. It follows that the proposition presented above is false; nor are things altogether as it signifies.

[4d. Insoluble IV]

Suppose that Socrates says 'Plato says something false,' and Plato says 'Socrates says something true.'

Once that hypothesis has been supposed, I ask whether the proposition said by Socrates is true or false.

If one says that it is true, then, since it signifies that Plato says something false, it is the case that Plato says something false.

But if one says that Socrates's proposition is false, then its contradictory is true – viz., 'Plato does not say something false.' And since Plato says that Socrates says something true, it follows that it is not false that Socrates says something true. Therefore, if it is false that Socrates says something true, it is not false that Socrates says something true.

The reply: Socrates's proposition is false, because it signifies that it is true {44va} (by the third thesis), and it signifies that it is false in virtue of the fact that it signifies that Plato's proposition is false, and Plato's proposition signifies that it is true. Nor is its contradictory 'Plato does not say something false,' which is equivalent to a disjunctive proposition made up of parts contradicting the parts of the conjunctive proposition equivalent to 'Plato says something false,' etc.

[4e. Insoluble V]

Suppose that there are only three propositions – viz., these: 'A man is a donkey,' 'God does not exist,' 'Every proposition is false' – and let the first be A, the second B, and the third C.

Then the question is whether C is true or false.

If one says that it is true, then things are as C signifies – that every proposition is false. Therefore, it is the case that every proposition is false. But C is a proposition; therefore, it is the case that C is a false proposition. Therefore, if C is true, C is false.

But if one says that C is false, then, since A and B are also false, it follows that it is the case that every proposition is false. And since on the hypothesis *A*, *B*, and *C* are all the propositions in the world and, further, it is the case that every proposition is false, and since *C* signifies that, therefore, things are as *C* signifies. Consequently, *C* is true. Therefore, if *C* is true, *C* is false.

The reply: *C* is false, because it signifies that it is true and that it is false; and, consequently, it is false.

And when it was said that if *C* is false, then every proposition is false, I grant that. When it is said further that things are as *C* signifies, I grant that. But [I do] not [grant] that things are however *C* signifies, because *C* signifies that it is true and that it is false, and that is not the case. Therefore, in that it signifies that it is false, things are indeed as it signifies; but in that it signifies that it is true, things are otherwise.

But you might say, 'Isn't it possible that it is true?'

I say no.

First doubt: On the contrary, it can be the case that every proposition false; for tomorrow perhaps only these two will exist: 'A man is a donkey' and 'God does not exist.' And this follows: It can be the case that every proposition is false, and, further, that is possible; therefore, that can be true.

Reply to the first doubt: I reply by denying the consequence 'That is possible; therefore, that can be true.' For ((*enim/autem*)) in order that a proposition be possible it is not required that it be able to be true; instead, it is enough that things can be as it signifies. Thus 'This proposition is negative' is possible, and yet it is impossible that it be true – for neither when it is, nor when it is not [can it be true], as is evident to anyone who considers it.

Similarly, in order that a proposition be necessary it is not enough that whenever it is framed it is true, since otherwise 'Some proposition is particular' would be necessary because it is true whenever it is framed, and yet it is not necessary. But it is evident that it is not necessary, since its contradictory, 'No proposition is particular,' is not impossible. Instead, in order that a proposition be necessary it is required and sufficient that it is impossible that things be otherwise than as it signifies.

Second doubt: There is some doubt whether this is a good consequence: 'Every proposition is affirmative; therefore, no proposition is negative.'

And one argues first that it is not [a good consequence]. For it is possible that the antecedent be true and impossible that the consequent be true; therefore, the consequence is not valid. I prove the premise: It is possible that 'Every proposition is affirmative' be true, for that is known of itself (for suppose that the proposition 'Every proposition is affirmative' is the only one in the world). But it is impossible that 'No proposition is negative' be true. For if it were ((*esset/est*)) possible that it be true, that would be either when it existed or when it did not exist. Not when it did not exist, for in order that any proposition be true it is required that it exist. Not when it existed either, for whenever the proposition 'No proposition is negative' exists, it is false in virtue of the fact that whenever it exists some proposition is negative, since it is negative itself.

One argues on the other side [as follows]. The opposite of the consequent destroys the antecedent; therefore, the consequence is good. This consequence holds good. Its antecedent is proved [as follows]: The opposite of the consequent is 'Some proposition is negative,' and from that this follows: 'Some proposition is not affirmative,' which {44vb} is the contradictory opposite of 'Every proposition is affirmative.' Therefore, etc.

Reply to the second doubt: The consequence is good. But when one says that it is possible that the antecedent be true although it is impossible that the consequent be true, I grant it; and when one says 'therefore, the consequence is not valid,' that is denied. For in order that a consequence be valid it is required and sufficient that it be impossible that things be as the antecedent signifies without things being as the consequent signifies. And so that is the way things are in the case under consideration. Thus if things are as 'Every proposition is affirmative' signifies, then things are also as is signified by 'No proposition is negative.' Nevertheless, I do indeed grant that in the consequence presented above the action performed by the consequent is incompatible with the action signified by the antecedent, but the action signified by the consequent is not incompatible with the action signified by the antecedent; rather, it necessarily follows. By 'the action performed by a proposition' we must understand the proposition's act of being or of not being; any things required for the proposition's being or not being are also said ((*dicuntur/dicitur*)) to be part of the action performed. But the action signified by the proposition is what we call things being or not being as the proposition signifies. And so when it is possible that the proposition be and at the same time that things be as the proposition signifies, the action performed is not incompatible with the action signified. On the other hand, if it is possible that things be as the proposition signifies and it is not possible along with this at the same time that the proposition be, then the action performed is discordant with and incompatible with the action signified.

First corollary: In connection with that solution I infer that in order that a consequence be good it is not required that the antecedent cannot be true without the consequent's being true. For this is a good consequence: 'Every man is an animal; therefore, a man is an animal,' and yet the antecedent can be true while the consequent is not true ((*non existente vero/existente falso*)), because the consequent can fail to exist while the antecedent exists. But when the consequent is not, it is not true. Therefore, etc.

Second corollary: Second, I infer that some consequence is good even though if its antecedent is true, its consequent is false. This is evident in the consequence presented above: 'Every proposition is affirmative; therefore, no proposition is negative.'

Third corollary: In the third place I infer that some consequence is good in which the antecedent can be true and it is impossible that the consequent be true even though the consequent is possible – as is evident in connection with the consequence 'Every proposition is affirmative; therefore, etc.' It is likewise evident as regards this one: 'No man is indicated; therefore this man ((*iste homo/Socrates*)) is not indicated (indicating Socrates).' In this consequence if the antecedent is true, it is impossible that the consequent be true, because neither when it exists nor when it does not exist [can it be true]. And so even though the consequent is incompatible with the antecedent as regards the action performed, it is not incompatible as regards the action signified. Thus, if things are as the antecedent signifies ((*significat/consignificat*)) it is impossible that things not be as the consequent signifies. The situation is similar as regards this consequence: 'This proposition is singular, and this one, and so on; therefore, every proposition is singular.' The consequence is good even though it is impossible that the consequent be true while the antecedent is true. And so a good consequence is one such that whenever things are as is signifiable by the antecedent it is impossible that things not be as is signifiable by the consequent (supposing that there is no new imposition of the terms, etc.).

[4f. Insoluble VI]

Suppose that Socrates says that Plato says something false, and Plato says that Cicero says something false, and Cicero says that Socrates says something false.

Then the question is whether Socrates says something true or something false.

If Socrates says something true, then Plato says something false; and if Plato says something false, Cicero says something true; and if Cicero says something true, Socrates says something false. Therefore, if Socrates says something true, Socrates says something false.

But if one says that Socrates says something false, then Plato says something true, and Cicero says something false; and if Cicero says something false, Socrates says something true. Therefore, if Socrates says something false, Socrates says something true.

The reply: Socrates says something false.

And when it was said 'then Plato says something true,' the consequence is denied. For Socrates says something false not only because he says that Plato says something false, but also {45ra} because in saying that Plato says something false he is saying that Cicero says something true, and in saying that Cicero says something true he is saying that he himself says something false. Now anyone saying any proposition by means of which he is saying that he says something false says something false in saying that proposition – as is clear enough from what has already been said. Thus with that hypothesis providing the means, Socrates does indeed say that he himself says something false.

For this reason one must know that some propositions can affirm that they are false or that they are not true in four different ways. In the first way, by themselves, without other propositions cooperating – as, for example, if I said 'I am saying something false' and nothing else; or suppose that this was written on paper: 'Every proposition written on paper is false.'

In the second way these propositions can affirm that they themselves are false or not true by asserting that other propositions are false, which assert that the original propositions are true – as, for example, if Socrates says 'Plato says something false' and nothing else, and Plato says 'Socrates says something true' and nothing else; or if this is written on paper: 'Every proposition written on parchment is false,' and this on parchment: 'Every proposition written on paper is true.'

In the third way some propositions assert that they themselves are false or not true by asserting that other ((*alias/aliquas*)) propositions are true, which assert that the original propositions are false – as, for example, if Socrates says 'Plato says something true' and nothing else, and Plato says nothing besides this: 'Socrates says something false'; or if ((*si/sic*)) this proposition is written on paper: 'Every proposition written on parchment is true,' and this one is written on parchment: 'Every proposition written on paper is false.' The first asserts that it itself is false in that it asserts that the second is true, which asserts that the first ((*primam/se*)) is false. (Occasionally this happens indeed with many propositions, as can be done in the proposed sophisma.)

In the fourth way some propositions assert that they themselves are false by asserting that other propositions are false that are altogether like them as regards the cause of truth and of falsity. Suppose, for example, that only this proposition is written on paper: 'A proposition written on parchment is false,' and only this other proposition is written on parchment: 'A proposition written on paper is false.' Obviously each of them asserts that it itself is false in that it asserts that one is false that is altogether like it as regards the causes of truth and of falsity; for no cause could be assigned for the one's being true rather than the other, or for the one's being false rather than the other, etc.

[4g. Insoluble VII]

Suppose Socrates says 'God exists,' and Plato says 'Only Socrates says something true,' and there are no other speakers in the world.

Then the question is whether Plato says something true or something false.

If one says that Plato says something true – on the contrary: If Plato says something true, then it is the case that Socrates says something true and no one other than Socrates says something true, since Plato says that only Socrates says something true. Further: No one [other] than Socrates says something true, but Plato is someone other than Socrates; therefore, Plato does not say something true – which was to be proved.

But if you say that Plato says something false, then, since on the hypothesis there are no more speakers besides Socrates and Plato, and since Socrates says something true, it follows that Socrates says something true and that no one other than he says something true. From this it follows further that only Socrates says something true. And, furthermore: Only Socrates says something true, and Plato says that only Socrates says something true; therefore, Plato says something true and, consequently, not false – which was to be proved.

The reply: Plato says something false, because he says a proposition that signifies that Socrates's proposition and no other is true; consequently, it signifies that it itself is not true. But any proposition that signifies that it itself is not true is false (by the sixth thesis). Therefore, Plato's proposition is false.

And when it is argued that therefore it is the case, as long as the hypothesis remains the same, that Socrates says something true and no one other than Socrates says something true, I grant it. And when it is argued further that therefore it is true that only Socrates says what is true, the consequence is denied.

But you might say, 'On the contrary, in that case one is arguing from the exponents to what is expounded.' {45rb}

I deny it, because in that case 'Only Socrates says something true,' the proposition uttered by Plato, does not signify only that Socrates says something true and that no one other than Socrates says something true; instead, it signifies along with this that Plato says something false. And so when one argues 'Socrates says something true, and no one other than Socrates says something true; therefore, only Socrates says something true,' one commits the fallacy of the consequent; there follows also the fallacy of reasoning *secundum quid et simpliciter* (assuming the hypothesis laid down at the beginning remains the same, etc.).

[4h. Insoluble VIII]

Suppose there are only three propositions in the world: 'A man is an animal,' 'God exists,' 'Every proposition besides an exceptive proposition is true'; and let the first be *A*, the second *B*, the third *C*.

Then the question is whether *C* is true or false.

If one says that it is true, then its exponents are true – viz.,

'Every proposition if it is other than an exceptive proposition is not true.' Therefore, this is true: 'An exceptive proposition is not true.' But there is no exceptive proposition other than *C* ((om. *ab*)), and therefore *C* is not true – which was to be proved.

But if one says that *C* is false, that is either because an exceptive proposition is not true or because ((*quia/quod*)) an exceptive proposition is true. One cannot say the first, because each of those that is not an exceptive proposition is true; therefore, the second – that an exceptive proposition is true. And, consequently, if it is false it is true – which is evidently absurd.

The reply: *C* is false because it signifies that it is false. For it signifies that what is other than an exceptive proposition is true, and since there is no exceptive proposition other than it, it signifies that it is not true and, consequently, false.

And when it was said that if it is false, etc., I say that it is false not because ((*quia/quod*)) any other exceptive proposition is true but because it signifies that it itself is true, and it is not true. Therefore, etc.

[4i. Insoluble IX]

Suppose that each man with the exception of Socrates says 'God exists,' and that Socrates says 'Every man besides me says something true.'

I say, briefly, that on that hypothesis Socrates says something false; for he says one proposition that says that it itself is true and that it itself is false, as is evident, etc.

[4j. Insoluble X]

Suppose Socrates says 'God exists,' and Plato says 'A man is an animal,' and Cicero says 'A man is a donkey,' and Marcus says 'The number of people who say something true is the same as the number of people who say something false'; and let the first be *A*, the second *B*, the third *C*, the fourth *D*.

Then the question is whether *D* is true or false.

If it is true, then two of the things that were said are true and two are false. But it is clear that the two said first are true; therefore, the other two things that were said are false, one of which is *D* itself. Therefore, if it is said that *D* is true, it follows that it is false.

But if one says that it is false, then, since *C* is also false, it follows that two are false. And just as many are true as are false; therefore, the number of people who say something true is the same as the number of people who say something false. Therefore, things are the way *D* signifies they are, and, consequently, *D* is not false – which was to be proved.

The reply: *D* is false.

And when it is said further that therefore the number of people who say something true is the same as the number of people who say something false, I grant it; also when it is said that things are the way *D* signifies they are, I grant it. And when it is said further that therefore *D* is true, the consequence is denied. For, as was said [above], in order that a proposition be true it is not enough that things are the way they are signified to be by that proposition, but it is required that however things are signifed to be by that proposition, so they are. But that is not the way it is in connection with this proposition.

[4k. Insoluble XI]

GOD EXISTS, AND SOME CONJUNCTIVE PROPOSITION IS FALSE.

And let this conjunctive proposition be *A*, its first part *B*, and its second part *C*; and suppose that there is no other conjunctive proposition in the world besides this one.

Then the question is whether *A* is true or false.

If one says that *A* is true, since for the truth of a conjunctive proposition it is required that each part of it be true, it follows that each part of *A* is true. And then, furthermore, *C* is true, and however *C* signifies, so things are. But *C* signifies that *A* is false; therefore, the way things are is that *A* is false. Therefore, if *A* is true, *A* is false.

But if one says that it is false – on the contrary: For then [since] it is enough for the falsity of a conjunctive proposition that one part be false, and since the first part, *B*, is not false, [it follows] that if *A* were false, *C* would be false. But I prove that that is not the case. For if *A* were {45va} false, things would be as *C* signifies them to be; and, consequently, *C* is true.

The reply: The conjunctive proposition *A* is false.

And when it was said that therefore either *C* or *B* is false, I grant it; also when it was argued that *B* is not false, I grant it. And when it was said further that therefore *C* is false, I grant it. And when it was said further that if *C* is false, *A* is false, [and] therefore things are as *C* signifies them to be, I grant it. And when it was said further that therefore [*C*] is true, the consequence is denied. Thus it is not that things are however *C* signifies; for it signifies that it [itself] is true and that it is false.

[4l. Insoluble XII]

A MAN IS A DONKEY, OR SOME DISJUNCTIVE PROPOSITION IS FALSE.

Let this disjunctive proposition be in the world, and let there be no other disjunctive proposition in the world; and let it be called *A*, its first part *B*, and its second part *C*.

Then either *A* is true or *A* is false.

If *A* is true, one part of it is true, since from the truth of a disjunctive proposition it follows that one part of it is true. But it cannot be said to be *B* – that much is clear. That leaves *C*. Then as follows: *C* is true; therefore, some disjunctive proposition is false. But there is none other than *A*; therefore, *A* is false. Therefore, if *A* is true, *A* is false.

But if one says that *A* is false, it follows that both its parts are false; for from the falsity of a disjunctive proposition it follows that both its parts are false. Consequently, *C* is false. But I prove that that is not the case. For if *C* is false, then, since *B* is false, it follows that *A* is false. Consequently, it follows that some disjunctive proposition is false. Then as follows: Some disjunctive proposition is false; therefore, things are the way *C* signifies them to be. And, furthermore, therefore, *C* is true.

The reply: *A* is false.

And when it is said further that both of its parts are false, I grant it; also when it is said further that if *C* is false, *A* is false, I grant it. And when it is said further that therefore things are the way *C* signifies them to be, I grant that. [But when it is said further that] therefore *C* is true, the consequence is denied. For although things are the way *C* signifies them to be, nevertheless it is not that things are however *C* signifies they are. For as regards its direct signification it signifies that *A* is false, and as regards its secondary signification it signifies that it itself is false. Consequently, as was said earlier, ('Every proposition signifying, etc.' [the sixth thesis]) *C* signifies that it is true and that it is false; consequently, it is false.

A doubt arises [here], because it was said [above] that the conjunctive proposition 'God exists, and some conjunctive proposition is false' is false. But, on the contrary, if that is the case, it follows that its contradictory is true, and yet it is false. The consequence holds good, and the falsity is proved as follows. For according to things said above, its contradictory seems to be this: 'Either no God exists, or no conjunctive proposition is false'; but that is false. The consequence holds good because all the parts of it are false.

Reply to the doubt: That is not its contradictory. In order to accept [something as] its contradictory, however, let us first see what 'God exists, and some conjunctive proposition is false' is equipollent to on the supposition that there is no other conjunctive proposition. And because that conjunctive proposition signifies that it is false, let it be called the negative proposition *A*. It follows that this will be acceptable: 'God exists, and some conjunctive proposition is false, and *A* is not false.' Therefore, one must take its contradictory in accordance with this; and it will be the following: 'Either no God exists, or no conjunctive proposition is false, or *A* is false.' But that is true because it is a single disjunctive proposition one or another part of which is true – viz., 'No conjunctive proposition is false, or *A* is false'; etc.

[4m. Insoluble XIII]

IF GOD EXISTS, SOME CONDITIONAL PROPOSITION IS FALSE.

Let this conditional proposition be in the world, and no other; and let it be *A*, its antecedent *B*, and its consequent *C*.

Then the question is whether *A* is true or false.

If one says that *A* is true, then [as follows]: Then things are as *B* signifies them to be [and] things are also as *C* signifies them to be;

for that is required for the truth of the conditional proposition if things are as *B* signifies them to be. It is clear *per se* that things are also as *C* signifies them to be; and, further, therefore, *C* is true. But *C* signifies that *A* is false. Therefore, if *A* is true, *A* is false.

But if one says that *A* is false, then as follows: If *A* is false, it is impossible that *B* be true unless *C* is true. This consequence holds good, because for the truth of *A* it is enough that *B* cannot be true without *C* – i.e., that things {45vb} cannot be as they are signified by *B* to be without things being as they are signified by *C* to be. The antecedent is proved as follows: If *A* were false, *C* would be ((*esset/est*)) true. Therefore, if *A* is false, *B* is not true unless *C* is true. This consequence holds good [and] its antecedent is proved as follows: If *A* is false, things are as *C* signifies them to be, because *C* signifies that *A* is false. And if that is the case, it follows that *C* is true.

The reply: *A* is false.

And when it was said that therefore things are as *C* signifies them to be, that is granted. And when it was said further that therefore *C* is true, the consequence is denied, because *C* signifying that *A* is false signifies that it itself is false. Consequently, it signifies that it is true and that it is false, and, consequently, by one or another thesis presented earlier it is false. Thus, even though things are the way *C* signifies them to be, it is not that things are however *C* signifies they are; but that is what would be required for *C* to be true, etc.

[4n. Insoluble XIV]

GOD EXISTS; THEREFORE, THIS CONSEQUENCE IS NOT VALID.

Let this consequence be *A*, its antecedent *B*, and its consequent *C*; and 'this' indicates the consequence put forward. Then I put forward consequence *A*, and I ask whether consequence *A* is valid or not.

If one says that it is valid, then, since its antecedent is true, it follows that its consequent is true. And if its consequent is true, then things are as its consequent signifies them to be. But its consequent signifies that consequence *A* is not valid. Therefore, consequence *A* is not valid.

But if one says that consequence *A* is not valid – on the contrary: If consequence *A* is not valid, it is possible that *B* be true while *C* is false. But that is false, which I prove as follows. For if *A* is not valid, things are as *C* signifies them to be, because *C* signifies that *A* is not valid; and, consequently, *C* is true. Therefore, *B* cannot be true unless *C* is true. Therefore, *A* is valid. Therefore, if *A* is not valid, *A* is valid. The first consequence is evident, for in order that *A* be not valid it is enough that *B* can be without *C*, if they were formulated. The last consequence holds good from the first to the last.

The reply: Consequence *A* is not valid.

And when it was said at the end that therefore *C* is true, the consequence is denied. And if someone said 'If *A* is not valid, then things are as *C* signifies them to be,' I grant that. But it is not the case that things are however *C* signifies they are. And, therefore, this does not follow: 'Things are as *C* [signifies] them to be; therefore, *C* is true,' etc.

Now we have to consider insolubles that stem from our inward actions, such as being deceived, being mistaken, being in doubt, pretending. And first let there be this insoluble:

[40. Insoluble XV]

Suppose that in Socrates's mind there is this: *Socrates is deceived*, and no other proposition, and let it be *A*; and suppose that Socrates believes that proposition to be true.

Then the question is whether Socrates in believing *A* to be true is deceived or not.

If one says that Socrates is deceived, it follows that *A* is false; for otherwise in believing *A* to be true he would not be deceived. Furthermore, this is false: 'Socrates is deceived'; therefore, Socrates is not deceived.

If one says the second, it follows that *A* is true. And this follows further: '*A* is ((*est/esse*)) true; therefore, Socrates is deceived.' Therefore, if Socrates is not deceived, Socrates is deceived.

The solution: In believing *A* Socrates is deceived.

And when it is said that therefore *A* is true, the consequence is denied, because *A* not only signifies that Socrates is deceived, but that Socrates is deceived and that he is not deceived, and that is false. And, consequently, *A* is false in virtue of the fact that it is not the case that things are however *A* signifies they are.

In just the same way, let *Socrates is mistaken* be in Socrates's mind, and he knows that to be mistaken is to believe something false to be true ((*verum/falsum*)) or to believe something true to be false. (And this is argued and solved in the same way as *Socrates is deceived*, etc.)

[4p. Insoluble XVI]

SOCRATES IS PRETENDING THAT HE IS A SOPHIST.

Suppose that to pretend is to show oneself to be as one is not, and that a sophist [is one who] shows himself to be as he is not. Then as follows: Socrates, who is not a sophist, can show himself to be a sophist (by conversion of the sophisma sentence, or by something of that sort), but because he is not one, it follows (by the description [or] nominal definition of pretending and the description [or] nominal definition of the term 'sophist') that he is pretending to be a sophist.

The opposite is argued [as follows]: The hypothesis posited implies [that the sophisma sentence is false]; therefore, [the sophisma sentence is false]. The consequence holds good, and the antecedent is explained as follows. If Socrates is pretending that he is a sophist, {46ra} then in pretending that he is a sophist, either he is a sophist or he is not. If he is a sophist, then he is not pretending that he is a sophist, because if anyone is truly what he shows himself to be, he is not pretending (by the description of pretending).

But if one says that he is not a sophist, it follows that he is not what he shows himself to be, since he shows himself to be a sophist. Furthermore, if he is not what he shows himself to be, he is a sophist (by the description [or] nominal [definition] of the term 'sophist'). Therefore, whatever one says, something incompatible seems to follow.

The reply: If we presuppose [this] signification of the terms, it is impossible that Socrates pretend that he is a sophist, as the argument on the other side already satisfactorily proves.

And when it was said that Socrates, who is not a sophist, can show himself to be a sophist, I deny it. For if Socrates to begin with is not a sophist, as soon as he shows himself to be a sophist; he is a sophist; etc.

[4q. *Insoluble XVII*]

IT IS POSSIBLE THAT SOCRATES KNOWS THAT HE IS MISTAKEN.

Suppose that to be mistaken is to assent or not to dissent falsely, or to believe something false to be true or something true to be false. And it is proved [as follows]: That Socrates is mistaken is possible; therefore, that Socrates knows that he is mistaken is possible. The antecedent is known, [and] the consequence holds good, because otherwise there would be a proposition that could be known by Plato that it would be impossible for Plato to make known to Socrates. For it is clear that 'Socrates is mistaken' can be known by Plato, and if it could not be known by Socrates, Plato could not make it known to Socrates.

One argues on the other side as follows: That Socrates knows that he is mistaken implies a contradiction; therefore, it is impossible. The consequence holds good, [and] the antecedent is proved [as follows]: For 'Socrates knows that he is mistaken; therefore, Socrates is not mistaken' follows, since nothing is known unless it is true. Likewise, this follows: 'Socrates knows that he is mistaken; therefore, he is not mistaken.' This is proved, because if he knows that he is mistaken, then he knows that he assents or does not dissent falsely; and if he knows that he assents falsely, he knows that what he assents to is false; and if he knows ((*scit/scitur*)) that, then he does not assent to it, and, consequently, he is not mistaken. Likewise, if he knows that he does [not] dissent truly, he knows that what he dissents from is true, and, consequently, he does [not] dissent from it; and, consequently, he is not mistaken.

Second, if Socrates knew that he was mistaken, then he would know ((*sciret/scit*)) that in judging that *A* should be done he was mistaken, and he will know he is mistaken in judging in that way. And let *B* be the mistaken judgment in which he judges that *A* should be done. Then as follows: Socrates knows that he is mistaken in judging that *A* should be done; therefore, Socrates knows that judgment *B*, in which he judges that *A* should be done, is mistaken. Then as follows: Socrates knows that judgment *B* is mistaken; therefore, Socrates knows that things are otherwise than he judges through judgment *B* (that *A* should be done). Therefore, if Socrates knows that he is mistaken in judging (in the mistaken judgment *B*) that *A* should be done, at one and the same time he judges that *A* should be done (and he does this by means of the mistaken judgment *B* that *A* should be done) – i.e., by means of the knowledge he has in virtue of the fact that judgment *B* is mistaken, and consequently there will be contrary judgments in the same thing. But that is impossible, and so it is impossible that Socrates knows that he is mistaken.

The reply: It is impossible that Socrates know that he is mistaken.

And when it was said that it is possible that Socrates be mistaken, I grant it. And when it is said that therefore it is possible that Socrates know that he is mistaken, the consequence is denied. And I grant further that some proposition can be known by Plato that it is impossible that Plato make known to Socrates [viz.,] that he is mistaken. But he can indeed say as much to him and argue that it follows that he knows that he was mistaken. Therefore, it is indeed possible that Socrates know that he was mistaken even though it is impossible that he know that he is mistaken, etc.

[4r. Insoluble XVIII]

Suppose that the proposition 'The king is seated, or some disjunctive proposition written on this sheet is in doubt for Socrates' is written on this sheet, and no other [proposition is written there] ((om. .*a*.)) [And] let it be posited that it is hidden from Socrates whether the king is seated or is not seated. Let it be posited further that Socrates is very learned in [every] art, and that he is looking at that proposition on this sheet.

Then the question is whether that proposition is known by Socrates to be true, known by Socrates to be false, or in doubt [for him].

One cannot say that Socrates knows it to be false; for if that is the case, it would follow that he knew each part of it to be false. But that is false. Its falsity is evident, since by the hypothesis he does not know its first {46rb} part to be false because the first part is in doubt for Socrates. Consequently, by the hypothesis, the first part [of the proposition] is not known to Socrates.

Nor can one say that Socrates knows that proposition to be true. For if he does, he would know at least one part of the disjunctive proposition to be true. But not the first part, by the hypothesis;

therefore, the second. But I prove that that is not the case; for if he knew the second part to be true, then the second part would be ((*esset/est*)) true because nothing is known unless it is true. Furthermore, if the second part is true, then things are as they are signified to be by the second part. But it signifies that the proposition presented above is in doubt for Socrates. Therefore, it is the case that the disjunctive proposition presented above is in doubt for Socrates. Consequently, that disjunctive proposition is not known by Socrates to be true – which was to be proved.

But if one says that that disjunctive proposition is in doubt for Socrates, then Socrates knows that it is in doubt for him, since he is very learned in every art; for an expert considering any proposition would of course know and say whether that proposition was in doubt for him or not. Then, further: Socrates knows that that proposition is in doubt for him; therefore, Socrates knows that things are as its second part signifies. And if that is the case, then he knows that the second part of the second disjunctive proposition is true. And if he knows that the second part of that disjunctive proposition is true, he also knows that that whole disjunctive proposition is true. Consequently, the disjunctive proposition presented above is not in doubt for Socrates – which was to be proved.

The reply: That proposition is in doubt for Socrates.

And when it was said that therefore Socrates knows that things are as its second part signifies, I deny it. For that reason, I say that the second part of that disjunctive proposition is in doubt for Socrates, but also that that disjunctive proposition is not in doubt for Socrates. Thus, as regards its direct signification it signifies that that disjunctive is in doubt for Socrates, but as a result of the combination of the consequent mentioned above ((*praedictae consequentis/praedictam consequentem*)) it signifies that the disjunctive proposition presented above is not in doubt for Socrates; for that follows from it together with the hypothesis posited. And so the second part of the disjunctive proposition presented above is false ((*falsa/faba*)) if it is considered as a single proposition by itself. And since Socrates is very learned in every art, he knows that the second part of the disjunctive proposition presented above is false. And since, on the hypothesis, its first part is in doubt for Socrates, it follows that the disjunctive proposition presented above is in doubt for Socrates.

[First objection:] But, on the contrary, if the disjunctive proposition presented above were in doubt for Socrates, it would follow ((*sequeretur/sequitur*)) that as long as the hypothesis posited before remains in force the contradictory of that disjunctive proposition would also be in doubt for Socrates. This is evident, because he cannot know one part of a contradiction to be true and be in doubt about the other part. But the contradictory of the disjunctive proposition presented above is 'No king is seated, and no proposition written on this sheet is in doubt for Socrates.' But Socrates knows that [this] second [proposition] is false, because he knows that its second part is false. But for the falsity of a conjunctive proposition it is enough that one part is false, and in order that a whole [conjunctive proposition] be known to be false, it is enough that one part of it be known to be false.

[Second objection:] In the second place, the second part of the conjunctive proposition contradicts the second part of the disjunctive proposition, but the second part of this conjunctive proposition is false; therefore, the second part of the disjunctive proposition presented above was true – the opposite of which was said [above].

Reply [to the first objection]: The contradictory of the disjunctive proposition presented above must be in doubt for Socrates. And I say, further, that the contradictory of the disjunctive proposition presented above was not correctly derived. In order to see this it is essential to know that the second part of that disjunctive proposition signifies or can signify that it itself is false when a certain hypothesis has been posited, although it does not signify this directly but signifies it by implication in accordance with the hypothesis that was posited, as was apparent. And, therefore, it signifies reflexively that it itself is true, or even that it is false; because if we suppose that the second part of that disjunctive proposition is true, we have to accept as equivalent to that disjunctive proposition the following proposition: 'The king is seated, or the disjunctive proposition written on this sheet is in doubt for Socrates.' *D* is true as long as the reflexivity is discounted. And the contradiction of the disjunctive proposition presented above has to be derived in accordance with this, and it is the proposition 'No king is seated, and no proposition written on this sheet is in doubt for Socrates.' Or *D* is not true.

On this basis [the reply] to the counterinstances is evident, because that proposition was granted [– viz.,] that the contradictory of the disjunctive proposition presented above is as in doubt for Socrates as is the disjunctive proposition it contradicts. For Socrates knows the second part of it to be {46va} true because the second part of it is a disjunctive proposition whose last part he knows to be true; but he is in doubt about the second part of the conjunctive proposition presented above, and consequently about the whole conjunctive proposition, since in order that a conjunctive proposition be in doubt it is enough that one part of it be in doubt.

In reply to the second [objection] I say that the contradictory of the second part of the disjunctive proposition was not derived correctly, as is already arguably evident from the things that have been said, etc.

[4s. Insoluble XIX]

Suppose that Socrates is in such a state that he does not want to attack Plato if Plato does not want to attack ((*vult invadere/invadit*)) him, and that Plato is in such a state that he does not want to attack Socrates if Socrates wants to attack him; and if Socrates does not want to attack him, [Plato] wants to attack him (viz., Socrates).

Then the question is whether Socrates wants to attack ((*vult invadere/invadit*)) Plato or not.

If not, then, by the hypothesis, Plato wants to attack Socrates. Further, Plato wants to attack Socrates; therefore, Socrates wants to attack Plato. Therefore, if Socrates does not want to attack Plato, Socrates wants to attack Plato.

But if one says that Socrates wants to attack Plato, then, by the hypothesis, Plato does not want to attack Socrates. Further, Plato does not want to attack Socrates; therefore, by the hypothesis, Socrates does not want to attack Plato. Therefore, if he wants to attack Plato, he does not want to attack Plato.

This is very much the same: Suppose that Socrates does not want to eat except when Plato wants to eat, and Plato does not want to eat when Socrates wants to eat.

Then the question is whether Socrates wants to eat or not.

If he wants to eat, then Plato wants to eat. Further, if Plato wants to eat, then, by the hypothesis, Socrates does not want to eat. Therefore, if Socrates wants to eat, Socrates does not want to eat.

But if one says that he does not want to eat, then, by the hypothesis, Plato wants to eat. Further, if Plato wants to eat, then, by the hypothesis, Socrates wants to eat. Therefore, if Socrates does not want to eat, Socrates wants to eat.

The reply: Each of those hypotheses is impossible, and so it is not surprising if a contradiction follows. All the same, each part of [each] hypothesis is possible even though it is not compatible with the other part, etc.

WALTER BURLEY
OBLIGATIONS (SELECTIONS)

Introduction

(For information on Burley's life and writings, see the introduction
to his *Consequences*, Translation 9.)

Burley's *Treatise on Obligations*, portions of which are translated
here, was written around 1302. It is a representative account of an
intriguing part of medieval logic from a relatively early stage of
its development. His treatment of obligations here is fundamental
for understanding the many and varied later fourteenth-century
accounts.

The notion of logical obligations developed in the context of the
dialectical disputation in the highly structured form inherited from
Aristotle's *Topics*. The job of the initiator of an obligational disputation (the 'opponent') is to present propositions to which his
designated interlocutor (the 'respondent') is obliged to respond in
certain ways. The opponent aims at trapping the respondent into
maintaining contradictory propositions, and the respondent aims
at getting through the stipulated time-period of the disputation
without having contradicted himself. The respondent's obligatory
responses are three: *granting* the proposition put to him by the
opponent, *denying* it, *'doubting'* it – i.e., claiming that his circumstances in the disputation do not support his granting or denying it.
The respondent may also draw a distinction among senses of an
ambiguous proposition put to him, but he must follow that *distinguishing* with granting, denying, or doubting the proposition in
each of the senses distinguished.

Obligational disputations became important in fourteenth-
century university education not only for the intellectual training
they afforded but also because they gave rise to certain dialectical
paradoxes that were philosophically interesting in their own right,
some because they seemed to challenge the laws of logic. Burley's

interest in the translated portions of his treatise is in such paradoxes and their solutions.

For further discussion of obligations, see CHLMP V.16, 'Obligations'; on disputation generally, see CHLMP I.1, 'Medieval Philosophical Literature,' and VII.27, 'The Oxford Calculators.'

Obligations (selections)

[Introduction]

{34} 0.01. There are two sides in a dialectical disputation, the opponent's and the respondent's. The opponent's job is to use language in a way that makes the respondent grant impossible things that he need not grant because of the *positum*. The respondent's job, on the other hand, is to maintain the *positum* in such a way that any impossibility seems to follow not because of him but rather because of the *positum*. Therefore, as regards the statable thing [at issue], the aim of both the opponent and the respondent is directed at whatever the respondent is obligated by.

0.02. And so the first thing we have to know is what an obligation is. It must be said that an obligation is a prefix belonging to the statable thing [at issue] in accordance with a certain condition. It is called 'obligation' as if to say 'bound by something else' (*ob aliud ligatio*). But because a genus cannot exist apart from its species, we should first divide obligation into its species. Obligation is divided in this way: It obligates [the respondent] either to [A] an act or to [B] a disposition; and these are both divided as follows. The obligation covers either what is complex [i.e., a proposition] or what is noncomplex [i.e., a term]. If [A1] it obligates to an act and {35} covers what is noncomplex, it is *petitio*. If [A2] it covers what is complex, it is *sit verum*. If [B1] it obligates to a disposition and covers what is noncomplex, it is *institutio*. If [B2] it covers what is complex, it obligates either to [B2.1] maintaining the complex as true, and then it is *positio*; or it obligates to [B2.2] maintaining it as false, and then it is *depositio*; or to [B2.3] maintaining it as uncertain, and then it is *dubitatio*. And so there are six species of obligation.

But because *institutio* is the imposition of a new signification on some utterance, and we have to presuppose what a word signifies in a disputation, we should turn our attention to *institutio* first and then to the rest.

[Institutio]

1.01. *Institutio* is introduced either for the sake of abbreviation or in order for us to conceal what is at issue. And *institutio* is subdivided, for trouble arises either because one utterance is imposed on one [thing] or because more than one utterance is imposed on one [thing], as happens in the case of synonyms. And each of these cases is subdivided, because one sort of *institutio* is absolute and another is dependent.

[*Absolute* Institutio]

1.02. Here, for instance, is an absolute *institutio*: 'Let '*A*' signify a man or a donkey.' In absolute *institutio* the following rule applies:

An institutio should never be allowed when what the utterance signifies depends on the truth or falsity of the proposition in which it is used.

For it goes the other way around: Truth and falsity depend on what the terms signify. And on this basis the following sophisma is solved.

1.03. Let '*A*' signify a donkey in a true proposition, a man in a false proposition, and the disjunctive [term] 'a man or not a man' in an uncertain proposition. Next, either you are *A* or not. If you are *A*, then the proposition ['You are *A*'] is true; therefore, '*A*' signifies ((*significat/est*)) a donkey, therefore, you are a donkey. If you are not *A*, then the proposition ['You are *A*'] {36} is false, and in a false proposition '*A*' signifies a man; therefore, 'You are a man' is false. If 'You are *A*' is uncertain, then '*A*' is the same as the term 'a man or not a man,' and in that case 'You are a man or not a man' would be uncertain.

1.04. The solution is evident, because an *institutio* should not be allowed when it makes what the utterance signifies depend on the truth of a proposition.

1.05. Here is another rule:

A part can never signify the whole whose part it is, even though it could appellate the whole whose part it is.

Therefore, an *institutio* should never be allowed when it makes a part signify [its] whole. And on this basis the following sophisma is solved.

1.06. Let 'A' signify that 'A' signifies what is false, and let the question be whether 'A' signifies what is true or what is false. If it signifies what is true, and 'A' signifies that 'A' signifies what is false, then that 'A' signifies what is false is true; therefore, 'A' signifies what is false. But, on the contrary, if 'A' signifies what is false, then that 'A' signifies what is false is true, and 'A' signifies that 'A' signifies what is false; therefore, 'A' signifies what is true. Therefore, if it signifies what is false, it signifies what is true.

1.07. The solution: 'A' cannot signify that 'A' signifies what is false, because a part cannot signify the whole whose part it is; nor can it signify what is interchangeable with the whole, or the contradictory of the whole, or its subcontrary.

1.08. Here is another sophisma: Let 'A' signify that 'B' signifies what is false. Let 'B' signify that 'C' signifies what is false. And let 'C' signify that 'A' signifies what is false. And let the question be whether 'A' signifies what is true or what is false. If it signifies what is true, then 'B' signifies what is false; therefore, 'C' does not signify what is false; therefore, 'A' signifies what is false. Therefore, if 'A' signifies what is true, it signifies what is false. But, on the contrary, if 'A' signifies what is false, 'B' does not signify what is false; and if 'B' does not signify what is false, 'C' signifies what is false; and if 'C' signifies what is false, 'A' does not signify what is false. Therefore, from the first, if 'A' signifies what is false, 'A' does not signify what is false. {37}

1.09. The solution: The *institutio* should not be allowed, because it is interchangeable with an *institutio* in which it is posited that 'A' signifies that 'A' signifies what is false.

1.10. Here is another sophisma. 'A' can signify everything that is not A; therefore, let 'A' signify everything that is not A. And I ask whether you are A or not. If you are, and A is only that which is not A, then you are not A. If you are not A, and 'A' signifies everything that is not A, then you are A.

1.11. The solution: The proposition 'Let "A" signify (or let "A" appellate) everything that is not "*A*"' is ambiguous in virtue of the fact that the negation can fall under the appellation or outside it. If it falls under the appellation, the *institutio* should not be allowed. If it falls outside it, the *institutio* should be allowed, and in that case it should be granted that you are *A* or are not *A* ((om. *non est causa*)). And in that case, '"*A*" appellates everything that is not *A*' should be denied, and this is true and should be granted. '"*A*" appellates everything that *was* not *A*.'

1.12. Here is another sophisma having to do with the act of appellating. '*A*' appellates every proposition not appellated by its subject and only such propositions. Next, *A* is a proposition. Either this proposition ['*A* is a proposition'] is appellated by '*A*' or it is not. If it is appellated by '*A*,' then it is appellated by its subject, and no such proposition is appellated by the utterance '*A*'; therefore, the proposition is not appellated by '*A*.' Therefore, from the first, if it is appellated by '*A*,' it is not appellated by '*A*.' But, on the contrary, if the proposition is not appellated by '*A*', then it is not appellated by its subject; but every such [proposition] is appellated by the utterance '*A*'; therefore, the proposition is appellated by the utterance '*A*.' Therefore, if it is not appellated by '*A*,' it is appellated by '*A*'.

1.13. The solution: The proposition is appellated by '*A*,' and it does not follow that it is appellated by its subject. Instead, the opposite follows, since '*A*' appellates only a proposition not appellated by its subject.... {41}

[Petitio]

2.01. *Petitio* is next. Like *institutio*, *petitio* covers what is noncomplex, and it seems to be the genus for every species of obligation. For anyone who posits something in a *positio* requires (*petit*) that it be granted, and anyone who posits something in a *depositio* requires (*petit*) that it be denied. (Therefore, reasonably enough, *petitio* comes directly after *institutio*.) But from this it appears that *petitio* is not a species [of obligation] distinct from other species, just as a genus is not numbered ((*ponitur/ponit*)) with [its] species. It must be said that *petitio* is distinct from other species [of obligation], because a *petitio* posits the performance of an act that is

mentioned in the statable thing [at issue], but the other species do
not require (*petunt*) this.

2.02. One sort of *petitio* is common, and another is dialectical; but
common *petitio* is not relevant here. A dialectical *petitio* is an expression that insists that in the disputation some act must be performed
with regard to the statable thing [at issue]. For example, 'I require
(*peto*) you to respond affirmatively to "God exists,"' and the like.
And *petitio* obligates [the respondent] to perform an action with
regard to the *obligatum*, while *positio* obligates [him] only to maintain [the *obligatum*]; and in this way *petitio* and *positio* differ. But, on
the contrary, when [the opponent] says, 'Let it be posited that you
are running,' he produces an obligation for you to perform an act
with regard to this proposition 'You are running' [– viz.,] by
granting it. Therefore, *petitio* does not obligate [the respondent to]
more than *positio* does. We have to say [in reply] that *petitio* per se
obligates [the respondent] to an act, *positio* only *per accidens*. Similarly, *petitio* obligates [the respondent] to perform an act expressed in
the statable thing [at issue], but *positio* always obligates [him] to
maintain something. So far it seems that *petitio* is not an obligation,
for to require is not to obligate, because, unless the respondent
consents, he is neither more nor less obligated in virtue of the
opponent's requiring [something of him]. We have to say [in reply]
that *petitio* is an obligation – not just any *petitio*, however, but {42}
only one that occurs with [the respondent's] consent.

2.03. One sort of *petitio* is absolute, and another is relative. Here
is an example of the first: 'I require you to grant that a man is a
donkey.' An example of the second: 'I require you to grant the first
thing to be proposed by me.'

2.04. [The following] rule is laid down:

> *What is impossible must not be granted unless there is a petitio that what
> is impossible be granted.*

But if a *petitio* has been produced requiring that what is impossible
be granted, then, if [the respondent] has consented to the *petitio*, it
is not absurd to grant what is impossible. On the basis [of this rule]
sophismata of the following sort ((*huiusmodi/huius*)) are resolved.

2.05. I require you to grant that a man is a donkey. Next, let 'A
man is a donkey' be proposed. If you grant it, you grant what is
impossible; therefore, [you have responded] badly. If you deny it,

the disputation is over; you were required to grant that a man is a donkey, and you have not granted it – therefore, [you have responded] badly.

2.06. The solution: Once the *petitio* has been admitted, 'A man is a donkey' must be granted; and it is not absurd to grant what is impossible when a *petitio* has been produced requiring that what is impossible be granted.

2.07. In connection with every obligation, three general rules are laid down, namely,

> [1] *Everything following from an obligatum must be granted* (where '*obligatum*' is interpreted as what has been granted or what must necessarily be granted);

likewise,

> [2] *Everything incompatible with the obligatum must be denied;*

likewise,

> [3] *One must reply to what is irrelevant in accordance with its own quality.*

2.08. These rules must be maintained in the case of *petitio*, too, if there is no *petitio* to the contrary. For example, I require you to grant one thing only ((om. *esse*)). Next, I propose 'God exists.' This must be granted because it is necessary. Next, let 'Something exists' be proposed. If you deny this, you deny something that follows [from what has been granted], for this follows: 'God exists; therefore, something exists.' If you grant it, the disputation is over. You were required to grant only one thing, and you have granted more than one; therefore, [you have responded] badly.

2.09. The solution: After the granting of 'God exists,' 'Something exists' need not be granted. And [this inference] is not valid: 'This follows; therefore, it must be granted' if there is a *petitio* to the contrary, and in the present case there is. But it need not be denied, either. It need not be responded to [at all], except {43} in such a way as to exculpate oneself.

2.10. Things are much the same with regard to the other sort [of *petitio*]. I require you not to respond to the first thing proposed by me. Next, I propose 'God exists.' If you grant this, the disputation is over; you have contravened what was required [and] therefore, [you have responded] badly. The conclusion is the same if you deny it or say that you are in doubt about it. If you do not respond, then, on the contrary; the proposition is necessary, and you should therefore grant it.

2.11. The solution: You should not respond to 'God exists' once you have admitted [this] *petitio*. It appears, however, that this *petitio* is not logical but, rather, extra-logical (*vulgaris*), [like] one of these: 'I require you to be silent,' 'I require you not to fulfill my requirement.'

2.12. Here is a sophisma: I require you to grant that a man is a donkey. Next, I propose 'You grant that a man is a donkey.' If you grant this, you grant what is false, and you were not required to grant this; therefore, [you have responded] badly. If you deny it, the disputation is over. The *obligatum* was that you grant that a man is a donkey, and you have not granted it; therefore, [you have responded] badly.

2.13. The solution: When 'You grant that a man is a donkey' is proposed, it must be denied, because you were not required to grant this but only that a man is a donkey; and so by granting this, you would satisfy the *petitio*.

2.14. Another sophisma: I require you to respond badly to 'God exists.' Next, I propose this to you: 'God exists.' Whatever the response, the answer is 'The disputation is over.' And the question is whether you responded well or badly. If you responded well, and you were required to respond badly, you have contravened what was required and, therefore, have responded badly. Therefore, if you have responded well, you have responded badly. But, on the contrary, you have responded badly; therefore, you have done what was required and, therefore, have responded well. Therefore, if you have responded badly, you have responded well.

2.15. The solution: The *petitio* should not be admitted, because no *petitio* should be admitted unless it is in the respondent's power to satisfy the requirement. But once this *petitio* has been admitted by anyone, he cannot satisfy it. Or, alternatively, once this *petitio* has been admitted {44} and 'God exists' is proposed, one should respond by saying that you are in doubt, since one should choose the lesser of two evils, and it is a lesser evil to respond in that way to what is necessary than to deny what is necessary. And when the question arises whether you have responded well or badly, it must be said that [you have responded] well as far as the requirements of the obligation go, but badly as far as the nature of reality goes.

2.16. Here is another sophisma: I require you to grant that the king is seated or is not seated (in such a way that there is a disjunction of the *petitio*). Next, I propose this to you: 'The king is seated.' If you grant this, you grant what is in doubt when you are not obligated to do so. Because although you are obligated to grant that the king is seated or is not seated, you are not obligated to grant that the king is seated. If you deny this, you deny what is in doubt when you are not obligated to do so; therefore, [you have responded] badly. If you respond by saying that you are in doubt, I propose this: 'The king is not seated.' If you grant this, you grant what is in doubt which you are not obligated [to grant], because although you are obligated to grant that the king is seated or is not seated, you are not obligated to grant that the king is not seated. If you deny it, you deny what is in doubt, which you are not obligated [to deny]. If you respond by saying that you are in doubt, the disputation is over. You were required to grant that the king is seated or is not seated, and you have done neither; therefore, [you have responded] badly.

2.17. The solution: Some people say that if someone requires a cow or a donkey, it is up to the man from whom it is required to give whichever one he likes, a cow or a donkey, and he thereby satisfies the requirement. Analogously, the respondent can grant whichever one he likes, and he thereby satisfies the requirement. Others say that the opponent must be asked whether he wants it to be in the respondent's power to grant either alternative indifferently. If he says yes, the respondent responds satisfactorily by granting whichever one he likes. But if [the opponent] does not want it to be in the respondent's power, he must make it definite which alternative the respondent must grant. And if he does not make it definite, the respondent should not admit the *petitio*, because in this obligation it must be made definite for the respondent.

2.18. Trouble arises from mixing *positio* with *petitio*, {45} as in the following case: I require you to deny the first thing proposed by me, and I posit that Socrates is running. Next, I propose 'Socrates is moving.' If you deny this, you deny what follows [from the *positum*]; therefore, [you have responded] badly. If you grant it, the disputation is over. You were required to deny the first thing proposed, but you have granted it; therefore, [you have responded] badly.

2.19. The solution: If the *petitio* was agreed to, then 'Socrates is moving' should be denied. And when *petitio* is mixed with *positio*, what follows from the *positum* is sometimes denied and the opposite of the *positum* is granted, if the *petitio* is of this sort.

[Positio]

3.01. Now that we have discussed *petitio* and *institutio* we have to discuss *positio*. *Positio*, as the term is used here, is a prefix to something statable [indicating that the statable thing] should be held to be true. And it is divided, because one sort of *positio* is possible and the other sort is impossible. And each of these is subdivided, because [the *positio*] covers either a simple or a composite statable thing. If it covers a composite statable, either it is a composite formed by means of a copulative conjunction – in which case it is called conjoined *positio* – or it is formed by means of a disjunctive conjunction and is called indeterminate *positio*. Likewise, sometimes there is a stipulation in a *positio*, and then the *positio* is dependent. *Positio cadens* and *positio renascens* are included under dependent *positio*.

[Possible Positio]

3.02. First, we have to discuss possible *positio*. And we must consider to begin with what must be posited in this sort of *positio*. It is important to know that in the case of possible *positio* what must be posited is a false contingent proposition, a true uncertain proposition, and sometimes a truth known to be true – for example, against shameless people who sometimes deny a truth known to be true, for [even] a truth known to be true is not always held to be true. {46}

3.03. Second, we should consider how this sort of *positio* is to be produced. It is produced in the following way: Suppose Socrates is black, and suppose it is posited that Socrates is white. The hypothesis, however, does not obligate but rather makes definite. And because I can be definite about the truth of one opposite and maintain the other opposite as true, the *positio* that posits that Socrates is white can be admitted even though the truth of the matter, as was already said, is that Socrates is black.

3.04. At the beginning of making a *positio*, we use the verb 'It is posited'; and at the end we use the expression 'The disputation is over' (*cedat tempus*). The respondent is obligated until 'The disputation is over' is said, unless the opponent and respondent agree otherwise. Therefore, we need an art to direct us in responding to the *positio* and to the things proposed from the time when 'It is posited' is said to the time when 'The disputation is over' is said. For the response to what is proposed after 'The disputation is over' is said will not be altered on account of the *positum*. And when 'The disputation is over' has been said, we should consider whether or not [the respondent] has responded well in the obligation, because we cannot judge this during the time of the obligation.

[Rules]

3.05. It is important to know that there are some rules that constitute the practice of this art and others that pertain to its being practiced well. First, we should discuss the rules that constitute the practice of this art. Rules concerning what is posited and what is relevant and irrelevant constitute the practice of this art. First, this rule is given concerning the *positum*:

> 3.06. *Everything that is posited and put forward in the form of the positum during the time of the positio must be granted.*

The clause 'put forward in the form of the *positum*' is used because if [something] is put forward in a form other than the form of the *positum*, it need not be granted. For example, if 'Marcus' and 'Tully' are names of the same man, and it is posited that Marcus is running, one need not grant that Tully is running. For that 'Marcus' and 'Tully' are names of the same man is either known or not known. {47} If it is known, and it is posited that Marcus is running, then it must be granted that Tully is running, because it follows. If it is not known, one should respond to 'Tully is running' by saying that one is in doubt. And the clause 'during the time of the *positio*' is used, because if it is put forward outside that time, it need not be granted.

3.07. There is the following objection to this rule. [First objection:] Suppose that, indicating two contingent contradictory [propositions], one posits 'The other one of these is true.' Next, let 'One or the other of these is true' be proposed. That is necessary and therefore must be granted. Next, let 'The other one of these is true' be proposed. This is posited and therefore must be granted, and it is put forward in the form of the *positum*. When it has been granted, let 'Each of these is true' be proposed. If you deny this, you deny what follows logically; therefore, [you have responded] badly. If you grant it, you grant what is impossible when the *positum* is possible; therefore, [you have responded] badly. And this occurs only because you grant the *positum* put forward in the form of the *positum*.

3.08. Furthermore, [second objection:] I want it to be the case that whichever of these is proposed first is the *positum* (indicating the same propositions as before). Then this is true according to the rule: 'Each of these must be granted if it is proposed first.' But one or the other of these is incompatible with the *positum*; therefore, something incompatible with the *positum* must be granted.

3.09. In reply to the first objection, when 'the other one of these is true' is proposed in second place, it should be denied. And this is not a case in which the *positum* is put forward in the form of the *positum*, because in the *positum* 'the other one' was an indefinite or indifferent name for both of these [propositions]; but when it is put forward in second place, 'the other one' is a relative name.

3.10. In reply to the second objection, the conclusion 'Something incompatible with the *positum* must be granted' does not follow. Instead, this follows: 'Something incompatible with the *positum* must be granted if it is proposed first.'

3.11. Here is another way of arguing [against the rule]. One or the other of these is true and the other one of them is possible. Let this be posited. And let 'One or the other of these is true' be proposed, and after that 'The other one of them is true.' This must be granted, because the *positum* is put forward {48} in the form of the *positum*; for in the *positum* 'the other one' is a relative. And then let 'Each of these is true' be proposed.

3.12. [In reply] it should be said that when one says, 'Let "One or the other of these is true and the other one of them is possible" be posited,' this *positio* should not be admitted, just as this one should not be admitted: 'Some proposition is possible' – and let some proposition be posited ((*ponatur/proponatur*)). [That is] because the respondent should be certain about what is posited, but in this case no proposition is determinately posited.

3.13. Suppose somone argues otherwise, however, in this way: 'One or the other of these is true, and "The other one of them is true" is possible.' In that case it should be said that 'One or the other of these is true, and "The other one of them is true" is possible' is false because of the second part; for the second part of the copulative proposition 'One or the other of these is true, and "The other one of them is true" is possible' is impossible.

3.14. Next [we have to discuss] what is proposed. Everything proposed is either relevant or irrelevant. If it is irrelevant, it must be responded to on the basis of its own quality; and this [means] on the basis of the quality it has relative to us. For example, if it is true [and] known to be true, it should be granted. If it is false [and] known to be false, it should be denied. If it is uncertain, one should respond by saying that one is in doubt. But if it is relevant, it either follows or is incompatible. If it follows, it must be granted. If it is incompatible, it must be denied. That is why [the following] rules are given.

> 3.15. [First rule:] *Everything that follows from the positum must be granted. Everything that follows from the positum either together with an already granted proposition (or propositions), or together with the opposite of a proposition (or the opposites of propositions) already correctly denied and known to be such, must be granted.*
>
> 3.16. [Second rule:] *Everything incompatible with the positum must be denied. Likewise, everything incompatible with the positum together with an already granted proposition (or propositions), or together with the opposite of a proposition (or the opposites of propositions) already correctly denied and known to be such, must be denied.* {49}

3.17. [Objection 1 against first rule:] One argues against the first rule [in this way]. Let this be posited: 'Nothing is posited to you.' Next, let 'Everything that follows from the *positum* must be granted' be proposed. This must be granted because it is a rule. Next, let 'Something follows from the *positum*' be proposed. This follows and therefore must be granted. Next, let 'Something is posited' be proposed. If you grant this, you grant the opposite of the *positum*; therefore, [you have responded] badly. If you deny it, you deny something that follows, because this follows: 'Something follows from the *positum*; therefore, something is posited.'

3.18. Furthermore, [Objection 2 to first rule:] Let this be posited to you: 'No animal is running.' Let this be posited to Socrates: 'A man is running.' Once this whole thing has been posited, I propose this: 'Some animal is running.' If you grant this, you grant the opposite of the *positum*. If you deny it, the disputation is over; you deny something that follows [from the *positum*]. Proof: For this is true: That some animal is running follows from the *positum*; because if it did not follow from the *positum*, it would not follow from what was posited to Socrates. And in that case that an animal is running would not follow from the fact that a man is running, and that is false.

3.19. In reply to the first of these [objections], one says that this must be denied: 'Everything that follows from the *positum* must be granted'; it is not necessary either. But this is necessary: If something follows from the *positum*, it must be granted.

3.20. In reply to the second [objection], I say that this does not follow: 'You have denied something that follows from the *positum*; therefore [you have responded] badly.' But this does follow: 'You have denied something that follows from what was posited to you; therefore, [you have responded] badly.'

3.21. Again, [Objection 3:] It is proved [as follows] that not everything that follows from the *positum* and the opposite of a proposition already correctly denied must be granted. Let this be posited: 'You are in Rome or that you are in Rome must be granted.' Next, let 'That you are in Rome must be granted' be proposed. This is false and irrelevant; therefore, it must be denied. Next, let 'That you are in Rome follows from the *positum* and the opposite of a proposition already correctly denied' be proposed. This is necessary, because this conditional is necessary: 'If either you are in Rome, or that you are in Rome must be granted, but that you are in Rome is not to be granted, then you are in Rome.' Once this has been granted – 'That you {50} are in Rome follows from the *positum* and the opposite of a proposition already correctly denied' – let this be proposed: 'That you are in Rome must be granted.' If you grant this, you have granted and denied the same thing; therefore, [you have responded] badly. If you deny it, the disputation is over; you have denied what follows according to the rule. Because if the rule is good, this follows: 'That you are in Rome follows from the *positum* and the opposite of a proposition already correctly denied; therefore, that you are in Rome must be granted.'

3.22. [In reply to Objection 3,] one says that this must be denied: 'That you are in Rome follows from the *positum* and the opposite of a proposition correctly denied'; it is not necessary either. Even if it is necessary that from the posited disjunction together with the opposite of one disjunct it follows that you are in Rome, it is nonetheless not necessary that that disjunction be posited.

3.23. We can give examples of the rules mentioned above.

3.24. [First rule:] Everything that follows from the *positum* must be granted. For example, let it be posited that Antichrist is white. Next, let 'Antichrist has a color' be proposed. This must be granted because it follows from the *positum* by itself.

3.25. Likewise, [first rule:] Everything that follows from the *positum* and an already correctly granted proposition must be granted. For example, suppose Socrates and Plato are black. Let it be posited that Socrates is white. Next, let 'Socrates and Plato are alike' be proposed. This must be granted, because it is true and irrelevant. Next, let 'Plato is white' be proposed. This must be granted because it follows from the *positum* and a proposition already correctly granted.

3.26. Likewise, [first rule:] Everything that follows from the *positum* together with already correctly granted propositions must be granted. For example, let it be posited that Antichrist has a color. Next, let 'Antichrist is not white' be proposed. This must be granted because it is true and irrelevant. Next, let 'Antichrist is not black' be proposed. This must be granted because it is true and irrelevant. Next, let 'Antichrist has an intermediate color' be proposed. This must be granted because it follows from the *positum* and propositions already correctly granted.

3.27. Likewise, [first rule:] Everything that follows from the *positum* and the opposite of a proposition already correctly denied must be granted. For example, suppose 'Socrates is white' is posited, and {51} let 'Socrates and Plato are not alike' be proposed. This must be denied, because it is false and irrelevant. Next, 'Plato is white.' This must be granted, because it follows from the *positum* ((om. *cum*)) and the opposite of a proposition already correctly denied.

3.28. Likewise, [first rule:] Everything that follows from the *positum* and the opposites of propositions already correctly denied must be granted. For example, suppose 'Antichrist has a color' is posited, and let 'Antichrist is white' be proposed. This must be denied, because it is false and irrelevant. Afterwards let 'Antichrist is black' be proposed. This must be denied, because it is false and irrelevant. Next, let 'Antichrist has an intermediate color' be proposed. This must be granted, because it follows from the *positum* and the opposites of propositions already correctly denied, as is evident.

3.29. On the same basis examples concerning what is incompatible are evident. For example, where something that follows [from the *positum*] is proposed, its opposite should be proposed. This will be incompatible, because if one of a pair of opposites is compatible, the other will be incompatible.

3.30. One argues [as follows] against the rule concerning what is irrelevant. It seems that one should not respond to an irrelevant proposition in accordance with its own quality. For suppose it is posited that you are in Rome. Next, 'My hand is closed.' This must be granted (supposing it is the case that my hand is closed). Next, let that come to be false. Then, let 'My hand is not closed' be proposed. This is true and irrelevant; therefore, it must be granted according to the rule, and yet its opposite was granted previously.

3.31. In reply it should be said that 'My hand is not closed' must be denied even though it is true. And that is because it is incompatible, since its opposite was previously granted.

3.32. The rule concerning what follows and what is incompatible must be understood either conjointly or dividedly. But the rule concerning what is irrelevant must be understood only conjointly. For in order for something to be irrelevant, it needs to be irrelevant to the *positum*. And if some propositions are already granted, [what is irrelevant] must be irrelevant to the *positum* together with all the propositions that are granted. But in order for something to follow, it is enough that it follows from the *positum* by itself, or from one proposition that is already granted, or from the *positum* together with propositions that are already granted. (And analogously for what is incompatible.) {52}

3.33. Next are rules that do not constitute the practice of this art but are just useful.

3.34. [First rule:] One rule concerning the obligational art is this:

One must pay special attention to the order [of the propositions].

The reason for this rule is that a proposition that is to be granted in one place is not to be granted in another place. Therefore, when some proposition is proposed, we should consider its order relative to propositions previously granted. For example, suppose it is the case that Socrates and Plato are black, and let it be posited that Socrates is white. Then if 'Socrates and Plato are alike' is proposed in first place, it must be granted, because it is true and irrelevant. And if 'Plato is white' were proposed after this, it would have to be granted, because it follows. If, however, 'Plato is white' were proposed in first place, it would have to be denied, because it is false and irrelevant. If 'Socrates and Plato are alike' were proposed after this, it would have to be denied because it is incompatible. And that is why a proposition that is to be granted in one place is to be denied in another; and that is why one should pay special attention to the order [of the propositions].

3.35. Here is another rule:

During the time of the obligation one should not give a definite answer to a question requiring a distinction ((distinguibilis/disciplinalis)).

This is evident in the following way. Suppose the truth of the matter is that Socrates alone is speaking, and let it be posited that Socrates is silent. And let 'Some man is speaking' be proposed. This is true and irrelevant; therefore, it must be granted. And if [the opponent] asks 'Who is this man [who is speaking]?' you must grant the opposite of the *positum* or something false and irrelevant if you respond. Because, if you say 'Socrates is speaking,' you grant a proposition incompatible with the *positum*. And if you say 'Plato, or Cicero, or *any* other man is speaking,' you grant a proposition that is false and irrelevant.

3.36. From this it is clear that an indefinite proposition is sometimes to be granted where no singular proposition is to be granted. For on the hypothesis supposed above, namely, that only Socrates is speaking, if in that case 'Socrates is silent' is posited and 'A man is speaking' is proposed, [the proposed proposition] must be granted [when it is proposed] in first place; but any singular [proposition proposed] in the same place must be denied. For 'Socrates {53} is speaking' must be denied because it is incompatible with the *positum*; and any of the other [singular propositions] must be denied because it is false and irrelevant.

3.37. Furthermore, it is clear that a singular proposition is sometimes to be granted when a universal proposed in the same place is to be denied. For example, suppose the truth of the matter is that every man other than Socrates is running and that Socrates is not running. And let this be posited: 'Socrates is running.' Then any singular [proposition falling under] the universal 'Every man is running' must be granted [when it is proposed] in first place; and yet the universal itself [proposed] in the same place must be denied. Any singular proposition must be granted, because one singular is posited, and each of the others is true and irrelevant. But the universal proposition is neither posited nor true and irrelevant.

3.38. Here is another rule, from our predecessors:

> *Outside the time [of the disputation] the truth of the matter must be acknowledged.*

One might ask why men who intend to argue say 'The disputation is over' and then argue outside and not during the time of the *positio*. In reply we have to say that during the time of the *positio* we cannot show that the respondent has responded badly, because the time in which we conclude that the respondent has responded badly has to be a time in which we accept only what is true, but during the time of the *positio* we need not grant what is true. Outside the time [of the *positio*], however, what is true must be granted; because when no obligation has been established, what is true must always be granted.

3.39. Likewise, when [a respondent] is under an obligation, he can without absurdity grant that he is responding badly; but he cannot do that outside the time [of the *positio*].

3.40. Here is another rule:

> *When a possible proposition has been posited, a proposition that is impossible per se must not be granted, and a proposition that is necessary per se must not be denied.*

3.41. But, on the contrary, let this be posited: 'That a man is a donkey must be granted.' Next, let 'A man is a donkey' be proposed. If you grant this, the point at issue has been made: You are granting a proposition that is impossible *per se*, when a possible proposition has been posited. If you deny 'A man is a donkey,' the disputation is over; you had to respond as if the *positum* were true. And if the *positum* were true, you would have had to grant ['A man is a donkey'], because anything must be granted [in the disputation] that must be granted as far as the truth of the matter goes.

3.42. In reply we have to say that 'A man is a donkey' must be denied. And you did not have to respond as if the *positum* were in fact true, because if the *positum* were in fact true, what is obligated would be something impossible. But one must not respond in the same way {54} when what is obligated is impossible as one does when what is posited is possible.

3.43. Likewise, when the *positum* is true, you would have to grant a proposition that you would not have to grant when the *positum* is false. For once 'You are in Rome' has been posited, if 'You are at *A*' (where *A* is some place in Rome) is proposed, and if 'You are at *B*' (and so on for all other places in Rome) is proposed in case the *positum* is false, each of these propositions must be denied when it is proposed in first place. On the other hand, if you were in Rome, and one of those propositions were proposed to you in first place – 'You are at *A*, or at *B* (and so on for the other places)' – it would have to be granted, because it would be true and irrelevant. And for this reason one must not respond to the *positum* and to propositions proposed in the same way when the *positum* is true as one does when the *positum* is not true.

3.44. Here is another way of arguing: It is possible that Socrates, who is not white, be white; let this be posited. And let 'Socrates is not white' be proposed. This must be granted because it follows [from the *positum*]. After this, let 'Socrates is white' be proposed. If you grant this, you are granting opposites when something possible has been posited; and [in that case] the point at issue has been made. If you deny it, you are denying something that follows, because this follows: 'Socrates, who is not white, is white; therefore, Socrates is white.'

3.45. The solution: If the modifying clause is included in the *positio*, the *positio* must not be admitted, because [in that case] an impossible proposition is posited. If it is not included in the *positio*, the *positio* must be admitted; and in that case nothing is posited except that Socrates is white. And then when 'Socrates is not white' is proposed, it must be denied; and it does not follow from the *positum*.

3.46. There is another way of showing that something impossible must be granted when a possible proposition is posited. It can happen in general (arguing outside the obligation) whenever it is posited that some false contingent proposition must be granted or that some true contingent proposition must be denied. For example, let this be posited: 'That you are in Rome must be granted.' Next, let this be proposed: 'Only this (indicating the *positum*) is what is obligated'. This is true and irrelevant; therefore, it must be granted. When it has been granted, let 'The disputation is over' be said; and let it be asked whether the *positum* was true or false. If one says that it was true, then, on the contrary, from the *positum* and a true proposition a false proposition followed. For this followed: 'That you are in Rome must be granted, and only this (indicating the *positum*) is what is obligated; therefore, you are in Rome.' If one takes the other side, namely, that the *positum* was false, then, on the contrary, that you are in Rome {55} followed from the *positum* and a true granted proposition; and it was true that everything of this sort had to be granted; therefore, 'That you are in Rome must be granted' was true, and this was the *positum*. Therefore, the *positum* was true.

3.47. The solution: Before the granting of the first proposition proposed, the *positum* was false; but after the granting of the first proposition proposed, it became true. And before the granting of the first proposition proposed, that you are in Rome followed from the *positum* together with a true irrelevant proposition, but not from the *positum* together with a true granted proposition. But not everything that follows from the *positum* together with a true irrelevant proposition must be granted. For once 'You are in Rome' has been posited, then 'You are a bishop' follows from the *positum* together with this true irrelevant proposition: 'That you are in Rome and that you are a bishop are alike [in truth value].' And yet 'You are a bishop' is not to be granted [if it is proposed] in first place, because this does not follow: The premises had to be granted; therefore, the conclusion had to be granted. Instead, this follows: The premises were granted; therefore, the conclusion had to be granted. After the granting of the first proposition proposed, however, the *positum* was true; and then a false proposition did not follow from the *positum* and a true proposition, but rather from the *positum* and a false proposition.

3.48. One must argue and respond in the same way when it has been posited that some true contingent proposition must be denied.

3.49. Here is another rule:

> When a possible proposition has been posited, it is not absurd to grant something impossible per accidens.

And this can happen in four ways: either because the *positum* becomes impossible, or because a granted proposition becomes impossible, or because a granted proposition becomes incompatible with the *positum*, or because a granted proposition becomes incompatible with another granted proposition.

3.50. An example of the first way: Suppose that you have never responded to the proposition that God exists, and let it be posited that you have never responded to the proposition that God exists. Next, let 'God exists' be proposed. This must be granted because it is necessary. Next, 'You have never responded to the proposition "God exists."' This must be granted because it is posited, and yet it is impossible *per accidens* because it is a negative false proposition concerning the past; and in the case under discussion it is supposed to have become impossible *per accidens*.

3.51. An example of the second way: Let it be posited that you are in Rome. And let 'You have never responded to the proposition that God exists' be proposed. This must be granted, because it is true and irrelevant (supposing that it is the case). Next, 'God exists.' This must be granted because it is {56} necessary. Next, 'You have never responded to the proposition that God exists.' This must be granted because it was granted before; and yet it is impossible *per accidens*.

3.52. An example of the third way: Let it be posited that you are seated. Next, let this be proposed: 'That you are seated and that you have never responded to the proposition that God exists are alike [in truth value].' This must be granted because it is true and irrelevant. Next, 'God exists.' This must be granted because it is necessary. Next, 'You have never responded to the proposition that

God exists.' This must be granted because it follows, and yet it is impossible *per accidens*. And in the granting of 'God exists,' the first proposition proposed becomes incompatible with the *positum*.

3.53. An example of the fourth way: Let it be posited that you are in Rome. Next, 'You are seated.' This must be granted, because it is true and irrelevant. Next, 'That you are seated and that you have never responded to the proposition that God exists are alike [in truth value].' This must be granted because it is true and irrelevant. Next, 'God exists.' This must be granted because it is necessary. Next, 'You have never responded to the proposition that God exists.' This must be granted because it follows, and yet it is impossible *per accidens*.

3.54. An objection to this rule: What is impossible must not be granted unless it is obligated, but what is possible does not obligate [anyone] to what is impossible. Therefore, when what is possible is posited, what is impossible must not be granted. Likewise, if something impossible is granted, this is only because of something granted before; but anything from which something impossible follows is badly granted.

3.55. In reply we have to say that the rule is most firmly established and is based on the following two rules.

3.56. [The first rule is:]

> If something is granted, it must always be granted during the time of the obligation.

3.57. The second [rule] is:

> What is possible and true in one place [in a disputation] is impossible in another place; but when it is true and irrelevant, it must be granted. Therefore, if it is proposed when it is impossible, it must be granted because it was granted before.

3.58. It is important to know, however, that what is impossible must never be granted except when it is obligated. Nevertheless, what is impossible must be granted even when nothing but what is possible has been posited. This occurs when a proposition that was granted before, when it was true, has become impossible. For in that case the impossible thing is obligated just because everything previously granted is obligated. {57} And it is not the case that that proposition was badly granted before, because when it was granted it was true.

3.59. On this basis many sophismata are resolved. For example, let *A* be the instant at which the *positum* is posited, and let it be posited that it is *A*. And let 'It is *A*' be proposed. This should be granted because it is the *positum*. And yet it is impossible *per accidens*. (And there is no absurdity here.)

3.60. Likewise, let *A* be the instant at which you respond to the first proposition proposed (and I want it to be the case that you are seated [when you respond]). And let this be posited: 'You are running or you respond affirmatively at instant *A*.' Next, let this be proposed: 'You are running.' This is false and irrelevant; therefore, it must be denied. Next, 'You respond affirmatively at instant *A*.' This must be granted, because it follows; and yet it is impossible *per accidens*.

3.61. Here is another rule:

> When a false contingent proposition is posited, one can prove any false proposition that is compossible with it.

[One can do so] in the following way: Let it be posited that you are in Rome. Next, let 'You are not in Rome or you are a bishop' be proposed. This must be granted, because it is true and irrelevant. Next, 'You are a bishop.' This follows. And in this way one can prove any false contingent proposition that is compossible with the *positum*.

3.62. Alternatively, let the *positum* be the same [as in the previous example], and let this be proposed first: 'That you are in Rome and that you are a bishop are alike [in truth value].' This must be granted, because it is true and irrelevant. Next, 'You are a bishop.' This must be granted because it follows. Or if the consequence is denied, let this be proposed in first place: 'That you are in Rome and that you are a bishop are alike in truth or in falsity.' This must be granted since it is true and irrelevant. Next, 'You are a bishop.' This must be granted because it follows.

3.63. The rule is proved in another way [as follows]: Let the *positum* be the same [as in the previous example], and let this be proposed: 'One or the other of these is true' (indicating 'You are not in Rome' and 'You are a bishop'). Next, 'You are a bishop.' This must be granted because it follows, for this follows: 'One or the other of these is true, and you are in Rome; therefore, that you are not in Rome is false; therefore, that you are a bishop is true; therefore, you are a bishop.'

3.64. Nevertheless, a proposition that is false and not compossible [with the *positum*] or a proposition that is impossible cannot be proved. For a proposition that is the same [in truth value] as the opposite of some proposition or other is incompatible with that proposition, and so is a proposition that is the same [in truth value] as an impossible proposition. {58}

3.65. An objection against the rule: A false proposition must never be granted unless it is obligated in some way. But one false contingent proposition does not obligate [the respondent] to infinitely many false propositions; therefore, when one false contingent proposition is posited, it is not the case that infinitely many false propositions can be proved. But there are infinitely many false propositions compossible with any given false proposition; therefore, etc. [A second objection:] Furthermore, the false proposition to be proved does not follow from the *positum* by itself; therefore, it follows from the *positum* together with some other proposition. This other proposition does not follow from the *positum*. And so it is either true or false. If it is false, it must be denied. And if it is true, the opposite of the *positum* and the opposite of this true proposition follow from the opposite of the false proposition to be proved. But the opposite of the false proposition to be proved is true, and the opposite of this true proposition is false; therefore, a false proposition follows from a true one.

3.66. In reply to the first [objection] we have to say that even if one false proposition does not obligate [the respondent] to infinitely many false propositions, one false proposition together with infinitely many true ones that can be proposed can obligate [the respondent] to infinitely many false propositions; and in this way infinitely many false propositions can be proved.

3.67. In reply to the second [objection] I say that the opposite of that true proposition (from which together with the *positum* the false proposition follows) does not follow from the opposite of the false proposition to be proved. But the opposite of a conjunction composed of the *positum* and that true proposition does follow from the opposite of the false proposition to be proved, and the opposite of that conjunction is true.

An objection against the way the rule is proved: A disjunction is not true unless one or the other part of it is true. Therefore, a disjunction is not to be granted unless one or the other part of it is to be granted. But neither part of [the disjunction] 'You are not in Rome or you are a bishop' is to be granted [if it is proposed] in first place, for one part of it is false and irrelevant and the other part is incompatible with the *positum*. [A second objection:] Furthermore, if 'You are in Rome' is posited and this is proposed: 'You are in Rome, and that you are in Rome and that you are a bishop are alike [in truth value],' it would have to be denied, and not because of 'You are in Rome.' Therefore, [it would have to be denied] because of this: 'That you are in Rome and that you are a bishop are alike [in truth value].' Therefore, this must be denied [when it is proposed] in first place. And so, that you are a bishop is not proved in accordance with the rule.

3.68. In reply to the first [objection] one says that a disjunction is to be granted when neither part is to be granted. A disjunction cannot be true and irrelevant when none of its parts is true and irrelevant; neither is it ever the case that a thing's being true is the same as its having to be granted. {59}

3.69. In reply to the second [objection,] some people say this must be denied [when it is proposed] in first place: 'You are in Rome, and that you are in Rome and that you are a bishop are alike [in truth value]'; and it must be denied by reason of the *positum*, and yet the *positum* must not be denied.

3.70. But this reply is false because the conjunction is false in respect of 'You are in Rome.' But that is not to be denied only because it is false, but because it is false and irrelevant. For this reason I reply in a different way, that the conjunction is to be denied, and not only because of the *positum* nor only because of a true irrelevant proposition. Instead, it is to be denied because it is false and does not follow; and therefore it is to be denied because of both [parts of the conjunction]. And yet neither part is to be denied [if it is proposed] in first place.

3.71. There is another way of proving that this – 'That you are in Rome and that you are a bishop are alike [in truth value]' – is to be denied [if it is proposed] in first place. For if this – '"You are in Rome" and "You are a bishop" are alike [in truth value]' – is to be granted, then 'you are in Rome' would have to be granted if it were proposed in first place; therefore, 'You are a bishop' would have to be granted if it were proposed in first place.

3.72. In reply we have to say that [that conclusion] does not follow, because this does not follow: 'The premises are to be granted; therefore, the conclusion is to be granted.' For one premise is to be granted because it is posited, and the other because it is true and irrelevant; and the conclusion is neither posited nor true and irrelevant.

3.73. Here is another rule:

> When a false contingent proposition concerning the present has been posited, one must deny that it is the present instant.

(But this should be understood as concerning a particular instant.) The rule is proved in the following way.

3.74. If something is false as regards the present instant, it is impossible that it be verified as regards the present instant. Therefore, if it is true, one must deny that it is [now] the present instant. Furthermore, let *A* be this instant, and let this be posited: 'Antichrist exists.' Next, let 'Antichrist exists at *A*' be proposed. This is false and irrelevant; therefore, it is to be denied. Next 'Antichrist exists at some instant other than *A*.' This follows from the *positum* and the opposite of a correctly denied proposition; therefore, it is to be granted. Next 'It is [now] *A*.' This is to be denied because it is incompatible. And in this way the rule is evident.

3.75. But on the contrary. [First objection:] Let *A* be this instant, and let this be posited: 'That it is [now] *A* is to be denied.' Next, 'It is [now] *A*.' If you deny this, the disputation is over. And it is asked whether the *positum* was false or true. If it was true, then that it is [now] *A* {60} was not to be denied, and you denied it ((om. *A*)); therefore, [you responded] badly. If it was false, then 'That it is [now] *A* is to be denied' was false; therefore, that it is [now] *A* was not to be denied, and you denied it; therefore [you responded] badly. If it is granted that it is [now] *A*, the disputation is over. The *positum* was either true or false. If it was true, then that it is [now] *A* was to be denied, and you granted it; therefore [you responded] badly. If it was false, then that it is [now] *A* was to be denied, [and] you granted it; therefore, [you responded] badly.

3.76. [Second objection:] Again, let it be posited that you do not respond uniformly. Next, 'It is [now] *A*.' This is to be denied, in accordance with the rule. Next, 'God exists.' This is to be granted because it is necessary. When it has been granted, one says 'The disputation is over.' And it is asked whether the *positum* was true or false. If it was true, then [you responded] badly in denying that it is now *A*. If it is false, then you failed to respond nonuniformly – which is false.

3.77. [Third objection:] Again, let *A* be the same as before, and let it be posited that you deny that it is [now] *A*. Next, 'It is [now] *A*.' If you grant this, you grant that it is the present instant, when a false contingent proposition has been posited. If you deny it, then the *positum* is true; therefore, although the *positum* is true, you deny that it is [now] *A*.

3.78. In reply to the first [objection:] When it is said that the *positum* was either true or false, I reply that it was neither the one nor the other, because positing that one must deny that it is the present instant is the same as positing that the *positum* is false, since these are interchangeable. And if 'The *positum* is false' is posited, it must not be granted that the *positum* is false or that it is true.

3.79. In reply to the second [objection], one says that before the granting of the second proposition proposed the *positum* was false, but after the granting of the second proposition proposed the *positum* was true.

3.80. As for the third [objection], one replies by denying 'It is [now] *A*.' And when it is denied, the *positum* is true. But when it was proposed, it was false; and so a change of hypothesis (*transcasus*) occurs.

3.81. Nevertheless, there is some doubt about which instant the rule is understood to be about. If it is understood with regard to the instant of the *positio*, it should undoubtedly be denied that it is [this instant], because that it is [this instant] is false when it is proposed. But if it is understood with regard to the instant that is occurring when it is proposed that it is [this instant], one can perhaps grant without absurdity that it is that instant. For once that has been granted, nothing follows except that what is impossible *per accidens* is granted when a possible proposition has been posited. {61} And once a possible proposition has been posited, it is necessary that what is impossible *per accidens* be granted, as is evident from the previous discussions.

3.82. We can, however, prove regarding any instant that it is not that [instant] if a false contingent proposition is posited. For example, let *A* be any instant you like, and let it be posited that Antichrist exists. Next, 'Antichrist exists at *A*.' This is false and does not follow; therefore, it is to be denied. Next, 'Antichrist does not exist at *A*.' This follows. Next, 'It is not [now] *A*.' This follows from the *positum* and a proposition correctly granted, for this follows: 'Antichrist exists and does not exist at *A*; therefore, at some ((*aliquo/alio*)) instant other than *A*; therefore, it is [now] some other instant; therefore, it is not [now] *A*.' And in this way, once a false contingent proposition regarding the present instant has been posited, one can prove regarding any instant that it is not [now] that [instant].

3.83. But it is evident that 'It is [now] the present instant' is not always to be denied when a false contingent proposition regarding the present instant has been posited. For let this be posited: 'Antichrist exists, and it is now *A*.' Next, let 'It is now *A*' be proposed. (Let *A* be this instant.) This should be granted because it follows, and so it should be granted regarding the present instant that it is [now]. But this counterexample is a sophisma, because this is impossible: 'Antichrist exists, and it is [now] *A*.' Maintaining the rule in every case, one should reply that 'Antichrist exists' and 'It is [now] *A*' are incompatible. And so, once 'Antichrist exists' has been posited, 'It is [now] *A*' should be denied as incompatible.

3.84. Here is another rule:

All responses must be directed to the same instant.

3.85. But on the contrary. [First objection:] Suppose someone asks which instant that is. It is either the instant of the *positio* or some other instant. And no instant can be given. For if one is given, let it be *A*. And let it be posited that Antichrist exists, and let 'Antichrist exists at *A*' be proposed. If it is granted, something false and irrelevant is granted; therefore, [you have responded] badly. If it is denied, let this be proposed; 'It is [now] some other instant.' This follows from the *positum* and the opposite of a correctly denied proposition. Next, 'It is not [now] *A*.' This follows; therefore, it is to be granted. Once it has been granted, the disputation is over. You have granted with respect to instant *A* that it is not [now] *A*, and that it is not [now] *A*, [said] with respect to instant *A* is impossible *per se*. Therefore, you have granted what is impossible *per se* when the *positio* laid down was possible.

3.86. [Second objection:] Similarly, let Socrates be white when the first proposition proposed is proposed, {62} and let him be black when the second proposition proposed is proposed. In that case, when 'Socrates is white' is proposed in first place, it must be granted; and if it is proposed in second place, it must be denied. But the same proposition is not to be granted and denied with respect to the same instant; therefore, not all responses are to be directed to the same instant.

3.87. [Third objection:] Again, let this be posited: 'You are in Rome or the king is seated.' Next, let 'The king is seated' be proposed. This is in doubt and irrelevant; therefore, one must respond by saying that one is in doubt. Next, 'You are in Rome.' This is false and does not follow; therefore, it must be denied. Next. 'The king is seated.' This follows from the *positum* and the opposite of a correctly denied proposition; therefore, it must be granted. But the same proposition cannot be certain and in doubt with respect to the same instant, and this proposition was at first doubted; therefore, not all responses are to be directed to the same instant.

3.88. The solution: The rule must be understood in the following way: One must respond to all propositions proposed as if they were proposed at the same instant, so that throughout the time of the obligation only those propositions that can be maintained with respect to the same instant should be granted. And because incompatible propositions cannot be maintained with respect to the same instant throughout the time of the obligation, incompatible propositions must not be granted. But it is not possible to assign a particular instant as the instant to which the response to all the propositions proposed should be [directed]. And yet one should reply to all the propositions proposed as if they were proposed at the same instant, and this is what the rule maintains. Moreover, the rule should be understood as concerning only affirmative and negative responses and not the response that one is in doubt, because that response does not contribute to the consequence [developed during the disputation].

3.89. Here is another rule:

> *When the positum is false, the proposition 'The positum is false' can be granted; and yet concerning what is posited one must never grant that it is false.*

For example, if it is posited that you are in Rome, and 'The *positum* is false' is proposed, it can be granted. But if 'That you are in Rome is false' is proposed, it must be denied.

3.90. One argues against this [in the following way]: Let it be posited that you are in Rome (and I want it to be the case that nothing else is posited). Next, 'The *positum* is false.' This should be granted *per se*. Next, 'Only this is the *positum*' (indicating the *positum*). This must be granted, because it is true on the hypothesis. Next, 'That you are in Rome {63} is false.' If you grant this, you grant concerning what is posited that it is false. If you deny it, the disputation is over; you deny something that follows. For this follows: 'The *positum* is false, and only that you are in Rome is posited; therefore, that you are in Rome is false.'

3.91. We have to reply by denying 'Only that you are in Rome is posited,' because it is incompatible [with what precedes it].

3.92. But on the contrary. [First objection:] Let this conjunction be posited: 'You are in Rome, and only that you are in Rome is posited.' Next, 'The *positum* is false.' This should be granted according to the rule, etc. But these propositions are incompatible *per se* – namely, 'You are in Rome, and only that you are in Rome is posited' and 'The *positum* is false.' [Second objection:] It is furthermore proved that this must not be granted: 'The *positum* is false.' This proposition is irrelevant, but one must respond to an irrelevant proposition within [an obligation] in the same way [as one would respond to it] outside [the obligation]. When nothing is posited, however, one must deny that the *positum* is false; therefore, when something is posited, one must deny that the *positum* is false.

3.93. In reply [to the first objection], we have to say that when the *positum* is false, 'The *positum* is false' must be granted if it is not incompatible, because every true proposition that is not incompatible must be granted. And so if the *positum* is false, and that it is false is not incompatible, then that the *positum* is false must be granted. So, if it is posited that you are in Rome, and it is false, 'The *positum* is false' must be granted, because it is true and not incompatible. But when 'You are in Rome, and only that you are in Rome is posited' is posited, then 'The *positum* is false' is incompatible. And for this reason 'The *positum* is false' must not be granted.

3.94. In reply to the second [objection], we have to say that with regard to an irrelevant proposition that has the same quality during [the obligation] as outside [it] one must respond in the same way during [the obligation] as outside [it]. But if the qualities are different, one must respond differently. For if it is posited that you are in Rome, and only during the time of the obligation the truth of the matter is that you are white, then if 'You are white' is proposed in the time of the obligation, it must be granted; and yet outside [the time of the obligation] it must be denied. It is the same way here, because when the *positum* is false, 'The *positum* is false' is true, and when nothing is posited, 'The *positum* is false' is false. For this reason it must be granted in the obligation but denied outside [it]. {64}

[How to Construct Sophismata]

3.95. The next topic is how to construct sophismata. The first thing we have to consider is this: If it is posited that certain propositions are alike [in truth value], they can be alike either in truth only, in falsity only, or indifferently in truth and in falsity. If they can be alike in truth only, then either one must be granted when it is proposed in first place. If they can be alike in falsity only, then either one must be denied when it is proposed in first place. If they can be alike indifferently in truth and in falsity, then one must respond to either one proposed in first place according to its own quality. By means of these considerations the responses associated with certain sophismata are evident.

3.96. Here is one [such] sophisma: Let it be posited that 'The decision has gone against you' and 'You do not know that the decision has gone against you' are alike [in truth value]. Next, 'The decision has gone against you.' This is false and obviously does not follow; therefore, it must be denied. Next, 'You do not know that the decision has gone against you.' This must be denied, because a proposition like it [in truth value] is denied. Next, 'You know that the decision has gone against you' ((om. *Debet concedi quia*)). This is the opposite of a correctly denied proposition; therefore, it must be granted. Next 'The decision has gone against you.' If you grant this, you have granted and denied the same proposition; therefore, [you have responded] badly. If you deny it, you deny something that follows, because this follows: 'You know that the decision has gone against you; therefore, the decision has gone against you.'

3.97. The solution is evident on the basis of what has been said. 'You do not know that the decision has gone against you' and 'The decision has gone against you' cannot be alike [in truth value] except in truth only. For this reason whichever of these is proposed first must be granted. And it is important to know that a consequent and the opposite of an antecedent cannot be alike [in truth value] except in truth only, because if they were alike in falsity, the consequent would be false, and so would the opposite of the antecedent. But if the consequent is false, the antecedent is false. Therefore, if the consequent and the opposite of the antecedent were alike in falsity, contradictories would be false at the same time. And for this reason whenever it is posited that a consequent and the opposite of an antecedent are alike in truth value, each of them should be granted. And in that way the sophisma is solved. And in this way there is an obvious solution to sophismata in which it is posited that subcontraries are alike [in truth value], since subcontraries cannot be alike [in truth value] except in truth only.

3.98. A sophisma is constructed in another way when it is posited that an antecedent and the opposite of a consequent {65} are alike [in truth value]. For example, let it be posited that 'No grammarian exists' and 'That God exists is granted by a grammarian' are alike in truth value. Next, 'No grammarian exists.' This is true and irrelevant; therefore, it must be granted. (Suppose that it is the case.) Next, 'That God exists is granted by a grammarian.' This should be granted, because a proposition which is like it [in truth value] is granted. Next, 'A grammarian exists.' If you grant this, you grant opposites. If you deny it, you deny something that follows: 'That God exists is granted by a grammarian; therefore a grammarian exists.'

3.99. The solution is evident on the basis of what has been said, for the two propositions 'That God exists is granted by a grammarian' and 'No grammarian exists' cannot be alike [in truth value] except in falsity only. And for this reason whichever of these is proposed first should be denied. And it is important to know that an antecedent and the opposite of a consequent cannot be alike [in truth value] except in falsity; because if they were alike in truth, the antecedent would be true and the opposite of the consequent would be true. But if the antecedent is true, the consequent will be true. Therefore, the consequent and the opposite of the consequent would be true at the same time, which is impossible.

3.100. Here is another sophisma: Let *A* be the proposition 'That the decision has gone against you and that you do not know that the decision has gone against you are alike [in truth value].' And let *B* be the proposition 'You are seated.' Let it be posited that *A* and *B* are alike in truth value. Next, 'You are seated.' This is true and irrelevant. (Suppose that that is the case.) Therefore, it must be granted. Next, let 'The decision has gone against you' be proposed. This is false and does not follow; therefore, it must be denied. Next, 'You do not know that the decision has gone against you.' This must be denied, because if *A* and *B* are alike [in truth value] and *B* is true, *A* will consequently be true. Therefore, that the decision has gone against you and that you do not know that the decision has gone against you are alike [in truth value], and that the decision has gone against you is false. Therefore, 'You do not know that the decision has gone against you' must be denied. Next, 'You know that the decision has gone against you.' This is the opposite of a proposition correctly denied; therefore, it must be granted. Next, 'The decision has gone against you.' If you grant this, you have granted and denied the same proposition; therefore, [you have responded] badly. If you deny it, you deny something that follows, because [this follows]: 'You know that the decision has gone against you; therefore, the decision has gone against you.'

3.101. The solution is evident on the basis of what has been said, for *A* and *B* can be alike indifferently in truth or in falsity. For this reason one must respond to each of them in accordance with its own quality when it is proposed in first place. And so, if 'You are seated' is proposed first, it must be granted; but in that case {66} 'The decision has gone against you' must be granted because it follows. And yet, if 'The decision has gone against you' were proposed in first place, it would have to be denied; and in that case, if 'You are seated' were proposed, it would likewise have to be denied.

3.102. Here is another way of constructing a sophisma: Let there be one conditional proposition whose antecedent is a conjunction and whose consequent is false. And let it be posited that the consequent and the opposite of the first part of the antecedent are alike [in truth value]. Next, let the consequent be proposed. It will apparently have to be denied. But first, the part of the antecedent that is not in the *positum* will be acquired. For example, let *A* be 'That Socrates is white must not be granted,' and let *B* be that Socrates is white; and let there be this conditional: 'If one must grant that Socrates is white, and if the only thing obligated is that *A* and *B* are alike [in truth value], then Socrates is white.' Then let it be posited that *A* and *B* are alike [in truth value]. Next, let this be proposed: The only thing obligated is that *A* and *B* are alike [in truth value]. This is true and irrelevant; therefore, it must be granted. Next, 'Socrates is white.' This is false and does not follow; therefore, it must be denied. Next, 'That Socrates is white must not be granted.' This must be denied, because the proposition like it [in truth value] is denied. Next, let this be proposed: 'One must grant that Socrates is white.' This must be granted, because its opposite is denied. Next, 'Socrates is white.' If you grant this, you have granted and denied the same proposition; therefore, [you have responded] badly. If you deny it, you deny what follows from a granted proposition and the opposite of a correctly denied proposition. For this follows: 'One must grant that Socrates is white, and the only thing obligated is that *A* and *B* are alike [in truth value]; therefore, Socrates is white.'

3.103. Some people reply to this [sophisma] by granting the first proposition proposed, and after the granting of it each of the propositions that are alike [in truth value] must be granted. But this solution cannot stand. For if the *positum* remains the same and the first and second propositions proposed are granted, then 'That Socrates is white is not to be granted' [is proposed]. This must be granted, because a proposition that is like it [in truth value] is granted. Next, 'One must grant that Socrates is white.' If you grant this, you grant opposites. If you deny it, you deny something that follows; for this follows: 'Socrates is white and the only thing obligated is that *A* and *B* are alike [in truth value]; therefore, one must grant that Socrates is white.' For if something is true and neither it nor its opposite is obligated, it must be granted. Furthermore, if the *positum* remains the same and the first and second propositions proposed have been granted, let 'That Socrates is white is not to be granted' be proposed. This must be granted, because a proposition that is like it [in truth value] is granted. Next,

'Something false is obligated.' This follows; {67} therefore, it must be granted. That it follows is evident. For if Socrates is white, and that Socrates is white is not to be granted, something false is obligated; for nothing true is not to be granted unless something false is obligated. Therefore, 'Something false is obligated' must be granted because it follows. Next, 'That *A* and *B* are alike [in truth value] is false.' If you grant this, you grant something incompatible with the *positum*. If you deny it, you deny something that follows, because this follows: 'Something false is obligated, and the only thing obligated is that *A* and *B* are alike [in truth value]; therefore, that *A* and *B* are alike [in truth value] is false.'

3.104. For this reason, it seems that one must reply in a different way, namely, that when the *positum* has been admitted, 'The only thing obligated is that *A* and *B* are alike [in truth value]' must be denied. For from this proposition and the *positum* something incompatible with the *positum* follows, since this follows: '*A* and *B* are alike [in truth value], and the only thing obligated is that *A* and *B* are alike [in truth value]; therefore, only what is true is obligated.' But these propositions are incompatible: '*A* and *B* are alike [in truth value]' and 'Only what is true is obligated.'

3.105. Here is another way in which a sophisma occurs. If you want to prove something, posit that it is the same [in truth value] as the first or the second proposition to be proposed, and then propose something true in the first place. For example, I want to prove that you are a donkey. I posit this: 'That you are a donkey is the same [in truth value] as the first proposition to be proposed.' Next, 'God exists.' This is necessary; therefore, it must be granted. Next, 'Only this is the first proposition proposed.' This is true (indicating the first proposition proposed). Next, 'You are a donkey.' This should be granted, because it follows from the *positum* together with a proposition correctly granted. For this follows: 'That you are a donkey is the same [in truth value] as the first proposition proposed, and that God exists is true, and only "God exists" is the first proposition proposed; therefore, that you are a donkey is the same [in truth value] as a true proposition.' Furthermore, therefore, that you are a donkey is true.

3.106. The solution: Once the *positum* has been admitted, 'God exists' should be granted; but that only 'God exists' is the first proposition proposed should be denied, because it is incompatible.

3.107. If it is posited that certain propositions are not alike [in truth value], one should consider whether one of them follows from the other or not. If neither of them follows from the other, one should respond to whichever of them is proposed in first place in accordance with its own quality. If one does follow from the other, [however,] the consequent should be granted whenever it is proposed, for the antecedent and the consequent cannot fail to be alike [in truth value] unless the consequent is true. For if the consequent were false, {68} the antecedent would be false; and in this way the antecedent and the consequent would not fail to be alike [in truth value]. By this means the resolution of the following sophisma is evident.

3.108. Let it be posited that 'Antichrist is running' and 'Antichrist exists' are not alike [in truth value]. Next, let 'Antichrist exists' be proposed. This is apparently false and irrelevant; therefore, it must be denied. Next, 'Antichrist is running.' This follows, because a proposition that is unlike it [in truth value] is denied. Next, 'Antichrist exists.' If you grant this, you have granted and denied the same proposition; therefore, [you have responded] badly. If you deny it, you deny something that follows, because this follows: 'Antichrist is running; therefore, Antichrist exists.'

3.109. The solution is evident. 'Antichrist exists' must be granted, because the antecedent and the consequent cannot fail to be alike [in truth value] unless the consequent is true.... {84}

[Depositio]

4.01. Having discussed *positio*, we must now discuss *depositio*. *Depositio* is a prefix to something statable [indicating that] something should be held as false. And for this reason, in making a *depositio* we guarantee the respondent the truth of [the proposition] that is the *depositum*; because if it were false it would have to be denied, even if it were not the *depositum*. Therefore, in order that it might be denied because of the obligation and not for any other reason, I guarantee the respondent the truth of the *depositum* by saying, [for instance,] 'It is true that Socrates is running, and let the *depositum* be that Socrates is running.' Therefore, because {85} *depositio* obligates [a respondent] to hold something as false, the *depositum* must be denied.

[Rules]

4.02. Thus the following is a rule concerning a *depositum*:

> *Every depositum that is in the form of a depositum and proposed during the time of the depositio must be denied.*

And because when a consequent has been denied the antecedent must be denied [also], and because the *depositum* must be denied, every proposition that is antecedent to the *depositum* by itself or together with a proposition that has or propositions that have been correctly granted and are known to be such must be denied. When an antecedent has been denied, its consequent can be equally well granted or denied; and so no rule is given concerning a proposition which is by itself consequent to a *depositum*. Instead, a rule is given only concerning the *depositum* itself, concerning a proposition antecedent to it, and concerning a proposition contradictory to it. Thus [it is a rule that]

> *every proposition contradictory to the depositum must be granted;*

but [it is also a rule that]

> *it is not the case that every proposition incompatible with the depositum must be granted,*

because incompatible propositions can be false at the same time. For this reason it need not be the case that if one is false, the other is true. But there is the following rule concerning a proposition that follows from propositions previously granted:

> *Every proposition that follows from a proposition or propositions previously granted must be granted.*

[It is also a rule that]

> *One must respond to an irrelevant proposition in accordance with its own quality.*

4.03. The same rules that were laid down in connection with *positio* should be upheld here [also]. For example,

> *In this art one should not give a definite answer to a question requiring a distinction ((distinguibilis/disciplinalis)).*

Likewise,

> one should pay special attention to the order [of the propositions]; and all responses must be directed to the same instant.

Likewise,

> when the depositum is a true contingent proposition, it is possible to prove any false proposition compossible with its opposite.

Likewise,

> when the depositum is a contingent proposition, one needs to grant what is impossible per accidens.

Likewise,

> when the depositum is a true contingent proposition concerning the present instant, one must deny that it is now that [instant].

4.04. Here is [another] rule:

> Whenever the depositum is that a true contingent proposition must be granted (or that a false contingent proposition must be denied), the proposition 'Only this is obligated' (indicating the depositum) must be denied when one has granted the proposition that had to be granted on the depositum (or when one has denied the proposition that had to be denied on the depositum).

This is because the *depositum* follows from 'Only this is obligated' together with a correctly granted proposition. By this means sophismata of the following sort ((*huiusmodi/huius*)) are solved.

4.05. Let the *depositum* be that it must be granted that you are seated, and let 'You are seated' be proposed. {86} This must be granted, because it is true and irrelevant. Next, let this be proposed: 'Only this is obligated' (indicating the *depositum*). This is apparently true and not incompatible; therefore, it must be granted. Next, 'That you are seated must be granted.' If you grant this, you grant the *depositum*. If you deny it, you deny something that follows from propositions that have been correctly granted, for this follows: 'You are seated, and the only thing obligated is that that you are seated must be granted; therefore, that you are seated must be granted.' For if something is true and nothing other than this is obligated, it must be granted.

4.06. The solution is evident, for 'Only this is obligated' (indicating the *depositum*) together with a proposition correctly granted implies the *depositum*.

4.07. Here is another rule:

> *Whenever the depositum regarding something impossible is that it must be denied, and regarding something necessary that it must be granted, the proposition 'Only this is obligated' (indicating the depositum) must be denied.*

This is because it is antecedent to the *depositum*.

4.08. For example, let the *depositum* be that 'A man is a donkey' must be denied, and let this be proposed: 'Only this is obligated' (indicating the *depositum*). This is apparently true and not antecedent to the *depositum*; therefore, it must be granted. But when it has been granted, let this be proposed: 'Only what is possible is obligated.' This clearly follows. Next, 'That a man is a donkey must be denied.' If this is granted, the *depositum* is granted. If it is denied, something that follows is denied, because this follows: 'Only what is possible is obligated; therefore, that a man is a donkey must be denied.'

4.09. The solution. 'Only this is obligated' (indicating the *depositum*) must be denied, because it is antecedent to the *depositum*. For if only this is obligated, then only what is possible is obligated; and if only what is possible is obligated, then that a man is a donkey must be denied.

4.10. One can argue in the same way if the *depositum* is that something necessary must be granted.

[How to Construct Sophismata]

4.11. The art of constructing sophismata in connection with *positio* is the same as the art of constructing sophismata in connection with *depositio* (and vice versa). For example, in connection with *positio*, when certain propositions are posited to be alike [in truth value], [then in connection with *depositio*] the *depositio* is that they are *not* alike [in truth value]. And the inference will be the same {87} in the two cases, because a *positum* that certain propositions are alike [in truth value] is the same as a *depositum* that they are not alike [in truth value]. Also, to use a certain proposition in a *positum* is the same as to use its opposite in a *depositum*. And if the *depositum* is that certain propositions are not alike [in truth value], one should make use of the following art.

4.12. One must consider whether the propositions that according to the *depositum* are not alike [in truth value] can be alike in truth only (in which case one must grant each of them when it is proposed), in falsity only (in which case each of them must be denied), or indifferently in truth and falsity (in which case one must respond to either one in accordance with its own quality when it is proposed in first place).

4.13. Because of this, it is evident that if the *depositum* is that a consequent and the opposite of an antecedent are not alike [in truth value], then either one proposed in the first place should be granted. And if the *depositum* is that 'The decision has gone against you' and 'You do not know that the decision has gone against you' are not alike [in truth value], and 'The decision has gone against you' is proposed, it should be granted. For if it is denied, you need to deny that you know that the decision has gone against you, and you need to grant that you do not know that the decision has gone against you. Thus one needs to grant that 'The decision has gone against you' and 'You do not know that the decision has gone against you' are not alike [in truth value], and so one needs to grant the *depositum*.

4.14. Similarly, if the *depositum* is that an antecedent and the opposite of a consequent are not alike [in truth value], then each of them must be denied when it is proposed, since an antecedent and the opposite of a consequent cannot be alike [in truth value] except in falsity [only].

4.15. If, on the other hand, the *depositum* is that a consequent and the opposite of an antecedent are alike [in truth value], then one must respond to each of them in accordance with its own quality when it is proposed in first place.

4.16. Similarly, if the *depositum* is that an antecedent and a consequent are alike [in truth value], the consequent must be granted whenever it is proposed; because if the consequent is denied, one needs to deny the antecedent. Thus one would need to grant that the antecedent and the consequent are alike [in truth value], and so the *depositum* would have to be granted.... {89}

[*Dubitatio*]

5.01. *Dubitatio*, as the term is used here, is a prefix to something statable [indicating that] something should be held as being in doubt. Therefore, the following is a rule concerning the *dubitatum*.

> 5.02. *To every dubitatum proposed during the time of the dubitatio {90} one must respond by saying that one is in doubt about it.*

5.03. Likewise,

> To whatever is interchangeable with the *dubitatum* and to whatever is contradictory to the *dubitatum* one must respond by saying that one is in doubt about it, since it is impossible to be in doubt about one of a pair of contradictories unless one is [also] in doubt about the other.

5.04. We can be in doubt about an antecedent and know the consequent to be true (for, seeing something from a distance, we [can] know that it is a body and be in doubt about whether or not it is an animal), and so one must grant a proposition consequent to the *dubitatum* if it is true. But if a proposition consequent to the *dubitatum* is false, one must respond to it by saying that one is in doubt about it, because it ought not to be denied either. For if the consequent is denied, one needs to deny the antecedent [also], and so one would need to deny the *dubitatum*. For this reason one must respond to a false proposition consequent to the *dubitatum* by saying that one is in doubt about it. Similarly, if the *dubitatum* is a consequent, one need not be in doubt about the antecedent. For we are in doubt about whether the king is seated, and yet we know that it is false that every animal is seated. Therefore, if a proposition antecedent to the *dubitatum* is false, it should be denied. If it is true, one must respond to it by saying that one is in doubt about it. For it must not be denied, since it is true, and it must not be granted either, in virtue of the fact that it is antecedent to the *dubitatum*. And if the antecedent is granted, one must grant the consequent [also], and thus one would need to grant the *dubitatum*. And so, if a proposition antecedent to the *dubitatum* is true, one must respond to it by saying that one is in doubt about it.

5.05. Hence, there are these rules: One must respond to the *dubitatum*, to what is interchangeable with it, to what is contradictory to it, to its consequent if it is false, and to its antecedent if it is true by saying that one is in doubt about it. But if the antecedent is false, it must be denied; and if the consequent is true, it must be granted. (And here we mean an antecedent and a consequent [which are] not interchangeable).

> 5.06. *One must respond to an irrelevant proposition in accordance with its own quality.*

5.07. It seems, however, that one must grant the opposite of the *dubitatum*, as in connection with the following hypothesis. Let the truth of the matter be that Socrates is white, and suppose that you know this well. Let the *dubitatum* be that Socrates is white. Next, 'You are in doubt whether Socrates is white.' This is false and known to be false; therefore, it must be denied. Next, 'You know that Socrates is white.' This must be denied, because it is antecedent to the *dubitatum*. Next, 'Socrates is not white.' {91} If you grant this, you grant the opposite of the *dubitatum*; and in that case we would have what we were after. If you deny it, the disputation is over. You have denied what follows from the opposites of propositions that were correctly denied. For this follows: 'You are not in doubt whether Socrates is white, and you do not know that Socrates is white either; therefore, Socrates is not white.' That this consequence is good is evident, for the opposite of one part of the antecedent follows from the opposite of the consequent together with the other part of the antecedent. For if Socrates is white and you do not know that Socrates is white, you are in doubt whether Socrates is white. And for this reason one must respond to 'You are in doubt whether Socrates is white' by saying that one is in doubt about it. For it should not be granted since it is false and known to be false, and it should not be denied either. For if it is denied, one needs to grant the opposite of the *dubitatum*, as we argued.

5.08. The rules presented previously in connection with *positio* and *depositio* are to be upheld here [also] – for example:

> *All responses must be directed to the same instant.*

Likewise,

> *one must pay special attention to the order [of the propositions] in the obligational art.*

Likewise,

> *one must not give a definite response here to a question requiring a distinction ((distinguibilis/disciplinabilis)).*

Likewise,

> *If the dubitatum is true, one must grant the proposition: 'The dubitatum is true.'*

(As regards that which is the *dubitatum*, however, one must never grant that it is true.) Likewise, if the *dubitatum* is a false contingent proposition, it is possible to be in doubt about any false proposition compossible with it. For example, let the *dubitatum* be that you are in Rome, and let this be proposed: 'That you are in Rome and that you are a bishop are alike [in truth value].' This must be granted, because it is true and irrelevant. Next, 'You are a bishop.' To this one must respond by saying that one is in doubt about it. For if this is granted, one needs to grant the *dubitatum*, and if it is denied, one needs to deny the *dubitatum*.

5.09. Here is a rule:

> *Whenever ((quandocumque/qualitercumque)) one is in doubt whether a true contingent proposition must be granted or whether a false contingent proposition must be denied, if 'One is in doubt whether it must be granted' has been granted, or if 'One is in doubt whether it must be denied' has been denied, then one needs to respond to the proposition: 'Only this is obligated' (indicating what is the dubitatum for you) by saying that one is in doubt about it.*

For otherwise the *dubitatum* would have to be granted or would have to be denied. For example, let the *dubitatum* be 'That you are seated must be granted.' Let this be proposed: 'You are seated.' This must be granted, because it is true and not antecedent to the *dubitatum*. Next, 'Only this is obligated' (indicating the *dubitatum*). This apparently must be granted since the truth of the matter is that it is true. Once this has been granted, {92} let this be proposed: 'That you are seated must be granted.' If you grant this, you grant the *dubitatum*. If you deny it, you deny something that follows, because this follows: 'You are seated, and the only thing obligated is that that you are seated must be granted; therefore, that you are seated must be granted.'

5.10. The solution to this is evident, because one must respond to 'This is the only thing obligated' by saying that one is in doubt about it.

5.11. Here is another rule:

> *Whenever the dubitatum regarding what is impossible is that it must be denied, or regarding what is necessary that it must be granted, one must*

*respond to 'This is the only thing obligated' (indicating the dubitatum)
by saying that one is in doubt about it.*

For example, let this be the *dubitatum*: 'That a man is a donkey must
be denied.' And let this be proposed: 'This is the only thing obligated' (indicating the *dubitatum*). If you grant this, you grant a
proposition antecedent to the *dubitatum*, because if this is the only
thing obligated, then only what is possible is obligated; and furthermore, therefore anything impossible must be denied. Thus that a
man is a donkey must be denied. If one denies 'This is the only
thing obligated,' one denies a proposition that is true and known to
be true and whose opposite is not obligated.

5.12. The solution is evident. One must respond to 'This is the
only thing obligated' by saying that one is in doubt about it.

5.13. It is important to note that any [expression] such as 'That
you are running is in doubt' [or] 'That you are seated is in doubt' is
ambiguous. For one sense is that it is in doubt whether 'You are
running' is true or not, and another sense is that the *dubitatum* is
'You are running,' that is, that you are obligated to hold 'You are
running' as being in doubt.

WILLIAM HEYTESBURY
THE COMPOUNDED AND DIVIDED SENSES

Introduction

William Heytesbury was born in Wiltshire, England, around 1313. By 1330 he was a fellow of Merton College, Oxford, with which he is traditionally associated. In 1371 he was Chancellor of the University (he may also have been Chancellor in 1353–54; the records are unclear), and he died in 1372. His works on logic were probably written between 1331 and 1339. The most influential, his *Rules for Solving Sophismata*, is usually dated 1335. Heytesbury's treatise on the compounded and divided senses of propositions, translated here, seems to have been written before his *Rules*.

This treatise, *De sensu composito et diviso*, gets its historical importance not only from the apparent fact that it represents the first attempt to provide a systematic treatment of the various modes in which the distinction between the compounded and divided senses had been recognized by Heytesbury's predecessors, but also from the undoubted fact that it became the sourcebook for much of the subsequent literature on these topics, attracting both imitators and commentators. If the treatise is original in its comprehensiveness, it seems derivative in most other respects; but that hardly counts as a flaw in an attempt to organize scattered, disparately treated material. There are plenty of genuine flaws in the treatise, however, as the attentive reader may discover. But whatever its shortcomings, it is and in many respects deserves to be the principal text of a very interesting and suggestive branch of late medieval linguistic analysis.

Heytesbury initially distinguishes nine modes of composition and division on the basis of the linguistic devices that give rise to the two senses, but in his more detailed discussions and illustrations of the modes he reverses the initial order of modes VI and VII, and he never discusses the last one he lists. The following revised list is a better guide to the treatise: (I) modal (or 'ampliative') words; (II) words producing confused supposition; (III) relative pronouns; (IV) words that can occur either categorematically or syncategorematically; (V) the conjunction 'and'; (VI) clauses such as 'it is the case that'; (VII) the disjunction 'or'; (VIII) epistemic and volitional verbs. His discussion of (VIII), by far the longest, leads into a discussion of obligational disputation, which concludes the treatise.

For all its subtle complexity, the doctrine of obligations (see Translation 12) is founded on considerations of the three propositional attitudes to which the respondent in a disputation can be disputationally obligated: granting, denying, or doubting (claiming that in the circumstances of the disputation he has no basis for either granting or denying) any proposition put to him by the opponent. The three verbs by means of which these propositional attitudes are expressed are all included in (VIII), and 'doubt' figures explicitly and prominently in Heytesbury's rules and examples, overshadowed only by 'know,' the primary epistemic verb. And since both granting and denying are properly based on knowing, all three basic disputational replies can be examined in a consideration of knowing and doubting. (For more on Heytesbury's treatment of knowing and doubting, see Translation 14.) Furthermore, the verb 'know' is the main verb in many of the most important obligational sophismata, the propositions with which obligational disputations are begun.

Besides making one of the three basic replies already mentioned, a respondent in a disputation may draw a distinction regarding the sense of an ambiguous proposition before offering one or the other basic reply to each of the senses, and Heytesbury's detailed analysis of the compounded and divided senses equips the respondent to make especially effective, widely applicable use of this technique.

For the importance of the distinction between the compounded and divided senses in medieval modal logic, see CHLMP V.17, 'Modal Logic.'

(This translation is based primarily on the edition of 1494. In some passages, indicated by '[with 1501],' we rely on the edition of 1501.)

The Compounded and Divided Senses

[1. Introduction]

[1a. Invalid Inferences from One Sense to the Other]

{2ra} When one is arguing from the compounded sense to the divided sense and vice versa, the consequence is often fallacious. Thus, none of these follows: [E1] It is impossible that you traverse this distance; therefore, you cannot traverse this distance. [E2] It is impossible that something white be going to be black; therefore, nothing white can be black. [E3] Each of these two contradictories can be true at some instant; therefore, it can be that each of these two contradictories is true at some instant. [E4] In each of two places you can be at some instant; therefore, it can be that you are in each of two places at some instant. [E5] You know one or the other of these to be true; therefore, one or the other of these you know to be true. [E6] You believe Socrates to be running; therefore, Socrates you believe to be running. [E7] The man appears to be a donkey; therefore, it appears that the man is a donkey. [E8] It is necessary that one or the other of these be true; therefore, [of] one or the other of these it is necessary that it be true. [E9] The soul of Antichrist necessarily will be; therefore, necessarily there will be the soul of Antichrist. [E10] Sometime it will be the case that the soul of Antichrist necessarily will be; therefore, the soul of Antichrist necessarily will be. [E11] You know proposition *A* to be true; therefore, proposition *A* you know to be true. [E12] You believe the king to be in London; therefore, this man you believe to be in London (indicating the king). [E13] You want to beat this man, and this man is a clerk; therefore, you want to beat a clerk. [E14] For every motion there is required a proportion of greater inequality; therefore, a proportion of greater inequality is required for every motion. [E15] Every man has a head; therefore, a head every man has. [E16] Immediately after this there will be some instant; therefore, some instant will be immediately after this. [E17] An infinite number is finite; therefore, a finite number is infinite. [E18] Four are two and two; therefore, four are two. [E19] They are white and black; therefore, they are white. [E20] It will be the case that you are every man who is in

Rome; therefore, you will be every man who is in Rome. [E21] It can be that Antichrist is a man who exists; therefore, Antichrist can be a man who exists. [E22] It is possible that you are every man existing in this house; therefore, you can be every man existing in this house. [E23] You are bound to pay him a penny; therefore, some penny you are bound to pay him. [E24] Now you begin to traverse some part of this magnitude; therefore, some part of this magnitude you begin to traverse. [E25] Socrates needs an eye in order to see; therefore, an eye Socrates needs in order to see.

And in such instances, which can be formulated by disputants in virtually every subject matter, a consequence from one sense to the other is invalid.

[1b. The Importance of the Inquiry]

Thus there is no caution by which one can be misled more often or more easily than the one having to do with the compounded and the divided sense; for many are the fallacies that reduce to division and composition. For that reason one must take pains to understand how the compounded and the divided sense occurs, and which is which. The two senses are often very much alike linguistically and entirely irrelevant to each other as regards meaning, truth and falsity, and the form of arguing.

[1c. The Modes of Compounding and Dividing]

The variety of compounding and dividing occurs in nine modes.

The first mode, as was shown by examples at the beginning, is dependent on the ampliative verb 'can' or on any similar {2rb} ampliative, such as 'is appropriate,' 'true,' 'possible,' 'impossible,' 'contingent,' and any others like them by means of which composition and division occurs.

The second mode is dependent on a term that has the power of producing confused supposition – e.g., such verbs as 'require,' 'need,' 'presuppose,' 'begin,' 'desire,' 'long for,' 'want,' 'owe,' 'be obliged'; [also] 'necessary,' 'always,' 'to eternity,' 'eternally,' 'immediately,' and so on.

The third mode is dependent on a relative term [such as] 'who,' 'which,' 'that,' 'of whatever sort,' 'whatever,' especially with respect to a common term that has merely confused supposition – as when one argues in this way, for example: 'Immediately after this there will be an instant that immediately after this will be; therefore, immediately after this there will be an instant, and it immediately after this will be.'

The fourth mode is dependent on a term that is sometimes taken categorematically and other times syncategorematically. The term 'infinite' (*infinitus, -ta, -tum*) is of that sort, [as is] 'whole' (*totus, -ta, -tum*). (The terms that were introduced adverbially before – viz., 'always,' 'to eternity,' 'eternally,' and the like – can be reduced to this mode.)

The fifth mode is dependent on the copula of conjunction, 'and' – as when one argues in this way, for example: 'Those men are in Rome and Ausonia; therefore, those men are in Rome.'

The sixth mode is dependent on the determination '[it is] the case' (*ita*) or 'as' (*sicut*) – e.g., 'it will be the case,' 'it was the case,' 'it is the case'; 'as it is,' 'as it was,' 'as it will be' – as when one argues in this way, for example: 'It is the case that Socrates will be as big as Plato; therefore, Socrates will be as big as Plato,' or vice versa.

The seventh mode is dependent on the disjunction 'or,' as is clear in the sophisma 'Every proposition or its contradictory is true.'

The eighth mode is dependent on verbal terms signifying an act of will or of intellect – e.g., it depends on the verbs 'know,' 'be uncertain,' 'believe,' 'want,' 'desire,' 'seek,' and so on.

The ninth mode is dependent on an accidental term placed in the subject with respect to a past-tense or future-tense verb in relation to the same term placed in the predicate ((*praedicati/praeteriti*)) with respect to the same verb – modes that can be reduced to composition or division, although this is more nearly the fallacy of *figura dictionis*. For example, 'A white thing will be a black thing; therefore, a black thing will be a white thing' does not follow.

[2. Mode I]

As for the first mode of bringing about composition and division that is presented here, the examples at the beginning are clear enough.

And it is important to know what the compounded and the divided sense is with respect to the first mode (as also with respect to the other modes and, generally, with respect to any of the modes that have been presented), and first of all in connection with the verb 'can' or [with what] would be a mode of it. (The term 'possible' is of that sort; [also] 'necessary,' 'necessarily,' or 'of necessity,' and so on.) Regarding them, it is important to know that when one is found in a proposition without a ((*aliquo/alio*)) modifying relative following it, the divided sense occurs. And then, in such a proposition, the ampliative verb is interpreted personally, as in 'You can traverse this distance,' 'You can be in Rome and Ausonia,' 'A white thing can be black,' and so on.

On the other hand, when the verb 'can' or a mode of it occurs altogether first in a proposition, the compounded sense occurs. And then the compounded sense signifies a possible instantaneous identity with respect to the composition following the term 'possible,' and in that case an ampliative term of that sort is interpreted impersonally there, as when one says 'It is possible that a white thing is black,' 'It is possible that you traverse this distance,' 'It can be that you are here and in Rome.' But the divided sense signifies a succession with respect to different times and to different parts of the same time.

Furthermore, in the compounded sense, it is denoted that the composition that you are here and in Rome, that you traverse this distance, is possible; and by means of the other proposition it is denoted that the composition that a white thing is black is possible. The same holds for other such propositions. {2va} The divided sense does not signify in that way, however; for the proposition 'A white thing can be black' indicates that something that now is white or can be white can be black.

The proposition 'You can traverse this distance' is verified through the proposition 'You have or can have the capacity in virtue of which it can be that you will traverse this distance,' and the same holds for other such propositions. When one argues from the divided sense to the compounded sense where the divided sense is verified through a succession of that sort with respect to different parts of time, a succession whose composition is [not] possible for a given instant, the consequence is invalid. But when one argues with respect to terms in virtue of which such a composition is possible through a given instant, and it is not the case that by means of some modifying relation something is denoted through the divided sense otherwise than through the compounded sense (or vice versa), the consequence will be valid. And it will be so generally in respect of simple terms that are not incompatible either *per se* or *per accidens*, as when one argues in this way: 'You can be a bishop; therefore, it can be that you are a bishop'; 'You can be in Rome; therefore, it is possible that you are in Rome'; and vice versa. On the other hand, 'It is possible that you be a man who is in Rome; therefore, you can be a man who is in Rome' does not follow because of the modification 'who [etc.].' Likewise, the reason why the consequence 'A white thing can be black; therefore, it is possible that a white thing be black' is invalid is that although the terms 'white' and 'black' are simple, they imply contrary dispositions. And so the composition 'A white thing is black' is not possible, although that would follow if the consequence were valid. The same sort of thing must be said about the term 'traverse this distance'; it is because it cannot be verified for the present instant regarding anything that the composition 'You traverse this distance' is not possible, just as 'A white thing is black,' etc., is not.

[3. Mode II]

When one argues from the compounded sense to the divided sense dependent on a term that has the power of producing confused supposition in a term, as was said before, the consequence is generally invalid – e.g., if one argues in this way: 'In order that you see there is required an eye; therefore, some eye it is required that you have in order that you see' ((om. *per oculum* [with 1501])). Likewise, this does not follow: 'I begin (desire, long, want, am bound, ought) to touch some point on body *A*; therefore, some point on body *A* I begin (desire, etc.) to touch.' Similarly, an argument using these terms does not follow: 'Of necessity ((*de necessitate/necessarium*)) (necessarily, always, to eternity, eternally, immediately) after any future instant whatever there will be some man; therefore, some man of necessity (to eternity, etc.) will be [after any future instant whatever].'

[4. Mode III]

Next, a consequence from the compounded sense to the divided sense in respect of relative terms is ordinarily invalid unless it is valid by reason of the subject matter. For none of these follows: 'You differ from a man who is in Rome; therefore, you differ from a man, and he is in Rome': 'Every animal that can bray ((*rudibile/ risibile* [with 1501])) is a donkey; therefore, every animal can bray ((*rudibile/risibile* [with 1501])) and it is a donkey'; 'Every proposition whose contradictory is false is true; therefore, every proposition is true, and its ((*et illius/cuius* [with 1501])) contradictory is false'; 'Every man is an animal that is rational; therefore, every man is an animal, and it is rational.'

At this point you should take note of two rules regarding relatives. The first rule is that the relative 'who,' 'which,' 'that,' or 'what' is sometimes expounded (by means of a conjunction, 'and,' and the relative term 'he,' 'she,' 'it') and sometimes not expounded. [It is not expounded] when a negation or a term including negation precedes it, when it refers to a term that has merely confused supposition, and when it precedes the main verb – as is evident in the propositions mentioned earlier in connection with the third mode.

The second rule is that when a relative is used in the same categorical proposition [with its antecedent], it supposits in the same way as its antecedent does – as in 'Every man is an animal that is rational' – but a relative used in another categorical changes its supposition – as in 'Every man is an animal, and it is rational.' {2vb} That is because a relative term must never be expounded in that way while it is referred to a common term that has merely confused supposition, or used after a negation, or used immediately after a distributed term, which occurs when the proposition is in the compounded sense. For in such propositions as 'Every proposition is true whose contradictory is false' the divided sense occurs, because the divided sense occurs when the relative follows the main verb. But if the relative is used immediately after a confused distributed term ((om. *immediate*)), the proposition is in the compounded sense – e.g., 'Every animal that can bray is a donkey.' In propositions such as 'Every man who is white is running,' however, the compounded sense occurs; for the compounded sense occurs when the relative precedes the main verb. (And either the former or the latter relative may be taken either in the nominative or in an oblique case.)

Notice also that the main verb is the one that renders that proposition finished or perfect. 'Every man who is running,' for example, is neither a perfect proposition nor a complete expression; when one says 'Every man who is running is white,' on the other hand, the expression has been adequately perfected. And so [in that case] the second verb is the main verb because the first one is impeded. If, however, one were to say 'Every man is who is running,' or 'Every man is running who is,' the first verb would be the main verb. And by this means one can tell which sense is compounded and which divided, etc.

It happens that sometimes both senses are true, and sometimes both are false; and so no general rule is laid down on that point. Sometimes, however, the divided sense is false when the compounded sense is true, or vice versa. Thus, in sophismata of this [third mode] sort, the divided sense is false and the compounded sense is true, but that is not the way it is in respect of other terms. And the reason why it happens that way in connection with relative terms is that what the compounded sense signifies, the divided sense also signifies, and the compounded sense signifies fewer things than the divided sense signifies. For this follows: 'Every man is running who is white; therefore, every man is running, and every man is white,' from which it clearly follows that 'Every man who is white is running' signifies no more than that every white man is running.

[5. Mode IV]

With respect to terms that are sometimes taken categorematically and other times syncategorematically, however, the consequence is fallacious when one infers the compounded sense from the divided sense. Thus none of these follows: 'Infinitely many equal non-communicating parts has Socrates; therefore, Socrates has infinitely many equal noncommunicating parts'; 'Infinitely many are finitely many; therefore, finitely many are infinitely many'; 'Infinite will this line be; therefore, this line will be infinite'; 'With infinite speed will Socrates move; therefore, Socrates will move with infinite speed'; 'Infinitely does movable object *A* exceed its resistance; therefore, movable object *A* exceeds its resistance infinitely'; 'In-finitely can this continuum be divided; therefore, this continuum can be divided infinitely'; and so on. The consequence is invalid because in the one proposition the term 'infinite' [or some form of it] supposits categorematically, in the other syncategore-matically.

Thus in general, when the term 'infinite' or any syncategorematic ((*sincathegorematicus/sincathegorematice* [with 1501])) term of that sort precedes the proposition entirely, so that there is no term ahead of it which is a determination in respect of that term standing syncate-gorematically, the divided sense occurs and [the proposition] sig-nifies dividedly. For example, 'An infinite number is finite' signifies that a number of some size is finite, and two times that number is finite, and three times that number, and four times, and so on infinitely. Likewise, 'Infinitely many equal noncommunicating parts has Socrates' signifies that some equal noncommunicating parts, etc., and not so finitely many does he have but that he has two times more, and four times more, and so on infinitely.

Similarly, it must be said generally that when that syncate-gorematic term comes first in any proposition, with nothing determinable {3ra} with respect to it preceding it, it is interpreted syncategorematically. But when a term determinable with respect to it precedes it when it occurs in the subject, it is interpreted categorematically, just as when it occurs in the predicate. Thus, when one says 'During an infinite time can this contingent be future,' 'infinite' is taken categorematically, and the proposition is impossible. For in the proposition 'During an infinite time this contingent can be future,' 'infinite' is taken categorematically, and the sense is 'During some infinite time can this be future.' And that is impossible, because in that case this follows: 'This can be future during an infinite time, and during all eternal time.' And so they include opposites.

Much the same must be said about such propositions as these: 'Infinitely many equal noncommunicating parts has Socrates; therefore, some infinitely many equal non-communicating parts has Socrates'; 'An infinite number is finite; therefore, some infinite number is finite.' For when the determinable ['some'] precedes the syncategorematic term, it supposits categorematically and determinately for some definite number. And so, in virtue of the fact that it is acknowledged that such things cannot be, such propositions are impossible.

[6. A Combination of Modes III and IV]

It should likewise be said that when this term is taken in the predicate and some relative is added to the term 'infinite,' a sophisma often results – as when one says 'Infinitely many are the equal noncommunicating parts of which one is a part of Socrates, infinite is some number that is finite; therefore, infinitely many are the equal noncommunicating parts of Socrates and those has Socrates, and infinite is some number and it is finite.' In this connection note also that that mode of arguing is invalid, as was evident before; for a relative term added to a term that has merely confused supposition must never be expounded in that way.

[7. Mode V]

If composition or division is produced in respect of the sign of conjunction 'and,' it can easily be ridiculed because the difference between the compounded and the divided sense is easy to see. Thus 'Two men are in this place and in this one; therefore, two men are in this place' does not follow. Likewise, neither of these follows: 'These two have pennies *A, B, C, D*; therefore, this one has pennies *A, B, C, D*'; 'Socrates can carry stone *A*, and Socrates can carry stone *B*; therefore, Socrates can carry stones *B* and *A*.'

It is in this connection that the fallacy of composition and division is usually assigned, in arguing from the singular number to the plural with respect to the verb 'can' – as when one argues in this way, for instance: 'Proposition A can be true at instant C, and proposition B can be true at instant C; therefore, A and B can be true at instant C'; 'Plato can be at some time in location A, and Socrates can be in location A; therefore, Socrates and Plato can be at the same time in location A.'

Some people can reply easily enough, however, by saying that when one argues from the divided sense to the compounded sense or vice versa depending on the sign of conjunction 'and' after a distributed term the consequence is invalid.

Similarly, when the conjunction 'and' links two terms placed in the subject, one of which is distributed and the other not, the reply is difficult – as when one argues in this way, for instance: 'All two and two are four, all two and two are three; therefore, three are four'; 'All two and three are five, all two and three are three; therefore, three are five'; 'Every man and two men are three men, every man and two men are two; therefore, two men are three.' And so on for the proofs.

With regard to such propositions, however, one can reply by denying the consequence. It is not a syllogistic inference because the major extreme is not concluded of the minor; for in the minor proposition the term 'two men' is placed in the predicate and is not the minor extreme but only a part of the minor extreme, and the minor extreme is a combination, or the combined term {3rb} 'two men and two men'; and the major extreme is the combined term 'two men and three men.' (And the same holds regarding the other examples.) And then one must conclude in this way: 'Therefore, two men and two men are two men and three men.' (Likewise as regards three men, and so on for the other cases.)

Suppose someone says that the consequences produced before are sufficiently evident because they are in syllogism and they are interchangeable with this mode of arguing: 'Whatever are two and two are four, and two and two are three; therefore, three are four.' (And the same holds regarding the other examples.)

The reply is that that inference is good enough, but its premises are incompatible and its conclusion is false. The reason why this last inference is good and the previous ones are invalid is this: [In this last inference] the subject of each premise is the composite term 'two and two,' and the subject is distributed; but that is not the way it is in the other, previous ones, because the manner of distributing is not the same in this case as in those, etc.

[8. Mode VII ((*Septimus/Sextus*))]

Next, one can construct in just the same way a sophisma dependent on the conjunction ((*coniunctione/conclusione* [with 1501])) 'or' by reason of distribution, as in the sophisma 'Every proposition or its contradictory is true,' 'Everything good or not good is to be chosen,' 'Every man or donkey is a donkey,' 'Everything evil or not evil is evil,' and so on for cases just like these.

The reply is just the same. For this does not follow: 'Every proposition or its contradictory is true, every proposition or its contradictory is false; therefore, a true proposition is false.' What does follow, however, is this: 'Therefore, that is false whose contradictory is true.' (And the same holds regarding others of that sort dependent on the conjunction 'or.') And so the fallacy of composition and division is very often committed in this way.

But if [the conjunction 'or'] occurs after a distribution, or a negation, or any term that has the force of negation in such a way as to distribute or produce confused supposition, then an argument from an inferior to its superior with negation or distribution is not fallacious, since in every case what is disjoined ((*disiunctum/disiunctus* [with 1501])) is superior to any part of it. And it is for that reason that 'You differ from a donkey; therefore, you differ from a man or from a donkey' follows ((om. *non*)).

[9. Mode VI ((*Sextus/Septimus*))]

When one argues compounding or dividing in a way that depends on the determination 'it is the case,' 'it was the case,' 'it will be the case,' 'it can be the case' with respect to a distributed term, with respect to a double composition or negation, or with respect to anything that has that sort of force – such as the term 'necessary' – that mode [of arguing] is often fallacious. For example, when one argues in this way: 'It will be the case that you are every man existing in this house; therefore, you will be every man existing in this house'; 'It will be the case that you will be as big as Plato is; therefore, you will be as big as Plato is'; 'It will be the case that the soul of Antichrist necessarily will be; therefore, the soul of Antichrist necessarily will be'; and so on.

The same thing happens with respect to double compositions dependent on the verb 'know' – as, for example, when one argues in this way: 'It will be the case that you know the soul of Antichrist necessarily to be; therefore, it necessarily will be'; 'It will be the case that you know yourself to be every man who is in this house; therefore, you will be every man who will be in this house.' The consequence is invalid, as was said before. And so, as was said before, it does not follow that it will be the case that the soul of Antichrist necessarily will be, nor does it follow that it will be the case that you will be every man existing in this house. And in that case, as has been said, the consequence is invalid.

Nevertheless, a [Mode VI] consequence is indeed valid with respect to a simple composition of a simple subject and a simple predicate: 'It will be the case that you will be a bishop; therefore, you will be a bishop'; 'It will be the case that you will be of such a sort; therefore, you will be of such a sort'; 'It will be the case that you will be bigger than Plato; therefore, you will be bigger than Plato.' And the reason [why these are valid] is that the determination ['It will be the case'] and the proposition are referred to the same instant; but that is not the way it is in the other cases.

[10. Mode VIII]

Next, an argument dependent on verbal terms signifying mental acts or acts of will – such as 'know,' 'doubt,' 'believe,' {3va} 'seek,' 'be uncertain,' 'want,' 'think,' 'want not,' 'desire,' 'perceive,' 'understand,' and the like – is often fallacious with respect to composition or division. For example, when one argues in this way: 'You know one or the other of these to be true; therefore, one or the other of these you know to be true'; 'One or the other of these you doubt to be true; therefore, you doubt one or the other of these to be true'; 'Your father you believe to be a donkey; therefore, you believe your father to be a donkey'; 'You know some proposition to be true that you doubt to be false; therefore, some proposition you know to be true that you doubt to be false'; 'The man appears to be a donkey; therefore, it appears that the man is a donkey'; 'You are uncertain that proposition *A* is true; therefore, proposition *A* you are uncertain is true'; 'Socrates the bishop you want to see; therefore, you want to see Socrates the bishop'; 'You desire to see the king; therefore, the king to see you desire'; 'You perceive one of these to be mute; therefore, one of these you perceive to be mute'; 'You understand some man to be going to come here; therefore, some man you understand to be going to come here'; and so on. For in all these the divided sense is irrelevant to the compounded sense, and vice versa; and it is for that reason that the consequence is bad.

In these propositions, then, the divided sense occurs when the verb signifying an act of intellect or of will comes between [the noun or pronoun in] that sort of [oblique] case and the verb in the infinitive mood – as when one says 'One or the other of these you know to be true,' 'Proposition *A* you believe ((*credis/scis*)) to be false.' By means of this sense it is denoted that one or the other of these is such that you know it to be true, and that *A* is a proposition you believe to be false.

When a verb of that sort comes first, however, the compounded sense occurs – as when one says 'You know one or the other of these to be true,' 'You believe proposition *A* to be false.' And this sense denotes that you know that one or the other of these is true, and that you believe ((*credis/scis*)) proposition *A* to be false.

Now it is clear enough that these two propositions are not interchangeable: 'One or the other of these is such that you know it to be true' and 'You know that one or the other of these is true.' Thus, the sense of the first proposition is that it is an indefinite or particular proposition whose subject supposits determinately for something – viz., for this one or for that one – in such a way that this follows: 'One or the other of these is such that you know it to be true; therefore, this one of these is such that you know it to be true, or that one of these is such that you know, etc.' And so of each part of this disjunctive proposition you can say that it is false, even though you do indeed know that one or the other of them is true; for in that case this does not follow: 'You know that one or the other of these is true; therefore, you know that this one of them is true.'

It can be said, therefore, that a consequence of this sort, arguing from the divided sense to the compounded sense, is invalid, unless it is valid by reason of the terms. For example, 'This you know to be true; therefore, you know that this is true,' and, (when anything at all has been indicated,) 'This you know to be *A*; therefore, you know that this is *A*.' And that is the way it is in such cases when in the divided sense the term ['this'] supposits in the absence of any ((*aliquo/alio*)) determinable.

Furthermore, when the determination is interchangeable with the predicate, there is a good consequence from the divided sense to the compounded sense. For example, 'This white thing you know to be white; therefore, you know that this white thing is white' does follow.

If the determinable is not interchangeable with the predicate, however, a consequence from the divided sense to the compounded sense is invalid. Thus, 'This white thing you know to be running; therefore, you know this white thing to be running' does not follow, although this one does indeed follow: 'This you know to be running; therefore, you know this to be running.'

The reason for this is that scarcely anything picked out by means of differentiae is such that it cannot be understood through the pronoun 'this' used by itself. And so in such cases when the term 'this' supposits by itself in the compounded sense as in the divided (and vice versa), the consequence is valid. (This always holds for a discrete thing and not for one that is common, unless perhaps ((*forte/sorte* [with 1501])) in respect of the verb 'doubt.' For in keeping with the fact that it can be maintained as readily believable, the following consequence is invalid: 'You doubt whether this is a man; therefore, this you doubt to be a man,' since the 'this' might stand for such a thing as is not but was a man.)

Furthermore, when one argues from the divided sense to the compounded sense when the term 'this' is kept in the predicate, when no {3vb} term at all that is known *per se* supposits in the same proposition, or when the subject is not a term known *per se*, the consequence is invalid. Thus, this does not follow: 'What is true you know to be this; therefore, you know that what is true is this'; 'Socrates you know to be this; therefore, you know that Socrates is this.'

On the other hand, each of these does indeed follow: 'A being you know to be this; therefore, you know that a being is this'; 'Something you know to be this; therefore, you know that something is this.' And the reason is that those transcendental terms are known *per se*, in virtue of the very fact that any thing is known to be, and also anything is known to be a being.

That is not the way it is with respect to other terms, however; for it is not in virtue of the very fact that Socrates is known to be that he is known to be Socrates or a man. And so, with respect to these terms as with respect to terms altogether ununderstood, such a consequence – in which one argues from the divided sense to the compounded sense – is invalid. Thus, I call such terms incompletely understood, and I mean those that are adequately understood with respect to some of their significates and adequately in doubt with respect to some of their significates. All those that are not transcendentals [or altogether ununderstood] are of this sort, etc.

The terms that I call altogether ununderstood are those that supposit on a hypothesis [of a disputation] and that in the absence of the hypothesis have no supposition known to me. For example, 'Suppose that *A* is one or the other of these, and that which of them is *A* remains hidden from you, and that each man is going to run in Beaumont tomorrow,' and so on. Thus, in connection with these terms, it is to be noted that universally if any ununderstood term is used in the predicate with respect to a verb signifying knowledge or doubt, such a proposition is to be denied, whatever it may be – as, for instance, if someone says 'This you know to be *A*,' 'Something you know to be *A*,' when it has been posited that one or the other of these is *A*, and that which of them is *A* is hidden from you.

On the other hand, if the same ununderstood term is used in the subject with respect to a term that is known *per se*, the proposition is often to be granted, even though the verb 'know' or a verb signifying certainty or discernment follows – as, for instance, if someone says '*A* you know to be a being,' '*A* you know to be something,' when it has been supposed that you know that one or the other of these (indicating a man and a donkey) is *A*, and that you do not know which of them is *A*.

But if this altogether ununderstood term is used in the subject with respect to the verb 'know' combined with a mediate term, the proposition is often to be doubted; and on a [disputational] hypothesis it is sometimes to be denied, and on a hypothesis it is [sometimes] to be granted. For suppose, as before, that you do indeed know that one or the other of these is *A* (indicating a man and a donkey), and that which of them is *A* is hidden from you, but that you know which of them is the man and which the donkey. Then, if the proposition '*A* you know to be a man' has been proposed, it is to be doubted; and likewise '*A* you know to be a donkey.' But if '*A* you know to be an animal' has been proposed, it is to be granted; for whichever of them is *A*, it is such that it you know to be an animal, since each of them you know to be an animal.

Again, the opponent [in a disputation] often commits a fallacy in proceeding from such a divided sense to such a divided sense as he believes to be its converse – as, for instance, in arguing '*A* you know to be Socrates; therefore, Socrates you know to be *A*,' and '*A* you know to be a donkey; therefore, a donkey you know to be *A*.' That consequence is invalid, but it does follow that something that you know to be Socrates is *A*, and that something that you know to be a donkey is *A*. And, as before, each of those is in doubt.

Again, it is customary to argue often in this way: 'Socrates you know to be this (indicating *A*); therefore, Socrates you know to be *A*,' even though that mode of arguing is never valid. For when one argues succinctly from a term that is better understood combined with the verb 'know' (and with the verbs 'believe,' 'discern') to any other term that is less well understood with respect to the same verb combined [with it], the consequence is invalid. For 'This I know or believe to be an animal; therefore, I know or believe this to be a man or a donkey' does not follow. And consequently it does not follow when the verb 'know' is combined with an altogether ununderstood term following it. Thus '*A* you know to be this (indicating *A*); therefore, *A* you know to be *A*' does not follow; although *A* you know to be this, nevertheless, nothing do you know to be *A*. For it was said before that a proposition in which a term altogether ununderstood is combined with the verb 'know' depending on the infinitive verb 'to be' is never true.

Suppose someone argues on the following grounds that it is: Suppose that *A* is in fact the proposition 'God exists,' and that you do not know that any proposition is *A* but instead {4ra} believe that no proposition is *A*. Even so, you know *A*. This is proved; for you know whatever is true to be true, and that true thing is *A*;

therefore you know that true thing to be *A*. Here the reply is to deny the consequence.

Likewise, if someone argues 'You are in doubt whether *A* is true, and nothing is *A* but "God exists"; therefore, you are in doubt whether "God exists" is true,' the consequence is denied.

And so a compounded sense of this sort occurs as a conclusion only by means of two premises, both of which are taken in the compounded sense. Thus, this does not follow: 'You know that every true one of these signifies precisely as is the case, but the proposition "The king is seated" signifies precisely as is the case; therefore, you know that it is true.' Instead, one has to add in the minor premise that you know that the proposition 'The king is seated' is a true one of these. Likewise, this does not follow: 'You know that every true one of these signifies precisely as is the case, but the proposition "The king is seated" is a true proposition; therefore, you know that that proposition signifies precisely as is the case.'

Similarly, this does not follow: 'You are in doubt whether that is seen by you, and that is a man (indicating that which is seen by you); therefore, you are in doubt whether a man is seen by you.' The consequence is invalid. Instead, one has to add that you know that that is a man.

Again, this does not follow: 'It can be that this is white, and this is black; therefore, it can be that a white thing is black.' Instead, one has to add in the minor premise that it is necessary that this be black.

Thus if the premises are accepted partly in the divided sense and partly in the compounded sense, or if one is in the compounded sense and the other is a simple assertoric proposition involving simple affirmation or simple negation, and if one concludes the compounded sense from them, the consequence is invalid, unless perhaps it is valid by reason of the terms. (I call a proposition simply accepted if it is simply categorical with a simple subject and a simple predicate, either affirmative or negative assertoric, without any term that gives rise to the compounded or the divided sense.) For example, when one says 'You know that everything future will be, and this is future; therefore, you know that this will be' (indicating Antichrist or any future contingent). But the minor premise in this case is a simply assertoric proposition, and the major premise is taken in the compounded sense. And that consequence does not follow in the compounded sense any more than it would in other cases.

If, however, one argues from a major proposition taken in the divided sense and a simply assertoric minor, drawing a conclusion in the divided sense, it will be valid. And in that case the inference is an expository syllogism, or nearly enough like one – as if it were one or another syllogism of this sort, as when one argues 'This you know to be true, and this is *A*; therefore, *A* you know to be true'; 'This you know to be running, and this is Socrates; therefore, Socrates you know to be running'; 'Everything future you know to be future, Antichrist is future; therefore, Antichrist you know to be future'; 'Everything true you know to be true, *A* is true; therefore, *A* you know to be true.' In these last two consequences the consequence is indeed valid, but the major premise is false, and so is the consequent.

But when one of such premises arranged in that way is known to be true and the other is known to be in doubt, the conclusion is to be doubted or, perhaps, granted. For example, when it has been supposed that one or the other of the propositions 'God exists' and 'A man is a donkey' is *A*, and that which of them is *A* is hidden, and one argues in this way 'This is known by you (indicating "God exists"), and this is *A*; therefore, *A* is known by you,' the conclusion is to be doubted, as is the minor premise.

On this basis [one can deal] with all argumentations that have to do with composition and division and depend on such verbal terms having to do with acts of mind, of will, or of intellect.

[11. Excursus on the Art of Obligation]

And so one must, in this art as {4rb} in any obligation, be altogether attentive to what follows and to what is incompatible. For to every irrelevant proposition that is proposed in first place one must reply just as one would reply to it if no hypothesis at all had been posited. It often happens, however, that a proposition is altogether irrelevant when proposed ((*proposita/posita*)) in first place but relevant enough in the second and third place. For it can happen that from it together with the opposite of [a proposition] that has been correctly denied there follows the opposite of the hypothesis, or the opposite of [a proposition] that follows from the hypothesis, or the opposite of [a proposition] that has been previously granted. And so it can happen that when a proposition is proposed in such a place [i.e., in the second or third place] it will have to be simply granted or denied, even though it had to be doubted previously. For that reason, no matter what hypothesis has been posited, when a proposition has been proposed in one sense or the other, one must observe very carefully whether it is relevant or irrelevant not only on the first or some other occasion on which it is proposed, but also whenever it is granted or denied. For after it has been granted or denied once, it will be more relevant than later (*infra*), unless its subject matter happens to be arranged in such a way that an overt change in the actual state of affairs occurs in the meantime. In that case the same proposition could correctly be granted and afterwards denied because of such a change having taken place in the actual state of affairs.

For example, when it has been posited that you are in Rome, let the proposition 'My hand is closed' be proposed when it is true, and let it be granted. Once it has been granted, suppose both my hands are opened. Then, when any time at all has passed, let the proposition 'Neither of my hands is closed' be proposed. It is plausible enough that this can be granted then because of such a change having occurred within the time of this sort of obligation. The opponent, however, does not get the correctness [of his case] clearly established from the fact that the same [proposition] has been both granted and denied within the time of the obligation. And it can be said that I did grant [the proposition] before but now want not to grant it; instead, I willingly deny it, and you could show it to be true.

If you should want an example having to do with the things said before, it is clear enough how the same proposition proposed on the hypothesis in first place is to be doubted or denied, but proposed in the second or third place is to be granted. For example, let this disjunctive proposition be posited: 'The king is seated or you are in Rome.' If the proposition 'The king is seated' is then proposed, it must be doubted since it is doubtful and irrelevant. Let the proposition 'You are in Rome' be proposed then. Since it is false and irrelevant, it must be denied. And if 'The king is seated' is then proposed again, it must be granted; for it follows from the *positum* together with the opposite of [a proposition] that was correctly denied, because 'The king is seated or you are in Rome, but you are not in Rome; therefore, the king is seated' does indeed follow. The consequence is good because one is arguing from a whole disjunctive along with the destruction of one part over the other part [as the conclusion], and when one argues in that way, the consequence is good, etc.

WILLIAM HEYTESBURY
THE VERBS 'KNOW' AND 'DOUBT'

Introduction

For information on Heytesbury's life and writings, see the introduction to Translation 13. The selection translated here is the second chapter, *De scire et dubitare,* of his *Rules for Solving Sophismata.*

Sophismata are puzzling propositions that, when interpreted on special hypotheses, appear to be supported by one set of arguments and opposed by another set, thus generating a paradox. Heytesbury's *Rules* is intended as a handbook for students, to sharpen their skills at dealing with the sorts of sophismata then being debated in the schools. Chapter I deals with insolubilia, or variations on the liar's paradox. Chapter II considers the logical and semantic effects of the verbs 'know' and 'doubt.' Chapter III deals with propositions involving relative terms, and the puzzles discussed involve the kind of reference (mode of supposition) of the relative term used in various ways in several sorts of propositions. Chapter IV considers propositions involving the verbs 'begin' and 'cease,' which generate puzzles about time and change. Chapter V, on maxima and minima, concentrates on the problems of setting limits to certain quantitative or qualitative continua, such as weight or heat. Finally, Chapter VI, on the three categories of place, quantity, and quality, is concerned with velocity and acceleration.

Chapter II, translated here, has to do with sophismata that generate paradoxes about knowing and doubting and may fairly be said to belong to what would now be called epistemic logic. The basic issue that motivates the discussion is whether anyone can know what is in doubt for him. Heytesbury begins by presenting seven arguments purporting to show that one can in fact know what is in doubt for him. After some general remarks about the compounded and divided senses of propositions, which figure importantly in

what follows, Heytesbury goes on to analyze and rebut each of the
seven initial arguments. He concludes the chapter with advice to
participants in obligational disputations (see the introduction to
Translation 12) in a way that suggests that the debate over epistemic
logic in which Heytesbury is here engaged may be part of a larger
debate over the rules of obligational disputations.

For a discussion of the logical roots of medieval sophismata, see
CHLMP IV.11, 'Syncategoremata, Exponibilia, Sophismata'; for
information on the use of sophismata in fourteenth-century education and natural philosophy, see CHLMP VII.27, 'The Oxford
Calculators.'

The Verbs 'Know' and 'Doubt'

[Introduction]

{12va} The word 'know' is used in many ways; but whether it is
taken[1] broadly or strictly, nothing is known by a person that is in
doubt for that person. Nevertheless, various hypotheses are formulated in order to prove it; for people argue to that conclusion in
many ways, as follows.

[Argument A1]

In the first place, suppose that any proposition that anyone is
considering that is not known to be true or known to be false by
him[2] is in doubt for him.

Then let it be posited that you know that A is one or the other of
these: 'God exists,' 'A man is a donkey'; and that you know one of
them – 'God exists' – to be necessary[3] and the other – 'A man is a
donkey' – to be impossible;[4] and that which of them is A is hidden
from you.

Then it is consistent with that hypothesis that you know
proposition A. It also follows that you do not know that A is true
and that you do not know that A is false; for in keeping with the

hypothesis you know that nothing is A besides 'God exists' or 'A man is a donkey.' And, by the supposition, every proposition you are considering that you do not know to be true or know to be false is in doubt for you.[5] Therefore, since it follows from the hypothesis that proposition A is of that sort, it follows from the hypothesis that A is in doubt for you.

But whatever is consistent with the hypothesis is consistent also with anything following from the hypothesis. Therefore, since it follows from the hypothesis that proposition A is in doubt for you, and it is also consistent with the hypothesis that you know proposition A (as was accepted earlier), and[6] the whole hypothesis is possible, it follows that these are consistent with one another: 'You know proposition A,' 'Proposition A is in doubt for you,' and 'One proposition is every proposition that is A.'

And so it follows that the same thing is known by a person that is doubted by that person – which is what we were aiming at.

[Argument A2]

One argues to the same effect in this way. Let it be posited that you know that A[7] is the true one of these, indicating these contradictories, which are in doubt for you: 'A king is seated,' 'No king is seated' – so that you know that whichever of them is A is true and that only that one is A (and vice versa) – and that although you know that A is the true one of them, you do not know which of them is A, just as you do not know which of them is true.

[Argument A2.1]

Once those things have been posited, let this consequence be formulated: 'If A is true, this is true'; and suppose that you know (along with the whole hypothesis) that A is indicated by the subject of the consequent. On that assumption the consequence is good, known by you to be good, and the antecedent 'A is true' is known by you; therefore, the consequent 'This is true' (A having been indicated) is known by you.

And that the consequent is in doubt for you is argued at once as follows: for whether 'A king is seated' or 'No king is seated' is

indicated, the proposition 'This is true' is in doubt for you since by
the hypothesis each of them is in doubt for you; therefore, whichever of them has been indicated, you do not know that it is true. It
follows, therefore, that 'This is true' is in doubt for you; for by
means of its subject only a proposition in doubt for you is
indicated.

And, as was argued earlier, 'This is true' is known by you.
Therefore, a proposition in doubt for you is known by you. Therefore, something in doubt for you is known by you – which is what
was to be proved.

[Argument A2.2]

Again, one argues on the same hypothesis in this way. Every
proposition you know to be true you know, but you know proposition A to be true; therefore, proposition A you know. And
proposition A is in doubt for you, because both 'A king is seated'
and 'No king is seated' are in doubt for you. But A is one or the
other of them; therefore, A is a proposition in doubt for you.
Therefore, the same thing is known by you and in doubt for you.

[Argument A3]

One argues to the same effect in this way. Let it be posited that you
know that this is this (indicating Socrates), and that you do not
know that this is Socrates, but you do know that the proposition
'This is this' signifies precisely that this is this, and also that the
proposition 'This is Socrates' signifies {12vb} precisely that this is
Socrates. For suppose that Socrates, whom you know to be a man,
is in front of you, and that you do not know him to be Socrates.

Once that has been posited, it follows that the proposition 'This
is Socrates' is in doubt for you; for as you are considering it (along
with the other details of the hypothesis that has been introduced),
you know that it signifies precisely as you doubt to be the case;
therefore, it is in doubt for you. The consequence is known, and
the antecedent follows from the hypothesis; therefore it follows
from the hypothesis that 'This is Socrates' is in doubt for you.

And that it is known by you is argued as follows; for[8] you know

that it signifies precisely as you know to be the case. I prove this:
For you know that it signifies precisely that this is Socrates, and
you know that this is Socrates; therefore, you know it. The consequence is evident, and the major premise is apparent in connection
with the hypothesis. And the minor premise is argued; for you
know the proposition 'This is this' (Socrates having been indicated);
therefore, however it signifies you know to be the case. But it
signifies that this is Socrates; therefore, you know it to be the case
that this is Socrates. And this follows: 'You know it to be the case
that this is Socrates; therefore, you know that this is Socrates.' And
if that is so, it follows that you know the proposition proposed to
you – viz., 'This is Socrates.'

And that proposition is in doubt for you, as was proved before.
Therefore, as before,[9] what is in doubt for you is known by
you.

[Argument A4]

Again,[10] you know that this is either Socrates or Plato, but you do
not know whether it is Socrates, nor do you know that [11] it is
Plato. And in that case the proposition 'This is Socrates' will be in
doubt for you.

And that it is known by you is argued as follows: For you know
that it signifies precisely as you know to be the case. The proof of
this is[12] that you know that this signifies precisely[13] that this is
Socrates or that[14] this is Plato, and you know that that is the case
because you know that this is Socrates or that this is Plato; therefore, you know the proposition. The consequence is evident, and
the minor premise is evident on the basis of the hypothesis. And
the major premise is argued [as follows]: For you know that
the proposition signifies precisely that this is Socrates, and you
know that this follows: 'It signifies precisely that this is Socrates;
therefore, it signifies precisely that this is Socrates or that this is
Plato,' because the argument goes from a part of what is disjoined
to the whole of what is disjoined[15] or from part of a disjunctive
proposition to the whole disjunctive proposition without negation
and without distribution.

Therefore, etc.

[Argument A5]

Again, suppose that you know what is indicated by the subject of the proposition 'This is a man,' and that you know that the proposition signifies precisely as its terms suggest, and that something you know[16] to be a man and nothing do you doubt to be a man.

Once that has been posited, it follows that 'This is a man' is known by you to be true or that it is known by you to be false. For since you know what is indicated[17] and nothing do you doubt to be a man, either that thing you know[18] to be a man or you know it not to be a man. But if you know it to be a man, and you know that the proposition signifies in precisely that way, it follows that you know the proposition. And if you know it not to be a man, and you know that the proposition signifies precisely that it is a man, it follows that you know that it[19] is false.

And that it is in doubt for you on this hypothesis is argued as follows: For when 'This is a man' has been proposed to you on the hypothesis, because that proposition was in doubt for you before the hypothesis and does not follow from the hypothesis, it is not to be granted because of the hypothesis. And for that same reason it is not to be denied. Therefore, it follows that it is to be doubted – and not because it follows from the hypothesis that it is in doubt for you, but because the truth of the matter is that it is in doubt for you.

But, as was argued earlier, you know it to be true or you know it to be false. Therefore, a proposition in doubt for you is known by you to be true or known by you to be false.

[Argument A6]

Again, let *A, B,* and *C* be three propositions of which two – *A* and *B* – are known to you while the third – *C* – is in doubt for you. And suppose that you do not know which of them is *A* or *B*, {13ra} and that which of them is in doubt for you is likewise hidden from you.

Once those things have been posited, it follows that one of those propositions is known by you, since both *A* and *B* are known by you.[20]

It also follows that each of them is in doubt for you, since

whichever one of them is indicated, you are in doubt whether it is
in doubt for you; for, on the hypothesis, when A is indicated, you
are in doubt whether it is in doubt for you;[21] for if you know that it
is not in doubt for you, then by the same reasoning it follows that
you would know that this (indicating B) is not in doubt for you.
And you do indeed know that one of those three is in doubt for
you; therefore, you know that this (indicating C) is in doubt for
you – which is contrary to the hypothesis, since the supposition is
that you do not know which of them is in doubt for you. It
follows, therefore, that, whichever of them is indicated, you are in
doubt whether it is in doubt for you.[22] This follows, too: 'You are
in doubt whether this is in doubt for you, and you know that this is
a proposition; therefore, this is in doubt for you.' The consequence
is argued in this way: Since you know that this is a proposition that
you do not know to be true and do not know to be false, it is in
doubt for you; nor do you believe it unhesitatingly.

It follows, therefore, that since one of these is known by you and
each of them (indicating the same ones) is in doubt for you, the
same thing is known by you and in doubt for you.

[Argument A7]

Again, you know that this is Socrates, and you are in doubt
whether this is Socrates (the same thing having been indicated). For
let it be posited that yesterday you saw Socrates and you still know
that the man you saw yesterday is Socrates. And suppose that you
see Socrates today and it is hidden from you that he is Socrates;
instead, you believe that the man you are seeing now is Plato.
Suppose, too, that you do not see anyone besides Socrates.

Once those things have been posited, you know that this is
Socrates (indicating the one you saw yesterday). For you would
unhesitatingly grant that this (indicating the one you saw yesterday)
is Socrates, since you do indeed know that the one you saw yesterday is Socrates[23] (for suppose, for the sake of the example, that you
know that you saw no one yesterday except the one who is Socrates). In that case it follows that you know that this is Socrates
(indicating the one you saw yesterday).

And (indicating the same one) you are in doubt whether this is

Socrates, because you are in doubt whether this (indicating the one you see now) is Socrates. And the one you see now and the one you saw yesterday are the same.

Therefore, you know that this is Socrates, and you are in doubt whether this is Socrates (the same thing having been indicated).

[General Reply]

I reply[24] to all these [preceding seven affirmative arguments] in general, and I maintain that none of them proves what it sets out to prove, nor is it possible that any hypothesis could do so.[25]

In order to clarify this it should be noted that certain propositions are sometimes accepted in the compounded sense [whereas others] just like them are taken in the divided sense and are not interchangeable with those accepted in the compounded sense.

Again, it is important to know that propositions of that sort occur especially in virtue of terms conveying an action or disposition of the understanding[26] – either being able to be or not being able to be, being necessarily or not being necessarily.[27] Of this sort are the terms 'know,' 'doubt,' 'understand,' 'imagine,' 'perceive,' 'want,' 'want not,' 'possible,' 'impossible,' 'necessary,' and so on as regards other terms that are like them.[28]

That such propositions occur with such [29] terms appears clearly enough in ordinary speech, as when one says 'I know A to be true' and 'A I know to be true.' Those propositions are very much alike, but they are not interchangeable; for the one is accepted in the divided sense, and the other in the compounded sense – just as in this case: 'Some proposition I doubt to be true' and 'I doubt some proposition to be true'; 'I understand or imagine some point to be the center of this body' and 'Some point I understand or imagine to be the center of this {13rb} body'; 'I perceive Socrates to be speaking' and 'Socrates I perceive to be speaking'; 'I want to give you my horse' and 'My horse I want to give you'; 'I want Socrates to be in the pit' and 'Socrates I want to be in the pit'; 'It is possible that a white thing be black' and '[Regarding] a white thing, it is possible that it be black'; 'It is necessary that every[30] man be an animal' and '[Regarding] every[31] man, it is necessary that he be an animal'; 'It is impossible that a seated man run' and '[Regarding] a seated man, it is impossible that he run.' And in this way it is obvious that there are many similar propositions, like the ones already put forward and others of that sort, that are not interchangeable because the one is taken in the compounded sense and the other in the divided sense. [That is] because the compounded sense rarely or never is interchangeable with the divided sense; instead, for the most part, however similar they are, they are nevertheless irrelevant to each other, as will appear below.

Again, it must be taken as a rule that when one of the terms mentioned above[32] (or a term like them) precedes or follows the entire dictum of a proposition, that proposition must be taken in the compounded sense. If, for example, someone says 'I know A to be true,' that whole proposition is taken in the compounded sense. And in that case it is interchangeable with the proposition 'I know that A is true.' And from this it follows that the proposition 'A is true' (or at least [33] some proposition signifying that A is true) is known by me.

But many of the terms listed[34] above do not very suitably follow after the entire dictum of such a proposition. For it would be improper to say 'A to be true I know' [or] 'Some proposition to be true I doubt.'[35] Some of them, on the other hand, can follow after the whole of such a dictum properly enough;[36] for it is all right to say 'That A is true is possible,' 'That a man is running is possible,' 'That a man is a donkey is impossible.'

Therefore, whether such a term precedes an entire dictum of that sort or follows it, the entire proposition[37] will be taken in the compounded sense.

As for the dictum of a proposition, I am speaking of it at present in just the way it was spoken of by those men who wrote that from every true proposition it follows that its dictum is true. For this follows: 'God exists; therefore, that God exists is true'; 'The man is white; therefore, that the man is white is true.' According to them, therefore,[38] the dictum of the proposition 'God exists' is the expression 'that God exists'; and the dictum[39] of the proposition 'The man is white' is the expression[40] 'that the man is white' according to those same people. And that, for the present, is what I mean [too].[41]

But when any of the terms mentioned above occurs in the midst of such a dictum – as, for instance, when one says 'A I know to be true,' 'Some proposition I doubt to be true,' 'A white thing can be black,' or '[Regarding] a white thing, it is possible that it be black,' then the whole proposition is taken in the divided sense. And what is denoted by the whole proposition when one says '*A* I know to be true' is that the proposition that is *A*, or that which is *A*, I know to be true. 'Some proposition I doubt to be true' – i.e., 'Something is a proposition that I doubt to be true.' 'A white thing can be black' – i.e., 'That which is white can be black or that which can be white can be black.' For it can be said in this way: '[Regarding] a white thing, it is possible that it be black' – i.e., '[Regarding] that which is white, it is possible that it be black'; but to have the divided sense explicitly[42] it is better to say that a white thing can be black.

And so it should be noted that in all the foregoing these two senses, the compounded and the divided, are not interchangeable. For '*A* I know to be true' and 'I know that *A* is true' are irrelevant to each other, because neither of them follows from the other. For it can be the case that the proposition that is *A* I know to be true even though I do not know that *A* exists in fact. For even if I believed that Socrates died twenty years ago,[43] so that I believed that it was now[44] impossible that Socrates exists, it still can be the case, consistent with this, that Socrates I know to be running in Beaumont. For in the divided sense a consequence of this sort is perfectly valid: 'This I know to be running, and this is Socrates; therefore, Socrates I know to be running'; analogously, 'This I know to be true, and this is *A*; therefore, *A* I know to be true.' For this follows: 'That which is *A*{13va} I know to be true; therefore, *A* I know to be true.' And so in the divided sense a consequence of this sort is acceptably valid: 'This I know to be true, and this is *A*; therefore, *A* I know to be true'; for if the premises and conclusion are understood in that way, the inference is an expository syllogism.

But if from those same premises someone concludes such a proposition[45] in the compounded sense, an argument[46] of that sort is not valid. For the following consequence is not valid: 'This I know to be true, and this is *A*; therefore, I know *A* to be true,' nor can it be concluded in an expository syllogism. In order to conclude that [proposition][47] one would, instead, have to accept two premises of which both are in the compounded sense or at least[48] in a sense interchangeable with or antecedent to the compounded sense, arguing in this way: 'I know this to be true, and I know this to be A; therefore, I know A to be true.' That consequence is good, but it is not an expository syllogism because it does not have the conditions of an expository syllogism, as is perfectly obvious.

Not even a consequence of the sort [49] in which both premises are taken in the compounded sense is universally valid – [when], that is, the one [is taken] with the verb 'know' and the other with the main verb of the proposition to be concluded. Thus this does not follow: 'I want to see the pope, and I know that only he is the pope; therefore, I want to see him'; 'I want to beat the priest,[50] and I know that only he is the priest; therefore, I want to beat him';[51] so also as regards others of that sort.[52] That sort of consequence is not valid, especially in respect of verbal terms having to do with the will.[53]

The reason for this is that in connection with such terms it is not required that you want the consequent, even though you know the consequence to be good and you want the antecedent. For this follows:[54] 'You are beating this man; therefore, you are beating the priest'; and you know this consequence to be good, and you want the antecedent and do not want the consequent. And the reason for this is that although you know the consequence to be good, you might wish it were not valid; for it happens very often that a person desires what he knows[55] it is impossible for him to get.

With other terms, however, an argument of that sort holds good for the most part. For this follows: 'You are in doubt whether A is true, and you know that only this is A; therefore, you are in doubt whether this is true.' This follows[56] likewise: 'You are in doubt whether this is true, and you know that only this is A; therefore, you are in doubt whether A is true'; 'You believe that Socrates is deceived, and you know that only this one is Socrates; therefore, you believe that this one is deceived.'

Now the reason why the term 'only' (or some exclusive term) is introduced into the proposition taken in the compounded sense with respect to the verb 'know' is that otherwise the antecedent could be verified for something other than the consequent, or the consequent could be verified not for that for which the antecedent is verified [but for something else]. For if one argues in this way – 'I am in doubt whether A is true, and I know that this is A; therefore, I am in doubt whether this is true' – the consequence need not be good.

For it is consistent that I should indeed know that this is not true and that[57] this is *A* and should [nevertheless] be in doubt whether *A* is true, because I am in doubt whether[58] it is an *A* other than this one that is[59] true. And so it could happen that the antecedent would be verified for something other than that for which the consequent is verified, and also that the consequent would not be verified for that for which the antecedent is verified – as when one argues in this way: 'I am in doubt whether this is true, and I know that this is *A*; therefore, I am in doubt whether *A* is true.' This mode of arguing is not valid, because it can happen that I know that an *A* is true that[60] is not this one. In this way, then, it is obvious how we have to add[61] such an[62] exclusive[63] or distributive term in order that this[64] mode of arguing with the aforementioned terms[65] be generally[66] valid.

It follows, therefore, that in connection with such[67] propositions and those similar to them the compounded sense is not interchangeable with the divided sense;[68] instead, they are for the most part irrelevant to each other.

Now that this has been seen, then, I reply to the arguments produced earlier.

[Reply to Argument A1]

First,[69] in reply to the first argument, when it is argued that the same thing is known by me and in doubt for me, I say, as before, that that is impossible.

And to the supposition, when it is supposed that every proposition that anyone is considering that he does not know to be true or know to be false is in doubt for him, the reply is that the supposition is[70] possible – for it is possible that [its] predicate be affirmed truly of [its] subject.[71] But it does not follow[72] that if there is a proposition that someone is considering {13vb} that he does not know to be true or know to be false, that proposition[73] is in doubt for him. For he may believe it firmly, unhesitatingly, in such a way that he unhesitatingly believes that he knows it – and it may nevertheless be false. And in that case he is considering it, and yet it is not in doubt for him (nor[74] does he know it to be true, nor does he know it to be false); or he believes it with such intensity that he is unhesitating about whether matters are in fact as it signifies, and so he is not in doubt. For suppose that someone who is not the king were to approach as the king ordinarily approaches, in similar circumstances, so that it would be generally said by everyone that he was the king; and suppose that he was like the king in all respects. I would so firmly believe that he was the king that I would believe that I knew that he was the king. And so[75] in that case I would not know[76] that he was the king or that he was not the king, nor would I be in doubt whether[77] he was the king.

Thus speaking broadly,[78] in such a way that[79] contingents of that sort[80] and accidental sensible characteristics[81] are [among the things that are] known, to know is nothing other than unhesitatingly to apprehend the truth – i.e., to believe unhesitatingly that it is so when (*et cum hoc quod*) it is so in reality. For in that way I know that Rome was a beautiful city, that there are many men in Oxford, that this one is awake, that that one is asleep, and so on.

But someone may argue against this by concluding that from this it follows that it is possible that on the basis of a hypothesis[82] a person may be in doubt whether he knows that this or that is the case. For[83] let it be posited that you believe firmly, unhesitatingly, that the king is in London. Then let the proposition 'The king is in London' be proposed. And since the truth of the matter is that it is in doubt for you and irrelevant, it follows that you have to doubt it. But on the basis of what is in doubt for you as regards this hypothesis you know that the king is in London. For you could not then correctly deny that you know the king to be in London, because, according to you, this follows: 'The king is in London, and you believe unhesitatingly that the king is in London; therefore, you know that the king is in London.' The major premise is in doubt for you, and the minor is the hypothesis; therefore, the consequent is not to be denied by you. Nor is it to be granted, either, since it is false and irrelevant. Therefore, it is to be doubted. And in that way[84] it follows that you[85] are in doubt whether you know that the king is in London – which was to be proved.

To this I reply that the conclusion is impossible and contains opposites. For this follows: 'You know that the king is in London; therefore, with certainty,[86] unhesitatingly, you apprehend or perceive that the king is in London.' This also[87] follows: 'You apprehend or perceive with certainty,[88] unhesitatingly, that the king is in London, and you are considering whether or not you perceive that you perceive in that way; therefore, you perceive that you perceive in that way.' The consequence is clear enough; for you would not on the basis of any evidence perceive that this or that is the case if you could not on the basis of the very same evidence perceive that you perceive that this or that is the case. And on that basis one argues as follows: 'You perceive that you perceive with certainty, unhesitatingly, that the king is in London; therefore, you perceive that you know that the king[89] is in London.'

One also argues similarly on the basis of the other part – viz., that if you are considering whether you perceive that this or that is the case, and you do not perceive that you perceive, then you do not perceive that this or that is the case. Therefore, if you are considering whether you know that this or that is the case, and you do not perceive that you know that this is the case, then you do not know that this is the case. One argues, therefore, in this way: 'You are considering whether you know that the king is in London, and you do not perceive that you know that the king is in London; therefore, you do not know that the king is in London.' That consequence is sufficiently evident on the basis of things already said. And then this follows: 'This consequence is known by you to be good, and the antecedent is known by you; therefore, so is the consequent.' Now, that the antecedent is known by you is evident, because in virtue of the fact that you doubt that you know, you know that you are considering whether you know and that you do not perceive that you know. And if that is the case, then in virtue of the fact that you doubt that you know, you know that you do not know and, furthermore, you do not know that you do not know, as a consequence of which you doubt that you know. It follows, therefore, that the proposition 'You doubt that you know' contains opposites – which is what was intended.

But as for the argument, once that hypothesis has been supposed, I grant[90] that when the proposition 'The king is in London' is proposed in first place one must reply by saying 'I am in doubt about it.' And as for the other [proposition], when 'You know that the king is in London' is proposed, one replies by denying it, because it is false and irrelevant. Moreover, that consequence is not valid: 'The proposition follows from the hypothesis and a proposition that is in doubt for you; therefore, it is not to be {14ra} denied by you.' On the contrary, even though it does follow from the hypothesis and a proposition known by me, given the hypothesis it would have to be denied. It is as if once the proposition 'I am in Rome' has been posited to me,[91] the proposition 'You are in Rome' follows from the hypothesis and a proposition known by me. For this follows: 'I am in Rome, and you are in the same building I am in; therefore, you are in Rome.' Nevertheless, the proposition 'You are in Rome' proposed in first place would have to be denied.

Thus it does not follow, nor is it a rule, that if a consequence is good,[92] known by you to be good, and the antecedent is in doubt for you, the consequent is not to be denied by you. And yet when a consequence is known by you to be good and it has been replied to[93] by doubting the antecedent, and the consequence is entirely irrelevant to the hypothesis and to all other things that have been granted and[94] denied (if things were that way during that time), the consequent is not to be denied. But in the case under consideration, the antecedent from which it would follow that you know that the king is in London is not in doubt for you. For[95] even though one part is in doubt for you and the other follows from the hypothesis, you know[96] that the whole conjunctive proposition is false, because you do indeed know that the hypothesis is false. For even though it is supposed that you unhesitatingly believe that the king is in London, the truth of the matter is that you know that you do not believe in that way. And so the argument does not go through.

And so I admit the first supposition – viz., that every proposition that anyone is considering, etc. – as possible, and not otherwise.

And as for the further argument, I admit the hypothesis, and I grant all of it up to the point at which it is said that from the hypothesis it follows that proposition A I do not know to be true and also that A[97] I do not know to be false – and I deny that. Moreover, I say that from the hypothesis the opposite follows. For it follows from the hypothesis that proposition A I know to be true or that proposition A I know to be false. Suppose also (as is said in the course of arguing in that same place) that I know proposition A together with the hypothesis.[98] I say that in that case it follows[99] that proposition A I know to be true.

And as for the argument in which it is argued that from the hypothesis it follows that I do not know A to be true, I grant it. And I deny the further consequence in which it is inferred from this that it follows[100] that A I do not know to be true; for the argument there is from the compounded sense to the divided sense, each of which[101] is on that hypothesis entirely irrelevant to the other. For the proposition that is A I know to be true, and I do not know that it is A. Thus, A I know to be true, and yet[102] no true thing do I know to be A; on the contrary, nothing do I know to be A, nor [is] A [something] I know to be A.

Suppose it is argued that A I do know to be A, because A I know to be this (indicating A); therefore, this I know to be A (by simple conversion).

Again, in this way: A you know to be the same as something, and A[103] you do not know to be the same as anything other than A itself; therefore, A you know to be the same as A itself.

Again, to the same effect in this way: A you know to be the same as itself; therefore, A you know to be the same as A itself.

For the first [of these three counterarguments], I deny the consequence 'A I know to be this; therefore, this I know to be A'; nor does it hold[104] by conversion. If you do want to convert that [proposition], however,[105] you have to convert it in this way: 'A I know to be this; therefore, what I know to be this is A.'

For the second [counterargument], I reply by denying the proposition 'A I know to be the same as A itself.' And this does not follow: 'A I know[106] to be the same as something, and A I do not know to be the same as anything other than A itself; therefore, A I know to be the same as A itself.' [That is] because A I know[107] to be the same as A itself or something other than A itself, and yet A I do not know to be the same as A itself, and A[108] I do not know to be the same as something other than A itself.[109] Nor does this follow: 'I know A to be the same as A itself; therefore, A I know to be the same as A itself,' because the argument there is from the compounded sense to the divided sense.

As for the other [counterargument], when it argues that A I know to be the same as itself, I grant it. For each of them – 'God exists' and 'A man is a donkey' – I know to be the same as itself, and A is one or the other of them; therefore, A I know to be the same as itself. And when it argues further 'therefore, A I know to be the same as A itself,' I deny[110] the consequence.

And so, since it follows from the hypothesis supposed that no proposition do I know to be A – indeed, that nothing do I know to be *A* – and that I know that only one or the other of those is *A*, and also that only this one of them – 'God exists' – is true, it follows that I do not know *A* to be true and also[111] that I do not know *A* to be false. And because it was added further, almost to excess, that *A* is 'God exists,' I grant, as before, that *A* I know to be true; and, further, {14rb} I deny that I know *A* to be true.

And if[112] on that basis it is argued that some proposition I know to be true that I do not know to be true, since *A* I know to be true and I do not know *A* to be true, I say that that does not follow but is simply impossible. For although proposition *A* I know to be true and I do not know proposition *A* to be true, still proposition *A* I know to be true, which I know to be true. It is possible, however, that I know some proposition to be true that I do not know to be true (although that does not follow on the hypothesis given); for I know some proposition in doubt for me to be true, and any [proposition] in doubt for me I do not know to be true, and so I know some proposition to be true that I do not know to be true and that I doubt to be true. But that is taken in[113] the compounded sense, and the preceding conclusion was taken in the divided sense. And so, when it is inferred on the first hypothesis from the two premises 'Proposition *A* I know to be true' and 'I do not know proposition *A* to be true' [that] therefore the same proposition I know and doubt, I say that the consequence is not valid. Nor does it follow from that hypothesis that *A* is in doubt for me. Instead, the opposite follows; for this follows: 'None of those is in doubt for you, *A* is one of those; therefore, *A* is not in doubt for you.'

When the first hypothesis has been supposed, but it is not also posited with that hypothesis which of the propositions is *A*, or when it has been supposed generally in that fashion that you know that some proposition is *A* and you do not know which,[114] then whether one proposes in first place '*A* is true' or '*A* is false' or '*A* is known by you' or '*A* is in doubt for you,' or any such[115] proposition is proposed in first place, it is typically denied by many people as false and irrelevant. For although it is supposed that *A* is one or the other of them, or that *A*[116] is some proposition, it does not follow from that [supposition] that *A* is true or that *A* is false, nor does anything of that sort follow from it. And the truth of the matter is that *A* is not a proposition but a vowel, and it is for that reason that each proposition such as '*A* is true' or[117] '*A* is false' and others like them proposed in first place is false and irrelevant and therefore to be denied.

But that reply is altogether sophistical. It does not attack the argument, nor does a person replying in that way have evidence against anyone doubting the same proposition[118] proposed in first place. For since the person replying in that way takes it to be the truth of the matter that[119] *A* is a vowel and not a proposition, someone else[120] can deny that.[121]

Likewise, because the person replying in that way[122] admits that *A* is a proposition, in his view it is possible that *A* is a proposition. For that reason, then, he[123] holds it to be obvious that *A* is not a proposition.

In reply to that, however, he can say that he does not admit it because it *is* possible that *A* is a proposition, but in order to consider the argument.

And in that case the other person can make the rejoinder that in carrying the argument on[124] he has to reply further, in a way more relevant to the point of the argument.

And so, when a general hypothesis of that sort has been supposed and nothing is posited about which proposition is *A*, I am in doubt whether *A* is true, whether *A* is false, whether *A* is known by me to be false, whether *A* is known by me to be true, whether *A* is known by me to be impossible, whether *A* is known by me to be necessary, and whether *A* is in doubt for me. In a general hypothesis of that sort, however, almost all the following sorts of propositions have to be doubted, no matter which place they are proposed in: '*A* I doubt to be true,' '*A* I know to be true,' '*A* I know to be known by me,' '*A* I know to be impossible,' '*A* I doubt to be impossible,' '*A* I know to be necessary.' And, in general, all these propositions have to be denied: 'Something true I know to be[125] *A*,' 'Something false I know to be *A*.'

Actually, in general, every affirmative proposition of that sort, in which such[126] an altogether ununderstood term determines the verb 'know,' has to be denied. I call a term altogether ununderstood that is not predicated truly and affirmatively of any thing by means of the verb 'know' – just like the term '*A*' in the hypothesis that has been supposed, since there is no thing you know to be *A*. But the fact that there is a term by which nothing I know is signified does not yet require that that term is altogether ununderstood by me, since the term may be affirmed truly of something[127] by means of the verb 'know.' For example, suppose it has been posited that I do not know what the term 'this' signifies or what is indicated by means of it; and yet 'A man I know to be this' is true because, perhaps, I myself[128] am indicated. And so if {14va} we are talking about an altogether ununderstood term, as we were before,[129] no proposition is to be granted in which such a term[130] is affirmed of anything else by means of the verb 'know' and the verb is directed to a person by whom the term is ununderstood. For example, suppose it has been posited that you know what A is and I do not know. In that case 'Something you know to be A' must be granted,[131] and 'Something I know to be A' must be denied.[132] And on this basis what was said goes through.

But, on the other hand, when a term understood in itself is affirmed of anything else by means of the verb 'doubt,' an affirmative proposition of that sort must be denied. I call a term understood in itself that is such that when it is affirmed truly of anything, a person by whom those terms are understood in themselves[133] is immediately certain that that is the case. The following terms are of that sort: 'in doubt for you,'[134] 'known by you,'[135] 'affirmative proposition,' 'negative proposition,' demonstrative pronouns used by themselves without a[136] determinable (e.g., the pronoun 'this'), and so on. Thus, there is no proposition that you doubt to be in doubt for you; on the contrary, it is in virtue of the very fact that a proposition is in doubt for you that you are certain that it[137] is in doubt for you. In the same way, when a proposition is known by you, you are certain that it is known by you. And when a proposition has been proposed, it is immediately certain whether it is affirmative or negative – at least in general, or almost always. It could happen, in [some] hypothesis, that an expression was a proposition, and you were considering[138] it, and you did not know[139] it to be a proposition and so [did not know it to be] either affirmative or negative.[140] And even given that you did know[141] it to be a proposition, it could be consistent [with this:] that you did not know[142] it to be affirmative or know[143] it to be negative because you did not understand[144] its terms – given, for instance, that you knew[145] it was a Greek, or Hebrew, or French[146] proposition. But this counterinstance means only that those terms mentioned above[147] are not understood in themselves, or at least that in a [certain] hypothesis it could happen that they were not understood in themselves, and that is not contrary to the rule.

Nor [is there] anything [of which] you doubt that it is this,[148] no matter what is indicated, because it is either this or[149] something other than this. If it is this, and this you know to be (because this you are considering, and this you know you are considering), then this you know to be this. The consequence is understood, because this follows: 'You know that this is; therefore, you know that this is this.' And this follows further: 'Therefore, this you know to be this.' And if that is the case, then neither this nor anything other than this do you doubt to be this. The consequence is understood, and the consequent is what was intended.

And it is no obstacle that the argument here is from the compounded sense to the divided sense, because when the term 'this' is a simple subject without a[150] determinable with respect to the verb 'know,' the compounded sense is interchangeable with the divided sense (and vice versa[151]). Moreover, when that is done[152] with any verb whatever, the propositions will be relevant [to each other] because the compounded sense follows from the divided sense. But the divided[153] sense is interchangeable with the compounded[154] sense not with any verb whatever but only with respect to the verb 'know.' For this follows: 'This I know to be white; therefore, I know that this is[155] white'; 'This I know to be Socrates; therefore, I know that this is Socrates';[156] and conversely: 'I know that this is Socrates; therefore, this I know to be Socrates,' and so on. This follows too:[157] 'This I doubt to be white; therefore, I am in doubt whether this is white'; 'This appears black; therefore, it appears that this is black.' But it does not follow conversely: 'I doubt whether this is white; therefore, this I doubt to be white'; 'It appears that this is black; therefore, this appears black';[158] for it can happen that I am in doubt whether this is white even though this does not exist in reality, and it can also happen that it appears to me that this is black even though this does not appear. And so when one argues in that way from the compounded sense to the divided sense, it is the fallacy of the consequent because it follows conversely and not this way.

And that is what was said above, that the compounded sense and the divided sense are rarely relevant to each other and very rarely interchangeable. They are relevant [to each other] only when such a term[159] used by itself without any determinable of that sort supposits in respect of a term effecting a difference of that sort among similar propositions of that kind. The terms recounted above are of that sort:[160] 'know,' 'doubt,' and so on; and this [holds] when we are speaking of a difference such that a false proposition results where before there was a true one (or vice versa) because of the change of the subject or the predicate into another term interchangeable with it. For it is understood that many propositions, some of which are taken in the compounded sense and[161] others in the divided sense, are interchangeable, such as {14vb} these: 'A white thing can be' and 'It can be that a white thing is';[162] 'Socrates can run' and 'It can be that Socrates is running,' and so on. But sophismata are not based on those, and so from the outset the discussion has not been about them.[163]

And, as was already said, although 'This I know to be white' and 'I know that this is white' are interchangeable, 'This animal I know to be white' and 'I know that this animal is white' are not interchangeable. Nor are they relevant [to each other]; for the term 'animal' is plainly not[164] interchangeable[165] with the predicate 'white' or, plainly, superior to it; for[166] wherever such a determinable term is plainly superior to the predicate or plainly interchangeable with the predicate, there[167] it does indeed follow. For this follows: 'This white thing I know to be white; therefore, I know that this white thing is white' (and vice versa); similarly, this follows: 'This colored thing I know to be white; therefore, I know that this colored thing is white' (and vice versa).

From the things that have now been said it is clear how one is to reply in connection with the first[168] hypothesis and the general hypothesis, always avoiding as impossible that what is known by anyone is in doubt for that same person.

[Reply to Argument A2]

I [now] reply to the second argument.[169] And I admit[170] all of it up to the consequence in which it is argued 'If *A* is true, this is true,' and[171] I grant that consequence. And when it is argued further 'The consequence is good,[172] known by you to be good, and the antecedent is known by you; therefore, the consequent is known by you,' I grant the consequence and deny the major premise. For I grant the consequence not because I know it to be good but because it follows that[173] if A is, this is (and vice versa). And so it follows from[174] the hypothesis that[175] if A is true, this is true. And so I grant the consequence[176] as following from the hypothesis, not because it is known by me to be good; for its being known by me to be good as long as it signifies in that way is explicitly incompatible with the hypothesis.

And as for the argument in which it is argued further that[177] I know the consequence to be good because I know that only A is indicated in the consequent, I say that that[178] does not follow. Indeed,[179] this does not follow: 'I know that the proposition "This is A" is true;[180] therefore, I know that this is A.' For[181] although I might know that that proposition was true (because I knew that only A was indicated by its subject and that the proposition signifies precisely in keeping with the combination of its terms), it does not follow that I would know that it signified that this is A. For just as this does not follow (as will become clear in the reply to the fifth argument) 'The proposition "This is a man" is in doubt for me; therefore, I am in doubt whether this is a man,' so also in the case under consideration this does not follow: 'The proposition "This is true" is known by me to be true; therefore, I know that this is true.' Nor does this follow: 'This proposition is known by me to be true; therefore, this proposition is known by me'; instead it is in doubt for me, and yet I know it to be true. And the reason [for this] is that even though I know that things are altogether as it signifies, and it signifies that this is A, or that this is true, still I do not know that it signifies that this is A, or that this is true.[182]

And if I am asked how it signifies to me since I know that it is true, I say[183] that it signifies to me that *this* is true, or that *this* is true, indicating A itself and its contradictory. Analogously, when Socrates or Plato are indicated[184] but in such a way that it is hidden from me whether Socrates is indicated or[185] Plato is indicated, although I know that only Socrates or Plato is indicated, then the proposition 'This is Socrates' signifies to me that *this* is Socrates (when Socrates is indicated[186]) or that *this* is Socrates (when Plato is indicated[187]). For[188] if I knew that that proposition[189] signified precisely that this is Socrates when Socrates is indicated,[190] then that proposition on that hypothesis I should not doubt but grant. And if I knew on that hypothesis that it signified that this is Socrates when Plato is indicated,[191] I should at once deny it. And so because I do not know precisely how it does signify on that hypothesis, I doubt it. And the situation is just the same in the case under consideration.

And if it is argued that this case and that one are not the same because on the hypothesis supposed I know that only *A* is indicated (as was posited and granted from the outset), the reply to this is that it was[192] never granted that I know which one is indicated, except because it was posited and follows from the hypothesis – not because it is true and irrelevant. But the truth of the matter is that it is false and follows. Similarly, that I know 'This is true' to be true when *A* is indicated[193] was granted not because of some argument explicitly drawn from the hypothesis but because it is possible in its own right and could be proved by adding several particulars compatible with that same hypothesis or one just like it. To that extent it follows explicitly that I might know the proposition 'This[194] is {15ra} *A*' or the proposition 'This is true' to be true, and know that it signifies in that way, and yet not know that this[195] is true, or that this is *A*, while continuously indicating the same thing as before – as things already said show clearly enough to be possible.

From this it follows, as was mentioned before, that there is a proposition that I know to be true, and yet it[196] is not known by me; instead, I know that it is in doubt for me.

And that that conclusion is possible is proved in the following way. Suppose it is posited that the proposition 'This is true' is interchangeable with the true one of these: 'A king is seated,' 'No king is seated,' and that you know that it is interchangeable with the true one of them.[197] In that case it is understood that you know that 'This is true' is true, and yet it is in doubt for you because you do indeed know that it signifies precisely as you doubt to be the case. Therefore,[198] you know it to be in doubt for you.

Similarly, suppose it is posited that the one of the two contradictories 'A king is seated' and 'No king is seated' that is now[199] true signifies that it is true and in addition signifies as it ordinarily does in general, and that you know that 'This is true' is interchangeable with the true one of them. In that case,[200] on the same basis as before,[201] you know 'This is true' to be true because you know that it is interchangeable with the true one.[202] Nevertheless, it is in doubt for you as before, because however it[203] primarily and principally signifies you doubt to be the case. Therefore that [proposition] you do not know. The consequence is evident, and the antecedent is taken explicitly from the hypothesis. The hypothesis is possible, however, because it is possible enough that you know the proposition '*A* is *B*' to be interchangeable with 'God[204] exists' or with '*A* man is a donkey'[205] even though you do not know with which one of them it is interchangeable. And it is just the same in the case under consideration. For that reason what was proposed before is granted as possible.

And on that basis it is apparent that one is not required to grant the antecedent of the second reduction[206] in the main argument – viz., this one, that every proposition that I know to be true I know. But because that antecedent is true and irrelevant for something supposed there, I grant it there.

And when it is argued further 'Every proposition that I know to be true I know, but I know proposition[207] *A* to be true; therefore, proposition *A* I know,' I deny the consequence. For although I know proposition *A* to be true, proposition *A* I do not know to be true. For although I know that proposition *A* is true,[208] the proposition that is *A* I do not know to be true, because neither of the propositions – '*A* king is seated,' 'No king is seated' – do I know to be true, and proposition *A* is one or the other[209] of them; and so proposition *A* I do not know to be true. So, just as neither of them do I know to be true (but I know that one or the other of them is true), just so proposition *A* I do not know to be true (but I know that proposition *A* is true).

And if on the basis of this one argues further that I know some proposition to be true that I do not know to be true (because I know proposition *A* to be true, which I do not know to be true), I grant the consequence and the consequent. For I know one of them to be true, and each of them I doubt to be true; therefore, I know some proposition to be true which I doubt to be true. Therefore, I know some proposition to be true that I do not know to be true.

And in that way the reply to the [second] reduction[210] is clear enough.

[Reply to Argument A3]

As for the third argument,[211] when it is argued that the same thing is known by me and in doubt for me, the reply is that it is not.

And, further, when it is posited that I know that this is this (indicating Socrates), and that I know that the proposition 'This is this' signifies precisely that this is this, and that it is hidden from me whether this is Socrates,[212] the reply is[213] that that hypothesis taken literally is not to be admitted, just as its second section is not to be admitted. For,[214] as was said in Chapter One, that[215] is not possible – viz., that the proposition 'This is this' signifies *precisely* that this is this; for if it signifies that this is this, it[216] signifies that this is, and that this is Socrates, and that this is a man.

For that reason, it is never admitted that any proposition signifies *precisely* that this or that is the case in such a way that the proposition signifies that this is the case and that it does not signify in any other way that it is [the case]. But, all the same, we ordinarily say that the proposition signifies precisely that this or that is the case because the proposition signifies in this way primarily and principally and does not signify[217] in any other way than [signifying] what follows from the fact[218] that that is the case. Thus in accordance with what we ordinarily say, these [claims] would be consistent: The proposition 'This is this' signifies precisely that this is this, and yet it signifies that this is Socrates. But because these [claims] are not consistent taken literally, {15rb} and the second follows from the first, I deny the first as impossible taken literally. And I grant that it is possible[219] that the proposition 'This is this' primarily and principally signifies precisely in this way, but by implication it signifies in another way.

And I reply in just the same way to the other [part of the hypothesis], when it is supposed that the proposition 'This is Socrates' signifies precisely that this is Socrates. For that is not possible in the way the words suggest, but it is possible that it signifies precisely[220] in this way primarily and principally.[221]

And then as for the further argument,[222] when it is argued that the proposition 'This is Socrates' is in doubt for me on that hypothesis, I grant it. And when it is argued that it is known by me because I know the case to be just as it precisely signifies primarily and principally, and just as primarily and principally I know it to signify,[223] the reply is to deny it. For it primarily and principally signifies that this is Socrates, and that this is the case I do not know.

And when it is argued that I do, because I know the proposition 'This is this' (Socrates having been indicated); and, therefore, however it signifies, that that is the case I know (or I know that that is the case, which is the same as far as I am concerned), and it signifies that this is Socrates; and, therefore, I know that to be the case – the reply is that the first consequence is not valid – viz., 'This proposition I know; therefore, however it signifies I know to be the case.' But this does follow: 'I know this proposition, and I know that it signifies in some way; therefore, however I know that it signifies I know to be the case.' And this follows, too:[224] 'I know this proposition, and I am considering whether things are altogether as it signifies; therefore, I know that things are altogether as it signifies'; and I grant that. And this does not follow further: 'I know that things are altogether as the proposition "This is this" signifies, and it signifies that this is Socrates; therefore, I know that this is Socrates.' For, as was said earlier, to conclude that conclusion one must take each of the premises in the compounded sense, or at least in a sense[225] interchangeable with the compounded sense. Thus, when one argues in this way – 'I know that things are altogether as it signifies, and I know that it signifies that this is Socrates; therefore, I know that this is Socrates' – the consequence is indeed valid. But on the hypotheses supposed the minor premise is false.

And so the argument works neither in the first way nor in this way.

[Reply to Argument A4]

In reply to the fourth argument, I admit all of it up to the claim that I know that the proposition 'This is Socrates' signifies precisely that this is Socrates or that this is Plato. I deny that. Nor does it signify in this way primarily and principally; instead, it primarily and principally signifies that this is Socrates. And this does not follow: 'It signifies primarily and principally that this is Socrates; therefore, it signifies primarily and principally that this is Socrates or that this is Plato'; rather, the opposite follows.

One[226] might argue against this in the following way: the disjunctive proposition 'This is Socrates or this is Plato' primarily and principally signifies precisely that this is Socrates or that this is Plato, and that simple proposition[227] is interchangeable with this disjunctive because the disjunctive follows formally from it and vice versa. For this follows: 'This is Socrates; therefore, this is Socrates or this is Plato.' And on the basis of what is in doubt for you this follows: 'This is Socrates or this is Plato; therefore, this is Socrates.' The consequence is argued in this way, since this follows: 'This is Socrates or this is Plato; therefore, this is,' and on the basis of what is in doubt for you this follows: 'This is; therefore, this is Socrates.' Therefore, on the basis of what is in doubt for you from the first one this follows: 'This is Socrates or this is Plato; therefore, this is Socrates.'

The reply to this is that things are interchanged in two different ways:[228] either broadly or strictly. Those things are said to be strictly interchangeable that imply each other formally through a single necessary middle: The two propositions 'A man is running' and[229] 'A risible thing is running' are interchangeable in that way, for they imply each other formally through the necessary middle 'If anything is a man, it is a risible thing' (and vice versa). The propositions 'This is' and 'This is Socrates' are also interchangeable in that way, since if this is, this is Socrates (and vice versa), and so on regarding such cases. Some things are said to be interchangeable broadly, however, in that they imply each other formally, but not through only one middle,[230] but through more than one middle. Thus the propositions 'God exists' and 'Something exists' can be said to be interchangeable in this way. For this follows formally: 'God exists; therefore, something exists'; and this also follows formally: 'Something exists; therefore, God exists,' because this follows formally: 'Something exists; therefore, either it is caused or it is something uncaused; and if it is caused, a cause in a [causal] series exists; and if a cause in a [causal] series exists, a first cause exists; and if a first cause exists, God exists; and[231] if it is something uncaused, God exists, since if it is something of that sort, it is God.' Therefore, this follows from the first one: 'If something exists, God exists'; and so[232] it follows that the two propositions[233] 'God exists' and 'Something exists' are interchangeable, using 'interchangeable' {15va} broadly.[234] But it is better to use the term 'interchangeable' strictly than to ampliate it to such a degree,[235] since it strikes the

hearer as absurd that the simple proposition 'God exists' is interchangeable with the disjunctive proposition 'Something exists, or a
stick is standing in the corner.'

Whether the locution is used in the first way or in the second
way, however, this consequence is not valid: 'These two propositions are interchangeable; therefore, in whatever way one of them
signifies primarily and principally, both of them signify primarily
and principally.' For the proposition 'A man is running' is interchangeable with the proposition 'A risible thing is running,' and 'A
man is running' primarily and principally signifies that a man is
running [and by implication that a risible thing is running], while
the other primarily and principally signifies that a risible thing is
running and by implication that a man is running.

And for that reason the argument introduced before does not
work.

[Reply to Argument A5]

In reply to the fifth argument, I admit all of it up to where it is
argued that I know the proposition 'This is a man'[236] or[237] I know it
to be false, and I deny that.

And as for the argument in which it is argued that that is the case
because I know what is indicated[238] and nothing do I doubt to be a
man, and so the thing indicated I know to be a man or that thing I
know not to be a man – the reply to that is to deny the consequence, since from that antecedent it does not follow that I am
considering whether that thing is a man or not. Even assuming that
I am considering it, it could be that I unhesitatingly[239] believe it to
be a man, and in that case if it is not a man I would not know it to
be a man, or doubt it to be a man, or know it not to be a man. And
so, if along with the earlier hypothesis it is supposed that I am
sufficiently considering whether it is a man or not, and that nothing
that is not a man do I unhesitatingly believe to be a man,[240] then I
do grant (as something following [from that amended hypothesis])
that that thing I know to be a man or that that thing I know not to
be a man.

I also deny the further consequence, in which it is argued 'This I
know to be a man, or this I know not to be a man, and I know
what is indicated by "this" and that the proposition "This is a man"

signifies primarily and principally in keeping with the combination of its terms; therefore, I know the proposition "This is a man"[241] or I know it to be false.' For from all the things supposed up to that point it does not follow that I know that the proposition 'This is a man' signifies that this is a man, because no matter what is indicated the following consequence is worthless: 'I know what is indicated by "this" in the proposition "This is a man";[242] therefore, I know that it signifies that this is a man.' And so, the main argument does not prove that conclusion, just as it does not [prove] the other thing – viz., that the proposition 'This is a man' is known by me and also in doubt for me – since from that hypothesis it follows neither that it is in doubt for me nor that it is known by me. But since it is true and[243] irrelevant that it is in doubt for me, I grant that; and I deny that it is known by me.

This may be argued against in the following way, however. If that proposition is in doubt for you, then you are in doubt whether things are altogether as it signifies; and it signifies that this is a man; therefore, you are in doubt whether this is a man. The consequent is contrary to the hypothesis.

I reply to this by denying each consequence. For this does not follow: 'You doubt this proposition; therefore, you are in doubt whether things are altogether as it signifies.' For it can be that I know that things are altogether as it signifies, and that I know it to be true (as was said above), and that it is nevertheless in doubt for me. This follows, however: 'It is in doubt for me; therefore, it signifies as I doubt things are, or I am in doubt whether things are altogether as it signifies.' And on the posited hypothesis I grant only the last part – viz., that I am in doubt whether things are altogether as it signifies.

I also deny the further consequence, in which it is argued 'I am in doubt whether things are altogether as it primarily and principally signifies, and it primarily and principally signifies that this is a man; therefore, I am in doubt whether this is a man.' For even though it does signify in that way, I do not know that it signifies in that way. And so, in connection with this hypothesis, I grant that the proposition 'This is a man' is in doubt for me, and I deny that it is in doubt for me whether this is a man (the same thing having been indicated). Instead, I know that this is a man or I know that this is not a man,[244] and whichever of those is proposed by itself in first place I reply to by saying 'I am in doubt about it.' Thus I am in doubt about the proposition 'I know that {15vb} this is a man,' likewise 'I know that this is not a man,' likewise 'I do not know that this is a man.'

And if it is argued on that basis that I am in doubt whether I know if this is a man, I reply that that is impossible. And if it is asked what I am in doubt about, I reply that I am in doubt regarding the proposition 'I know that this is a man' – not because I am in doubt whether I know if this is a man, but because I am in doubt about the way in which the proposition 'I know that this is a man' signifies.[245] Thus, in the absence of any hypothesis at all, if the proposition 'This is a man' has been proposed to me without having been made definite, I am in doubt about it, and I grant that it is in doubt for me. And when the proposition 'You are in doubt whether this is a man' is proposed thereafter, I am in doubt about it, and also about the proposition 'I know that this is a man,' and, in short, each such proposition I am in doubt about. Nevertheless, perhaps neither that proposition nor any of them signifies as I doubt things are, but as I know them to be or know them not to be; but [I am in doubt about it] because I do not know the way in which it signifies or that things are altogether as it signifies.

For that reason one should never reply by saying 'I am in doubt about it' in response to any proposition in the compounded sense with respect to any of the terms 'know,' 'not know,' 'doubt,' 'believe,' 'perceive,' 'want not,' 'want,' 'desire,' except in virtue of such a demonstrative term as 'this' or 'that' (and so on as regards such demonstrative terms), and even then very rarely. For [one] never [replies 'I am in doubt about it'] in virtue of any of them except when the truth of the matter is that one does not know[246] what such a demonstrative term signifies – and even then not always when one is in doubt about what that term signifies, but [only] when the simple demonstrative term supposits with respect to one or another understood term, not when it supposits with respect to an altogether ununderstood term. For example, assuming that you do not know what is indicated [by the demonstrative term], do not know anything to be A, and do not know anything not to be A, in that case 'You know that this is A' is not to be doubted, nor is 'You are in doubt whether this is A' or 'You know that this is not A.'[247]

But the reason one replies to the propositions 'You know that this is a man,' 'You are in doubt whether this is true,' 'You believe that this is impossible,' and the like by saying 'I am in doubt about it' when[248] the truth of the matter is that one does not know what[249] is indicated is[250] that when[251] the demonstrative term supposits[252] in respect of an understood term as regards many of its supposita, and one does not know whether it indicates what is known to be a man or what is known not to be a man or what is doubted to be a man, or what is known to be true or what is doubted to be impossible, in that case and for that reason such propositions as 'I know that this is a man,' 'I am in doubt whether this is a man,' and the like, are doubted. And yet when a term such as 'this' supposits in respect of an altogether ununderstood term such as 'A' (when nothing is known to be A nor is anything known not to be A), whatever may have been indicated, one knows at once that that is not known to be A or known not to be A. And for that reason the proposition 'You know that this is A' is not to be doubted, nor is 'You know that this is not A.' (And you may develop a reply[253] just like this one for cases just like these.)

Nevertheless, the preceding sophisma can be strengthened in this way. For the proposition 'This is a man' is proposed, and let it be posited that you know yourself to be a man and what is indicated by 'this,' and that you know also that that proposition signifies precisely that this is a man – that is, so that you know that it signifies in this way and it does not signify in any other way than [signifying] what follows from the fact that this is a man. Once that has been posited, when that proposition is proposed[254] it cannot be denied, since it may be one that follows; for this may follow:[255] 'You exist; therefore, this is a man.' Nor is it to be granted, because on the basis of what is in doubt for you it is impossible. And so if it is said to be in doubt for you, then one argues in this way. The proposition 'This is a man' is in doubt for you, and you know that it signifies precisely that this is a man; therefore, you are in doubt whether this is a man. Once that consequent has been granted, let the proposition 'You know that this is a man' be proposed, and[256] it would have to be doubted in connection with the things said before. Therefore, the propositions 'You know that this is a man' and 'You are in doubt whether this is a man' would stand together, because you grant the one and doubt the other.

I reply to this, and I say that when 'This is a man' is proposed, it is to be doubted – i.e., one must reply {16ra} to it by saying 'I am in doubt about it.' And, further, when it is accepted that that proposition is in doubt for me, I reply to that, too, by saying 'I am in doubt about it,' for I am in doubt whether it is incompatible with the hypothesis that that is in doubt for me. For if I am indicated, these propositions, signifying in that way, do not stand together: 'I know myself to be a man,' 'I know that the proposition "This is a man" signifies precisely that this is a man,' and 'That proposition is in doubt for me.' And so whenever 'This is a man' is proposed in connection with that hypothesis, I should reply to it by saying 'I am in doubt about it,' and also to 'That proposition is in doubt for me.' And to the other propositions[257] – 'I know that this is a man,' 'I am in doubt whether this is a man,' 'I know that this is not a man' – I should reply by saying 'I am in doubt about it,' exactly as in connection with the previous hypothesis. (And no absurdity directed against this follows.)

[Reply to Argument A6]

As for the sixth argument, when it is posited that *A, B,* and *C* are three propositions of which two – *A* and *B* – are known to me, whereas the third – *C* – is in doubt for me, and that it is hidden from me which of them is in doubt for me, I deny the hypothesis. For it is impossible that I should doubt any proposition that I doubt myself to doubt.

And as for the proof, when it is argued that that is the case, because it is possible that I know that one of these [men] is Socrates and I do not know which of them is Socrates, and so, by the same reasoning, it is possible that I know that one of these three propositions is in doubt for me and I am in doubt about which of them is in doubt for me, I reply to that by denying the consequence. For, in virtue of the fact that there is a proposition I am in doubt about and I am considering whether or not I am in doubt about it, I know[258] myself to be in doubt about it.

Thus, let it be posited that there are three propositions of which one is known by me to be necessary relative to this instant, another in doubt for me and contingent, and the third known by me to be impossible – e.g., these three: 'God exists,' 'The king is seated,' 'A chimera exists' – and that those three propositions are subsequently arranged in such a way that I do not know which of them is necessary, which is contingent, or which is impossible, although I do indeed know that one is necessary, another contingent, and the third impossible, and I am considering all of them at once. As long as that hypothesis is in effect, not only is 'The king is seated' in doubt for me, but each of them is in doubt for me. Nor am I in doubt about which of them is in doubt for me, even though I am in doubt about which of them is the contingent proposition 'The king is seated'; but the proposition that earlier I knew to be necessary will at that time be in doubt for me. And[259] just the same sort of thing is said[260] regarding propositions A, B, and C on the hypothesis supposed.

Someone may argue against this in the following way, however. For it is possible that you are in doubt about some proposition that you do not know you are in doubt about and that you do not [even] know to be a proposition, as happens in the case of a layman [who knows no Latin]. And in that case, then it is posited that you are considering whether the proposition doubted by you in that fashion is in doubt for you or not; and[261] you will not at once know it to be in doubt for you, in virtue of the fact that you still do not know it to be a proposition. For some time, therefore, you will be hesitant about whether[262] it is in doubt for you, and yet you will continuously be in doubt about it. Therefore, etc.

The reply to this[263] is that as soon as such a person considers[264] whether the proposition is in doubt for him,[265] if for that time he is in doubt[266] about it, he knows[267] it to be in doubt for himself.[268]

And if it is argued that that is not so, because a layman would not at once recognize what is a proposition, or what it is to be in doubt about a proposition, the reply is that immediately after he knows how to consider and to discriminate, he would know whether or not such a proposition was in doubt for him; but he might not know at once how to consider and to discriminate whether[269] or not the proposition was in doubt for him. And so this is not incompatible with the reply that was given.

And it must be noted, all the same, that if any proposition is in doubt for you that you know to be a proposition, and you are considering whether or not it is in doubt for you, that proposition you do know to be in doubt for you.

And that suffices for the negation of the hypothesis supposed in the main argument.

[Reply to Argument A7]

As for the seventh and last argument, in which it is argued that I know that this is Socrates and I am in doubt whether this is Socrates (the same thing having been indicated), the reply is that that is impossible and does not follow from the hypothesis supposed there. For this does not follow: 'I know that the man I saw yesterday is Socrates, and no one did I see yesterday except that {16rb} man; therefore, I know that that man is Socrates,' because even though no one did I see yesterday except that man, I do not know it but may perhaps believe that that is so.[270]

And if it is asked why in that case I granted the proposition 'This is Socrates' (the one I saw yesterday having been indicated), since it does not follow that I know that this is Socrates even though I know that the one I saw yesterday is Socrates, the reply is that I do not grant that as known, but as following. For this follows: 'The one I saw yesterday is Socrates, and no one did I see yesterday except him; therefore, he is Socrates.' Suppose, for example, that this is Socrates and that that is hidden from me. In that case I would grant that this is Socrates not because I know that this is Socrates (since that is incompatible with the hypothesis), but because it follows that this is Socrates. And it is just the same in the case under consideration.

And suppose that it is argued that it does not follow from the hypothesis that this is Socrates, because nothing is supposed in it except that Socrates is indicated, and it does not follow from that that this is Socrates. For 'therefore, this is Socrates' does not follow when Socrates has been indicated[271] only by the pronoun 'this,' since these stand together: 'Socrates alone is indicated, and yet this is a donkey.' It is in that connection that the following sophismata work: 'Every man who is white is running, and each of them is seated (all white men having been indicated)'; 'This is Socrates (someone other than Socrates having been indicated[272])'; 'This is false (and I am indicating only a proposition just like "This is false")'; and so on regarding others[273] of that sort, all of which are based on the fact that this sort of consequence is not valid: 'Only such-and-such is indicated; therefore, this is such-and-such (anything at all having been indicated).'

The reply to this is to grant[274] that this consequence is not valid taken literally: 'I am indicating a white man; therefore, this man is[275] white (anything at all having been indicated).' But it would be[276] too shameless to raise a counterinstance in any such case except where an argument requires a counterinstance of that sort. And although[277] such a proposition as 'This is white' is granted when it is said that[278] a white thing is indicated, it is not granted as following from the proposition 'A white thing is indicated,' but because by that proposition it is made definite that this is white, at least as far as ordinary understanding is concerned, even though not literally. Analogously, in connection with the given hypothesis this does indeed follow: 'I am indicating Socrates; therefore, this is Socrates,' since this follows: 'I am indicating Socrates; therefore, Socrates exists,' and this follows: 'Socrates exists; therefore, this is Socrates,' for that something other than what now[279] is Socrates could[280] be Socrates is no less false than that Socrates can be a donkey. And so that counterinstance proves nothing, just as the hypothesis and the main argument prove nothing.

The way one has replied before in connection with the hypotheses that have been set forth is also the way one must reply, in accordance with the very same principles, in connection with any hypotheses at all, which can be infinitely varied depending upon the opponent's wishes.

[Objections to the Reply to Argument A1]

Nevertheless, someone may argue[281] in the following way against one thing that was said above: If the compounded sense followed from the divided sense where the subject is a simple demonstrative pronoun – as when one argues 'This I doubt to be true; therefore, I doubt whether this is true' – on the same reasoning this would follow: 'These I believe to be true; therefore, I believe that these are true' [or] 'These some men believe to be true; therefore, some men believe these to be true.' But one argues that that is not the case. For let it be posited that there are two propositions each of which you believe to be true, but you believe that they are three propositions and that the third of them is false. In that case those two you believe to be true, because each of them you believe to be true; but you do not believe that those two are true, because you do not believe that they are two[282] or that they are true.[283]

For a second [objection], let it be posited that only one proposition and no more does Socrates believe to be true, and one other proposition and no more does Plato believe to be true. In that case, let the two propositions believed by Socrates and by Plato be picked out, and it follows that they are believed by those men to be true, and yet those men do not believe that they are true. Therefore, etc.

[Rejoinders to the Objections]

Here is the reply[284] to these [objections], and first to the first. And the consequence 'These I believe to be true; therefore, I believe that these are true' is granted,[285] whatever may have been indicated. And as for the hypothesis supposed,[286] it is said to be possible enough, for that same thing happens almost universally when someone believes himself to believe something false. For everything believed by him he believes to be true, but he does not believe that everything believed by him is true; instead, [he believes] that some [of it] is false. And he does not believe all things {16va} believed by him to be true, nor all things believed by him does he believe to be true, taking the term 'all things' collectively. Thus, this does not follow: 'Each of these Socrates believes to be true; therefore, these Socrates believes to be true.' Nor does this follow: 'Each of these Socrates believes to be true; therefore, he believes each of these to be true.' And so, it is evident that in connection with the hypothesis supposed this consequence is not valid: 'Each of those two I believe to be true; therefore, those two I believe to be true.' Thus, in connection with that hypothesis those [propositions] I neither believe to be true nor [believe to be] false; rather, those [propositions] I believe not to be true.

As for the second [objection], when it is argued that those are believed by some men to be true and it is not believed that those are true, the reply[287] is that that conjunctive proposition is impossible[288] and does not follow from the hypothesis supposed there. For the consequence is not valid: 'Socrates believes this proposition to be true, and Plato believes that[289] proposition to be true; therefore, Socrates and Plato believe the propositions to be true.' Nor does it follow that those propositions Socrates and Plato believe to be true, because that is the same as the one before.

But if someone argues that it does follow, because this follows: 'Socrates believes that, and Plato believes that; therefore, Socrates and Plato believe those', and so, by the same reasoning, this follows: 'Socrates believes this[290] to be true, and Plato believes[291] that to be true; therefore, those Socrates and Plato believe to be true,' I say that it does not follow. And the reason for the difference is that the antecedent 'Socrates believes this[292] to be true' denotes a composition that the proposition 'Socrates believes this proposition' does not denote. Thus, this follows:[293] 'If[294] Socrates and Plato believe these propositions to be true, then each of those men believes them to be true,' for this follows: 'Socrates and Plato believe them to be true; therefore, they believe it to be the case that they are true; therefore, each of them believes it to be the case.' For otherwise it would follow that it would be possible that Socrates and Plato would know that the situation is of some sort and yet neither of them would know it to be of this sort. And then it could be that Socrates and Plato would know some one simple proposition, such as the proposition 'These are true,' and neither of them would know it. And so it would follow that they would know some[295] proposition about which they would be in doubt. For if each of them is in doubt about the proposition, it follows that they both are in doubt about it. And that is impossible; therefore, so is the antecedent from which that follows, or anything that is antecedent to that antecedent.

Thus it is granted that there are many propositions each of which is known and believed to be true even though no[296] propositions are believed to be true, and that many men know many propositions of which, or of any of which, they cannot know them to be in reality.

And so it is sufficiently apparent that that objection does not succeed, and that the other one does not yield a conclusion.

[Concluding Remark]

It is especially advantageous in this subject matter for the respondent to attend not only to the content but also to attend carefully to the words of the hypothesis posited and to their order, and that he should examine with care the difference (which he readily recognizes) between[297] the compounded sense and the divided, and that he reply on the basis of a hypothesis to no irrelevant proposition otherwise than he would reply to it in the absence of a hypothesis.

The material of the second chapter may be developed in that way, then. And now follows the third, which is to be passed through more briefly than the others.[298]

Emendations

[We have emended the text of the Venice edition of 1494 by drawing on variants found in six of the manuscripts. Each emendation listed here is drawn from at least one of the manuscripts, and most are drawn from a majority of the manuscripts. Readings dependent on three or fewer manuscripts are followed by '*'. Each emendation is preceded by the reading in Venice 1494.]

1. dicatur] sumatur
2. quam ille nescit esse veram nec scit esse falsam] quae non est scita esse vera ab isto nec scita esse falsa
3. esse veram et necessariam] esse necessariam
4. esse falsam et impossibilem] esse impossibilem
5. eidem dubia] tibi dubia
6. et cum hoc totus] et totus
7. quod sit] quod *A* sit
8. sic tu] sic quia tu
9. te item] te ut prius item
10. item posito quod scias] item scias
11. scias an hoc] scias quod hoc
12. quod probo] probatio*
13. illa significat] illa praecise significat
14. vel hoc] vel quod hoc
15. disiunctivae ad totam disiunctivam] disiunctivae ad totum disiunctum vel ad totam disiunctivam
16. scias aliquid] aliquid scias
17. per subiectum illius propositionis hoc est homo, et aliquid scis esse hominem] *om.*

18. scis illud] illud vel scis
19. istam propositionem esse] istam esse
20. te per casum et] te et
21. dubium probo quia] dubium quia
22. quia demonstrato *A* in casu isto dubitas an illud sit tibi dubium] *om.*
23. demonstrato illo quem heri vidisti] *om.*
24. respondetur] respondeo
25. aliquam propositionem esse scitam et eandem esse dubiam] *om.*
26. animae] intellectus
27. vel impossibile esse vel non esse] *om.*
28. multis] terminis qui similes sunt eisdem
29. his] huiusmodi
30. est hominem] est omnem hominem
31. et hominem] et omnem hominem
32. istorum terminorum] istorum dictorum terminorum
33. vel aliqua] vel saltem aliqua
34. accepti] recitati
35. veram aliqui] veram dubito aliqui
36. competenter] satis proprie
37. propositio dicta accepta] propositio accepta
38. autem] igitur
39. et istius propositionis] et dictum huius propositionis
40. albus hominem] albus est haec oratio hominem
41. et sic de aliis] secundum eosdem et ego intelligo istud de praesenti
42. expressius] expresse
43. per quatuor annos praeteritos] viginti annis elapsis
44. quod esset] quod iam esset
45. conclusionem] talem propositionem
46. consequentia non valet huiusmodi] non valet huiusmodi argumentum
47. concludendum argumentum istud] concludendam istam
48. vel in] vel saltem in
49. ista] talis*
50. istum] sacerdotem
51. sacerdotem] istum
52. multis aliis] aliis huiusmodi
53. actum voluntatis] voluntatem
54. in casu] *om.*
55. quod tamen scit] quod scit
56. similiter tu] similiter sequitur tu
57. et hoc] et quod hoc
58. quia unum] quia dubito an unum*
59. potest esse] sit
60. et quod *A*] quod
61. oportet] oportet addere
62. istum] huiusmodi

63. ponere] *om.*
64. talis] iste
65. arguendi] arguendi cum illis terminis praedictis
66. quod valeat] quod generaliter valeat
67. his] huiusmodi
68. convertuntur sensus compositus et divisus] convertitur sensus compositus cum sensu diviso
69. ad primum] primo ad primum
70. suppositio bene est] suppositio est
71. non tamen est necessaria neque universaliter vera] *om.*
72. sequitur tamen] sed non sequitur
73. illa sit] illa propositio sit
74. et nec] nec
75. tamen] et ideo
76. nescire] nescirem/nec scirem/non scirem*
77. quod] an
78. de scire] *om.*
79. communiter] *om.*
80. sciuntur contingentia] sciuntur huiusmodi contingentia
81. contingentia] contingentia et sensibilia accidentalia
82. isto] *om.*
83. quod probatur] *om.*
84. et si sic] et sic
85. tu scias regem esse Londonis et quod dubitas] tu dubitas
86. et] *om.*
87. Londonis sequitur] Londonis et sequitur
88. percipis absque] percipis certitudinaliter absque
89. quod est] quod rex est
90. conceditur] concedo*
91. tunc] *om.*
92. et] *om.*
93. tibi] *om.*
94. vel] et
95. quamvis una] quamvis enim una
96. enim] *om.*
97. propositionem] *om.*
98. quod *A* propositio sit illa Deus est] quod ego sciam *A* propositionem cum casu
99. dico tamen tunc quod sequitur] dico quod sequitur tunc
100. hoc quod] hoc quod sequitur quod
101. sensus] *om.*
102. et nullum] et tamen nullum*
103. et non] et *A* non*
104. valet] tenet
105. unde] sed
106. *A* esse] *A* scio esse

107. scio A] A scio
108. tamen] *om.*
109. ab A] ab ipso A*
110. negatur consequentia] nego consequentiam
111. et quod] et etiam quod
112. ulterius] *om.*
113. accipitur sensu] accipitur in sensu
114. sit] *om.*
115. alia] *om.*
116. quod sit] quod A sit
117. verum A] verum sive A
118. eandem primo] eandem propositionem primo
119. scilicet] *om.*
120. aliquis] alius*
121. et tunc clausa est ianua contra primum] *om.*
122. ex quo respondens] ex quo sic respondens/ex quo respondens sic
123. sic] ipse
124. consequenter arguendo quod] quod consequenter arguendo
125. est] esse
126. determinat terminus] determinat talis terminus
127. alio] *om.*
128. ego] ego ipse
129. scilicet de isto termino] *om.*
130. omnino ignotus] *om.*
131. a te] *om.*
132. a me] *om.*
133. talis terminus est de se notus] illi termini sunt de se noti
134. dubium] tibi dubium
135. scitum] scitum a te
136. alio] aliquo*
137. ista propositio est] ista est
138. consideraret aliquis] considerares
139. nesciret] nescires
140. esse sciret] *om.*
141. sciret] scires
142. sciret] scires
143. sciret] scires
144. intelligeret] intelligeres
145. sciret] scires
146. hebraica sed] hebraica vel gallica sed
147. termini non] termini praedicti non
148. similiter nec aliquis dubitat hoc esse hoc] nec aliquid dubitas esse hoc
149. illud est] *om.*
150. alio] aliquo
151. econtrario] econtra
152. verbo fiant tales] verbo hoc fiat istae

153. compositus] divisus
154. diviso] composito
155. scio hoc esse] scio quod hoc est
156. scio hoc esse Socratem] scio quod hoc est Socrates
157. similiter] *om.*
158. et sic de multis] *om.*
159. etiam] *om.**
160. sicut] *om.*
161. composito aliquae] composito et aliquae
162. Socrates] *om.*
163. ab initio non erat sermo] non erat locutio ab initio
164. homo] non
165. convertibilis palam] palam convertibilis
166. tamen] enim
167. praedicato illud bene] praedicato illo ibidem bene
168. iam dicto] primo
169. principale] *om.*
170. admittendo] et admitto
171. verum concedo] verum et concedo
172. bona et scita] bona scita
173. sequitur si] sequitur quod si
174. in] ex
175. sequitur si] sequitur quod si
176. concedo illam] concedo consequentiam illam
177. scilicet scio] scilicet quod scio
178. quod non] quod hoc non
179. hoc] immo
180. propositio] *om.*
181. non] enim*
182. quocumque demonstrato] *om.*
183. dicendum] dico
184. demonstrato Socrate et Platone] demonstrando Socratem et Platonem
185. et] vel*
186. demonstrato Socrate] demonstrando Socratem
187. demonstrato Platone] demonstrando Platonem
188. tamen] enim
189. illa praecise] illa propositio praecise
190. demonstrato Socrate] demonstrando Socratem*
191. demonstrato Platone] demonstrando Platonem
192. est] erat
193. demonstrato] demonstrando
194. hoc esse est] hoc est
195. nescirem est] nescirem quod hoc est
196. propositio] *om.*
197. et lateat te quid illorum sit verum isto posito] *om.*
198. sequitur quod tu] *om.*

199. quae est] quae iam est
200. notum est] *om.*
201. quod] *om.*
202. istorum] *om.*
203. propositio] *om.*
204. Socrates] Deus
205. est quamvis] est asinus quamvis*
206. deductionis] reductionis
207. porpositionem] propositionem
208. est propositio] propositio est
209. aliqua] altera
210. deductione] reductione
211. tertium cum] tertium argumentum cum
212. demonstrato Socrate] *om.*
213. dico] dicitur
214. sicut superius] sicut enim superius
215. enim] *om.*
216. etiam] *om.*
217. aliter quam] aliter significat quam
218. sequitur ipsam significantem quod] sequitur ad hoc quod
219. hoc] *om.*
220. illa sic] illa praecise sic
221. quod hoc est Socrates] *om.*
222. argumenta] argumentum
223. principaliter huic] principaliter et sic illum primo et principaliter scio significare
224. sequitur scio] sequitur etiam scio
225. vel convertibili] vel saltem in sensu convertibili
226. sed] *om.*
227. scilicet hoc est Socrates] *om.*
228. converti dupliciter dicuntur] converti est dupliciter
229. currit risibile] currit et risibile
230. necessarium] *om.*
231. etiam] et
232. si] *om.*
233. illa] ista duo
234. debet] de
235. proprie quam improprie] proprie quam tantum ampliare ipsum
236. esse veram] *om.*
237. quod] *om.*
238. per subiectum istius hoc est homo et aliquid scio esse hominem] *om.*
239. libere et] *om.*
240. non hominem nec aliud quod non est homo credam esse] *om.*
241. esse veram] *om.*
242. et scio istam significare praecise iuxta compositionem terminorum] *om.*

243. verum impertinens] verum et impertinens
244. est non] non est
245. quia nescio qualiter illa significat nec scio quod ita est totaliter sicut illa significat] *om.*
246. nescio] nescitur
247. tamen in conclusione respondetur dubitando ad istas propositiones tu scis quod hoc est hoc] *om.*
248. talibus est cum] talibus cum
249. quid in rei veritate] in rei veritate quid
250. demonstratus quia] demonstratur est quia
251. ibi] cum
252. supponitur] supponit
253. rationem] responsionem
254. propositio quia] propositio proposita quia
255. ex casu] *om.*
256. tunc similiter] et
257. consimiles istis] *om.*
258. statim] *om.*
259. dubia consimiliter] dubia et consimiliter
260. dico] dicitur
261. tunc] *om.*
262. non quod] numquid*
263. hic] huic
264. consideres an talis] consideret talis an ista
265. tibi] sibi
266. dubites] dubitet
267. tu scis] ipse scit
268. tibi] sibi
269. ideo non statim sciret] *om.*
270. Plato] *om.*
271. demonstro Socratem] demonstrato Socrate
272. et solum demonstratur alius] demonstrato alio
273. omnibus] *om.*
274. dicitur quod] dicitur concedendo quod
275. est homo] homo est
276. esse] esset
277. et conceditur] et cum conceditur
278. quando demonstratur] quando dicitur quod demonstratur
279. aliquid quod non] aliud quam nunc
280. possit] posset
281. arguit fortiter unus] arguitur forte aliquis
282. verae] *om.*
283. nec quod sint falsae] *om.*
284. respondeo] respondetur
285. concedo illam consequentiam] conceditur illa consequentia
286. casum dicitur] casum suppositum dicitur

287. hic] huic
288. illud totum est impossibile] illa copulativa est impossibilis
289. hanc] illam
290. illam] hanc
291. Plato illam] Plato credit illam*
292. propositionem] *om.*
293. bene] *om.*
294. sequitur Socrates] sequitur si Socrates
295. unam] *om.*
296. non illae] nullae
297. diligenter attendat et examinet diversitatem quae discernat velociter inter] diligenter examinet velociter quem distinguat inter
298. residuum] residua

BOETHIUS OF DACIA
THE SOPHISMA 'EVERY MAN IS OF NECESSITY AN ANIMAL'

Introduction

Not much is known about Boethius of Dacia beyond the facts that he was a Dane who was a master of arts in Paris around 1270 and that he was one of the main proponents of the Latin Averroism or Radical Aristotelianism condemned in the Condemnation of 1277. His works include treatises on the highest good, on dreams, and on the eternity of the world, a treatise on speculative grammar, and various treatises on natural philosophy, besides his books on logic.

The sophisma in the selection translated below develops out of the sentence 'Every man is of necessity an animal.' Boethius raises four questions more or less closely associated with it: (1) is it true when no man exists? (2) is knowledge destroyed when the things known are destroyed? (3) does a term lose its connection with what it signifies when its significata are destroyed? and (4) is the nature of a genus in its species something actual other than the final differentia of the species?

In dealing with the first question, Boethius presents a number of arguments to show that the proposition 'Every man is an animal' is necessarily true and therefore also true when no men exist. On the negative side of the sophisma, Boethius gives an analysis of truth as composition in discourse that reflects composition in reality; when man and animal are not compounded in reality, the proposition 'Every man is an animal' is not true either. After the initial round of arguments on either side, the bachelor (who may be thought of as a graduate student working with Boethius) presents his own position, that the sophisma sentence is true. Arguments against the bachelor's view are followed by Boethius's own determination of the question. He holds that the sophisma sentence is false, because eternal (i.e., necessary) truth has to be caused by things that are themselves necessary and indestructible. His replies to arguments on the other side include some interesting discussions of the nature of necessity and of truth.

The arguments concerning the second question have to do with the nature of knowledge. The bachelor's position is that knowledge is destroyed when what was known is destroyed because knowledge involves truth and truth depends on the composition in reality that corresponds to that truth. Boethius determines the question by saying that knowledge is not destroyed when the things known are destroyed if the things known have causes and principles on the basis of which they can be known. He goes on to discuss the kind of knowledge we have of a thing when we know it in its causes and principles.

As for the third question, Boethius holds that an utterance can signify even when its significata have been destroyed, because utterances, like thoughts, are independent of the existence of their objects. Just as we can have a thought of Socrates even though Socrates no longer exists, so the utterance 'Socrates' can signify after Socrates is destroyed; it signifies not what Socrates is, but rather what he was. (There is no record of the bachelor's position on the third question.)

The issue in the fourth question is whether there is one thing in whiteness, for example, that is responsible for its being the color white and another that is responsible for its being a color. That is, is the genus (color) of something (the color whiteness) something actually distinct from that thing's final differentia (whiteness), the characteristic that differentiates it from other species within the same genus? Here the bachelor and Boethius come to the same conclusion: The genus is not something actually distinct from the final differentia. In Boethius's view there is only one substantial form in Socrates, for example, and that form is both the form of human being and the form of animal, so that one and the same substantial form is responsible for Socrates's being animal and for Socrates's being human.

For further reading on the relationship of propositions to extralinguistic reality, see CHLMP IV.10, 'The Semantics of Propositions'; the epistemology of the Modists, a group to which Boethius belongs, is discussed in CHLMP VI.23, 'Intentions and Impositions'; and the general metaphysical issue of Question 4 in this selection is considered in CHLMP VI.20, 'Universals in the Early Fourteenth Century.'

The Sophisma 'Every Man Is of Necessity an Animal'

EVERY MAN IS OF NECESSITY AN ANIMAL.

Four questions are raised regarding this sophisma. The first has to do with its truth: Is it true when no man exists? Second: When the real things [the first proposition is about] have been destroyed, must the knowledge anyone had of those things be destroyed? Third: When those real things have been destroyed, must the term lose its connection with what it signifies? Fourth: When a genus is predicated of a species, is the nature of the genus existent in the species something actually existing other than the final differentia of the species?

First Question

Is 'Every man is of necessity an animal' true when no man exists?

[The Disputation]

As for the first, one argues as follows that the proposition is true [when no man exists].

[The Affirmative Arguments]

[A1] As Aristotle indicates in *Posterior Analytics* I (4, 73b16–18), being *per se* and being necessary are the same. But the proposition is *per se*, for any part of a definition is predicated of what is defined in the same way as the definition is predicated of what is defined. Therefore, this proposition is necessary. Therefore, it is true (by the Topic *from a species to the genus*).

[A2] The same conclusion is argued for as follows: By a syllogism based on opposed propositions, every animal is a substance, some man is not a substance; therefore, some man is not an animal. But, according to Aristotle in *Prior Analytics* II (5, 64b7–10), the conclusion of a syllogism based on opposed propositions is not possible (since, as is said there, it is contrary to fact). Therefore, 'Some man is not an animal' is impossible. Therefore, its contradictory – 'Every man is an animal' – is necessary. Therefore, this proposition is true when no man exists.

[A3] The proposition 'Every man is an animal' is either necessary or not. If it is necessary, I have what I am aiming at. If it is not necessary, it can be false. But if 'A man is an animal' were false, 'A man is a man' could be false. (The reason for this is that if a consequent is falsely stated of anything, any antecedent [of that consequent] is falsely stated of the same thing.) But if 'A man is a man' can be false, then 'A man is not a man' or 'A man is a non-man' can be true. But that is impossible, because in those propositions one opposite is stated of the other opposite. Therefore, 'A man {1–2} is a non-man' cannot be true. Therefore, neither can 'A man is a man' be false; and so it is necessary. And if a man is of necessity a man, he is of necessity an animal. Therefore, the first proposition is true.

[A4] In *Topics* IV (2, 123a15–18), Aristotle says that if anything is put forward as the genus of something, we have to consider whether the species to which that genus is assigned can lose that genus, since if the species can lose what is assigned as a genus, then what is assigned is not a genus. But *animal* is the genus of *man*. Therefore, the subject 'man' cannot lose the predicate 'animal.' Therefore, the first proposition is necessary, because that is what it signifies.

One argues to the opposing conclusion in the following way.

[The Negative Arguments]

[N1] We encounter three sorts of composition: the composition that is in reality itself, the composition that is in thought, and the composition that is in discourse. [These three sorts of composition are ordered] in such a way that in every case the truth that is in a subsequent composition comes from the truth of the prior composition as from its cause. For who can produce true composition in discourse unless in his thought there is a true composition from which the composition belonging to the discourse comes? And how will the composition in his thought be true unless there is a composition just like it in reality? For if there is division in reality and composition in his thought, the composition belonging to the thought will be false.

On that basis one argues as follows. The composition in thought is related to the composition in reality as the composition in discourse is related to the composition in thought. But the composition in discourse cannot be true unless there is a true composition in thought from which it comes. Therefore, neither can there be a true composition in thought unless there is such a composition in reality. But when no man exists, *animal* is not compounded with *man*. Therefore, neither thought nor discourse that compounds *animal* with *man* can be true when the composition that occurs in reality is lacking, because that composition is the basis and the cause of each subsequent truth – i.e., [the truth] of thought and of discourse.

And on that basis it is clear that some people – saving their peace – said less than is necessary when they said that once every man has been destroyed and every animal has been destroyed, the terms ['animal' and 'man'] signify the same as they signified before, even though *man* and *animal* are not what they were. For that reason, they say, the proposition is true.

But that is not the cause of truth; {1–3} for Aristotle, in explaining which statement is true and which is false (*Categories* 5, 4b8–10), says that an expression is called true (or false) because the reality is (or is not), and not because the terms signify the same. Therefore, that is not the cause of truth.

[N2] Necessity is truth nailed down (*veritas fixa*). But we do not find truth nailed down in any transmutable thing insofar as it is transmutable. Therefore, neither [do we find] its necessity [in such circumstances]. But *man* and *animal* are transmutable things because they are material things, and the matter in anything is that by which the thing can both be and not be (considered in connection with privation), as is said in *Metaphysics* VII (7, 1032a20–22). Therefore, as before, the first proposition is false.

[The Bachelor's Reply]

[The Bachelor's Position]

The reply to the question is that the proposition is true.

The reason for this is that being and not being are accidental to a thing, and so the essence of man remains always, whether or not there is a man. Therefore, since *man* and *animal* make a proposition of this sort true by their essence and not by the accident of their being or not being, the expression will be true whether or not there is a man (and likewise as regards an animal).

And so it seems we can offer an analogy. Socrates makes the locution 'Socrates is a substance' true by his essence, not by the accident that is his whiteness; and so when that accident has been removed, the expression will still be true.

The arguments are replied to as follows.

[The Bachelor's Rejoinders to the Negative Arguments]

[N1r] When the argument says that there are three sorts of composition – of things signified in discourse, of thoughts in the soul, and a third composition of real things – the Bachelor granted it. And he also said that the composition belonging to discourse is not true unless the composition belonging to thought is true. But – so he said – there need not be a similar composition in reality in order for the composition belonging to thought to be true.

[N2r] He replied to the second argument in this way: When the argument said that necessity is truth nailed down, he granted it. He also granted that nothing is nailed down in transmutable things insofar as they are transmutable. *Man* and *animal*, he said, are transmutable as regards being and not being, which he said {1–4} are accidents of theirs, but untransmutable as regards their essences, in virtue of which they make the expression true. And it is for that reason that it is a necessity and a nailed-down truth that a man is an animal.

[Against the Bachelor's Reply]

[Arguments Against the Bachelor's Position]

The [Bachelor's] position is argued against as follows:

When it is said that *man* and *animal* make the locution true in virtue of their essences after they have been destroyed – on the contrary: The essence of man exists after his destruction no more than it existed before his generation, but the essence of man before his generation was nothing except in the passive potentiality of matter and the active potentiality of an agent, like every [other] material form. Therefore, just as *man* and *animal* did not make the expression 'A man is an animal' true in virtue of their essences before their generation, when their essence was nothing, neither will they make it true after they have been destroyed.

As for his claim that being is accidental to essence, one argues as follows. It is either a separable or an inseparable accident. If it is a separable accident, then the being ((*esse/essentia*)) of a man can be removed from the man while he exists, in which case he can be and not be at the same time – which is impossible. But if it is an inseparable accident, then when a man is destroyed as regards his being he will be destroyed as regards his essence – which is the contrary of what he said.

Again, if being is a thing added to essence, then a simple essence, to which no accident and no real thing is added, would not have being – e.g., God and the Intelligences – which is impossible. For the being of eternal things is the cause of things that can be generated, as is said in *Metaphysics* VII (cf. XII 6, 1071b3–1072a18) and II (1, 993b27–30) and in the *Liber de causis*.

One argues against [the Bachelor's] resolution of the [negative] arguments as follows.

[Arguments Against the Bachelor's Rejoinders]

[N1rR] When he says that a true composition belonging to thought does not require a similar composition in reality – on the contrary: If something is not of necessity required by a thing in reality, then the opposite [of that which is not required] is compatible with that thing. {1–5} Therefore, if a true composition in thought does not require a similar composition in reality, a division in reality is compatible with that composition in thought. Therefore, a composition belonging to thought can be true when it compounds things that are divided in reality – e.g., *man* and *donkey* – which is impossible.

[N2rR] One argues against his resolution of the second argument as follows: If the essence of man and the essence of animal were to remain when every man and every animal had been destroyed, they would remain either in the matter or in the form. Not in the matter, since when a man has been destroyed, the matter of the man is under an opposing form; for the destruction of one thing is the generation of another. Therefore, if the same matter would at that same time be the essence of man, then opposites would be in the same thing [at the same time]. Nor would *man* be destroyed, even after his destruction, since the essence of man existing in the matter would constitute *man*.

Nor [would they remain] in the soul, since for the essence of natural things to make expressions true, it is not enough that the essence be in the soul; it must be in matter. Otherwise, if one were to conceive in one's soul of Socrates and of a white thing, it would be true that the one was compounded with the other even if in reality the situation were the opposite. And, furthermore, when every animal has been destroyed and every man has been destroyed, there is no soul in which the essence of man could remain. Even though the intellect can be separated from the body, when separated it is not the soul. For according to Aristotle in *De anima* II (1, 412a19–b6), the soul is the actualizing of a natural organic body that has life potentially; and according to Al–farabi [in his commentary] on the *Liber de causis* (iii.35, Pattin p. 53), vivifying the body is a distinguishing characteristic of the soul.

[The Determination of the Question]

[An Alternate Reply along with its Refutation]

Once those things have been disproved in that way, some people reply differently to the question, maintaining that the first proposition is true. Their reason is that a man can neither be nor be thought unless he is and is thought to be an animal.

All the same, since it is not necessary that a man be or that a man be thought, that reason is unsatisfactory even though it is impossible that a man be or be thought without being or being thought to be an animal.

[The Master's Reply]

Instead, we have to say that 'Every man is of necessity an animal' is false, whether or not a man exists. For according to {1–6} Aristotle in *Metaphysics* IX (10, 1051a34–1052a11), as truth is caused by reality, so eternal truth is caused by eternal things and untransmutable truth by untransmutable things, which are always in one [and the same] disposition. But truth that is transmutable and not necessary is caused by real things that are not necessary and can be destroyed. Therefore, since *man* and *animal* are transmutable real things that can be destroyed, and nothing in them is indestructible except for prime matter (which is thoroughly indestructible, as is proved in the *Physics* [I 9, 192a28–29]), and the proposition' 'Man is of necessity an animal' is not made true on the basis of prime matter, it follows that no untransmutable or even necessary truth is caused by the real things *man* and *animal*.

Again, a man is an animal because the matter that belongs to the man has been transmuted [to conform] to the form of animal. As a fire is fire because the matter that belongs to the fire has been transmuted [to conform] to the form of fire, so a man is an animal because the matter that belongs to the man has been transmuted [to conform] to the form of animal. In this way, therefore, when the transmutable matter is free from every form it can be transmuted [to conform] to, the man will be a non-animal because the matter that belongs to the man has been transmuted from the form of animal. But that is not necessarily an animal, because it is a non-animal. Therefore, etc.

Again, everything that can be destroyed as regards its substantial form and as regards every one of its dispositions can be destroyed as regards every predicate inhering in it essentially or accidentally. A man can be destroyed as regards his substantial form and every one of his dispositions. Therefore, he can be destroyed as regards every predicate inhering in him. Therefore, no predicate inheres in him necessarily. Therefore, the first proposition is false.

Let no one object to my saying that a man can be destroyed as regards his substantial form. For even though the intellect is an eternal substance, it is not an eternal form, since it does not always inform Socrates's matter. But if the intellect is not a form, there is no basis for an objection.

I grant the arguments proving that the first proposition is false. {1–7} To the arguments on the other side I reply as follows.

[The Master's Rejoinders to the Affirmative Arguments]

[A1R] When the argument says that being necessary and being *per se* are the same, and that the proposition, 'A man is an animal' is *per se* and therefore necessary, we have to reply in the following way: As contingent inherence is inherence whose predicate can be varied with respect to the subject while the subject remains [in existence], so necessary inherence is inherence whose predicate cannot be varied with respect to the subject while the subject remains [in existence]. And it is that sort of being necessary and being *per se* that are the same. For such a predicate has its cause in the subject while the subject remains [in existence]; but when the subject has been destroyed, the predicate does not have its cause in the subject, since the cause on the basis of which the subject made the expression true was the essence of the subject. But when *man* has been destroyed, there is no more essence of man than there was before the generation of *man*, which was the essence of man in potentiality only. And so, when *man* has been destroyed, the proposition is neither necessary, nor *per se*, nor true.

In another way, that is called necessary whose nature is such that it is, is not in any other way, and cannot be in any other way. And what is necessary in that way is found among entities that do not have in themselves principles of transmutation – i.e., in things that are separated from matter, since there is no transmutation without matter. A proposition need not be necessary in this way in order to be *per se*.

And it is apparent that 'A man is necessarily an animal' is not true when no man exists. For the truth of discourse involving the combination [of subject and predicate] is its signification, by which it is made like the reality. But when no man exists, the signification of that discourse is not like the reality, because *man* is not, nor is *animal* in *man* in the composition belonging to reality, but only in the composition belonging to the discourse. Therefore, when no man exists, the signification of this discourse is not the truth.

Again, Aristotle in *Metaphysics* IV (7, 1011b23–1012a28; cf. VI 4, 1027b20–23) proves that truth is in the one or the other part of a contradiction and argues as follows. The affirmative proposition signifies the composition of being to being, [and] the negative signifies the division of that being from the same being. But it is impossible that a being be at the same time compounded with some being and divided from that same being. Therefore, if {1–8} the affirmative proposition is true because of the composition of being to being that it signifies, the negative is false because of the division of being from being; and if the negative is true because of the

division of being from being, the affirmative is false because of the
composition of being to being which it signifies. And it is important to know that Aristotle proves the truth of the affirmative or the
negative discourse solely on the basis of whether a real thing is
compounded with another thing or divided from it. But when no
man and no animal exist, bring your intellect to bear on the nature
of that reality, and let us see if the essence of man and the essence of
animal are anything other than what they were before [man and
animal] were generated. But they were nothing then, for *man* did
not exist, nor did *animal* inhere in it. Therefore, neither are they
anything in the case under consideration, since [in it] they are no
more than they were then.

[A2R] In reply to the second argument, when it says that 'Every
animal is a substance, some man is not a substance; therefore, some
man is not an animal' is a syllogism based on opposed propositions,
the conclusion of which must be impossible, and that therefore
'Some man is not an animal' is impossible, and that therefore its
contradictory – viz., 'Every man is an animal' – is necessary, we
have to say what Aristotle says in *Prior Analytics* II (5, 64b7–10),
that [the conclusion of] a syllogism based on opposed propositions
is contrary to fact – i.e., when the conclusion removes a thing from
itself (for the conclusion of every syllogism based on opposed
propositions is negative). But he does not say that its conclusion
must be impossible. On the contrary, its conclusion can be true,
when it divides in the discourse things that are divided in reality.
That is the way it is in the case under consideration, for when every
man has been destroyed, *man* and *animal* are not compounded in
reality. Thus, even though one or the other premise of a syllogism
based on opposed propositions is necessarily false when one argues
on the basis of contraries (or both may be false, as sometimes
happens when one argues on the basis of contraries), its conclusion
can be true – i.e., a conclusion that signifies that things are divided,
when they are divided in reality. For what is true can follow from
things that are false.

[A3R] As for the third argument, when it says that the proposition 'A man is an animal' is either necessary or not, I say that it is
not necessary. When you say 'Therefore, the first proposition can
be false,' I grant it. And when you go on to say that therefore 'A
man is a man' can be false because if a consequent is falsely stated of

anything, any antecedent [of that consequent] {1–9} is falsely stated of that same thing, I say that 'A man is a man' is false when no man exists because [in that case] it is merely a composition belonging to discourse for which there is no corresponding composition in reality. And when the argument goes on to say that therefore 'A man is not a man' can be true, I say that it *is* true when no man exists because [in that case] the division belonging to the discourse has no opposing composition in reality. For if I ask you why the proposition 'Socrates is not running' is false when Socrates is running, you will reply that it is because there is a composition in reality that is opposed to the division belonging to the discourse, a composition that makes the proposition false. And if you do not reply in that way, then you cannot reply.

[A4R] As for the fourth argument, when you say that a species cannot lose its genus, that is true as long as the species exists. It is impossible that its genus should be varied with respect to it while it exists, for the reason why it does not lose its genus is that then the genus would sometimes be in the species and sometimes not while the species existed, in which case it would be not the genus but an accident. But that the species should lose its genus as a result of the destruction of its substance is not impossible, but necessary. For look – doesn't a man lose his substance as a result of his destruction? Because what is acquired by generation is lost by destruction, and so if the essence of a man or of a donkey is acquired by generation, it is lost by destruction. Therefore, if a donkey has this sort of genus – *animal* – causally on the basis of its essence alone, then, when it loses its essence as a result of destruction, it is necessary that it lose the genus *animal* and all [the other] things that inhere in it causally on account of its essence.

But if you want to say that the essence and form of the species *donkey* is not acquired as a result of generation, then the form of *donkey* existed before [the donkey] was generated. Therefore, [it existed] either separated from the matter or not. Not separated from the matter, because then it would be like one of Plato's Ideas; furthermore, according to Aristotle, material forms are not separable from matter. If you say that the form of *donkey* is actually in the matter before the donkey is generated, that is not possible; for nothing is transmuted [to conform] to that which it [already] has in actuality. Therefore, if in the donkey's being generated the matter

{1–10} is transformed to the form of *donkey*, then the essence or form of *donkey* was not actually in the matter before the donkey was generated.

Again, you say that the essence of *donkey* is not acquired as a result of [the donkey's] being generated. In that case I ask you: What is acquired as a result of generation? Plainly not the matter, since it exists before anything is generated and after everything is destroyed. If you say that it is the composite [of matter and form] that is generated *per se* and acquired as a result of generation (as Aristotle says in *Metaphysics* XI [cf. XII 3, 1070a10–35] and Albert says in commenting on that book [7.2.7, ed. Cologne 16.2: 348.19–21; cf. 11.1.6, ed. Cologne 16.2: 467.13–14]), then the form, which is one part of the composite, is also acquired as a result of generation, although accidentally. You don't want to reply that the essence of things that can be generated is eternal, not susceptible to destruction or generation, do you? To talk that way is to fail to know what it is that is expressed by the name. {2–1}

Second Question

When the real things have been destroyed, must the knowledge of those things be destroyed?

The second question is whether when the real things [the first proposition is about] have been destroyed the knowledge of those things must be destroyed.

[The Disputation]

That the knowledge must be destroyed is argued in the following way.

[The Affirmative Arguments]

[A1] Aristotle says in the *Categories* (7, 7b29) that if there is no knowable thing, there is no knowledge. But real things are knowable, and when they have been destroyed, they are not real things. Therefore, [when they have been destroyed] there is no knowledge [of them].

[A2] Aristotle says in the *Posterior Analytics* (II 7, 92b5–8; cf.

Physics IV 1, 208a30–31) that of that which is not no one can know what it is – e.g., no one can know what a goat-stag or a fligax is. Therefore, it seems that the existence of what is knowable is required if there is to be any knowledge.

[A3] When a cause has been destroyed, its effect is destroyed. But real things are the causes of our knowledge. Therefore, when the real things have been destroyed, it is necessary that the knowledge we had of them be destroyed. The major premise is apparent in itself. The minor premise is explained as follows. In the *Liber de causis* it is written that the knowledge that belongs to the first cause is the cause of all real things, for all things come from the first principle by way of cognition. But our knowledge is caused by the real things. Therefore, etc.

[A4] Again, all knowledge is of being. But when the real things have been destroyed, those very things are not being. Therefore, there cannot be knowledge of them [when they have been destroyed]. The major premise is evident on the basis of what Aristotle says in *Metaphysics* IV (1–2, 1003a21–1005a18), that, as the whole of philosophy has to do with the whole of being, so the parts of philosophy have to do with the parts of being.

The opposing side is argued for in the following way.

[The Negative Arguments]

[N1] A thing has one sort of being in matter and another in the soul (for real things are in the soul in virtue of imagination, memory, and thought), and the one sort does not depend on the other. For it need not be the case that if things are in matter in virtue of their substance, they are also in the soul in virtue of cognition – or vice versa, since many things have being in the soul (the chimera and the like) that do not have being in matter in virtue of their substance. {2–2}

On that basis one argues as follows: Whenever a thing has two sorts of being neither of which depends on the other, when that thing has been destroyed in respect of one of its sorts of being, it need not be destroyed in respect of its other sort of being. Therefore, since a real thing has its being in matter in virtue of its essence and substance and in the soul in virtue of cognition, and since the one sort does not depend on the other (as we have seen), when the thing has been destroyed as regards its being in matter, it need not be destroyed as regards its being in the soul. But the being of a real thing in the soul in virtue of its causes, principles, and elements is the knowledge of the thing. Therefore, etc.

[N2] Moreover, the knowledge of a thing is the soul's habit that comprehends that thing by means of everything that is required for knowing that thing. Therefore, anything without which that habit is in the soul is something without which there is complete knowledge of the thing. But such a habit can be in the soul independently of the existence of the real thing outside the soul. For, what prevents our knowing completely from what causes, at what time, and in what part of the sky an eclipse of the sun or the moon must take place, and how long it must last, even though the eclipse *is* not? – and analogously as regards plants, animals, and other things. Therefore, the destruction of the real things need not be the occasion of destroying the knowledge we had of them.

[The Bachelor's Reply]

[The Bachelor's Position]

The reply to this was that when the real things have been destroyed, it is necessary that the knowledge we had of them be destroyed. And the reason is that knowledge is not just any habit belonging to the soul, but a habit that is true. But once the real things have been destroyed, the habit remaining in the soul regarding them is not a habit that is true, because nothing in reality corresponds to it. Therefore – so he said – it is not knowledge but error and imagery.

The arguments on the opposing side must be replied to in the following way.

[The Bachelor's Rejoinders to the Negative Arguments]

[N1r] When the argument said that a thing has two sorts of being, in matter and in the soul, he granted it. When the argument said that the one sort does not depend on the other, he said that the being of the thing in the soul [that] is not knowledge of the thing, but imagery, does not depend on [the thing's] being outside the soul, but the being of the thing in the soul that is knowledge of the thing does depend on the thing's being outside the soul. And when the argument said that the chimera does not have being outside the soul but inside the soul, he said that that is not knowledge of the chimera but an image of the chimera and mere imagination. {2–3}

[N2r] In reply to the second argument, when it said that the knowledge of a thing is the soul's habit that comprehends that thing by means of everything that is required for knowing that thing, he granted it. When it went on to say that that habit is [in the soul] without the being of the thing outside the soul, he said that that was not true. And when it went on to say ((*cum dicebatur/tu dicis* [var.])) that there is no eclipse now and yet I can have knowledge of it, he said that that is not the case, since such a habit regarding an eclipse is not knowledge.

[Against the Bachelor's Reply]

[Arguments against the Bachelor's Position]

The [Bachelor's] position is argued against as follows:

If it is necessary that the knowledge of the things be destroyed when the real things have been destroyed, then that very habit, numerically the same, existing in the soul, which earlier was knowledge and necessary, would then be turned into error and a misdirected habit. For he said that once the real things had been destroyed, the same habit that there was earlier would be kept in the soul and would remain, but it would then not be knowledge but error. The consequent is impossible. For although numerically one and the same opinion is sometimes true and sometimes false, as Aristotle says (*Categories* 5, 4a22–28), that is not possible as regards the habit that is knowledge, since where there is falsity there is no necessity.

Moreover, as the causes, principles, and elements are related to their effect, so is the cognition of the causes, principles, and elements related to the cognition of the effect that is to be produced. But the causes, principles, and elements of any effect, when they exist in reality, necessarily lead to a cognition of the effect with a cognition of the causes. Therefore, a cognition of the causes, principles, and elements of any effect, once that cognition has been produced in the soul, necessarily produces a cognition of the effect. But [even] when the thing does not exist, there can be in the soul a cognition of that thing's causes, principles, and elements – the principles and causes from which such a thing must come to be if it comes to be. Therefore, etc.

One argues against [the Bachelor's] resolutions of the [negative] arguments in the following way.

[Against the Bachelor's Rejoinders]

[N1rR] He says that when the thing itself does not exist outside the soul, the being of the thing in the soul is not knowledge of that thing but error. In that case, anyone who produces in his soul a cognition of an eclipse on the basis of its causes and a cognition of thunder on the basis of the appearance of the clouds when those things [i.e., the eclipse and the thunder] do not exist outside the soul produces error and not knowledge in his soul. And anyone who lectures on the *Meteorology* when those {2–4} phenomena are not actually occurring is teaching error and not knowledge. And the same habit of the soul can on a single day become both error and knowledge. All these things are absurd; therefore, so is the antecedent. It follows also that if the eclipse is not occurring, the mathematicians have no more knowledge of it than does any ignoramus.

[N2rR] [His] resolution of the second argument is argued against as follows: Anyone who has in his soul the entire habit having to do with syllogism as taught in the *Prior Analytics* – i.e., how a syllogism must be constructed, how an assertoric syllogism works, how a syllogism including 'necessarily' works, how a converse, a circular, an ostensive syllogism works, how a syllogism leading to an impossibility works – [such a person] has complete knowledge of the syllogism even if no syllogism exists and none will ever be constructed.

If you say that this habit is not knowledge of the syllogism, then what sort of habit is it? It is not opinion regarding the syllogism, since opinion regarding a thing is not acquired through its necessary causes, and the habit we are talking about is acquired regarding the syllogism through its necessary causes. Therefore, it follows that it is complete knowledge of the syllogism.

If you say that that habit is error and not knowledge regarding the syllogism, that is astounding and unthinkable. The reason is that everyone who is in error regarding anything has to be corrected regarding it and can acquire a better habit regarding it – e.g., a doctor who errs in medicine and a harpist who errs regarding the principles of his art. But anyone who has the entire habit having to do with syllogism as taught in the *Prior Analytics* and has it as it is taught there cannot acquire a better habit having to do with syllogism, nor can he be corrected regarding the syllogism itself, its principles, or the act of syllogizing. Therefore, that habit would not be ((*fuerit/fuit*)) error, even if no syllogism existed. Therefore, if such a habit cannot be error, as has been proved, or opinion (since opinion is not a habit acquired through the necessary causes of a thing), it follows that it will be knowledge. Or else you must tell us *what* [that] habit [will be].

(To this there was no reply.)

[*The Determination of the Question*]

[*The Master's Reply*]

As for the question, we have to reply that when the real things have been destroyed, the knowledge of the things need not be destroyed if those things have causes and principles on the basis of which they can be known. For as the causes of an effect lead to the effect, so a cognition of those causes, when it has been produced {2–5} in the soul, necessarily leads to a cognition of that effect in the soul. Thus [the soul] has knowledge in the way the thing has causes and known principles. For when the eclipse (or animal, or plant) is not in existence, there is no knowledge of them in which one knows that they exist (since that is false). But there is knowledge of them remaining in the soul in which one knows from which causes, principles, and elements any of those things would have to be produced if it were to be produced, such that it would be impossible for any of them to be produced from other [causes, principles, or elements]. There is also knowledge of them in which one knows the mode of generation of any of them from its principles, such that it would be impossible for it to be produced from its principles in any other way. Ask yourself if you can have this cognition of a plant, or the rainbow, or the tide, or any other effect while they do not exist. As for me, I think that otherwise we would in fact not have any knowledge in this way of the rainbow ((*aliter sic re vera scientiam de iride non haberemus/per principia vera scientiam de iride non habemus* [var.])) or of an eclipse when they are not in existence. That is why when *man* and *animal* have been destroyed there is no knowledge of *man* in which one knows that a man is an animal (since that is false, as was clearly established in the preceding problem). But when *man* has been destroyed there can remain knowledge in the soul, knowledge in which one knows regarding *man* from which principles and elements and in what way *man* is generated, and from which ones it is impossible [that *man* be generated]. (Many other reasons could be added to this one, but because they are touched on in arguing about truth in *Metaphysics* II [1, 993a30–b31], I omit them for the sake of brevity.)

I grant the disputation offered on behalf of the other [i.e., the negative] side. To the arguments for the opposing conclusion I reply as follows.

[The Master's Rejoinders to the Affirmative Arguments]

[A1R] When the argument says that the knowledge is destroyed when the knowable thing has been destroyed, that is true if the knowable thing remains in no way at all. But things destroyed as regards their being in matter can remain as regards their being in the soul. And it is when they have that sort of being that knowledge of them exists, as we have seen.

[A2R] When the second argument says that of what does not exist – e.g., goat-stag and fligax – no one can know what it is, that is true as regards what does not exist at all, in the sense that neither it nor the causes from which its being is possible have being in reality. But not everything that does not exist is of that sort. For an eclipse, when it is not in existence, has causes in reality from which its being is not only possible but even necessary, so that it is in virtue of those causes that knowledge of it remains with the soul. {2–6}

[A3R] As for the third argument, when it says that the effect is destroyed when the cause has been destroyed, we have to say that there are two kinds of causes (as far as the resolution of this argument is concerned). One is a cause that is required not only for the production of the effect but also for its conservation. Regarding such a cause, that proposition is true, as is evident *per se*. For example, a light is required not only for light to be produced in the air but also for light to be conserved in that same air. The other is a cause that is required only for the production of the thing. For example, the person who makes a statue is required for the statue's being produced but is not required for the conservation of the statue. And the proposition is not true regarding this sort of cause, since nothing prevents the statue's remaining when the sculptor has been destroyed. It is in this way that real things are the causes of our knowledge, for things generate knowledge and cognition in our soul when we contemplate them, but the things themselves are not required for the conservation of our knowledge. That is why we have knowledge and cognition of future things in the possibility associated with their causes, of past things through memory. [As for the knowledge and cognition] of things considered absolutely, regardless of any difference of time and the other conditions with which the perception of things is received, I say that we have cognition of this sort through the intellect. But the cognition of things under the conditions by which one individual differs from another is through the production of images (*phantasia*).

[A4R] In reply to the fourth argument, when you say that all knowledge is of being, we have to say that either that [known] being must be actual, or it must be such that while it does not have being [in actuality] it does have causes and principles from which its being is necessary or possible – as is evident, since an eclipse is not, and yet its being will result necessarily from its causes. (I say 'or possible' because of things that can be generated, since not every thing that can be generated will be generated, even though it has causes from which its being is possible.)

The things that have already been said ought to be enough for this problem. {3–1}

Third Question

When the real things have been destroyed, is it necessary that the terms lose their connection with what they signify?

The third question was whether when the real things have been destroyed it is necessary that the terms lose their connection with what they signify.

[The Disputation]

That they do lose their connection is argued in the following way.

[The Affirmative Arguments]

[A1] Boethius says (*On Division*, PL 64, 889D [see Translation 1]) that if the subject thing is not, the utterance stops designating. But when the real things have been destroyed, the [subject] things are not. Therefore, the utterance stops designating.

[A2] Again, the thing, the thought, and what is signified by the utterance are altogether the same, since the thing itself is what is thought, and what is thought is signified by means of the utterance. But when the real thing has been destroyed, obviously it does not exist. Therefore, neither do the thought or what is signified by the utterance exist. But if what is signified by the utterance does not exist, the utterances must lose their connection with what they signify.

The opposing conclusion is argued for as follows.

[The Negative Argument]

[N] The form of a thing that can be generated is itself in the matter through the essence, in the soul through the cognition of it and not through its essence (for the stone is not in the soul, but the idea of the stone, as Aristotle says in *De anima* III [8, 431b29–432a1]), and it is in the utterance through signification. And the thing's being in the matter, its being in the soul, and its being in the utterance signifying it are different [from one another], and none of them depends on the others or on either one of the others.

On that basis one argues as follows. More than one kind of being is appropriate to any one essence, and no one of those kinds of being is dependent on any other. [Therefore,] when the essence has been destroyed as regards one of those kinds, it need not be destroyed as regards another. But since more than one kind of being is appropriate to a thing that can be generated, and none of them is dependent on any other – i.e., the being of reality in the matter, the being of thought in the soul, and the being of signification in the utterance – when the essence of the thing has been destroyed as regards its being in the matter, it need not be destroyed as regards its being in the soul or as regards its being of signification in the utterance. The major premise is evident, since Socrates's being and his being white are different kinds of being one of which does not depend on the other, and so when Socrates has been destroyed as regards his being white he need not be destroyed as regards {3–2} his being absolutely. The minor premise is also evident, since even though a thing after its destruction is not the same as before, I can think of it and imagine it the same as before, and so I can also signify it by means of an utterance; for whatever can be thought can be signified by means of an utterance.

[The Determination]

[The Master's Reply]

In reply to the question we have to say, briefly, that when the real things have been destroyed it is not necessary that the terms lose their connection with what they signify. The reason for this is not that it is necessary that a thing be signified by the utterance after the thing has been destroyed; on the contrary, that happens to it accidentally. Nor is the reason for this that it is necessary that the thing be signified ((*significari/significare*)) by means of some particular utterance; for just as there is no thing that an utterance is incompatible with, so there is no thing that it is determined to signify. But when the things have been destroyed, the terms need not lose their connection with what they signify; and the reason for this is that the utterance's signifying does not depend on the thing's being, because when one thing does not depend on another thing, if that other thing does not exist, it is possible for the first [and independent] thing to exist. Therefore, etc.

But obviously the utterance's ((*vocis/vocum*)) signifying does not depend on the thing's being, and for the following reason. Being and not being are opposed with respect to the same thing, [and] being signified and not being signified are opposed [with respect] to the same thing. But just as a thing's being and its not being signified by means of an utterance are not opposed (since many things are that are nevertheless not signified by means of an utterance; therefore, etc.), not being and being signified by means of an utterance are not opposed as regards the same thing. For we see that 'Socrates' does not signify that which Socrates *is* after his destruction (since after his destruction, when the substantial form of Socrates is nothing, the utterance 'Socrates' would signify nothing); instead, after Socrates's destruction 'Socrates' signifies such a being as Socrates once *was*, even though such a being *is not* Socrates in reality.

Again, what is possible for the intellect in thinking is possible for utterances in signifying, since whatever can be a thought can be what an utterance signifies, and in the [same] way. But when the real thing has been destroyed, conceiving of that thing is possible for the intellect as it was earlier; for it is possible to think the thing after its destruction. Therefore, it is also possible to signify the thing by means of an utterance as it was earlier. {3–3}

Again, anything that is not incompatible with any signified thing can signify a thing whether or not the thing itself exists. There is nothing signified that an utterance is incompatible with, just as there is nothing signified that it determines for itself. Therefore, an utterance can signify a thing whether or not the thing exists.

To the arguments on the opposing side we have to reply as follows.

[The Master's Rejoinders to the Affirmative Arguments]

[A1R] When you say that if the subject thing is not, the utterance, etc., I say that if the verb 'is' is predicated as a third ingredient, the proposition is true. And Boethius understands it in that way, so that its sense is this: If a thing is not subjected to the significant utterance and its signified thing, the utterance stops designating. But if 'is' is predicated as the second ingredient, the proposition is false, so that its sense is this: If the thing is not, the utterance stops designating – as is commonly said.

Another reply can be made. If the way in which the thing is not is such that the thing has no being at all – neither in matter through its essence, nor in the soul through cognition, nor in an utterance through signification – the utterance stops designating. That is true. But if the way in which the thing is not is such that it does not have being in matter, it need not be the case that the utterance stops being significant; for the thing can have being in the soul and in a significant utterance while it has no being in matter, as we have seen.

[A2R] In reply to the second argument, when he says that the thing, the thought, and what is signified by the utterance are altogether the same, it is true that the thing in the matter, the thought, and what is signified by the utterance are numerically the same thing, but the being is different in each case. For the thing's being thought, its being signified by the utterance, and its being a real thing are not the same; and so when the thing has been destroyed insofar as it is a real thing in matter, it need not have been destroyed insofar as it is what is signified by the utterance. {4–1}

Fourth Question

Is the nature of the genus existent in the species something actually existing other than the final differentia of the species?

Fourth, since the proposition 'A man is an animal' predicates the genus of a species, the question is whether the nature of the genus in the species is something actual other than the final differentia of the species.

[The Disputation]

One argues in the following way that it is.

[The Affirmative Arguments]

[A1] You say that the nature of the genus existent in the species is not anything actual distinct from the final differentia only because what is added to any actual substance is an accident of that substance. Therefore, if *animal* in *man* were something actual other than the final differentia of *man*, then the final differentia of *man* added to it would be an accident of it. But that is impossible; the differentia that completes the species cannot be an accident.

If that is what you say, your account is unacceptable [for the following reasons]:

That in which the soul of a plant or an animal is generated is some actual substance, and yet the animal's [or plant's] soul is not an accident [of that substance]. Therefore, this account [of yours] notwithstanding, the nature of the genus existent in the species can be [something] actual other than the final differentia of the species.

Again, the sort of substance that remains after the destruction of an animal's soul was in the animal's substance before the destruction of its soul. But an actual substance remains after the destruction of the animal's soul – viz., a perceived body. Therefore, a form that is added to an actual substance need not be an accident. Therefore, that account [of yours] notwithstanding, the nature of the genus existent in the species can be something actual other than the final differentia of the species.

[A2] Furthermore, Porphyry says (*Isagoge*, ed. Busse, 10.22–11.1) that a differentia is that by which a species exceeds the genus. Therefore, there is an actual substance [to which the final differentia is added]. {4–2} For the fundamentally prime matter is not the genus, since it is not predicated of *man* in respect of what [*man* is]. Therefore, if the genus is an actual substance, and the differentia is also actual, and the differentia is (as Porphyry says) that by which the species exceeds the genus, it follows that the nature of the genus is something actual other than the final differentia.

The opposing conclusion is argued for as follows.

[The Negative Argument]

[N] If it had to be the case that the nature of the genus existent in the species were something actual other than the final differentia of the species, then in that that is a simple form – e.g., [in] that that is color, or whiteness – there could not be anything that has the character of a genus or that has the character of a differentia. And then in that simple thing there would be no genus and differentia, in which case whiteness would not be a species in a genus, nor would color (and so on as regards others [of that sort]). The consequent is false, because *quality* is a possible genus of *color*, and *color* is the genus of *whiteness*, and there are also specific differentiae in them. The consequence is evident, because in what is simple (considered as something simple) we do not find anything distinct from anything else [in it]. The falsity of the antecedent ((*antecedentis/consequentis*)) [is apparent], because nothing that is one is made out of entities that are two in actuality; but every species is something that is one, and it is made out of a genus and a differentia; therefore, the one of them is not something actual distinct from the other.

[The Bachelor's Reply]

[The Bachelor's Position]

The reply made to this [by the Bachelor] was that the nature of the genus existent in the species is not something actual other than the differentia of the species. And he said this because of the argument that was offered in support of that side [of the disputation].

Then he replied to the [opposing] arguments. {4–3}

[The Bachelor's Rejoinder to the First Affirmative Argument]

[A1r] When the argument said that the only reason the genus existent in the species is not something actually existing other than the final differentia of the species is that in that case the differentia of each and every species would be an accident because it would be added to the genus, which is something actually existing, he granted it.

When the argument said further that a substantial form can be added to something actually existing – e.g., the soul of a man or ((*vel/et*)) the soul of a plant, [a substantial form] that is generated in the seed, which is an actual substance – he said that it is true that that in which an animal's soul is generated is an actual substance, but it is destroyed at the generation of the animal.

And when the argument said that therefore when the animal's soul is destroyed an actual substance remains – i.e., the perceived body – and so the animal's soul was in that actual substance before the destruction of the soul, he said that that was not true. Instead, the substance that remains is generated in actuality at the destruction of the animal's soul.

[Against the Bachelor's Position]

One argues against the [Bachelor's] position as follows.

[BR1] The name of a genus – e.g., the name 'animal' – is not the name of the matter alone, because the matter is not predicated of the composite in the first way of speaking *per se*. Therefore, the name of the genus must signify a substantial form. But the only substantial form in a species is the final differentia of the species. Therefore, either [the name of] the genus signifies the substantial form of only one species, and so [the genus] could not be predicated of any other species; or it signifies the substantial form of each and every species, and so [the genus] will be predicated of none of them. The reason for this [latter claim] is that the name of a genus predicates what it signifies; and so if it signifies the form of one species as also the form of another, it would predicate the forms of all the species equally primarily of any species of which it was stated.

[BR2] Again, names that signify altogether the same are synonyms. Therefore, if the genus were not something actual other than the form of the species, the parts of the definition would be synonymous names. In that case just as much would be conveyed by the name of the genus as by the whole definition. And these things are evidently impossible. {4–4}

[BR3] One argues in the third place that what is signified by [the name of] the genus – e.g., 'animal' – must be one because the word belonging to the genus must be one. But what is signified by 'animal' is an actual substance. Therefore, it must be one actual substance. But it cannot be the one form of any one species alone, nor can it be the forms of all the species, as was proved above. (And, in any case, all the forms of all the species are not one actual substance.) It follows, therefore, that [the name of] the genus signifies an actual substance existent in every [one of its] species, which is something other than any differentia of a species. (And that may have been Porphyry's view as well as the view of some of the moderns.)

(To these arguments there was no reply.)

[The Determination]

[The Master's Reply]

In reply to the question, we have to say that the nature of the genus existent in the species is not something distinct from the differentia of the species. [The name of] the genus signifies the quiddity and essence of the species, which is one and simple, for the quiddity of one thing is one. But if the name of the genus were to signify something actual distinct from the differentia of the species, it would not signify the essence and quiddity of the species. Therefore, etc. (And this is what Aristotle says in *Physics* II [3, 194b26–30], that all the parts of a definition pertain to the form of the thing defined.)

Furthermore, if the nature of the genus were something actual other than the differentia of the species, then a simple name would not have a genus and differentia, because nothing in it would be distinct [from anything else in it]. For you cannot say that there is one thing is whiteness whereby it is white, another whereby it is a color, another whereby it is a passible quality, a fourth whereby it is a quality, a fifth whereby it is an accident, and a sixth whereby it is itself. Instead, it is in virtue of one thing that all those things are in it. And that is Aristotle's position in *Metaphysics* VII (12, 1038a33) when he says that {4–5} in the substance of a thing there is no order. (What he calls the substance of a thing is all the things predicated of a species in a predication expounding its essence.) Furthermore, in *Metaphysics* VII (4, 1029b22–1030a17) Aristotle proves that an accident must not be included in a definition, arguing in the following way. All the parts of a definition are the same in virtue of the essence. But if the accidents *white* and *black* were included in the definition [of *man*], they would not be the same as *man* or the same as each other in virtue of the essence, nor would they be predicated of *man* in the first way of speaking *per se*. It is on that basis that he concludes that accidents must not be included in the definition of a substance. And on the basis of Aristotle's major premise here it is clear that the parts of a definition pertain to the essence [of the thing defined]. Therefore, the genus and the differentia are the same in reality. The major premise – the one that says that all the things included in a definition are the same in virtue of the essence – is evident; for they are predicated of the thing defined in the first way of speaking *per se*, and in virtue of the essence they are the same as one another. Obviously Aristotle means that the genus existent in the species is not something in the species other than the final differentia of the species.

Then again, all the things that pertain to the simple essence of a thing are the same in reality. Now the genus and the differentia predicate that essence of the species, for they are predicated of the species itself in the first way [of speaking *per se*]. The major premise is evident in itself, because the genus and the differentia are predicated of the species in the first way of speaking *per se*. They do not pertain to the essence of the subject and things that are predicated in the fourth way of speaking *per se*.

Thus, since the genus is the name of the aggregate, the other part [of the definition] is the essence of the species, the same as the differentia of the species signifies, even though more is signified under the word belonging to the genus, under [the name of] the characteristic distinctive of the genus.

But you will ask at once: How can he consider the name of the genus [to be] in the species, since the genus is the whole nature (*ratio*) of the species?

Then we have to say in reply that the numerically single form that is the form of Socrates picked out individually is itself the human form. And the same is also the form of animal, since the form of Socrates is the form of animal. And the same is also the corporeal form, since the form of Socrates is the form of body (because Socrates is a body). And that form, numerically one and the same, is the substantial form. Therefore, if a form numerically one and the same is the form of Socrates, and human, and animal, and corporeal, and substantial, {4–6} and [the form] of being; then by that [form] insofar as it is human, Socrates is a man (since it is in virtue of something's having the human form that it is called a man), by it insofar as it is the form of animal Socrates is an animal, insofar as it is corporeal Socrates is a body, insofar as it is substantial Socrates is a substance, and by it insofar as it is the form of being he is a being. And so by a form numerically one, Socrates has all the things that are in the predicamental line of substance, from the individual to the highest genus. And they are not many in reality because there is no order in the essence of a real thing, as is written in *Metaphysics* VII (12, 1038a33). But Socrates's form being substantial is not its being corporeal, its being corporeal is not its being animal, its being animal is not its being human (since in that case every form of animal would be human, which is false), nor is its being human its being Socrates's.

The reason for this is that Averroes, the Commentator, [in commenting] on *Metaphysics* V (in the new [Latin] translation) claims that there must be more than one distinguishing characteristic for the same thing, and that there must be different names for it in accordance with those various distinguishing characteristics. Now the completeness [of Socrates's being] in his species through his substantial form, which is the distinguishing characteristic of subsisting under his accidents, is appropriate to Socrates, and the name 'substance' is appropriate to him in accord with that distinguishing characteristic. And because he shares that distinguishing characteristic with many things, that name is more common than the others. Another completeness [of being] in Socrates through the same form is the intersection [in him] of three dimensions at right angles in the same point. And that is why the name 'body' is appropriate to Socrates in accord with that distinguishing characteristic, because the nature of body considered as body is that in it there is an intersection of three dimensions at right angles. Insofar as that form is a distinguishing characteristic of perceiving, the name 'animal' is appropriate to him, because an animal is an animal on account of perception. And insofar as the act of reasoning or any other proprium of *man* stems from that form, the name 'man' is appropriate to him. And because that distinguishing characteristic is more {4–7} specific than all [the others], that name is more specific than all the others. Nevertheless, those names are not names of those things themselves, but of the thing itself.

To the arguments on the opposing side we have to reply as follows.

[The Master's Rejoinders to the Affirmative Arguments]

[A1R] When [the argument] says that the nature of the genus existent in the species is not something in actuality because in that case the differentia added to it would be an accident, we have to say that that is not the reason. Instead, the reason is that the form signified by [the name of] the genus and the form signified by [the name of] the differentia belong to one simple actuality. That is why the nature of the genus existent in the species is not something actual other than the differentia of the species.

[A2R] As for the second argument, when it says that the differentia is that by which the species exceeds the genus, we have to say that the excess consists in the fact that the distinguishing characteristic seen in the form of the species insofar as it is what is signified by [the name of] the differentia is more specific than it is insofar as it is what is signified by [the name of] the genus. Nevertheless, in reality it is undivided.

Porphyry may have believed that the nature of the genus in the species was something actual other than the differentia of the species, but I know that that is false (as is clear from what has gone before).

The solution of the arguments raised against the Bachelor's argument is apparent on the basis of the things we have said.

INDEX